Driving Social Innovation

How Unexpected Leadership is Transforming Society

Published in the United States of America.

Fielding University Press is an imprint of Fielding Graduate University. Its objective is to advance the research and scholarship of Fielding faculty, students, alumni and associated scholars around the world, using a variety of publishing platforms. For more information, please contact Fielding University Press, attn. Jean-Pierre Isbouts, 2020 De la Vina Street, Santa Barbara, CA 93105. Email: fup@fielding.edu. On the web: www.fielding.edu/universitypress.

Library of Congress Cataloging-in-Publication data
1. Social Sciences – Social Change – Driving Social Innovation

Driving Social Innovation

How Unexpected Leadership is Transforming Society

Edited by
Marie Sonnet
Theresa Southam
Patrice Rosenthal

Fielding Institute for Social Innovation

Institute for Social Innovation
Striving for sustainable and just solutions to social problems

Praise for "Driving Social Innovation"

An insightful book about rethinking leadership in the context of dramatic social change. The authors offer new and fresh perspectives to consider in research and in governance. A must read in uncertain times.

— *Roxane de la Sablonnière, Professor, Department of Psychology, University of Montreal*

This excellent edited collection provokes and inspires new and different ways of making sense of leadership research and practice. Conventional leadership thinking continues to overly invest in the heroic leader, disregarding the significance of collective and individual leadership practices. Contributors to this book offer fresh perspectives that provide a rethinking of leadership through exploring the intersections of precarity, unexpected leadership and social justice. A must read for anyone wishing to better understand leadership thought in the context of 21st Century challenges.

— *Jackie Ford, Programme Director, Durham University Business School, United Kingdom*

Precarity and rapid change create a vacuum in which leadership needs to arise, and often does, from sources and forms that are unexpected. This book illustrates how important such leadership can be, especially in pursuit of social justice, interdependence, and adaptation to change. Sampling across the diverse set of chapters in this volume will reward the reader with surprise and insight into why unexpected leadership matters and is needed in pursuit of a better world.

— *Charles McClintock, Director, Institute for Social Innovation, Fielding Graduate University*

What the past 24 months of dealing with the Covid-19 pandemic has exposed is the precarity, vulnerability and insecurity of young researchers whose career and future hangs in the balance. This book weaves through leadership in varying contexts, guiding us on managing social changes, precarity and uncertainty in a changing and transforming world. Every young researcher who cares deeply

about their career development, leadership, and how to play an active role in their community and the academia should put this book on their required reading list.
— Palesa Natasha Mothapo, Head of Postdoctoral Research Support, Division for Research development, Stellenbosch University, South Africa

Dedication

This monograph is dedicated to groups who encourage unexpected leaders during times of precarity and change. These groups make the world more just and equitable. In these chapters, you will learn about groups like the Graduate Students of Color Association at Merrimack College, the Crones Counsel, Open Works, L'Arche, ARISE, Transforming Care, The Backbone in Tanzania, Citizens4Change, the Presencing Institute, the Minnesota COVIDSitters, the Association of Black Psychologists, Fielding Somatics, Phenomenology & Communicative Leadership community of practice, the American Society for Public Administration, the "Voyagers," BRIDGES Idaho, and Fielding Graduate University's Institute for Social Innovation. May you be as inspired as the editors are by these groups' foresight and perseverance.

Acknowledgements

The editors would like to acknowledge the unwavering support of the Director of the Institute for Social Innovation (ISI) at Fielding Graduate University, Dr. Charles McClintock. Under his sponsorship, we issued the call for chapter proposals to our ISI Fellows and received the outpouring of scholarship reported in this volume. Dr. McClintock gave shape and form to our theme—driving social innovation through *unexpected leadership*. We offer this volume in fulfillment of ISI's mission to find just and sustainable solutions to social problems.

With great appreciation, we also want to acknowledge our chapter reviewers, who gave generously of their time and expertise. They are Kathleen Allen, Peter Eichten, Allison Davis-White Eyes, Judy Stevens-Long, Mark K. McBeth, Mary McCall, David Rehorick, Daryl Rowe, Maryam Sani, Sarah Wallis, David Blake Willis, and Sergej van Middendorp. Thank you.

Finally, we express our gratitude to Joan V. Gallos, who graciously and insightfully begins this volume.

Table of Contents

Section Two: Challenging How to Lead During Precarity

Foreword

Finding Leadership in All the Right Places

Leadership matters. It always does. It mobilizes people and resources to get things done. Calls for leadership abound from every corner in today's fast-paced, technology-driven, increasingly complex world—cries for more leadership, better leadership, stronger leadership, principled leadership, inclusive leadership, transformational leadership. It is easy to understand why. A world characterized by wars and divisions, a global pandemic and its devastating implications, attacks on science and truth, and widespread inequity and injustice craves hope and a path to better days. At its best, leadership delivers both.

In the words of Harold Shapiro (2005), the former president of both the University of Michigan and Princeton, good leadership is a noble venture—a proactive social and ethical activity that launches a unique form of cooperative moral action. It asserts a positive vision and a pathway to a brighter future and mobilizes the energy and efforts needed to pursue the vision and stay the course in the face of inevitable resistance and fear of the unfamiliar. Leadership takes us into new territories to tackle difficult challenges that have no one right answer or widely accepted way forward. Lasting solutions to complicated problems, as leadership guru Ronald Heifetz (1994) reminds us, are only possible when those impacted engage on the issues and learn, adapting their values and understandings over time to match a new reality. Leadership takes patience and persistence, as well as time to grieve the loss of the world we thought we knew (Gallos & Bolman, 2021). It succeeds when it inspires us to think in creative and unconventional ways and to summon the courage to change ourselves and our systems. In precarious times, nothing matters more.

While leadership is too often thought of as a solo enterprise—the work of a charismatic superhero who will save the day—leading is a highly social endeavor anchored in human development. Understanding leadership as process, not person—as a series of steps and strategies that encourage collective reflection, adaptation, and social change—enables us to see that the full power and possibility of leadership transcends the work of any one person. Leadership is not limited to position in a hierarchy or restricted to those who possess a special title, formal authority, educational pedigree, or certain demographic characteristics. At its core, leadership promotes (a) *collective action* in service to (b) *shared or compatible goals* in a (c) *context of uncertainty*. It is all about deliberate strategies for engaging others who must be part of the solution and inspiring them to undertake what must be done for change. There are many vital roles in such a multi-dimensional social process, and they are open to all who understand the patience, persistence, and investments required and, nonetheless, choose to step forward. There are, for example, many ways to launch collective action, encourage learning, build shared goals, identify relevant constituents, support others in times of uncertainty, and manage planned change (Gallos, 2006a). There is no rule saying that all must be done by one person or one kind of person. Leadership can come from individuals or groups, whether they sit at the head or the foot of the table. What matters is respect for the process, an ethic of inclusivity, and acceptance that those who choose to lead will learn and change too as their work with others unfolds.

Casting aside outdated beliefs about the heroic leader also expands our individual and collective agency. We no longer need sit in wait for a superhero to hear our plea. We live and work among a host of individuals who have the right stuff to take us toward progress, and we may choose to step forward ourselves. A world gone terribly wrong—where we no longer seem able to connect across our differences or even recognize the same facts and truths (Haidt, 2022)—needs all the help it can get. To exclude those who lead from the edge, in unexpected places, without credentials, or with non-traditional methods is done at our peril. It's a *permanent white-water world* (Vaill, 1996), where it can be exhausting just staying afloat.

How then do we bring leadership and the resulting workable innovations and sustainable changes to our organizations, groups, or communities when we live amid powerful forces beyond our control? When riding white water, we can't change the shape and direction of that river. Instead, we must learn to read the currents and adapt to what's around us. Can we catch rushes, glide the rapids with new confidence and elan, and use—rather than fight—the energy in the flow around us to get where we and our institutions need to go? Consider three basics as a starting point.

First, accept that we lead in a permanent white-water world and that much of what we've learned about leading may be inadequate to our current task. We are not paddling canoes on a calm and protected lake where we can go where we want, when we want. We are being tossed and pummeled by a world with real winners and losers and no shared vision of equity and social justice. Step one is to name our reality. It helps to see the forces that we are up against so we can prepare for a long and arduous journey. Knowledge is power.

Step two is to fortify for the myriad opportunities and challenges ahead. We do that best when we let go of beliefs that zap our confidence or hold us back and take honest inventory of all we can bring and do. We may also need to strengthen the skills and competencies at the core of contemporary leadership. These include basic abilities to understand and manage groups and organizations as rational structures, political arenas, wellsprings of human talent, and cultures of hope so as to engage them in their full complexity (Gallos & Bolman, 2021). We can benefit in every situation with strong abilities to manage conflict productively, to marshal an agenda against the interests of others, to deal positively with people whom we find difficult, to embrace and leverage a group's diversity into its competitive advantage, and to facilitate strong teamwork.

Step three flows from two: Replace unhelpful beliefs and time-worn strategies with new ways of understanding and working in turbulent times. Peter Vaill (1996), for example, sees traditional leadership success coming from three paths:

- Work longer and harder (i.e., become a *workaholic*).
- Study longer and harder (i.e., become a *technoholic*).
- Be more politically astute and competitive (i.e., become a *poweraholic*).

These approaches may not hurt. But, in a world of constant turbulence and change, we can work as much as we want, study and search for the one right answer for as long as we choose—and try to outmaneuver and control everyone around us for as long as we can—and that one right answer will still elude us. Complex problems don't have simple technical solutions, and what got us into the rapids won't necessarily get us back on solid ground.

Vaill suggests an alternative: Learn to work differently and smarter—not just longer and harder and craftier—in four important ways:

1. **Work collectively smarter:** Come together with others for new ideas, insights, different perspectives, a fresh set of eyes, and the sustaining energy of colleagues. This requires identifying others who share your dreams and visions, as well as those who will challenge them in productive ways. Develop new and stronger strategic alliances with old and new friends and envision potential partners of all kinds. Working collectively smarter means mastering the art of interdependence—and James Thompson's classic, *Organizations in Action* (2003), is still viewed as the gold standard for strategies. Skills in facilitating productive discussions, learning from each other's experiments and mistakes, and putting competition to bed will help, too. It takes time to develop well-functioning.
2. **Work collaboratively smarter:** Working cooperatively in a world of growing needs and shrinking resources makes good sense. Time, energy, skills, and finances are tight. Pool your resources. Two hands work faster than one. Working collaboratively smarter also provides opportunity to fine-tune your teamwork skills: communicating clearly, actively listening to others, giving good feedback, setting shared goals, establishing boundaries, respecting the diversity of your colleagues, and more.
3. **Work reflectively smarter:** White water requires constant vigilance and agility. Scan for obstacles and openings, watch how we steer at every turn, assess in real time what's working and not, and switch strategies as needed and quickly. Such self-awareness and self-reflection will keep us on top of our game. Working reflectively smarter is working mindfully. And *reframing*—looking at the landscape from multiple perspectives and through the eyes of clients, workers, funders, bosses, partners, potential competitors, and critics (Gallos, 2006b)—deliberately broadens our options and keeps us from being blindsided by inattention to key constituents or subtle environmental shifts.
4. **Work spiritually smarter:** Leaders need to sustain hope and resilience in the face of hard work and even in times when it feels that all may be lost—and to help others do the same. That means finding meaning in small wins and defining failure and false starts as learning opportunities. It requires finding ways to build your own and others' strength and confidence—you'll need both

on those hairpin turns! Management scholar Burt Nanus (2008) suggests the need for a strong head and a strong heart: head to forge a compelling vision for a bright future (no matter how tentative) and small pockets of order in the chaos and uncertainty; heart to infuse the work with care and compassion and to handle conflict and differences productively.

Closing Thoughts

As I write this foreword, the United States continues its reckoning with questions of economic and social justice that have haunted the nation since its founding. Hundreds of thousands of people in large and small cities across the country and around the world have taken to the streets—even in the middle of a global pandemic—to protest the unlawful killing of unsuspecting Black men and women across America and to demand justice. It is a sign of progress in which we can take comfort during the most trying of times: the nation and the world awakening to the realities of systemic racism and injustice—policies and practices that maintain racial inequity "that many people had until now refused to see" and continued "by reflex" to deny (Kendi, 2020). Yet today, new national polling reported on the morning news found only 38% of American voters affiliated with a major political party were willing to disqualify a candidate from receiving their vote because the candidate made racist remarks (MSNBC, 2022). Leadership in times of social upheaval is tough work, and there are always ups and downs. Still the poll figures are disheartening. How do we create a more just world? Who and what can lead to lasting change? Leadership scholars and activists struggle with the answers. Still, there is ample reason for hope. The essays in this creative volume illustrate why.

Whether we lead the parade or work from the sidelines, we are needed to move our organizations and our world forward. We are all in the business of creating the future every day. Progress is aided in good ways when unexpected leaders arise from among our ranks and demonstrate strong leadership across a broad range of areas and issues that advance the human condition. How simply wonderful to see everyday women and men—many without formal roles or leadership training and often with demographic profiles counter to stereotypic images of "a real leader"—transforming lives, families, organizations, industries, communities, and nations through their honest efforts and hard work. Could we ask for more?

The leadership stories profiled and probed in this volume show just that, and the theories from them advance discussions of leading and social change that stretch back to the beginning of written history (and oral traditions before that). The authors write from their diverse experiences in faith-based communities, educational institutions, small towns, and vibrant spaces of innovation and wisdom, and their narratives stretch our understandings of who, when, where, and how to lead effectively. More importantly, they confirm that leadership opportunities are indeed open to all who seek them. Each essay asks us to look beyond persistent stereotypes and see who can and should lead us to better days. Each implicitly challenges us to answer why we are not leading to the best of our capacities, every day, in the arenas that matter to us most. Taken together the chapters shine a light on the significant contributions of all those whose efforts have been overlooked, under-valued, or falsely attributed to someone else and, as such, have lacked the support or encouragement to keep going for even bigger impact. Leadership is all about making the world a better place and advancing human capacities. We do just that—whether we achieve a grand vision or fall short of even a modest one—when we engage others in open and respectful ways in the fundamental human process of learning, adaptation, and growth. Could we ask for more?

April 2022

Joan V. Gallos
Brookline, Massachusetts

References

Gallos, J. V. (Ed.). (2006a). *Organization development.* Jossey-Bass.

Gallos, J. V. (2006b). Reframing complexity: A four-dimensional approach to organizational diagnosis, development, and change. In J.V. Gallos (Ed.) *Organization development.* Jossey-Bass, pp. 344-362.

Gallos, J.V. and Bolman, L. G. (2021). *Reframing academic leadership* (2nd edition). John Wiley & Sons.

Haidt, J. (2022, April 11). Why the past 10 years of American life have been uniquely stupid. *The Atlantic.* https://www.theatlantic.com/magazine/archive/2022/05/social-media-democracy-trust-babel/629369/

Heifetz, R. A. (1994). *Leadership without easy answers.* Belknap/Harvard University Press.

Kendi, I.X. (2020, August 5). The end of denial. *The Atlantic.* https://www.theatlantic.com/press-releases/archive/2020/08/ibram-x-kendi-on-the-end-of-denial/614962/

MSNBC (2022, April 27). *Roadblocks for voters.* https://www.msnbc.com/morning-joe/watch/gop-voters-less-concerned-with-homophobic-racist-remarks-than-dem-voters-poll-finds-138717765778

Nanus, B. (2008). Finding the right vision. In J. V. Gallos (Ed.), *Business leadership* (2nd edition), Jossey-Bass.

Shapiro, H. T. (2005). *A larger sense of purpose: Higher education and society.* Princeton University Press.

Thompson, J. D. (2003). *Organizations in action: Social science bases of administrative theory* (1st edition). Routledge.

Vaill, P.B. (1996). Learning as a way of being: Strategies for survival in a world of permanent white water. Jossey-Bass.

Introduction

The world, in tumult over the last few years, seems completely different and too much the same. Precarity, always present in the world, now seems its defining feature. Social justice, always too lacking, commands new urgency and attention. And leadership, a perennial object of fascination, needs a new look. There are surprising and intriguing developments at play—if they can be seen. This volume brings together chapters that focus on the intersection of these three forces—precarity, social justice, and unexpected leadership. Unexpected leaders influence others individually and collectively, regardless of social status or position, to meet needs in a particular setting.

In creating this volume, we sought to answer the call of Bolman and Deal (2017) to enlarge and extend the classic leadership literature to meet 21st-century challenges. These challenges result from uniquely converging forces: the exercise of leadership under intense and complex conditions, a demand for social justice in the pursuit of the full potential of every person and their communities, and dramatic, accelerating global change. As these chapters show, no domain is immune to these challenges. They pursue precarity and possibility in social, political, economic, environmental, health, and educational spaces.

Bolman and Deal (2017) called for a new generation of leaders and managers who will exercise diverse and multi-frame thinking. They called for a new generation who will be wise leaders, artistic managers, playful theorists, architects, catalysts, advocates, and prophets. These would be "pioneers who embrace the fundamental values of human life and the human spirit" and who would help avoid "misdirected resources, massive ineffectiveness, and unnecessary human pain and suffering" (p. 422). How will such leaders flourish? In precarious times, where those with the fewest resources suffer the most (Thrift & Sugarman, 2019), new, integrated thinking about leading toward justice is critical. Leaders at all levels in all domains, particularly unexpected leaders, are called to place social justice at the heart of their efforts.

The chapters in this collection attend to these challenges. The chapters come from various perspectives. They address different topics and contexts.

In their own ways, they explore three linked questions. First, what is the nature of precarity in the contemporary world? What is the stuff of precarity—who is affected, how, and why? Second, what are the social justice imperatives and possibilities inherent in these contexts? What might it mean in practice to build support for thriving human capabilities (Nussbaum, 2011)? Third, in these contexts, what might leadership look like? In the chapters comprising this volume, leadership looks different, sounds different, feels different. It is not classic. Rather, it is unexpected.

In this monograph, Institute for Social Innovation (ISI) scholar-practitioners explore leading toward greater social justice in diverse, precarious, fast-changing settings. The ISI was established in 2002 by Fielding Graduate University to help individuals as well as nonprofit, business, and government organizations address societal problems via research, professional development, and organizational consulting. ISI professionals include Fielding alumni, faculty, and students who conduct action-oriented research, train organizational leaders, lead community dialogues, and provide customized organizational consulting. The chapter authors in this volume are in pursuit of these objectives.

The monograph is arranged in two sections. In Section 1, the authors explore conditions in community and educational contexts that call for—and some generate—unexpected leadership. In Section 2, the authors explore how theories of unexpected leadership can be set into action. We learn about opportunities that precarity can bring to leaders who are willing to grow and change. A bridge chapter nods both ways.

We open in Chapter 1 with an exploration by Sonnet and Spearman of precarity in higher education and how this challenge was met in one doctoral program with informal, plural, circular leading by students themselves. In Chapter 2, Southam and Harman illuminate a distinctive, powerful, and care-oriented leadership of older women who embrace the archetype of the crone. In Chapter 3, Wilson argues for the power of intentional leadership in the context of an urban makerspace that fosters youth workforce development. In Chapter 4, Parker describes how the absence of leadership to improve school indoor air quality through accreditation requirements contributes to a persistent threat to student health and to failures in educational equity. In Buckley's Chapter 5, precarity is experienced by adults with disabilities and their caregivers in a "care-less society," ameliorated by a local project providing communities of care. Gebhardt's Chapter 6 rounds out the exploration of unexpected leadership in educational and community settings through a focus on change-making in small communities. Gebhardt discusses the "bloom-where-you-are-planted" approach of change leadership and how it is practiced by returning folk, faith groups, older women, and others. These chapters are united in arguments for an ethic of care and community—brought forth less by singular leaders and more by participative, non-positional, shared, and unexpected leadership.

The bridge Chapter 7 takes us to Tanzania and an exploration of these issues in the particular context of this country and through the lens of Theory U (Scharmer, 2009). McAlpine explores Ujasiri as a mindset and a leadership capacity that spurs action by citizen protectors, who step forward to protect women and children from violence in the community. Subsequent chapters discuss ways of thinking about leaders and leading that could advance human capabilities and thus increase social justice.

In Chapter 8, Curran and Thompson elaborate a distinctive form of leadership, termed generative team leadership, that they argue emerged from the "void" created by the pandemic. They theorize about this form of leadership and posit real-life illustrations of teens, communities, and corporate teams that fill the needs of the moment and form a new social fabric.

In Chapter 9, Eugene et al. focus on intersections between COVID-19 and a heightened awareness of racial injustices, propelling the need for dramatic social change. They call for psychologists to step into a new role as transformational leaders, leveraging their individual and institutional influence to address inequities that prevent more optimal life. Eugene et al. advocate for specific policies and practices to move the field towards equity and anti-racism. In Chapter 10, Haddad and Marlatt focus on apex leaders—heads of nations and large corporations whose decisions and actions have an outsized impact on the world. They describe a mentoring program and a developmental dynamic, grounded in transformative phenomenology and designed to increase the self-awareness of these leaders, with the goals of improving their decision-making and affecting positive, transformational change in the world.

In Chapter 11, Smendzuik-O'Brian uses an autoethnographic approach to explore the political precarity of the last few tumultuous years. She engages with the experience of public servants in the United States, asking how moral principles about the nature of civil society, political processes, and political leaders might be gleaned from religious traditions and from U.S. political traditions. She addresses how these principles can aid public service leaders to create contexts for the development of human capabilities.

We invited the authors of these chapters to explore the nature of precarity in our uncertain and teetering contemporary world. We asked them to consider how the work of Martha Nussbaum (2011) may help illuminate the pursuit of social justice in these contexts, and we invited authors to take a new look at leadership and what leading toward social justice might look like during turbulence. In their various ways, the authors have done just this. Their accounts are full of precarity and pain—and many are full of a rather surprising optimism with a focus on caring. The chapters show us unexpected leaders, who, in turn, show us better ways.

In an epilogue, we consider what the chapters have had to say about the three concepts of precarity, social justice, and leadership. We share what we have learned, adding to the scholarship of all three domains. What are the lessons for scholar-practitioners working at the intersection of precarity, social justice, and leadership? We invite you to read on and find out.

Patrice Rosenthal, Theresa Southam, and Marie Sonnet

References

Bolman, L. G., & Deal, T. E. (2017). *Reframing organizations: Artistry, choice, and leadership.* Jossey Bass.

Nussbaum, M. (2011). *Creating capabilities: The human development approach.* Harvard University Press.

Scharmer, O. (2009). *Theory U: Leading from the future as it emerges* (Kindle Edition). Berrett Koehler.

Section One

Unexpected Leading in Community and Educational Settings

Chapter 1

Leading from the Edge: Precarity, Resilience, and Success in an Informal Academic Support Community

Marie Sonnet
Institute for Social Innovation Fellow

Reid Spearman
Institute for Social Innovation Fellow

Precarity is a state in which security, necessities, and predictability are strained, and conventional assumptions are challenged (de la Sablonnière et al., 2013). Such a state is often accompanied by dramatic social change where "a rapid event leads to a profound societal transformation and produces a rupture in the equilibrium of the social and normative structures and changes/threatens the cultural identity of group members" (de la Sablonnière, 2017, p. 2). We think it is fair to say that the political, medical, environmental, and societal events of the 2020–2022 era, compounded by existing social fissures, have resulted in such ruptures. This is the context of our informal doctoral student support group study. During profound disruption, there are also precious opportunities for creativity (Bilder, 2014), questioning assumed knowledge, and advancing social justice, which is defined as strengthening human capabilities (Nussbaum, 2011).

While the phenomenon called *leadership* may be required to achieve such advancement, the dominant models of singular leading are inadequate for meeting the challenge of achieving greater social justice during precarity. In his introduction to a special issue of *Leadership*, Tourish (2020) asserted that the scale of the COVID-19 crisis revealed a "crisis of leadership theory and practice" (p. 261) and urged that

> Critical leadership studies has an important contribution to make in challenging self-serving theories of business that have come to guide much leadership decision-making. We have an opportunity to do research that really matters and participate in vital conversations about how the theory and practice of leadership can contribute to better outcomes from the coronavirus crisis, and others, still to come. (Tourish, 2020, p. 261)

To contribute to these conversations, we identified an example of *plural leadership* in the graduate education sector that was not explicitly invited by formal leaders or expected to complement their change leadership or response.

Plural leadership has been studied as a form of distributed leadership where the focus is the combined influence of multiple leaders in organizational situations (Canterino et al., 2020). More richly, Denis et al. (2012) described plural leading "not as a property of individuals and their behaviors, but as a collective phenomenon that is distributed or shared among different people, potentially fluid, and constructed in interaction" (p. 212). In their review, Denis et al. found that relevant literature contained four streams of scholarship about plural leading: (a) sharing leadership for team effectiveness, (b) pooling leadership at the top to direct others, (c) spreading leadership within and across levels over time, and (d) producing leadership through interaction. The fourth stream highlights Uhl-Bien's (2006) relational theory of leadership—leadership is an emergent organizing process and is relationally generated as a product of interactions and communications between people in a given context.

We saw evidence of relational leading in a set of doctoral students bound by a common academic objective and initiating their own responses to change and precarity at the edges of the formal school structure. We call this *leading from the edge*, echoing chaos theorist Norman Packard (1988) and complexity theorist Ralph Stacey (1996). We propose that in this space between chaos and adaptation—where flexibility, creativity, agility, and innovation emerge—a kind of fluid, unexpected, everyday leading increases human capabilities. Halifax (2018) described edge states as places of both peril and promise. Amidst precarity, perspective and resilience and compassion can foster academic success.

We examined this form of leading by investigating the experience of a subset of doctoral students in a small (1,071 students as of spring 2021) non-profit graduate university with a distributed learning model. The school population was 78% female and 64% over 39 years old. Faculty and students work virtually and in-person across a global platform. It is part of the school's mission to foster a more just and sustainable world.

An entry cohort of 21 new students met in the fall of 2017. An existing student served as an advisor. To stay in touch and provide mutual support, the student suggested utilizing the WhatsApp free multiplatform messaging application. The cohort agreed to create a virtual, 24/7 meeting place using this tool. As they discussed their intentions with other students, cohort members agreed that any student could be invited to the group, share access to conversations on WhatsApp, and view collected resources on Google Docs. They selected a group name, which we will report as the *Voyagers*. As of January 2022, there were 67 students and alumni in this peer network which is not sanctioned, trained, or formally convened. It is an organic web of loosely connected individuals who can reach out to peers when they want to. We wanted to find out: Does self-designed peer support in graduate education address precarity and increase social justice? These are our specific questions:

- During 2020–2021, what kinds of precarity did participants in the Voyagers experience?
- As a result of the Voyager experience, were human capabilities, as Nussbaum (2011) described them, strengthened?
- If so, with what kind of leading?
- What are the implications for graduate student success during precarity?

We first discuss (a) the nature of pursuing a doctoral degree, (b) the growing commitment to student health and well-being as a critical success factor, (c) the role of institutional and peer support, (d) Nussbaum's (2017) capabilities approach as a theoretical framework, and (e) the idealized model of singular, unitary leadership.

Pursuing a Doctoral Degree

Pursuing a doctoral degree is itself a precarious undertaking. It can comprise "precious moments of enthusiasm" and "a great many negative emotions" resulting in a balance of inspiration and exhaustion (Stubb et al., 2011, p. 33). There is a long median time to the doctoral degree in American graduate schools, with the shortest completion time ranging from 6.3–7.0 years for science and engineering (S&E) degrees. For non-S&E doctoral degree completion, median times range from 7.9 years for psychology and social sciences degrees to 12.0 years for education degrees (National Science Foundation Survey of Earned Doctorates, October 2021).

Persistence is not enough. Using aggregate and pre-COVID data, authors showed that in North American graduate schools, between 40% and 50% of enrolled doctoral students do not finish their degrees (Geven et al., 2018; Sverdlik et al., 2018; Cassuto & Weisbach, 2021), with variation by discipline ranging from 24–67% (Gardner, 2009). The attrition rate for minority students was reported at 70% (Brunsma et al., 2016), with nearly two-thirds of African American/Black doctoral candidates not completing their degrees (Joseph, 2012). Even allowing for expected attrition, long completion times and high rates of non-completion have severe economic and psychological costs that can be considered unacceptable (Gardner, 2009). The implications for doctoral student well-being are consequential.

Doctoral Student Stress

Stress for doctoral students comes from various sources, including long working hours, difficulty balancing the demands of scholarship with other obligations, the high cost of postsecondary education, and uncertainty of postgraduate employment (Hish et al., 2019). Events, even ones we choose (e.g., a new job or a doctoral program), can cause stress when they upset our balance and require an adjustment. Adjustment periods are taxing and increase a person's susceptibility to the effects of stress (Pearlin et al., 1981). Stress can also result from problems that persist over time. Chronic strains tend to erode a person's concept of self. Erosion occurs when individuals make judgments that lower their self-worth or feel they can no longer master the internal and external pressures that life imposes on them. Doctoral students have been shown to experience *imposter syndrome*, which captures both negative perceptions of self-worth and distorted views of one's abilities (Sverdlik et al., 2020). Lower self-esteem and perceived mastery can lead to a greater vulnerability to stress symptoms (Hish et al., 2019).

Stress affects the way students feel emotionally, influencing their ability to think clearly and perform well academically (Duraku & Hoxha, 2018). Doctoral students under stress are at increased risk for depression, anxiety, and burnout (Evans et al., 2018). In their study of economics PhD programs, Barreira et al. (2018) found that 25% of students who had been in their programs for five years or more experienced symptoms of depression and anxiety that were severe or moderate. During 2020–2021, students unexpectedly experienced remote events and virtual classes, a mode of delivery whereby instructors (largely untrained in online and/or virtual educational delivery) attempted to teach. In a survey of 208 graduate STEM degree-producing U.S. institutions, Stewart et al. (2021) reported that 71% put 90% or more of their classes online. Research and internships were disrupted. In addition to significant hardships, especially for vulnerable students, this type of learning can be "extremely isolating" (Posselt, 2021, p. 7). Stewart et al. (2021) reported that feelings of loneliness were the most frequently reported concern (37%), followed by other mental health concerns (33%).

Stress Mediators

Personal resilience and good mental health are crucial to student retention. Resilience can be described as "positive adaptation to negative life circumstances, and the relative stability (or swift recovery) of psychosocial, mental, and physical functioning following exceptionally stressful periods or situations" (Thoma et al., 2020, p. 216). Resilient students are better able to retain or recover good mental health in the face of adversity and can persist through academic challenges and setbacks (Eisenberg et al., 2016). Strengthening resilience and developing coping skills are personal strategies a student can employ, but doctoral students need broader support.

Choosing a faculty advisor experienced in academic mentoring and advising in addition to research can be crucial to completing a doctoral program (Hunter & Devine, 2016). Conversely, the lack of good mentor relationships is a characteristic shared by those who experience high levels of anxiety or depression (Evans et al., 2018). Faculty mentors are part of a support network that helps to cultivate significant, positive, long-lasting relationships and *belonging.*

The need to belong can be as imperative as the need for food, and being deprived of belonging may represent an intolerable situation (Baumeister & Leary, 1995). Strayhorn (2019) offered this definition of belonging: "a feeling or sensation of connectedness, and the experience of mattering or feeling cared about, accepted, respected, valued by, and important to the campus community or others on campus such as faculty, staff, and peers" (p. 4). Belonging is critical to building the sense of community that students need to deal with the many sources of stress inherent in doctoral studies (Greene, 2015). Sverdlik et al. (2020) found that perceived scholarly belonging mitigated the experience of being an imposter. When doctoral students share experiences connected to a common purpose, cohesive support networks providing significant benefits may develop (Pilbeam et al., 2013). Networks provide opportunities for discussion, comparing progress in an academic program, and emotional support. It takes a university community to graduate doctoral students.

Fostering Graduate Student Success: An *All Hands* Effort

Research on graduate student success has shifted from a prime focus on student socio-demographic and individual characteristics to examining institutional characteristics (Castelló et al., 2017; Eisenberg et al., 2016; Posselt, 2018, 2021; Skopek et al., 2020). This shift recognizes that universities can create environments where a focus on the socio-psychological well-being of students makes student completion more likely (Stubb et al., 2011). Recommended efforts include institutional support and peer support.

Institutional Support

The Council of Graduate Schools (2021) issued a call to action for graduate deans to support graduate student mental health and well-being with three goals: (a) Reduce attrition due to psychological and emotional distress, (b) raise degree attainment rates for both majority and underrepresented student groups, and (c) achieve greater graduate student and alumni satisfaction with the supportiveness of the graduate program environment. As of August 13, 2021, 166 graduate deans had signed a statement of commitments, with nurturing a positive and inclusive learning environment as a first principle.

Promoting health and well-being must be seen as an "all hands issue" (Posselt,

2021, p. 9) where everyone has a role to play in creating healthy cultures and responding to issues as they arise. Posselt noted that this is a "counter-cultural" (p. 9) recommendation, as such an objective is often seen as the responsibility of an office or a center and not everyone's responsibility. This distribution of accountability flows to students, too. Stubb et al. (2011) concluded that peer groups, for example, "can function as important and meaningful communities for students" (p. 47).

Along with other community members, peers can add to the experiences of adequate support and shared control that minimize the destructive friction between students and the learning environment that could lead to dropping out (Pyhältö et al., 2012). Using exit surveys of 1,406 students who completed doctoral programs between 2006 and 2008, Sowell (2009) reported that social environment and peer group support comprised one of six factors contributing to student completion. Others were financial support, mentoring/advising, family support, program quality, and professional/career guidance.

Peer Support

Two of the promising programs mentioned by Eisenberg et al. (2016) as addressing student resilience, mental health, and academic success are peer-based: the Student Support Network at Worcester Polytechnic Institute (WPI) and the Wolverine Support Network at the University of Michigan (UM). Both programs train students in peer support. At UM, students are trained by Counseling and Psychological Services to lead weekly meetings for both undergraduate and graduate students. At WPI, the Student Development and Counseling Center provides a Student Support Network training course for students "who may find themselves in the role of a trusted listener or helper for their peers." According to the WPI website, 10 other universities have adopted this curriculum. These formal programs sponsored by institutional support services leverage the value of peer support and have clear benefits. They may also require infrastructure unavailable at many schools.

Tackling a common hurdle directly, the Office of Education at Columbia University's Mailman School of Public Health began a WritingWorks peer support program for doctoral students in October 2021. The students at all stages of dissertation writing are assigned to writing clubs where peers generate support, accountability, and guidance in self-designed modes, including group writing.

At Merrimack College, students founded the Graduate Students of Color Association (Roumimper & Falk, 2021), where members are encouraged to co-create a counter space for processing, healing, and growth. A faculty advisor assists the group. Roumimper and Falk (2021) noted that "a formal student group is ideal because it provides institutionalization and a mechanism for institutional resources and support … new graduate students have a base from which to continue from year to year rather than having to recreate the group" (p. 1101). The urge to default to institutionalization is one we will question in this chapter.

By creating a healthy community that supports student agency and self-determination, along with validation, support, and role models that can act as resources, peer support can affect the social determinants of well-being related to graduate school completion (Posselt, 2021). We wanted to find out how participants in the Voyagers described their precarity and their supports. We do so in the context of a theoretical framework from Nussbaum (2011).

A Theoretical Framework: Core Mission—Human Development

To situate our study in the mission of the university and the pursuit of greater social justice, we noted Posselt's (2021) assertion that "the quality of social networks, norms, and trust within organizations can be thought of as critical tools in ensuring the conditions of freedom and security within which human rights are protected" (p. 5). Schools are such organizations. Strengthening the well-being of students increases justice, equity, and inclusion and links to an educational institution's core mission—human development—enabling people to "live full and creative lives, commensurate with their equal human dignity" (Nussbaum, 2011, p. 185). This developmental process creates a more just and sustainable world. We also recognize that this may be an idealized mission of the university. Financial and competitive pressures have shifted the educational focus of higher education in many schools to employability and career goals rather than classic human development goals (Healy et al., 2022). Still, for those institutions committed to increasing social justice, it is important to pursue how this is done with actual students.

Countering dominant approaches (e.g., White, Western, male) that emphasize the pursuit of wealth as the measure of development, Nussbaum (2011) argued for a theoretical paradigm in the development and policy world known as the *capabilities approach.* The imperative is to address "urgent human problems and unjustifiable human inequalities (p. xii), particularly "entrenched social injustice and inequality" (p. 19). Quality of life is defined as the presence of capabilities, which are "freedoms or opportunities created by a combination of personal abilities and the political, social, and economic environment" (p. 20).

Table 1
Nussbaum's (2011) Central Capabilities

Central Capability*	Description
Life	Ability to reach end of normal human life without reductions due to avoidable mental and physical challenges
Bodily health	Adequately nourished and sheltered
Bodily integrity	Opportunities to move with security. Safe from aggression and assault
Senses, imagination, and thought	Access to learning. Experiencing and producing work of one's own choice
Emotions	To love, grieve, long for, be angry and feel gratitude as a result of healthy attachments to others and place
Practical reason	Able to conceive of good and critically plan one's life with purpose
Affiliation	Show concern with and towards others without discrimination on the basis of sex, race, sexual orientation, ethnicity, religion, or nationality
Living in concern for and relation to other species	Living with concern for animals, plants and other living and non-living parts of the world
Play	Laughing and enjoyment
Control over one's environment	Participating in political choices that govern one's life and having equitable rights to property, work, and recognition

Note. Adapted from Nussbaum, M. (2011). Creating capabilities: The human development approach, Harvard University Press, pp. 33–34.

* Bolded entries are those in focus for this study

Nussbaum offered ten *central capabilities* (p. 33) that can be seen as "goals" (p. 169). Organizations, including educational institutions, could use these goals to aim and assess their pursuit of human development and thus their contribution to social justice. For this study, we were particularly interested in exploring student growth in four of these capabilities shown as bolded in Table 1: senses, imagination, and thought; emotions; practical reason; and affiliation. We also wanted to examine leading toward capability growth and greater social justice on the virtual campus in light of the prevailing paradigm of singular leadership.

The Idealized Model of Singular Leadership

Even as scholars assess the failures of leadership in the face of the global pandemic (Lagowska et al., 2020; Sufi, 2021; Tourish, 2020, Wieland, 2020), the ideal of an optimal set of individual leadership styles, traits, and behaviors persists. Scholars urge leaders to develop positive leadership traits such as protecting employees, offering optimism, providing timely and transparent communication, and displaying self-sacrificing behaviors and empathy (Wieland, 2020). Leaders should display a transformational leadership style that fosters superior positive relationships with subordinates, performance motivation, and commitment (Sufi, 2021). Leaders should even sound the part (Truninger et al., 2021). While the myth of the singular hero leader has long been questioned (Senge, 2000), the pursuit of the leader "made for this moment" endures.

Tourish (2020) observed that when there is radical uncertainty, there is less information, less expertise, and fewer resources. In this environment, leaders rise who exploit uncertainty, offer simple solutions, and engage in *incompetent* leadership, *denialist* leadership, *panic* leadership, *othering* leadership, and *authoritarian* leadership (pp. 266–267). "Mainstream leadership theories are of little help" (Tourish, 2020, p. 261). This creates an imperative for leadership scholars to imagine new models.

Prior to the COVID-19 pandemic, Bolman and Deal (2017) were already calling for a new generation of leaders who would be "pioneers who embrace the fundamental values of human life and the human spirit" and would help avoid "misdirected resources, massive ineffectiveness, and unnecessary human pain and suffering" (p. 422). They called for artistic managers, playful theorists, architects, catalysts, advocates, and prophets. The need for *pioneers* conflicts with the definition of the post-COVID-19 era leader as offered by Kurt and Erdoğan (2021)—"A person who can attract attention by affecting people both physically and mentally, appealing to their feelings, motivating and uniting them towards a specific goal, and making them do what they want" (p. 1).

Complicating this blunt dissonance is an assertion rooted in social identity leadership theory (Hogg & van Knippenberg, 2003) that people want a leader:

> People simply need leadership—to help resolve self-uncertainty. The formal title and role of "leader" make explicit a structural role relationship within a group that assigns the leader a greater degree of perceived authority than the rest of the group (see Fiske, 2010) to determine group prototypicality, define the group's identity, and thus determine individual members' social identity. (Rast et al., 2012)

Rast et al. (2012) utilized uncertainty-identity theory (Hogg, 2007) to study how uncertainty affected the selection of a student leader. While there was a preference for a prototypical leader, uncertainty reduced resistance to a non-prototypical leader because, under uncertainty, any leader was better than no leader.

That longed-for "leader" is the idealized singular leader. Does this default model contribute to the leadership failures during precarity? Can a need for leadership be met when the leader is not a formal, singular, selected individual? Relationships—rather than authority, superiority, or dominance—may be essential (Uhl-Bien, 2006). Perhaps, during precarity, leaders are enablers, not controllers (Plowman et al., 2007).

To explore enabling leadership that impacted targeted central capabilities (Table 1), we chose four established leadership models (servant, inclusive, distributed, and authentic) in the singular leadership canon and identified eight outcomes related to the targeted capabilities. We wanted to know if these outcomes were experienced in our study setting where there was a plural, non-hierarchal, more circular form of leading. The four selected leadership models and eight associated outcomes are

- **Servant leadership** (Ragnarsson et al., 2018)

(1) experiencing care and compassion

(2) help toward achieving goals

• **Inclusive leadership** (Randel et al., 2018)

(3) experiencing a sense of belonging

(4) making a valued contribution

• **Distributed leadership** (Tian et al., 2016)

(5) experiencing self-empowerment

(6) a climate of trust

• **Authentic leadership** (Avolio et al., 2004)

(7) experiencing greater positive emotions about the work

(8) receiving reliable information.

In summary, we suggest that an organic peer community may derive its effectiveness from being inside the formal entity, yet outside of it, too. Leading from this edge is also a form of leading on the edge of disruption, where the impact of internal pressures related to pursuing the PhD and external events like the 2020-2021 pandemic collide. In that collision, space for unexpected, spontaneous, and generous leadership is created. Without a prescribed hierarchy, needs can be heard as they arise. Students can receive a response that is both crowd-sourced and personal, exceeding the capacity of a formal student services function. We wanted to examine this type of leading, particularly during precarity, as an undervalued form of leadership.

Method

Our Population

As of August 11, 2021, our population comprised 67 people who retained an affiliation with the group. They were primarily from one university school and were approximately 30% of its doctoral enrollment. All had initially asked to be included in email communications from the Voyager listserv and to have access to a Google Drive that houses shared resources related to achieving milestones in the doctoral timeline. A subset of these persons, approximately 43, also asked for access to the WhatsApp social media channel. Groups of participants, varying in size from 5 to 15, attend a monthly First Friday Zoom call to socialize, share updates, discuss experiences, hear from guest speakers, and exchange advice and encouragement. Interest groups on topics like student technology solutions and writing and publishing pop up, and those meetings are open to anyone interested.

Students interact with the Voyagers at various times in their academic program, reflecting both the use of group connections and the often-solo nature of the doctoral experience. That is, direct contact with a support group may vary with the academic cycles of individual and group work. We noted that approximately 50% of those who identify as Voyagers are *active*, defined as present in contact channels in the prior three months, or 33 people at the time of our survey. Defining active participation prompted our interest in understanding the value of the group to those who are not active. Being part of a network may provide valued support even if little or no assistance is provided (Baumeister & Leary, 1995).

Original Cohort

Table 2 shows the status (December 2021) of the original 2017 cohort of 21 students. Using 20 as the denominator due to a student's death, 17 have persisted for a retention rate of 85%, with six earning their doctoral degree within 4 years. All remain connected with the Voyagers. Dr. Spearman is one of the original cohort students, and Dr. Sonnet joined the group as an alumna in 2019.

Table 2
December 2021 Status of the 2017 Voyager Cohort

2017 Cohort		%	Retention
Deceased	1	5%	
In Program	10	46%	
Graduated	6	29%	85%*
Master's Only	1	5%	
Withdrawn	3	14%	
Totals	21		
Gender (F)	17	81%	
Gender (M)	4	19%	
Totals	21		

* 17 (85%) of a possible 20 students are retained over 4 years.

Study Design

To secure rich experiential data for our exploratory study, we chose a mixed-methods approach that would (a) gather quantitative data through a survey that also encouraged text comments and (b) collect additional qualitative data from focus group discussions and individual interviews. The quantitative data, analyzed using the IBM Statistical Package for Social Sciences (SPSS) Statistics 28 package, allowed us to summarize and compare participant experiences and counterbalance narrative data, which could be skewed to those more active in the Voyagers or more positive about their experience.

Narrative data were analyzed using thematic analysis methodology (Braun & Clarke, 2012), allowing us to see and make sense of reported experiences and find commonalities relative to our research questions. As co-researchers, we could leverage the analytical skills of two scholars and provide a crosscheck for bias. We used both inductive and deductive approaches to data coding and analysis and sought inter-rater agreement to increase confidence in our results (McDonald et al., 2019).

We secured university Institutional Review Board approval (IRB; #21-0506) to ensure participant protections, including informed consent, voluntary engagement, and agreement to use pseudonyms to protect privacy. The listserv administrator sent an invitation to join the study to all 67 names on the August 2021 Voyager listserv. The invitation invited volunteers to complete a SurveyMonkey survey, participate in a focus group, and/or schedule an individual interview. A reminder invitation was sent twice in the following two-week period. Survey responses were collected anonymously; volunteers for focus groups or interviews were asked to contact Dr. Spearman via email with their preferred date and time.

Using survey design protocols (Hinkin, 1998), 24 items with 4-point Likert ratings were developed in four categories: precarity (6 items), resilience (2 items), leadership outcomes (8 items), and the five Nussbaum (2011) capabilities (7 items). Each item offered the opportunity to say more in a text response, providing additional qualitative data, and included a Not Applicable response option. Some may feel they have no experience of an item, which would be valuable data. One demographic question asked the length of time the respondent was associated with the Voyagers. For privacy purposes, no other demographic data were collected.

We developed a semi-structured interview guide (Adams, 2015) with questions that would facilitate conversation and elicit valuable qualitative insight around three areas of inquiry: (a) the experience of precarity during the COVID-19 period, (b) resilience strategies, and (c) the impact of the Voyager connection. We conducted meetings via Zoom and the Zoom transcription feature produced meeting transcripts that were converted into Word documents. Focus group discussions were 60 minutes long; individual interviews were approximately 45 minutes long.

The technique used to code the data was in vivo coding. In vivo coding is the practice of assigning a label to a section of data, such as an interview transcript, using a word or short phrase taken from that section of the data. The researchers chose this coding method to increase the likelihood that the data analysis accurately represented the meaning of the experiences described by participants by creating codes using their own words (Saldaña, 2016). The primary object of the coding process is to move from the many disassociated ideas contained in the raw data to more abstract concepts that can describe the data in a more general way for the development of assertions or theories (Saldaña, 2016).

Working independently, we recorded the codes by hand using the transcript documents, selecting words and phrases relevant to research questions, assessing their frequency, and working iteratively to extract categories and develop themes. After the data were hand-coded, a second-level coding method called pattern coding allowed us to aggregate or disaggregate codes into categories. Categories are more significant larger segments of the data that have similar characteristics. Each of us then identified themes. A theme is a broad unit of information composed of more than one code or category combined to constitute a shared idea—a recurring topic or meaning that represents a phenomenon (McDonald et al., 2019).

One researcher used a primarily inductive method, a "bottom-up approach" (Braun & Clarke, 2012, p. 58) that derives codes and themes from the content of the data themselves. The other researcher employed a primarily deductive approach, where the analyst brings concepts, ideas, and topics to the data that are used for coding and interpretation. In this case, those concepts were precarity, resilience, the experience of established leadership outcomes, and the central capabilities. "In reality, coding and analysis often use a combination of both approaches" (Braun & Clarke, 2012, p. 58).

Findings

We received 17 survey responses, representing approximately 52% of the estimated active 33 participants at the time of the survey. We conducted two focus groups—with five participants and then three—and conducted four individual interviews for a total of 12 in-person contributors, 10 women (83%) and two men (17%). Of the 17 survey respondents, 11 (65%) were part of the Voyagers for 3 or 4 years. Five (29%) indicated 2 years, and one marked less than 1 year. We report survey results by section: precarity, resilience, leadership experience, and the central capabilities. We then present focus group and interview results.

Survey Results

COVID-19 Precarity

In the survey results (N=17), the reported impact of the pandemic on educational success during 2020–2021 was distributed across weak to very strong ratings. Nine respondents (45%) reported weak and moderate impact; eight (47%) reported strong and very strong impact. We queried for more specifics about the types of impact.

Seven (41%) participants indicated that their mental health had a strong or very strong impact on their academic success, as did their physical health. Seven (41%) reported that the physical health of others had a strong or very strong impact on their academic success. Six (35%) indicated that the mental health of others had a strong or very strong impact on their academic success. The impact of finances was rated by eight (47%) respondents as having a strong or very strong impact on their educational success.

Resilience

We defined resilience in the study context as a personal capacity to accomplish academic work during the study period. This capacity was rated as weak or moderate by nine (45%) respondents and strong or very strong by eight (47%). Personal support systems were rated as strong or very strong by 10 (59%)

participants and moderate or weak by seven (41%).

The Voyager Leadership Experience

Table 3 displays survey results about the experience of leadership outcomes as related to the Voyagers. We extracted these outcomes from four established leadership models. We show the data to capture the distribution and diversity of respondent experience. The higher the mean score (out of four possible points) and the lower the standard deviation around that mean, the stronger the experience.

We considered a Not Applicable response an abstention; that is, the respondent excluded themselves from that experience. The number of abstentions indicated how common the experience was. No experience was universal, as all items had at least one Not Applicable response. The most common experience was "As a result of the Voyagers, I experience care and compassion" with a mean of 3.63 and a standard deviation of 0.50. One respondent reported this was Not Applicable, representing the fewest abstentions in the data.

Table 3
Respondent Experience of Outcomes Related to Four Established Leadership Models

As a result of the Voyagers:	*M*	*SD*	Strongly Disagree	Disagree	Agree	Strongly Agree	Not Applicable
Servant Leadership Outcomes:							
I experience care and compassion.	**3.63**	**0.50**			6	10	1
I receive help toward achieving my goals.	3.64	0.63		1	3	10	3
Authentic Leadership Outcomes:							
I experience greater positive emotions about my academic work.	3.60	0.74		1	5	8	3
I receive information that is reliable.	3.53	0.83	1		4	10	2
Distributed Leadership Outcomes:							
I experience self-empowerment.	3.38	0.65		1	6	6	4
I experience a climate of trust.	3.53	0.83	1		4	10	2
Inclusive Leadership Outcomes:							
I feel a sense of belonging.	3.26	0.88	1	1	6	7	2
I feel I can make a valued "uniquely me" contribution.	3.29	0.73		2	6	6	3

Responses to Central Capabilities (Nussbaum, 2011)

Table 4 provides survey results related to our respondents' experience of the five central capabilities (Nussbaum, 2011). Using the same approach to the data, the items with the highest mean scores, low standard deviations, and fewest Not Applicable responses were under the capability, affiliation: "I feel treated as a dignified being whose worth is equal to that of others" and "I am more able to imagine the situation of another."

Two items under the capability, senses, imagination, and thought, received the most abstentions: "I am more able to use my own thinking to produce works of my own choice" and "I am able to participate more effectively in choices about my actions." The item "I have less anxiety in my life" had the lowest mean score in the dataset (3.07), with two Disagree responses and three abstentions, revealing a wide range of experience. This variation is also shown for the item under the capability, practical reason: "I am more able to engage in critical reflection about the planning of my life." We were particularly interested in this experience variation.

Narrative Data Results

After reviewing our independently obtained thematic analysis results, we found that narrative data from survey comments and interview transcripts directly converged toward a set of three themes and subthemes. These are shown in Table 5. We will look at data related to each of these themes, recapping first the relevant quantitative results and then offering examples of narrative statements.

Table 4

Respondent Experience of Central Capabilities (Nussbaum, 2011) Items

Central Capability As a result of the Voyagers:	*M*	*SD*	Strongly Disagree	Disagree	Agree	Strongly Agree	Not Applicable
Affiliation: I feel treated as a dignified being whose worth is equal to that of others.	**3.64**	**0.63**		1	3	10	3
I am more able to imagine the situation of another.	**3.62**	**0.51**			5	8	4
Emotions: I have less anxiety in my life.	**3.07**	**0.62**		2	9	3	3
I can show emotions (such as grief, longing, gratitude, and justified anger).	3.45	0.52			6	5	6
Practical reason: I am more able to engage in critical reflection about the planning of my life.	**3.09**	**0.51**		1	8	2	6
Senses, imagination, and thought: I am more able to use my own thinking to produce works of my own choice.	**3.20**	**0.79**		2	4	4	7
Control over one's environment: I am able to participate more effectively in choices about my actions (such as participation, speech, and association).	**3.33**	**0.50**			6	3	8

Table 5

Thematic Analysis of Narrative Data: Themes and Related Subthemes

Themes and Subthemes
1. Overcoming hardship through shared experience. *Subtheme*: Experiencing positive emotions about academic work
2. Increasing capacity through intellectual exchange *Subtheme*: Experiencing self-empowerment
3. Building lasting relationships through meaningful connection *Subtheme*: Feeling a sense of belonging

Overcoming Hardship Through Shared Experience

The lowest mean score of 3.07 in the dataset belongs to the item, "As a result of the Voyagers, I have less anxiety in my life." Figure 1 presents the dimensions of precarity reported. While not everyone experienced the same level of personal disruption, multiplied burdens involving family, school, work, self, and others were most frequently noted. Concurrently, 13 (76%) agreed or strongly agreed that as a result of the Voyagers they experience greater positive emotions about their academic work; one disagreed, and three abstained. Respondents identified strategies they used to "get through," which we noted as markers of resilience.

Narrative data provide detail about the experience of precarity while pursuing a doctoral degree during the COVID-19 crisis. Here are sample statements that include anonymous comments from survey respondents and interview comments denoted by an assigned pseudonym.

No one fared well. To a person, everyone dealt with all of the psychological

Figure 1
Reported Dimensions of COVID-19 Precarity

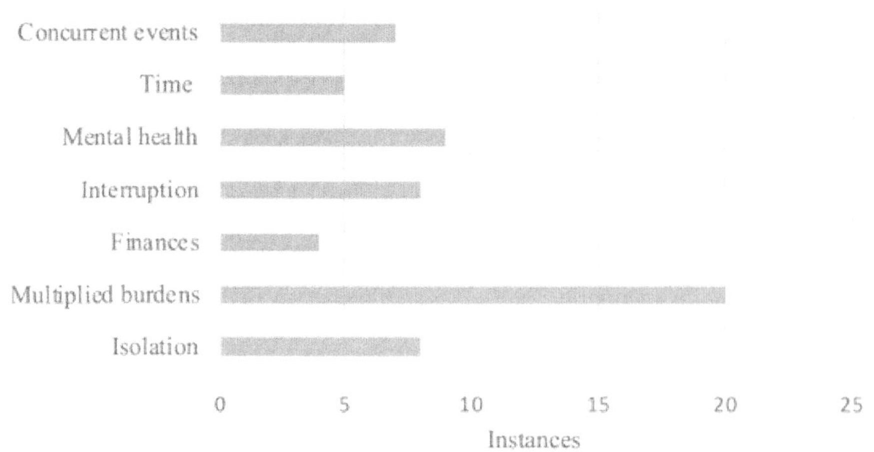

baggage of forced confinement. (Anonymous)

Too much togetherness made it hard to concentrate on the task at hand. (Anonymous)

It made [subject] recruitment very difficult and added months to the completion of data collection. (Anonymous)

I was doing most of my research online, so it did not impact me. (Anonymous)

The COVID pandemic impacted my participation in intensives and sessions at school which are a huge part of what makes my educational program successful. The day-to-day course participation and interactions with faculty and staff did not suffer as the modality didn't have to change. We were already set up to attend school online. What suffered and I believe hindered my progress was the face-to-face offerings. Places where the magic happens and ideas are born collectively amongst friends and food. (Anonymous)

I was dealing with multiple factors of border closures (airport closed/ seaports closed). It was so awful to be separated from my family and support system. (Anonymous)

Ill family members and one who died of Covid certainly threw everything off the rails. (Anonymous)

The fatigue with Zoom and the fatigue with being online for work and Zoom and school was very pronounced. (Hannah)

The bandwidth was gone so everything wound up being late. I mean this has cost me tens of thousands of dollars. I really felt like I was drowning; I was going under. (Ava)

It's just it's been this whole 2020 and 2021 have been really, really rough. (Olivia)

During the same period, respondents reported coping strategies and positive emotions about academic work.

I pushed through and it was tough. (Anonymous)

Being tenacious and adaptable helped me to persevere through this unprecedented time. It was through self-determination that I stayed on track. (Anonymous)

Working on my dissertation gave me a point of focus other than work, and other than the pandemic. I had plenty to occupy my mind and not panic about the pandemic. Being occupied also gave me more of a balanced mind when I did turn my attention to the pandemic, which helped me stay calm and not panic. (Anonymous)

The flexibility of working from home provided the opportunity to take frequent short walks that helped me physically with the gym closed. The mental break of stepping away let me come back refreshed and able to focus. (Anonymous)

My friendships with colleagues from my cohort, my committee, family, and friends helped the difficult times a lot less difficult. (Anonymous)

I was fortunate that I was employed throughout. Thus, I was able to afford tuition. (Anonymous)

Since professional activity reduced, I have more time and energy to put into dissertation work. (Anonymous)

I actually started getting my outdoor hike leader training done so I could do some hikes in nature, for people who are nervous to go out on their own. (Isabelle)

Through trials and tribulations, I've learned and built a foundational support system, because I know that life gets rough so I had these things in

Figure 2
Reported Dimensions of Resilience

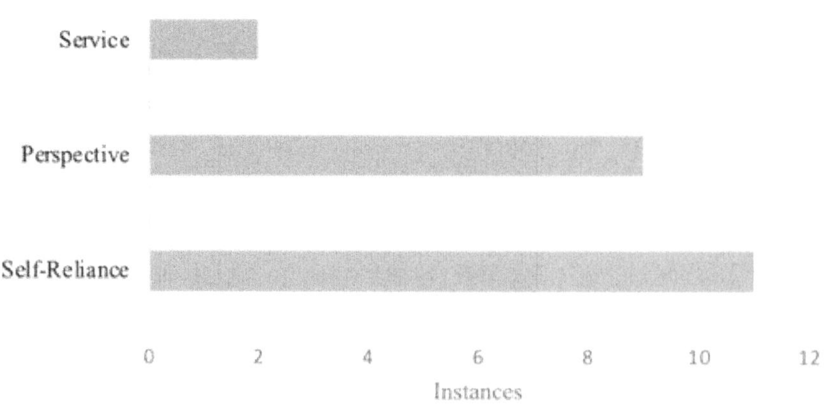

place. (Madison)

Figure 2 presents reported dimensions of resilience found in the narrative data. We noted self-reliance, developing perspective, and finding ways to serve.

Increasing Capacity Through Intellectual Exchange

According to survey data, 14 (82%) respondents agreed or strongly agreed that as a result of the Voyagers they receive reliable information; one strongly disagreed, and two selected Not Applicable. Thirteen (76%) survey respondents agreed or strongly agreed that they receive help toward achieving their goals; one disagreed, while three abstained. Twelve (71%) survey respondents agreed or strongly agreed that as a result of the Voyagers they experience self-empowerment; one disagreed, and four indicated Not Applicable. Narrative data supply more details.

Hearing about the success of others helps me be successful. (Anonymous)

I still struggle but I am more confident today than I was before. Voyagers listen to my ideas and provide legitimate feedback that helps me to see myself through others' eyes. I have huge self-esteem/confidence issues. (Anonymous)

Yes! The group doesn't do the work for you, but they tell you how and where to get started. That's a BIG help! Motivation, motivation, motivation, because I don't want to let the group down. (Anonymous)

Then this group gave me the confidence to just step up and do that. (Madison)

My confidence in how to live my life differently came from the fact that I could try on all these different hats with all these different people. (Emma)

You're gonna finish you know just out of pure spite some time. I got 10 people that are going to grab me and throw me a life preserver. You're not gonna let me quit. (Ava)

I feel really emboldened because heck if they're if they're being resilient against all those things, certainly, I could speak up a little bit here. (Georgia)

We had kind of had this little committee meeting with Voyagers and I said, this is what bothers me and I need to just kind of vent this out to you, and they all kind of looked at me and said, then you just say no. (Emma)

We all bring ourselves, our authentic selves, to the table, I think, as we go through the dissertation process and that may sit well with us individually and it might not, but to have the peer support that comes from a place of nonjudgment, I think helps each of us, as I speak for myself, to find our own true way. (Sophia)

Building Lasting Relationships Through Meaningful Connection

Sixteen (94%) survey participants agreed or strongly agreed that as part of the Voyagers they experience care and compassion. One reported Not Applicable. This item was the most highly rated and universally reported.

Fourteen (82%) survey respondents agreed or strongly agreed with experiencing a climate of trust; one strongly disagreed, and two reported Not Applicable. Thirteen (76%) participants agreed or strongly agreed that they are more able to imagine the situation of another, with no disagreement but four abstentions. Thirteen also agreed or strongly agreed that they "feel treated as a dignified being whose worth is equal to that of others"; one disagreed, and three abstained. Thirteen (76%) respondents agreed or strongly agreed that, as a result of the Voyagers, they experience a sense of belonging; one strongly disagreed, one disagreed, and two abstained. Twelve (71%) participants indicated that they agreed or strongly agreed that they make a valued, "uniquely me" contribution to the group; two disagreed, and three reported Not Applicable. Narrative data supply more detail:

One of the most important ways we help each other is to share our work. Having an example to follow makes the principles we're trying to learn easier to understand. (Anonymous)

I know I can always drop in and be welcomed. (Anonymous)

I returned to school after a long hiatus, and so the people I had connections with were long gone. The Voyagers gave me a new "anchor group" or cohort to connect with. (Anonymous)

I not only wanted to graduate but to have an alum group. The Voyagers have been just the ticket! (Anonymous)

Watching others progress and graduate and help celebrate has been motivating. (Anonymous)

Anytime I have a question, there is someone there to answer. Anytime I am looking for some assistance with direction, there is someone there. If I need something read for clarity, there is someone there. (Anonymous)

I just love the positive regard I receive from others. (Anonymous)

This is the biggest piece for me. Helping me to feel that connection and especially during COVID where we did not have in-person sessions. Also reminding me that I am not 100% crazy for pursuing a doctoral degree. (Anonymous)

I am perhaps not your ideal Voyager as I participate lightly. It is helpful to know that an active community is available when I have questions. I also appreciate knowing that others are encountering inconsistencies and difficulties with the system. (Anonymous)

I feel like the relationships within the Voyagers have helped because they were real. I wasn't doing this alone. I'm not doing this alone. (Charlotte)

Voyagers really created that virtual world where you could share resources and tips and see what's on the other side and get ideas and demystify processes. It was just so helpful and it did form that community that you don't have. (Ava)

It's been a delight for me to be a part of supporting other folks when they've had some challenging times. (Charlotte)

The First Fridays are good. You can tell it's good. I mean it's good for me, but you can tell it's kind of good for everyone to connect. (Noah)

Discussion

Precarity, Resilience, and Support

Our first aim was to understand the precarity experienced by doctoral students pursuing their degree during the COVID-19 pandemic. Data revealed a range of experiences from "I really felt like I was drowning; I was going under" (Ava) to "I was doing most of my research online so it did not impact me" (Anonymous), but the narrative descriptors yielded seven dimensions of precarity (Figure 1), with the largest set describing the pressures of multiple burdens.

Respondents shared how they managed to persist. They showed resilience through peril by using perspective—"We are barely holding on, and I know others who are in such worse positions than us (Anonymous)"—and sheer grit—"Being tenacious and adaptable helped me to persevere through this unprecedented time. It was through self-determination that I stayed on track" (Anonymous). Support systems were identified as strong or very strong by 59%

of survey respondents, and the root "support" was mentioned 53 times in the narrative transcripts. Descriptions of the Voyager connection as part of a support system ranged from the very personal, "I received lots of love and support from the Voyagers, unsolicited you know" (Madison), to the more bold, "There was this fearlessness there about giving you advice that was not necessarily what I would get out of a student services department which might be really careful" (Georgia), to the light "Enjoy the online support" (Anonymous). The informality of the Voyager support appears to offer a "Come and get what you need and if you don't need anything you still belong" experience. "Support" can mean what you need it to be.

> I am a member but not an active participant in the Voyagers. I truly appreciate the group as being open and accessible for its members to participate in the ways and the at the level of their need and comfort. All are welcome. All are valued. All receive the same level of information and opportunities. All are loved for who they are. The Voyagers provide students with connections that go beyond having been in courses together or having the same mentor. The diversity of the group has meant there is always someone who can help out, steer you in the right direction for information —if they don't have it themselves —and a boundless source of ideas when questions arise. It is a remarkable group. I don't know of any other group like it. (Anonymous)

Capabilities as a Source of Increased Justice

Advancing social justice is part of this university's mission. We wanted to know if participating in an informal network of support could also advance social justice. Social justice is a complex field of research, and the concept has many definitions (see Sabbagh & Schmidt, 2016), so we turned to Nussbaum's goal-oriented framework of social justice as advancing human capabilities. We queried our participants about the presence of four of the ten capabilities in the framework (Table 1) as a function of their Voyager experience. We found strong evidence of three of those central capabilities: (a) affiliation, (b) emotions, and (c) senses, imagination, and thought. Using Nussbaum's definitions in Table 6, we concluded the Voyager experience does increase social justice.

Table 6
The Voyager Experience Strengthens Three Human Capabilities (Nussbaum, 2011)

Capability	Definition
Affiliation	Show concern with and towards others without discrimination on the basis of sex, race, sexual orientation, ethnicity, religion, or nationality
Emotions	To love, grieve, long for, be angry, and feel gratitude as a result of healthy attachments to others and place
Senses, imagination, and thought	Access to learning. Experiencing and producing work of one's own choice

Leadership Outcomes as Community Outcomes

We also wanted to observe if outcomes related to established leadership models could be generated absent an official, singular leader. The Voyagers are not "leaderless," but those who do the leading are fluid, plural, informal, and enabling. There are no membership rules or requirements to enforce. "Groupness" depends mainly on individual and mutual initiative, from inviting students to connect to sending birthday cards to setting up a Voyagers Present's Zoom topic. As shown in Table 3, we looked for evidence of eight outcomes from four established leadership models (servant, authentic, distributed, and inclusive) that could support the three central capabilities. In the survey results, four of the eight outcomes had the most "Strongly Agree" survey responses (10). These are shown in Table 7. In the narrative results, three of the eight outcomes had especially strong support. These are shown in Table 8. We concluded that desired leadership outcomes can result from *community leadership* rather than just singular leadership.

Table 7
Survey Results: Experience of Leadership Outcomes in the Voyager Community

Leadership Type	Outcomes
Servant Community	I experience care and compassion. I receive help toward achieving my goals.
Authentic Community	I receive information that is reliable.
Distributed Community	I experience a climate of trust.

Table 8
Narrative Results: Experience of Leadership Outcomes in the Voyager Community

Leadership Type	Outcomes
Inclusive Community	I feel a sense of belonging.
Authentic Community	I experience greater positive emotions about my academic work.
Distributed Community	I experience self-empowerment.

Effects on Student Persistence

We found evidence that enhanced capabilities and community outcomes mediate stressors related to low graduation rates and long completion times. During precarity, "anxiety" was not greatly mitigated, and "control" was not greatly enhanced, but there was valuable student retention. In the university unit where the Voyagers are situated, the 2018-2019 two-year retention rate was 68%, and the time to completion was an average of 6.40 years; 36% of students finished in 4 years. The original 2017 Voyager cohort has been retained at 85% and 7 members (35%) have received their degrees in 4 years. It would be interesting to follow the completion rates of newer Voyagers who will pursue their studies during ongoing precarity in higher education.

Variation in Student Experience

It was important to show the range of student experience in the context of a diverse and deliberately fluid community, particularly as captured through the survey. Not everyone is having the same experience, but people could be having the experience they want or need in the context of a group connection. Voyager leave rates have not been officially kept, largely because there have been few requests to be removed from the group. Primarily due to the frequency of mobile notifications, there are occasional requests to leave WhatsApp and only to receive email communications.

Results do not fall along the time the respondent is affiliated with the Voyagers. For example, one respondent affiliated for 2 years described involvement as "light" and abstained from six questions. The same respondent reported agreement on care and compassion, help towards achieving goals, more positive emotions about academic work, reliable information, and self-empowerment. Another respondent affiliated for 4 years abstained from four questions and disagreed strongly about a climate of trust and greater positive emotions noting changes in the group over time. Personal and group dynamics unexamined in this study are clearly community factors.

Implications for Leading and Practice

In an exchange during one of our interviews, a participant who works in higher education exclaimed about the Voyagers: "I don't know quite how I would bring that … I never even thought about bringing it to my own institution" (Georgia). We propose that the idealized model of formal, essential, and highly prized singular leadership engenders not only a bias against but a blind spot towards other forms of leading that are critical during precarity. Peer leading at the institution in focus was appreciated, but its independent development was unexpected. While peer support at universities may be encouraged, it is likely organized and sanctioned as part of formal university offices, services, and departments, ostensibly so they can be carried from one year to another, but also for oversight and control. Power dynamics come into play.

The Voyagers are at the edge of formal entities, operating within university systems but as outsiders, too. This status could be threatening to formal authority. We noted skepticism ("Who are these people?") or attempts to assign the singular leadership model ("Oh, yes, that's Bill's group") because the Voyagers do present as a community. Sustained presence has had an impact. After 4 years, university administrators now invite a Voyager to talk to new student cohorts about peer support, and they call on the Voyagers to "ring the bells"—attending Voyagers ring a bell—at the end of a graduate's final dissertation defense.

Just as we question the formality of leading as its signature characteristic, we also question the formality of "membership." Belonging, we found, was much more a driver of meaning to the Voyagers than being a "member." We have deliberately avoided this term. Since language is important, we suggest "affiliate" which conveys an associate or a colleague in a more circular model of plural leading. An affiliate also reflects Nussbaum's central capability of affiliation, which received broad support in our study.

Study Limitations

The co-researchers are affiliated with the Voyagers; one is a founding student. Our connections could contribute to bias in several ways. We could skew the results positively, implicitly dissuade negative feedback, and depress participation for privacy concerns. While we earnestly attempted to minimize such bias, it may be present.

Participation in the study was lower than expected, so its representativeness can be questioned. We attribute this to timing (the study took place at the busy end of a term), the very informality of the group (not used to requests and requirements), and the relationships members may have with the researchers. The pandemic itself created a barrier as scheduling more Zoom meetings was undesirable.

The study invitation asked the Voyagers to complete the survey "and/or" participate in a focus group or individual interview. This offer may have appeared too complex. Interestingly, seven people accessed and consented to the survey but did not answer any questions. There was curiosity but not participation.

Future Research

We would like to see if an outside study team would generate more or different responses in our population. Since students at this university, as in our sample, are predominantly women, it would be interesting to determine if a Voyagers group is particularly consistent with women's ways of knowing and learning (Gallos, 1993), providing an essential community of support and confirmation to women. This study could also be repeated in university settings to examine other models of peer support, assessing peer support as part of their promised commitment to creating "a graduate education system that supports the academic success and well-being of all students" (Council of Graduate Schools, 2021, p. 1).

As educational institutions grapple with the impacts of the COVID-19 pandemic, particularly the decline in first-year enrollment of men, Latinx, and Native American students and the persistent gap related to Black high school students (Grawe, 2022), and differentiate themselves in a precarious and competitive environment (Basko, 2022), the premise that actions on campus strengthen human capabilities and advance social justice could be explored. A researcher could ask "Is this action or initiative or group strengthening human capabilities and thus advancing social justice?" For those institutions competing primarily on program content or skill development, what advantage would accrue to a stated focus on human development and social justice?

Plural, circular, non-hierarchal, fluid leading could be better developed in our leadership canon, particularly in response to precarity and radical uncertainty. Leadership concepts like Uhl-Bien's (2006) relational leading could be applied to increasing organizational and personal resilience capacity rather than fostering dependence on the talents of singular leaders. Leading that enables belonging could be studied as a way of bringing Indigenous wisdom into prevailing Western paradigms. The impact of perceived belongingness on academic success, informed by the work of Sverdlik et al. (2020), could be examined. We might explore whether the social identity promised by a designated "leader" is also or even better created by groups pursuing shared goals over time through mutual support. Finally, we could pursue how to foster this type of leading, or does it only evolve out of the unexpected affiliation of individuals?

Conclusion

We determined that belonging to the Voyagers yielded three of the five central capabilities queried and strengthened social justice. We found evidence of desired outcomes associated with established leadership models, but as a product of the community: care and compassion, help, information, greater positive emotions, trust, self-empowerment, and belonging. Informal, plural, circular leading from the edge had concrete benefits. While the lived experience of this dynamic during the social, medical, and political upheaval of 2020-2021 was varied, it was accompanied by evidence of resilience and academic persistence. Variations in the experience of affiliation surprised us. We did not expect, for example, that belonging would not necessarily mean social participation. Listening, accessing, tuning in, and simply knowing that others are sharing your experience might suffice. The variety of this experience, as in other complex systems, may be an unseen but essential strength. Fostering organic, unofficial, and unexpected forms of leading may be essential, too.

Meet the Authors

Marie Sonnet, PhD is a scholar-practitioner with 20 years of experience in quality and process improvement, change management, project management, training, and consulting. She learned that when improvement projects failed to meet and sustain objectives, human dynamics were often a root cause. Marie researched workgroup beliefs and behaviors present when an organization is able to meet the challenges of planned and unplanned change. She found that a collective capacity for resilience is built up by everyday experiences that add to or diminish a generative response. An organization can deliberately foster or unwittingly deter this capacity. Change response, especially under precarious circumstances, is especially enhanced by fostering emergent leadership close to the problems and close to the experiences of real people. This research on leading from the edge continues to explore how to do this. msonnet@email.fielding.edu

Reid Spearman, PhD has been using the education and skills acquired during a quality management career spanning more than two decades to help businesses comply with company policy, procedures, and best practice standards. He brings order to chaos by combining his expertise with an interpersonal relations-based approach to addressing identified challenges. Reid is an ASQ Certified Manager of Quality and Organizational Excellence (CMQ/OE) and has been a certified Project Management Professional (PMP) since 2006. He has a Master of Science degree in Quality Assurance (MSQA) from Southern Polytechnic State University (SPSU) and received his PhD in Organizational Development and Change (ODC) from Fielding Graduate University. Reid's most recent line of academic research concerns how organizations based on non-traditional peer networking can meet the personal and educational needs of doctoral students, which can be especially helpful in distance learning programs and during times of uncertainty like the COVID-19 global pandemic. cspearman@email.fielding.edu

References

Adams, W. C. (2015). Conducting semi-structured interviews. *Handbook of practical program evaluation, 4*, 492–505.

Avolio, B., Gardner, W., Walumbwa, F., Luthans, F., & May, D. (2004). Unlocking the mask: A look at the process by which authentic leaders impact follower attitudes and behaviors. *The Leadership Quarterly, 15*, 801–823. https://doi.org/10.1016/j.leaqua.2004.09.003

Barreira, P., Basilico, M., & Bolotnyy, V. (2018). Graduate student mental health: Lessons from American economics departments [Working Paper, November 4, 2018]. Harvard University. https://scholar.harvard.edu/sites/scholar.harvard.edu/files/bolotnyy/files/bbb_mentalhealth_paper.pdf

Basko, A. (2022, February 24). Stop playing it safe: The peril of the generic college. *The Chronicle of Higher Education*. https://www.chronicle.com/article/stop-playing-it-safe-the-peril-of-the-generic-college

Bilder, R. (2014). In K. Schwartz (May 6), On the edge of chaos: Where creativity flourishes [Blogpost]. *Mind/Shift*, KQED. https://www.kqed.org/mindshift/35462/on-the-edge-of-chaos-where-creativity-flourishes

Bolman, L. G., & Deal, T. E. (2017). *Reframing organizations: Artistry, choice, and leadership.* Jossey-Bass.

Braun, V., & Clarke, V. (2012). Thematic analysis. In H. Cooper (Ed.), *APA Handbook of Research Methods in Psychology: Vol. 2. Research designs* (pp. 57–91). American Psychological Association.

Brunsma, D. L., Embrick, D. G., & Shin, J. H. (2016). Graduate students of color: Race, racism, and mentoring in the white waters of academia. *Sociology of Race and Ethnicity, 3*(1), 1–13. https://doi.org/10.1177%2F2332649216681565

Canterino, F., Cirella, S., Piccoli, B., & Shani, A. B. (2020). Leadership and change mobilization: The mediating role of distributed leadership. *Journal of Business Research, 108,* 42–51. https://doi.org/10.1016/j.jbusres.2019.09.052

Cassuto, L., & Weisbuch, R. (2021). *The new PhD: How to build a better graduate education.* Johns Hopkins University Press.

Castelló, M., M. Pardo, A. Sala-Bubaré, and N. Suñe-Soler. 2017. Why do students consider dropping out of doctoral degrees? Institutional and personal factors. *Higher Education, 74* (6), 1053–1068. https://doi.org/10.1007/s10734-016-0106-9

Columbia Mailman School of Public Health. (2021, October 13). Let's write our dissertations together: Peer support program launches for doctoral students. *Targeted New Service.* https://www.proquest.com/wire-feeds/columbia-mailman-school-public-health-lets-write/docview/2581213871/se-2?accountid=33310

Council of Graduate Schools. (2021). *A call to action for graduate deans: Supporting mental health and well-being for graduate students.* https://cgsnet.org/ckfinder/userfiles/files/CGS%20Mental%20Health%20Statement%20and%20Signatories_081321_Final.pdf

Denis, J. L., Langley, A., & Sergi, V. (2012). Leadership in the plural. *Academy of Management Annals, 6* (1), 211–283. https://doi.org/10.5465/19416520.2012.667612

De la Sablonnière, R. (2017). Toward a psychology of social change: A typology of social change. *Frontiers in Psychology, 8,* 397. https://doi.org/10.3389/fpsyg.2017.00397

De La Sablonnière, R., French Bourgeois, L., & Najih, M. (2013). Dramatic social change: A social psychological perspective. *Journal of Social and Political Psychology, 1*(1), 253–272. https://doi.org/10.5964/jspp.v1i1.14

Duraku, Z., & Hoxha, L. (2018). *Self-esteem, study skills, self-concept, social support, psychological distress, and coping mechanisms effects on test anxiety and academic performance,* (July – December),1-9. https://doi.org/10.1177/2055102918799963

Eisenberg, D., Lipson, S., & Posselt, J. R. (2016). Promoting resilience, retention, and mental health. *New Directions for Student Services, 156*, 87–96. https://doi.org/10.1002/ss.20194

Evans, T., Bira, L., Gastelum, J., Weiss, L., & Vanderford, N. (2018). Evidence for a mental health crisis in graduate education. *Nature Biotechnology, 36*(3), 282-284. https://doi.org/10.1038/nbt.4089

Fiske, S. T. (2010). Interpersonal stratification: Status, power, and subordination. In S. T. Fiske, D. T. Gilbert, & G. Lindzey (Eds.), *Handbook of social psychology* (5th ed., pp. 941–982). Wiley.

Gallos, J. V. (1993). Women's experiences and ways of knowing: Implications for teaching and learning in the organizational behavior classroom. *Journal of Management Education, 17*(1), 7–26. https://doi.org/10.1177/105256299301700101

Gardner, S. K. (2009). Student and faculty attributions of attrition in high and low completing doctoral programs in the United States. *Higher Education, 58* (1), 97–

112. https://doi.org/10.1007/s10734-008-9184-7

Geven, K., J. Skopek, and M. Triventi. (2018). How to increase PhD completion rates? An impact evaluation of two reforms in a selective graduate school, 1976–2012. *Research in Higher Education, 59* (5), 529–552. https://doi.org/10.1007/s11162-017-9481-z

Grawe, N. (2022, January 20). Higher ed's evolutionary—not revolutionary—pandemic response. *The Chronicle of Higher Education.* https://www.chronicle.com/article/higher-eds-evolutionary-not-revolutionary-pandemic-response

Greene, M. (2015). Come hell or high water: Doctoral students' perceptions of support services and persistence. *International Journal of Doctoral Studies, 10*, 501-518. http://ijds.org/Volume10/IJDSv10p501-518Greene0597.pdf

Halifax, J. (2018). *Standing at the edge: Finding freedom where fear and courage meet.* Flatiron Books.

Healy, M., Hammer, S., & McIlveen, P. (2022). Mapping graduate employability and career development in higher education research: a citation network analysis. *Studies in Higher Education, 47*(4), 799-811. https:// doi.org/10.1080/03075079.2020.1804851

Hinkin, T. R. (1998). A brief tutorial on the development of measures for use in survey questionnaires. *Organizational Research Methods, 1*(1), 104–121.

Hogg, M. A. (2007). Uncertainty–identity theory. In M. P. Zanna (Ed.), *Advances in experimental social psychology* (Vol. 39., pp. 69–126). Academic Press.

Hogg, M. A., & van Knippenberg, D. (2003). Social identity and leadership processes in groups. In M. P. Zanna (Ed.), *Advances in experimental social psychology* (Vol. 35, pp. 1–52). Academic Press.

Hunter, K., & Devine, K. (2016). Doctoral students' emotional exhaustion and intentions to leave academia. *International Journal of Doctoral Studies, (11).* 35-61. http://ijds.org/Volume11/IJDSv11p035-061Hunter2198.pdf

Joseph, J. (2012). From one culture to another: Year one and two of graduate school for African American women in the STEM fields. *International Journal of Doctoral Studies, 7*, 125–142. https://doi.org/10.28945/1571

Kurt, Y., & Erdoğan, D. (2021). Leadership in the post-COVID-19 era: New leaders of the new normal. In *Global Perspectives on Change Management and Leadership in the Post-COVID-19 Era* (pp. 199-217). IGI Global. https://www.igi-global.com/chapter/leadership-in-the-post-covid-19-era/274205

Masten, A. S. (2001). Ordinary magic: Resilience processes in development. American Psychologist, 56(3), 227–23

McDonald, N., Schoenebeck, S., & Forte, A. (2019, November). Reliability and inter-rater reliability in qualitative research: Norms and guidelines for CSCW and HCI practice. *Proceedings of the Association for Computing Machining on Human-Computer Interaction.* No. CSCW, Article 72. https://doi.org/10.1145/3359174

National Science Foundation. (2021, October). *National Science Foundation Survey of Earned Doctorates.* https://ncses.nsf.gov/pubs/nsf22300/report/about-this-report

National Student Clearinghouse Research Center. (2021, October 26). *Fall 2021*

Enrollment. https://nscresearchcenter.org/stay-informed/

Nussbaum, M. (2011). *Creating capabilities: The human development approach.* Harvard University Press.

Packard, N. H. (1988). Adaptation toward the edge of chaos. In J. A. S. Kelso, A. J. Mandell, & M. F. Schlesinger (Eds.), *Dynamic Patterns in Complex Systems* (pp. 293–301). World Scientific. https://www.worldscientific.com/doi/abs/10.1142/978 9814542043#page=304

Pilbeam, C., Lloyd-Jones, G., & Denyer, D. (2013). Leveraging value in doctoral student networks through social capital. *Studies in Higher Education, (38)*10. 14721489. https://doi.org/10.1080/03075079.2011.636800

Plowman, D. A., Solansky, S., Beck, T. E., Baker, L., Kulkarni, M., & Travis, D. V. (2007). The role of leadership in emergent, self-organization. *The Leadership Quarterly, 18*(4), 341–356.
https://doi.org/10.1016/j.leaqua.2007.04.004

Posselt, J. (2018). Normalizing struggle: Dimensions of faculty support for doctoral students and implications for persistence and well-being. *The Journal of Higher Education, 89*(6), 988–1013.

Posselt, J. R. (2021). *Promoting graduate student well-being: Cultural, organizational, and environmental factors in the academy.* Council of Graduate Schools. https://cgsnet.org/wp-content/uploads/2022/01/CGS_Well-being-ConsultPaper-Posselt.pdf

Pyhältö, K., Toom, A., Stubb, J., & Lonka, K. (2012). Challenges of becoming a scholar: A study of doctoral students' problems and well-being. *International Scholarly Research Notices, 2012*, 1–12. https://doi.org/10.5402/2012/934941

Ragnarsson, S., Kristjánsdóttir, E. S., & Gunnarsdóttir, S. (2018). To be accountable while showing care: The lived experience of people in a servant leadership organization. *Sage Open, 8*(3). https://doi.org/10.1177/2158244018801097

Randel, A. E., Galvin, B. M., Shore, L. M., Ehrhart, K. H., Chung, B. G., Dean, M. A., & Kedharnath, U. (2018). Inclusive leadership: Realizing positive outcomes through belongingness and being valued for uniqueness. *Human Resource Management Review, 28*(2), 190–203.
http://dx.doi.org/10.1016/j.hrmr.2017.07.002

Rast III, D. E., Gaffney, A. M., Hogg, M. A., & Crisp, R. J. (2012). Leadership under uncertainty: When leaders who are non-prototypical group members can gain support. *Journal of Experimental Social Psychology, 48*(3), 646–653. https://doi.org/10.1016/j.jesp.2011.12.013

Roumimper, K. R., & Falk, A. F. (2021). Peer support of graduate students of color through a formal graduate student association. In M. Khosrow-Pour (Ed.), *Research Anthology on Empowering Marginalized Communities and Mitigating Racism and Discrimination* (pp. 1089–1107). IGI Global. https://www.igi-global.com/chapter/peer-support-of-graduate-students-of-color-through-a-formal-graduate-student-association/277613

Sabbagh, C., & Schmitt, M. (2016). Past, present, and future of social justice theory and research. In C. Sabbagh & M. Schmitt (Eds.), *Handbook of social justice theory and research* (pp. 1–11). Springer. https://bit.ly/3jTUGwr

Saldaña, J. (2016). *The coding manual for qualitative researchers.* SAGE.

Senge, P. (2000). *The leadership of profound change.* SPC Ink. http://www.spcpress.com/pdf/other/Senge.pdf

Skopek, J., Triventi, M., & Blossfeld, H. P. (2020). How do institutional factors shape PhD completion rates? An analysis of long-term changes in a European doctoral program. *Studies in Higher Education.* https://doi.org/10.1080/03075079.2020.1744125

Sowell, R. S. (2009). *Ph.D. completion and attrition: Findings from exit surveys of Ph.D. completers.* Council of Graduate Schools. https://cgsnet.org/data-insights/diversity-equity-inclusiveness/degree-completion/ph-d-completion-project/

Stacey, R. D. (1996). *Complexity and creativity in organizations.* Berrett-Koehler Publishers.

Stewart, D. W., Devoran, A. K., Neumeister, A. K., Knepler, E., Grigorian, K., & Greene, A. (2021, January). Graduate schools respond to COVID-19: Promising pathways to innovation and sustainability in STEM education. [White paper]. *NORC at the University of Chicago.* https://www.norc.org/PDFs/Graduate%20Studies%20COVID/NORC_COVIDWhitePaper_2021_FINAL.PDF

Strayhorn, T. L. (2019). *College students' sense of belonging: A key to educational success for all students.* Routledge.

Stubb, J., K. Pyhältö, and K. Lonka. (2011). Balancing between inspiration and exhaustion: PhD students' experienced socio-psychological well-being. *Studies in Continuing Education, 33* (1), 33–50. https://doi.org/10.1080/0158037X.2010.515572

Sverdlik, A., Hall, N. C., McAlpine, L., & Hubbard, K. (2018). Journeys of a PhD student and unaccompanied minors. *International Journal of Doctoral Studies, 13,* 361-388. https://doi.org/10.28945/4113

Sverdlik, A., Hall, N. C., & McAlpine, L. (2020). PhD imposter syndrome: Exploring antecedents, consequences, and implications for doctoral well-being. *International Journal of Doctoral Studies, 15,* 737–75

Thoma, M., Höltge, J., Eising, C., Pfluger, V, & Rohner, S. (2020). Resilience and stress in later life: A network analysis approach depicting complex interactions of resilience resources and stress-related risk factors in older adults. *Frontiers in Behavioral Neuroscience, 14.* 216. https://doi.org/10.3389/fnbeh.2020.580969

Tian, M., Risku, M., & Collin, K. (2016). A meta-analysis of distributed leadership from 2002 to 2013: Theory development, empirical evidence and future research focus. *Educational Management Administration and Leadership, 44* (1), 146–164. http://doi.org/10.1177/1741143214558576

Tourish, D. (2020). Introduction to the special issue: Why the coronavirus crisis is also a crisis of leadership. *Leadership, 16*(3), 261–272. https://doi.org/10.1177%2F1742715020929242

Truninger, M., Ruderman, M. N., Clerkin, C., Fernandez, K. C., & Cancro, D. (2021). Sounds like a leader: An ascription–actuality approach to examining leader emergence and effectiveness, *The Leadership Quarterly, 32*(5), 101420. https://doi.org/10.1016/j.leaqua.2020.101420

Uhl-Bien, M. (2006). Relational leadership theory: Exploring the social processes of leadership and organizing, *The Leadership Quarterly, 17*(6), 654–676. https://doi.org/10.1016/j.leaqua.2006.10.007

Wieland, S. (2020). Constituting resilience at work: Maintaining dialectics and cultivating dignity throughout a worksite closure. *Management Communication Quarterly, 34*(4), 463–494. https://doi.org/10.1177/0893318920949314

Worchester Polytechnic Institute. *Student support network manual/consultation request form for college campus professionals.* https://fs28.formsite.com/webteamwpiedu/ssn-professional/index.html

Chapter 2

The Croning of Older Women: Developing Crone-Informed Senses, Imagination and Thought

Theresa Southam
Institute for Social Innovation Fellow

Isabelle Harman
YellowBird Ghostwriter

Women have unique leadership styles. For example, they are more democratic and participative (Eagly & Carli, 2003), and relational and empathetic (Mills, 2020). Studies abound about how women and men leaders differ, but research on differences amongst women is difficult to find. This chapter explores how older women lead. Based upon the responses of 84 participants, this study describes the unique qualities of age 55+ leaders, including those who would call themselves crones and those who are unfamiliar with the term.

The term *crone* refers to people who have adopted a consciousness, associated with the feminine, where all things are interconnected, an ethic of care and kindness is enacted, and forms of resistance are used on behalf of the common good (Lewis McCabe, 2004). Older adults—women and men—often lead in less recognized, yet fundamental settings, that contribute to thriving communities (Hodgkin, 2012). In this chapter, we will challenge not only the notion of leadership—its meaning and context—but also how a unique approach to aging, the conscious development of the crone archetype, heightens social justice during times of precarity. Crones use their senses, imaginations, and thoughts, one of the core capabilities of human development and freedom (Nussbaum, 2011), to work for social justice. Figure 3 summarizes settings in which research participants lead, including as volunteers and with families and friends.

Figure 3
Word Cloud Summarizing the Contexts in which Research Participants Lead where the Larger Bolder Words Represent More Common Responses

Crones are Not a Disease

When most people hear the word "crones" they think of Crohn's, a painful disease related to inflammation of the digestive tract. When crone is explained as an archetype, "a pre-existent form in the collective unconscious that embodies instinctive ways of channeling wisdom, inner knowing, and intuition" (Ott, 2011, p. ii), there can be discomfort amongst both women and men. A crone reawakening over the last two decades is partly an extension of feminist struggles and arguments and partly a result of a particular kind of continuous development in later life, for example, commitments to kindness, the common good, and a belief that everything is interconnected. For those who identify as crones this usually results in a rejection of misogyny, sexism, and ageism (Rikke, 2019).

The 21st century is a precarious time for those who are not White and male. Older women face not only sexism and misogyny, but also ageism. Despite this reality, arisings of the crone archetype such as the Crones Counsel, [1] popular books like *Crones Don't Whine* (Bolen, 2003), and reflection on the crone archetype and reenactment of ceremony in the academy persist (Grudzen, 2018; Payerle, 2016; Ronn & Daugaard, 2005). White men's privilege is being revealed as "socially constructed and psychically embedded" (Flood & Pease, 2005, p. 17), but not insurmountable for older women who resist. The Inquisition and witch trials may be over, but too many women are still raped, tortured, and silenced for defying religious and societal norms (Human Rights Watch, 2021). Women are likely proceeding cautiously as they reclaim leadership attributes that historically led to persecution.

Older adults in North America, if they are involved in popular culture in any way, such as television, radio, newspapers, and social media, will see that how to "age well" and "successfully" is discussed widely. Older adults are to avoid disease-related disability, embody high mental and physical function, and actively engage with life (Rowe & Kahn, 1998). In a review of large studies of successful aging, the consistent measures were absence of disability, physical functioning, social engagements, cognitive functioning, and absence of depression (Depp & Jeste, 2006). The measures appear laudable. How can one argue with good health? Yet there are many challenges related to the construct.

Many researchers are challenging either the rightness of the measures themselves or the idea of measuring successful aging (Katz & Calasanti, 2015; Moody, 2004; Rubinstein & de Medeiros, 2015) For example, Liang and Luo (2012) pointed out challenges with successful aging including its busy ethic "overlooks the deeper concern of quality experience" (p. 328), its capitalist and consumerist nature prevails over a more harmonious view of well-being, and its values are North American and not inclusive of other cultures.

On top of the pressures of society related to what it means to age well, many older adults still do not receive basic supports. Nussbaum (2011) created ten capabilities, basic rights that she proposed citizens of a healthy, functioning nation would provide. One of these rights, even for the aged, is bodily health. Yet, Nussbaum and Levmore (2017) pointed out that there are still several million poor older adults in the United States who cannot afford what the rest of the population can.

Older women, endeavoring to adopt the crone archetype, long dismissed due to socially constructed definitions and self-imposed restraint, have their work cut out for them. Crones must resist tropes of popular culture and pursue harmonious ways of being, while maintaining basic capabilities such as bodily health. In Figure 4, Nelly is expected by her children to live independently while also facilitating volunteer activities in her community and remaining committed to her family. Both visions of independence and integration can result in high expectations for older adults during precarious times—a pandemic, climate crisis, and the resulting challenges to mental health and survival.

Figure 4
Photo of Nelly Leading a Grandmothers for Africa Fundraiser

Source: Theresa Southam. Used with permission.

Despite these many social pressures, financial challenges for many, and the fear of being "discovered" as a crone, there is a resurgence of the archetype that some women leaders are actively, sometimes secretly, developing through membership in societies, reading, and wisdom circles (Crones Counsel, 2021; Kinkead, 2015; Kreilkamp, 2012).

"Croning" is a project of redefinition and personal empowerment with the following attributes: (a) believing all humans are connected with each other and other species, (b) encouraging an ethic of care, and (c) participating in forms of resistance in order to support the common good (Lewis McCabe, 2004). Gebhart (Chapter 6) has found that although women in his community call themselves by different names—wise woman, elder, or grandmother—many assume the attributes of crone and are powerful forces of change in their communities.

About the Study

This study is modelled after Tacol (2016), who asked, "What is it like to be a Western Buddhist?" (p. 378). Research participants were recruited through interlocuters, such as university alumni and groups related to women's leadership and development. Responses to an adaptation of Tacol's *Life Situations Questionnaire* were gathered from 84 participants. These were mostly women; data included responses from one man and another participant who identified as non-binary. Participants included those who were unfamiliar with the word crone (n=17) and those who are familiar with and identified with the word crone (n=68). These responses were used to better understand the senses, imagination, and thoughts of older women leaders.

We wanted to know, "What is it like to be a crone leader during precarious times?" What we found was that older women, especially crones, may lead differently and unexpectedly. The data analysis methods used relate to the concept of *corpus linguistics*, an analysis utilized when there is a "need for internal cohesion of a 'body of facts'" (Mey, 2017, p. 186). We began with the digital survey tool, Qualtrics, to collect responses to ten prompts that form the Life Situations Questionnaire, to conduct rudimentary analyses, which included the average age of participants, and to generate a word cloud related to context for leadership (Figure 3). All participants, but one from Australia, were from North America. Approximately one-third were from Canada and, of those, mostly from British Columbia. The rest were from the United States, distributed evenly between the eastern, middle, and western states. There were large numbers of respondents from Massachusetts, Arizona, and California, likely due to the influence of the interlocuters.

After a careful reading of the responses to each prompt, corpus linguistics analysis methods—including word frequency lists, N-grams, and concordances—were created. This was done by using raw data from Qualtrics that was converted into files that could be analyzed with the open-source program AntConc. Concordances are "a collection of the occurrences of a word form, each in its own textual environment, where textual environment equates to the immediate co-text on either side of the search item" (Cheng, 2011, p. 73). Although the data from this study formed relatively small corpuses, such as 10–15 pages single-spaced per prompt, the word frequency lists, N-grams, and concordances revealed aspects of crone leadership which could not be ascertained from manual analysis.

The Contexts, Activities, and Organization of Crones

Since the participants from the study live in western cultures, they are largely situated in individualistic and neoliberal paradigms. Resistance to these paradigms, evident in the results you will read below, is remarkable given that it can be unsafe to be a resistant woman, let alone an aspiring crone, in such cultures. As Nussbaum and Levmore (2017) said, "(S)tereotyping of women … and other disadvantaged groups has typically been a major way of keeping them subordinated" (p. 13). This includes, the authors pointed out, discounting certain types of contributions such as transgenerational friendships and care for the planet, family, other humans, and nonhumans.

Yet older women and men persist in developing their social generativity and interconnectedness despite the devaluing of these activities in western societies. "(S)ocially oriented sharing of individual resources is often regarded as an important criterion of quality of life in old age" (Bukov et al., 2002). These authors go on to distinguish three types of social sharing activities in the oldest of the old: collective, productive, and political, observing that if an older person is involved in one type, then they are likely involved in another. The most common resource shared, according to Bukov et al. (2002), is time. They concluded that "an increase in social participation in old age can be expected for the future. This increase should be especially large for women" (p. 516). Perhaps developing and acting upon crone consciousness will propel part of this trend towards even greater social sharing and interconnectedness with the earth.

Social justice has been defined as the maintenance of capabilities such as senses, imagination and thought, emotions, affiliation, and living in concern for and relation to other species (Nussbaum, 2011). Social justice also encompasses "a struggle to equalize unequal power relations and call into question hegemonic assumptions and processes" (Grain & Land, 2017, p. 47). Since inequity has increased during these precarious times, social justice becomes an important lens.

For crones, equitable access to all is a basic principle of their gathering and supporting each other (Crones Counsel, 2021). The Counsel, for example, provides low cost, virtual ceremonies around the stages of life (maiden, mother, matriarch, and crone), the environment (phases of the moon, seasons), and the sharing of what has and can be (wisdom circles). These ceremonies for crone development maintain and support the capabilities of all participants. Crone development is considered a challenge to contemporary perspectives and is a crucial, yet missing, perspective that must be included to gain a holistic understanding of the challenges of this era (Grudzen, 2018). Individual and small group work empowers women to address the larger work of equalizing power relations and challenging hegemony.

Crones and Conscious Aging

In her seminal work on women's experiences and ways of knowing, Gallos (1993) found that in her university, many students did not have the ability to coherently and with confidence define who they were. Socially constructed and defined roles, including wife and mother, were ingrained in their psyche to the point where some could not define themselves beyond those roles (p. 8). These same women recognized the importance of mastering themselves and developing the intellectual courage to speak, write, and define their positions. They did not want to feel a sense of emptiness if they were no longer in roles that were familiar and comfortable (p. 12).

Crone development is a means for older women to discover who they are and to find their voice by reimagining their relevance to religion and spirituality. They are also interested in accessing other ways of knowing, including transcendence, relating to death in positive and healthy way such as life review, and memories rooted in the feminine.

Spirituality and Religion

Recent literature on aging discusses the Rowe and Kahn (1998) concept of *successful aging.* One of the challenges to successful aging has been its individualistic and me-centered nature. In a study of older women who identified as spiritual and/or religious, three major themes emerged related to aging successfully. The first theme is personal agency, which includes contributing to society and living as well as dying authentically. A participant from this study summed up the last two themes:

> To be successfully old is to have a picture of yourself as a contributing member of the group that you are part of however small or large. That is, to be significant to those people, and to be self-expressive continually of your spirituality, your thinking, of your emotional, personal, and physical being. (p. 202)

In fact, a lot of pressure has mounted on older adults to do more. Doing "more" is often expressed as measurable activities like volunteering and caring for children or your peers. Yet, less measurable contributions such as "being fully present," active listening, kind words, and feedback based on experience go unrecognized (Southam & Corley, 2020). "Unfortunately, most gerontological studies of elders doing good for others tend to focus on voluntarism and the health benefits for individuals that accrue from such activities" (McFadden, 2008, p. 135). These studies fail to recognize that a rich, contemplative, spiritual, and/or religious life also results in benefits for the families and communities to which the older women belong.

Learning from Transcendence

While actualizing the self is an important aspect of crone development, transcending one's mind, body, and spirit can also be a way of adding an alternate perspective to oneself and community. In her study, Cook-Greuter (2000) described transcendence as "a state of consciousness that one can enter but leaves upon returning to ordinary reality" (p. 232). Activities that older women can engage in that may lead to transcendence include deepening spiritual and religious practices, embracing ongoing "relationships" with people who have died, letting go of possessions, integrating the head and heart, appreciating our shared humanity, and realizing the fluid nature of knowledge (Southam, 2020).

Embracing Death and Envisioning What We Have Yet to Do

In his book *The Five Invitations: Discovering What Death Can Teach Us,* Frank Ostaseki (2017) reminded us of what many seem to forget: We all die. Western culture avoids death (Bartalos, 2009; Cosco et al., 2013). A crone embraces the circle of life, including death. She cultivates five habits of mind: (a) don't wait, (b) welcome everything, push away nothing, (c) bring your whole self to the experience, (d) find a place of rest in the middle of things, and (e) cultivate a *don't know* mind (Ostaseski, 2017). Crones assume these habits of mind through practice and with support from other crones. One of the practice tools is a focus on legacy-leaving through life review. The crone asks, "What have been the turning points in my life," "What have I learned from these turning points," and "What is it that I want to leave as my legacy now?" She can use spiritual life review techniques to accomplish this circle of life approach (Stinson, 2013).

The Importance of Early Memories Rooted in the Feminine

In a study of early memories of nature, O'Donoghue (2006) found that a feminist research methodology, memory-work, revealed different values in developing adults depending on whether they originated in the mother or father.

> Initial analysis of these memories showed predictable and gendered patterns of socialization, reflecting dominant values in relation to nature. For example, fathers defined many of our experiences in the natural world and taught us that nature was separate from the human realm and subject to control. Additional analysis of the memories moved us below this layer of socialization. We found sensual connection with the elements and discovered the influence of our mothers. (p. 345)

A lot of the memories of a crone originate in the feminine and mother.

The matriarchically defined heritage is honored in each participant's opening comments during gatherings. If the main parent and nurturer was the father, the feminine imprint or identity and memory may be different. In crone gathering, memories of father do come up, but they are not prompted. Methods like memory-work have also been problematized as it is difficult to escape hegemony no matter the method (Onyx & Small, 2001). However, memories of mothers and the feminine bear further consideration in the lives of crones.

Crones Enact Aspects of Leadership

In transformational leadership, "leaders and followers engage with each other through a shared purpose in ways that transform and elevate their motivation, conduct, and ethical aspirations" (Simola et al., 2010, p. 180). Crones participate in a form of transformational leadership when they participate in wisdom circles. The "leader" rotates as each crone shares their life's journey and plans their next steps (Sage-ing International, 2019). The leaders of the wisdom circles, who refer to themselves as facilitators, or members of the "motherboard," change from circle to circle and, in this way, there are neither leaders nor followers in the traditional sense.

A crone in Dr. Southam's community who read an early draft of this chapter expressed the need to reconsider how the West defines leadership as one informed by the influence of patriarchal worldviews. Instead, we should consider this to be insufficient and limited. Maintaining this worldview dismisses and, to an extent, hides the depth of understanding brought forth by women, particularly crones (A. McKenzie, personal communication, January 1, 2022).

Another crone from Dr. Southam's community, also after reading an early draft, shared the following:

> I saw visions of an old way of being in community … This way of the crone is in my blood memories. I feel something that has been sleeping in the Earth for far too long arising as a tangible energy into our consciousness, our feelings of nature, our bodies, and our hearts. (L. Moore, personal communication, January 3, 2022)

An Ethic of Care

Simola et al. (2010) proposed an *ethic of care* as a moral compass for transformational leaders. An ethic of care places less emphasis on autonomy and separation (Devine et al., 2008) and instead emphasizes interdependence based on truth to self. While applying an ethic of care, truth to others is a result of clearly communicating what one knows to be true (truth to self).

> Crones develop high and distinct individuality as evidenced by the ability to address or confront nuances and truths that may not be popular but contribute to the common good or to shared wisdom. Crones are willing to NOT fit into the norms and stereotypes, yet not necessarily to be labeled as the rebels or outlaws. This is a form of leadership and truth saying. (L. Reid, personal communication, December 31, 2021)

Rather than arbitrating amongst competing needs, an array of solutions that supports each party are sought by crones.

The notion of an ethic of care was first coined by Carol Gilligan in her book, *In a Different Voice* (1993), as a paradigm of inclusion and health stemming from the feminine. In studies of older women responding to case studies related to elder abuse, the women favored protection over autonomy, again more closely associating with an ethic of care than an ethic of justice (Dakin, 2013). A study of moral doctors, those who serve as physicians and wisdom advisors and turn structural inequalities into moral and ethical issues, in China uncovered a remarkable phenomenon whereby the skills and labor of retired women are not only expended in leisure and family, but also in a quasi-public role where they receive status, respect, and purpose (Wen et al., 2020).

The study found that these women physicians' application of an ethic of care actually challenged structural inequalities created by the governments that employ them. A crone from Dr. Southam's community said she envisions the equivalent of "moral doctors" in Canada for advising on standards of health care and services for seniors. She would call these wisdom advisors or compassionate truthsayers (L. Reid, personal communication, December 31, 2021).

Leadership Styles

We have seen evidence of four leadership styles. These are (a) believing all humans are connected with each other and other species, (b) encouraging an ethic of care in transformational leadership, (c) the Chinese moral doctors participating in forms of resistance in order to support the common good, and (d) the concept of humble leadership. Humble leaders foster cultures of development, mistake-tolerance, transparency, accurate awareness, recognition, and openness. The 87 research respondents demonstrated accurate awareness informed by a transcendent stance, promoted mistake-tolerance followed by active relational repair, recognized each other's value as well as the contributions of their colleagues, friends, and families' ancestors, mentors, teachers, and guides, and, finally were open to the viewpoints of other generations.

One of the authors (Theresa Southam) of this chapter has witnessed all of these aspects in the quarterly gatherings of the Crone Counsel in 2021(Crones Counsel, 2021). Storytelling at the forefront of the gatherings leads to a culture of development as these are teaching stories where mistakes are lessons. No person is held up as better than others since leadership is shared and rotated. Leaders are transparent about their own mistakes and learning.

In the wisdom circles that follow the storytelling, listeners are expected to be attentive but not to comment or become counselors themselves. They are instructed to listen carefully and be aware of their own triggers and trauma. Crones are recognized for their volunteer work for the Counsel. Openness is valued as participants share deeply. Participants often share how quickly they form trust and safety in the wisdom circles. This last point leads to the correlation between humble leadership and psychological safety which has been shown to be crucial to a group's cohesion and value (Wang et al., 2018).

Although attributes of transformational and humble leadership are evident in the crone, the whole notion of leadership may be flawed for many women who believed in more collective, collaborative, shared processes of development and learning (Gallos, 1995, 2017). For crones, although efforts to lead could be recognized, mentors, teachers, guides, and ancestors should be included in the development of leaders. Each crone has been and will be in each role at different times in their lives. This outlook adopts many learning from indigenous ways of being and knowing (Battiste, 2011; Nganga & Beck, 2017; Salis Reyes, 2019).

Additionally, leadership has been characterized by attributes long associated with men. Women find themselves in a labyrinth when they attempt to be leaders (Eagly & Carli, 2018). In fact, for women, being in the labyrinth of personal development may be the point. After all, labyrinths have long been places of healing and insight.

Imaging the Crone

In a social media post from the group Wild Woman Sisterhood, which has 2,363,400 followers, crone images like the one in Figure 5 are posted and described as,

> Radiant, luminous "crone" woman. During ancient times, the crones, hags, and witches were frequently sages, leaders, midwives, and healers in their communities and were revered for their wisdom and knowledge. As history evolved and a patriarchal society took hold, the definitions of the crone (the crowned one), the hag (the holy one), and the witch (the wise one) were distorted. (Wild Woman Sisterhood, 2015)

Figure 5

A Social Media Post from Wild Woman Sisterhood (2015, October 24)

However, crones in Theresa's community reacted negatively to Figure 5 as the image appears to be an "airbrushed" representation of a wrinkle-free and ageless woman. In another photo proposed for this article an older woman appears in a cluttered environment that hints of poverty. Given the perilous history of crones and the tenuousness of reactivating the crone archetype we will do well to choose representations of the contemporary crone carefully so that they represent the everyday nature of crones in our communities. In Figure 6 you see a representation of crone and daughter, crone and maiden, as they enjoy a moment in the heat of summer.

Figure 6
Crone, Lee Reid and Daughter, Keira Daniels, On a Summer's Day

Source: Elizabeth Cunningham. Used with permission.

Results: What It's Like to Be a Crone

In order to identify what it might be like to be an older woman leader and a crone, the following themes were explored in the survey: working in teams, mortality, nature and the environment, perception of past and future, and what older women feel when leading poorly or well. Participants told stories in response to the prompts. We summarize the findings from the study including any differences identified between women who self-identify as crones and those who are unfamiliar with the concept of crone.

In summary, crone leaders may

- have a less individualistic and more collective outlook, for example referring often to the common good as their legacy;
- demonstrate a more transcendent stance, including an orientation towards spirituality;
- foster a leadership or group dynamics focus of relational repair which largely goes unrecognized and is undervalued, and thus is "unexpected leadership";
- develop a worldview where humans and nature are not separate but interconnected;
- express their earliest memories sensually and commonly remember their mothers and the feminine,
- locate wisdom not individually but with mentors, teachers, guides, and ancestors; and
- be skilled in social generativity as well as intergenerational relations.

In the remainder of this results section, the reader will find a summary of responses to all 10 prompts provided to the research participants. We summarize words used most often as well as explanatory quotes by both groups: those unfamiliar with the concept of being a crone *(n*=17) and those self-identifying as crones (*n*=68). The findings are in relation to constructs such as death, working in teams, nature, relationship to future and past, and leadership. Frequently used words were analyzed in clusters and are presented in tables. Depending on the size of the cluster selected by the researcher, not all the uses will appear in the tables. Parameters for analysis were defined to include (a) a word associated with only two other words and (b) limiting the size of phrase chosen to no more than five words.

1. **When someone dies, I feel…**

Both groups used the words loss, sad, relief, grief, shock, peace, and reflection. Both also pointed out that the feelings depended on the type of death, for example, sudden, sick, and suffering. Those unfamiliar with the concept of crone commented on how death can make life precious. Crones added that they

- could be motivated by death,
- used pain to grow,
- saw death and life as a cycle and circle, and
- felt activities like journaling and self-reflection are important.

2. **I feel about my own death…**

Both groups used words related to fear, including being afraid and not afraid, and their own death being inevitable. There were descriptions in both groups related to leaving a legacy including in the crone group:

- contributing to the greatest common good and
- relying on religion, faith, and spirituality.

One crone said her own death would be like "melting into that infinite pool of energy, love, and light." The word "peace" was used repeatedly as well as "gratitude." The word "more" was used 25 times in response to this prompt. The clusters in Table 9 show how death is both feared and appreciated. For example, one is afraid of the ending and has more gratitude.

3. **I feel about another person working against me…**

In both groups, feelings of disappointment, anger, and betrayal were expressed. Also discussed was a desire to understand their own responsibility in the situation and the other person better. Participants asked of the other person's motivations: "Are they jealous? Do they have poor self-image?" Reactions ranged from avoidance and secrecy about the transgression to repairing the relationship. Crones leaned more towards repair, saying,

The actions of others are not my responsibility. It is my responsibility to let them know that I know.

I recognize that whatever story I might have about the situation, there are many, many more stories that I will never know that are also relevant (untold, unheard, unknown, untellable stories).

Reflection enables us to honestly question our own behavior and seek improvement.

Table 9
Use of the Word "More" in Response to Prompt "How I feel about Death"

	"More" Cluster
1	More a clear separation between
2	More about aspects of getting
3	More about it and seem
4	More afraid of the ending
5	More centered on living deeply
6	More curious about it then
7	More experiences and enter into
8	More gratitude for all I
9	More in the present and
10	More months or another year
11	More painful for those I
12	More peaceful understanding of death
13	More summers behind me than
14	More than just a distant
15	More years but I know

I am [...] invested in community building based on deep feminine relational connections.

Several crones provided two- and three-step processes of repair, including letting go of any resentments and connecting with the other person.

4. **When other people take credit for my work, I feel...**

Both groups acknowledged the importance of noticing and appreciating. One crone advised not to forget that every day! Both groups also spoke to the collective nature of producing anything and so, as a result, gratitude and acknowledgment of others must be part of taking credit. One crone said,

> I feel it is an appropriate response if one takes credit for their work as long as they include those who assisted them and that they honour where their own knowledge and wisdom originated ensuring to give credit to these influences such as teachers, guides, mentors, and ancestors.

In the crone group, taking credit is seen as an opportunity for reflection and focus on what makes a better world. Humility and modesty were discussed in both groups as important, but not at the risk of false humility, where one crone said an opportunity is lost "to have a conversation about WHY I had done that incredible thing."

5. **A recent experience of nature that was sad…**

Participants unfamiliar with the word crone focused more on how nature impacts humans, for example, a volcano exploding on a town, mudslides killing humans, wildfires, hurricanes, and tornados leaving people homeless. There were a few who spoke of feeling sad for nature's sake.

> I swim in sea water that is too warm for the salmon; I gag breathing forest fire smoke in the summers.
>
> I weep for our messed-up world ravaged by capitalist greed that destroys watersheds, oceans, forests, and the diversity of living things.
>
> I recently saw just one butterfly and just a few fireflies. They used to arrive in great numbers. So did the bees.

In the crones there were a lot of stories about the integration of humans and the environment. For example, crones said,

> Human insensitivity to/exploitation of the non-human living beings—the breakage of connections deeply disturbs me.
>
> We are nature, but somehow have lost our soul's connection to the web in which we are embedded.
>
> Nature has always also been my favorite, uniquely unbiased teacher. It reminds us of cycles (rather than linear conceptions of growth) and our interconnectedness.

The following stories describe crones trying to be part of nature where and how they lived.

> We have a bit of woods behind our house and this spring we had the joy of watching a family of fox pups discovering the world. They would often romp and play in our backyard. It was sad to see how quickly they grew up – and soon they disappeared into the deep woods. I liked feeling that we were in this life together – I miss them.
>
> I am always sad when it seems necessary to kill anything. I tend to carefully catch insects of all kinds and put them outside again. An invasion of red ants in my home led to direct combat – bashing them with a shoe – and finally to chemical warfare with a powerful spray around outdoor areas where they

entered. I didn't like any of this.

6. **Your earliest memory of nature...**

The overall feeling in these early memories is sensual. Smells, sounds, and feelings are prominent. You can see the sensual nature of these early memories as well as the interconnections between the grass and the dew, amongst the pines, and between the wind and the trees in these clusters:

• smell of the flowers and vegetables was

• smell of sweet grass and dew drop covered

• smell of the forest filled with pine trees

• the wind whispered through them stirring the smell

The word magic is also used four times. Here are two separate magical memories:

It was summer. As a child I can recall lying in the grass and was quietly watching bees buzzing in the clover. I put my cupped hand over one of them. It crawled over my arm without harming me. I thought I was magic! In retrospect, I realize I was just lucky. And quiet.

I wasn't much of bug-loving kid, but there was something magical about catching the lightening bugs and holding them in your cupped hands and watching them light up. They weren't scary – they didn't bite, weren't creepy-crawling like spiders, just a harmless creation of God that brought a bright little light to a little girl on warm summer nights.

There are also memories related to "mothering" both from biological mothers and being protected from nature.

• An early memory of nursing

• Being dipped in the ocean by my Mum. It was fun. I remember the waves washing over my toes - cold and wet.

• My mother was very unhappy and had become abusive and no longer nurturing. In front of our home was a beautiful old willow tree. I used to run to it and lean face forward against it. I felt its heartbeat, its essence and the most motherly love coming from it (the Willow) into me. Even writing this now it still brings me to tears as one of the most profound moments of my life. That tree became my solace for over two years.

Nature is viewed as safe and protective, for example, long grass to hide in or a large rock to lean on.

7. **How do you feel when you think about the future?**

Participants who do not identify as crones expressed a continuum of reactions to the future from positive, optimistic, and hopeful to worried and concerned. Growing hate and divisiveness amongst humans were mentioned as worrisome. Crones also spoke about feeling everything from hope to trepidation. Many spoke of living "in the moment" as in the quote,

> There are so many things happening in the world that are heartbreaking--wars, the climate crisis, migration, systemic racism and other injustices, extreme poverty alongside mind-boggling wealth, greed, shortsightedness, consumerism … the list goes on. There are also so many things happening that are heart expanding--individuals, groups and organizations dedicated to mindfully, lovingly, and compassionately working on behalf of all the above things and more that I've mentioned. I tend to focus my energies much more on the latter than the former.

One woman titled herself a "climate action warrior." Clusters associating the words "hope" were:

- hope and faith in the young people who
- hope and I think we are obliged to
- hope in the face of the unknown seem
- hope that something will happen to push
- hope the ideal can survive and be better

The use of "hope" is oriented toward wishes for the common good including responsibility, for example, for obligation and faith that something will happen. The use of worry is oriented towards others:

- worry about the state of the world because
- worry for my kids and students and all
- worry that we are making such a mess

8. **How do you feel when you think about the past?**

Many participants spoke of the past being full of lessons, for example, feeling ashamed of White privilege. If lessons are learned, participants may feel grateful, for example, for challenging privilege and living in a more equitable world. Crones went on to discuss what to do about feelings of both pride and regret about the past:

> I have very mixed feelings—some pride and some regret.
>
> As feelings from the past arise in me, I now like to take them out and give them a good "look see."
>
> Whatever the musings that come forward, I like to separate behaviours from life essence. I feel again whatever emotions arise, sit with them, honor them, and do my best to then let them go. This may need to happen several times before I can truly release a feeling especially when it is related to how we treat ourselves, one another, and our planet.
>
> To learn from the history of others is very important to me … to not repeat and reenact the dysfunction of the past … to inspire courage and initiative in others. So that there is a future.
>
> I am only interested in my past if there are learnings and lessons to be gleaned; patterns to be changed. I am repairing deep attachment trauma in my history, which invites the telling of stories and research into my ancestry. The process brings up rage and grief and fear […] and brings ecstasy and soul.

9. **What do you feel in your body when you lead well?**

Participants unfamiliar with crones spoke of feeling content, exhilarated, endorphins, and eustress. Similar to the responses related to leading poorly, those identifying as crones went further than the individual impacts of their leading, speaking often of what leading means for the collective—expressed as "openness" and "connection."

> An open heart, an open mind and a nervous system that is in tune with the energy of those I'm with
>
> I hope you don't mind me saying it is not really about ME leading well, I much prefer to talk about a way-finding process or a collaborative going forward.
>
> Mmmmm - a sense of connection. A sense of joy and something emerging from the whole, that is more and better than what I or any one of us could do alone."

Interestingly, the word "light" was used seven times. Related words such as feeling "lifted," "bright," and "powered" were also used. Participants correlated well-circulating energy and leading well including:

- the creation of a hum,

- experiences of transcendence, and
- energy tingling from the fingertips.

In response to "What do you feel in your body when you lead well?" the words "light" and "connection" were used frequently. The use of "light" indicates transcendence as the light originates from inside of the body, as in this cluster of examples:

- light between the vertebrae
- light is emanating from
- my eyes light
- feel like a light
- more space and light

The use of the word "connection" in relation to leading emphasizes the importance of interconnectedness, collaboration, and cooperation in leading. Although terms like collaboration and cooperation are discussed in the leadership literature, words like "connection" and "light" are used less frequently and thus the embodiment of leading in crones is, again, unexpected. Clusters related to connection include:

- a sense of connection
- connection and communion with
- connection to the people
- high sense of connection

10. **What do you feel in your body when you lead poorly?**

People who do not identify as crones spoke of feeling defeated and saddened if they hurt someone in the process of leading. Several referred to the need, after leading poorly, for self-reflection, evaluation, being brave, and learning lessons. Crones went further than individual improvement, saying that their overall goal after leading poorly is to repair social relations and to continue to work towards the larger goal of serving the common good. Some participants reject the notion of leadership when it means pushing agendas on others or forcefully being at the wrong place at the wrong time.

> I can't relate to this question. I normally don't think of myself as a "leader" and do not like the term.
>
> I continue to grapple with how I may best serve my family, friends and community especially as energy level seems to lower with aging.

These clusters deepen our understanding of the senses, imagination, and thoughts of women leaders, including those who would call themselves crones.

Summary, Contributions, and Future Studies

The contexts, activities, development, and organization of crones can be set within the perspective of conscious aging. Crone development, according to the research participants in this study, includes embracing spirituality and/or religion, learning from transcendence, embracing death, envisioning, and committing to what is left to be done, and embracing early memories rooted in the feminine. These attributes are verified by other researchers as significant for older women's development (Corbett, 2013; Erikson & Erikson, 1997; McCann Mortimer et al., 2008; Mlecz, 2018; Onyx & Small, 2001).

Crones enact forms of leadership such as transformational and humble leadership. However, many of the research participants in this study do not relate to the concept of leadership at all. Crones concern themselves with social justice, tending to collectivist positions and criticism of moral orientations congruent with individual autonomy. Crones are aligned with leadership and social justice when the moral orientation underlying the context is one of an ethic of care.

This study demonstrates differences between the collectivist outlooks of crone leaders and women's leadership defined using a patriarchal mindset. For crones there is a focus of relational repair, adopting worldviews where humans and nature are interconnected, remembering mothers and/or other sources of feminine wisdom including mentors, teachers, guides, ancestors, and being skilled in social generativity, especially through intergenerational relations.

The literature has largely restricted older women's crone leadership development to the personal. This study demonstrates how women embracing the crone archetype increase the sustainability of their community by contributing social, environmental, and economic benefits. This challenges the disregard for the implications of crone development in western society at large. By disrupting the norms of neoliberal societies, crones may play an important role in reducing inequitable structures and relationships not only amongst humans, but also with all other creations in the universe.

In a second phase of this study, a theory of communication, the *coordinated management of meaning* (Wasserman & Fisher-Yoshida, 2017), will be utilized to further explore the nature of crone generativity. The research will seek to understand: What is the nature of the social worlds that crones want to see in the future?

This current study challenges whether the conventional, traditional construct of leadership is relevant for older women leaders who have embraced the crone archetype. There were some unexpected reactions to leadership in this study. For example, "leading" well may be felt in ways that are not in the classic leadership literature, such as circulating energy, transcendence, and connection. Views about leaders' roles may also differ from classic leadership since conducting relational repair, healing collective trauma, and being an activist were key activities for crones.

Crones think about social justice in times of precarity and act on their reflections. Wars, the climate crisis, forced migrations, and racism are met with mindfulness, love, and compassion. When confronted with contemporary traumatizing events or historical trauma, crones prefer to fully experience the associated rage, grief, and fear, so that they may go on to act and feel "lifted," "bright," and "powered."

Crones demonstrate a way of organizing that does not rely heavily on a few privileged voices. The views of our most prominent leaders are largely emblematic of the hegemony. Prioritizing the views of a larger more inclusive representation of "leaders," including the unexpected leadership of older women crones bears consideration. More diverse moral orientations such as an ethic of care will result in more inclusive societies.

In 2021, songwriter Sharen Van Etten rereleased an album with the song "Love More." The song is about "regaining control of one's life, the finale to a feminist album about reclaiming one's voice and returning to love in the wake of trauma" (Pelly, 2021, para 10). "Love more, love more, love more" could serve as a mantra for not only crone leaders but also other leaders. Older women leaders who have embraced the crone archetype challenge conventional, traditional constructs of leadership. Leadership is no longer about "more stuff, more money, more things" but rather about mending, healing, and maintaining our humanity and, with humility, humanity's interconnection with all that surrounds us.

End Note

[1] See https://www.cronescounsel.org/

Meet the Authors

Theresa Southam, PhD is a 2020 Fielding graduate in human and organizational development. Her research debunks the myth that the world is facing a grey tsunami in the growing demographic of older adults. In fact, when older adults age consciously, their everyday kindnesses contribute to more sustainable communities. Recently she expanded her research as a Fielding Institute for Social Innovation Fellow to include trauma-informed teaching and learning. As department head of the Teaching and Learning Centre at Selkirk College, she is a 2020-2021 BC Campus Research Fellow and the recipient, with College of the Rockies, of the BC Campus Award for Excellence in Open Education. Theresa has contributed blog posts, book reviews, and published a blog and portfolio piece, *Is Being an Ally Enough*, for the Association for Anthropology, Gerontology and the Lifecourse. Her dissertation was *27,000 Sunrises: Everyday Contributions of Grateful and Giving Age 70+ Adults*. tsoutham@email.fielding.edu

Isabelle A. Harman, MA is a Realtor® in Pennsylvania and the owner/founder of YellowBird Publishing, LLC. She is a graduate of Fielding Graduate University's Master of Art—organization systems and Chapman University's Master of Art—organization leadership. For over thirty years, she served first on active duty in the U.S. Army and then as a military spouse. As a result, she evolved and embraced the role of crone/wise woman as she helped other military spouses navigate the unique challenges of being married to a member of the armed services, particularly during a prolonged era of war following the tragic events of 9/11/01. Isabelle is currently editing a book of fairy tales and writing a business communication book. She continues to grow as a crone by working toward closing the generation gap to bring the depth of experience, knowledge, and leadership of the crone/wise woman to the forefront of consciousness. isabelle@yellowbirdghostwriter.com

References

Bartalos, M. K. (Ed.). (2009). *Speaking of death: America's new sense of mortality.* ABC-CLIO.

Battiste, M. (2011). *Reclaiming Indigenous voice and vision.* UBC press.

Bolen, J. S. (2003). *Crones don't whine: Concentrated wisdom for juicy women.* Conari Press.

Bukov, A., Maas, I., & Lampert, T. (2002). Social participation in very old age: Cross-sectional and longitudinal findings from BASE. *The Journals of Gerontology: Series B, 57*(6), 510–517. https://doi.org/10.1093/geronb/57.6.P510

Cheng, W. (2011). *Exploring corpus linguistics: Language in action.* Taylor & Francis Group. http://ebookcentral.proquest.com/lib/fielding/detail.action?docID=957932

Cook-Greuter, S. R. (2000). Mature ego development: A gateway to ego transcendence? *Journal of Adult Development, 7*(4), 227–240. https://doi.org/10.1023/A:1009511411421

Corbett, L. (2013). Successful aging: Jungian contributions to development in later life. *Psychological Perspectives, 56*(2), 149–167.

Cosco, T. D., Blossom, S. C. M., & Brayne, C. (2013). Deathless models of aging and the importance of acknowledging the dying process. *Canadian Medical Association Journal, 185*(9), 751–752.

Crones Counsel. (2021). *Celebrating wise women.* https://www.cronescounsel.org/

Dakin, E. (2013). Protection as care: Moral reasoning and moral orientation among ethnically and socioeconomically diverse older women. *Journal of Aging Studies, 28*, 44–56. https://doi.org/10.1016/j.jaging.2013.12.001

Depp, C. A., & Jeste, D. V. (2006). Definitions and predictors of successful aging: A comprehensive review of larger quantitative studies. *The American Journal of Geriatric Psychiatry, 14*(1), 6–20. https://doi.org/10.1097/01.JGP.0000192501.03069.bc

Devine, J., Camfield, L., & Gough, I. (2008). Autonomy or dependence – or both?: Perspectives from Bangladesh, *Journal of Happiness Studies, 9*(1), 105–138. https://doi.org/10.1007/s10902-006-9022-5

Eagly, A. H., & Carli, L. L. (2003). The female leadership advantage: An evaluation of the evidence. *The Leadership Quarterly, 14*(6), 807–834. https://doi.org/10.1016/j.leaqua.2003.09.004

Eagly, A. H., & Carli, L. L. (2018). *Women and the labyrinth of leadership.* Routledge.

Erikson, E. H., & Erikson, J. M. (1997). *The life cycle completed (extended version).* W. W. Norton.

Flood, M., & Pease, B. (2005). Undoing men's privilege and advancing gender equality in public sector institutions. *Policy & Society, 24*(4), 119–138. https://doi.org/10.1016/S1449-4035(05)70123-5

Gallos, J. V. (1993). Women's experiences and ways of knowing: Implications for teaching and learning in the organizational behavior classroom. *Journal of Management Education, 17*(1), 7–26.

Gallos, J. V. (1995). On management education for women: Faulty assumptions, new possibilities. *Selections - Graduate Management Admission Council, 11*(2), 24. https://go.exlibris.link/3YjzGdyD

Gallos, J. V. (2017). Women's experiences and new ways of knowing: Implications for an Inclusive and equitable world. *Journal of Management Education, 41*(5), 643–648. https://doi.org/10.1177/1052562917718225

Gilligan, C. (1993). *In a different voice: Psychological theory and women's development.* Harvard University Press.

Grain, K. M., & Land, D. E. (2017). The social justice turn: Cultivating'critical hope'in an age of despair. *Michigan Journal of Community Service Learning, 23*(1).

Grudzen, M. (2018). Rituals as portals of transcendence in the lives of older adults. *Journal of Religion, Spirituality & Aging, 30*(2), 112–129. https://doi.org/10.1080/15528030.2017.1312725

Hodgkin, S. (2012). 'I'm older and more interested in my community': Older people's contributions to social capital. *Australasian Journal on Ageing, 31*(1), 34–39. https://doi.org/10.1111/j.1741-6612.2011.00528.x

Human Rights Watch. (2021). *"I thought our life might get better": Implementing Afghanistan's elimination of violence against women law.* https://www.hrw.org/report/2021/08/05/i-thought-our-life-might-get-better/implementing-afghanistans-elimination

Katz, S., & Calasanti, T. (2015). Critical perspectives on successful aging: Does it "appeal more than it illuminates"? *The Gerontologist, 55*(1), 26–33.

Kinkead, S. S. (2015). *On becoming a crone* (Publication No. 1691295) [Doctoral dissertation, Fielding Graduate University]. ProQuest Dissertations & Theses Global.

Kreilkamp, A. (2012). *Origins of crone chronicles.* BBI Media. http://www.cronemagazine.com/cc_origins.html

Lewis McCabe, G. C. (2004). *Morphing the crone: An ethnography of crone culture, consciousness and communities* (Publication No. NQ99206) [Doctoral disssertation, York University (Canada)]. ProQuest Dissertations and These Global.

Liang, J., & Luo, B. (2012). Toward a discourse shift in social gerontology: From successful aging to harmonious aging. *Journal of Aging Studies, 26*(3), 327–334. https://doi.org/10.1016/j.jaging.2012.03.001

McCann Mortimer, P., Ward, L., & Winefield, H. (2008). Successful ageing by whose definition? Views of older, spiritually affiliated women. *Australasian Journal on Ageing, 27*(4), 200–204. https://doi.org/10.1111/j.1741-6612.2008.00305.x

McFadden, S. H. (2008). Mindfulness, vulnerability, and love: Spiritual lessons from frail elders, earnest young pilgrims, and middle aged rockers. *Journal of Aging Studies, 22*(2), 132–139. https://doi.org/10.1016/j.jaging.2007.12.013

Mey, J. L. (2017). Corpus linguistics: Some (meta-)pragmatic reflections. *Corpus Pragmatics, 1*(3), 185–199. https://doi.org/10.1007/s41701-017-0017-8

Mills, K. (2020, September 9, 2020). Speaking of psychology (No. 115). *In The challenges faced by women in leadership with Alice Eagly, PhD.* American Psychological Association. https://www.apa.org/research/action/speaking-of-psychology/women-leadership-challenges

Mlecz, J. A. (2018). *Exploring death to understand life: Examining the relationships between self-transcendence, spirituality, and death anxiety* (Publication No. 10749000) [Psy.D. dissertation, College of Saint Elizabeth]. ProQuest Dissertations and Theses Global.

Moody, H. R. (2004). From successful aging to conscious aging. In M. L. Wykle, P. J. Whitehouse, & D. L. Morris (Eds.), *Successful aging through the life span : Intergenerational issues in health* (pp. 55–67). Springer. http://ebookcentral.proquest.com/lib/fielding/detail.action?docID=423273

Nganga, C. W., & Beck, M. (2017). The power of dialogue and meaningful connectedness: Conversations between two female scholars. *The Urban Review, 49*(4), 551–567. https://doi.org/10.1007/s11256-017-0408-y

Nussbaum, M. C. (2011). *Creating capabilities: The human development approach.* Harvard University Press.

Nussbaum, M. C., & Levmore, S. (2017). *Aging thoughtfully: Conversations about retirement, romance, wrinkles, and regret.* Oxford University Press.

O'Donoghue, R. (2006). Locating the environmental in environmental education research: a review of research on nature's nature, its inscription in language and recent memory work on relating to the natural world. *Environmental Education Research, 12*(3-4), 345–357. https://doi.org/10.1080/13504620600799117

Onyx, J., & Small, J. (2001). Memory-work: The method. *Qualitative Inquiry, 7*(6), 773–786. https://doi.org/10.1177/107780040100700608

Ostaseski, F. (2017). *Five invitations: Discovering what death can teach us about living fully*. Pan Macmillan.

Ott, J. S. (2011). *The crone archetype: Women reclaim their authentic self by resonating with crone images* https://sophia.stkate.edu/cgi/viewcontent.cgi?article=1016&context=ma_hhs

Payerle, M. (2016). The croning ceremony. *The Journal of Traditions & Beliefs, 3*(1), 11.

Pelly, J. (2021). *Sharon Van Etten epic Ten.* Pitchfork. https://pitchfork.com/reviews/albums/sharon-van-etten-epic-ten/

Rikke, S. (2019). "How lucky you are never to know what it is to grow old". *Nordlit, 0*(42). https://doi.org/10.7557/13.5012

Ronn, V., & Daugaard, K. (2005). The crone conspiracy. *International Journal of the Humanities, 3*(1).

Rowe, J. W., & Kahn, R. L. (1998). *Successful aging: The MacArthur Foundation study.* Pantheon.

Rubinstein, R. L., & de Medeiros, K. (2015). "Successful aging," gerontological theory and neoliberalism: A qualitative critique. *The Gerontologist, 55*(1), 34–42.

Sage-ing International. (2019). *Wisdom Circles.* https://www.sage-ing.org/get-involved/wisdom-circles/

Salis Reyes, N. A. (2019). "What am I doing to be a good ancestor?": An indigenized phenomenology of giving back among native collegegGraduates.

American Educational Research Journal, 56(3), 603–637. https://doi.org/10.3102/0002831218807180

Simola, S. K., Barling, J., & Turner, N. (2010). Transformational leadership and leader moral orientation: Contrasting an ethic of justice and an ethic of care. *The Leadership Quarterly, 21*(1), 179–188. https://doi.org/10.1016/j.leaqua.2009.10.013

Southam, T. (2020). *27,000 sunrises: Everyday contributions of grateful and giving age 70+ adults* (Publication No. 27739045) [Doctoral dissertaion, Fielding Graduate University]. ProQuest Dissertations and Theses Global.

Southam, T., & Corley, C. (2020). Living from the inside out: The value of conscious aging and the foray (4A+) "beyond self" paradigm. *Journal of Certified Senior Advisors, 80*(3).

Stinson, A. M. (2013). *Spiritual life review with older adults: Finding meaning in late life development* Scholar Commons. http://scholarcommons.usf.edu/etd/4778

Tacol, L. (2016). "What is it like to be a Buddhist?" *Interdisciplinary Description of Complex Systems, 14*(4), 378–396. http://dx.doi.org/10.7906/indecs.14.4.6

Wang, Y., Liu, J., & Zhu, Y. (2018). Humble leadership, psychological safety, knowledge sharing, and follower creativity: A cross-level investigation. *Frontiers in Psychology, 9*, 1727–1727. https://doi.org/10.3389/fpsyg.2018.01727

Wasserman, I. C., & Fisher-Yoshida, B. (2017). *Communicating possibilities: A brief introduction to the coordinated management of meaning (CMM)*. Taos Institute Publications.

Wen, M., Zhang, S., & McGhee, D. (2020). Utilizing the moral nobility of older Chinese women in governance: The uses of humility, empathy, and an ethics of care in moral clinics in Huzhou city. *The British Journal of Sociology, 71*(2), 300-313. https://doi.org/10.1111/1468-4446.12736

Wild Woman Sisterhood. (2015, October 24). *Wild woman sisterhood.* https://www.facebook.com/WildWomanSisterhood/photos/radiant-luminous-crone-woman-during-ancient-times-the-crones-hags-and-witches-we/536027519880170

Chapter 3

The Role of Intentional Leadership in Makerspaces: A Social Justice and Capabilities Approach

Gail Wilson

Institute for Social Innovation Fellow

Our nation's leaders and their leadership strategies—good or bad—help define the health of our country. In times of precarity, such as a worldwide pandemic, all institutions, organizations, and businesses must look closely at the disruptions and deficits in their systems, processes, and policies. Although there are many factors that can mitigate or impede the nation's future outlook and outcome, one way to mitigate societal upheaval is to understand the heart of leadership.

Building on my dissertation, *Makerspaces: Making STEAM Work in Urban Spaces* (Wilson, 2021), I found that what I called intentional leadership (IL) permeated the success of the makerspace teen program at the study site. It is a concept that expressed each leader's commitment to fulfilling the organization's mission to "make tools, technology and the knowledge to use them accessible to everyone" (Open Works, 2020). I used an ethnographically-oriented social science approach and framed the methodology in social justice, specifically distributional and relational justice (Gewirtz, 1998; Comstock et al., 2008). These foundational studies revolutionized my understandings of the role that social justice played on people, place, and systems that impact the lives of all individuals. The inclusion of the adult administrators' voices gave me a window into the larger role leadership played in advancing the organization's vision and how it was applied in practice.

Exploring that phenomenon revealed that when educational programs are designed deliberatively and intentionally (Haber-Curran & Owen, 2013) and with an ethical foundation (McClellan, 2013), they have the potential to create an environment where young people can learn, grow, and thrive. Intentional leadership was an unexpected finding in my research because my initial focus was on the experiences of the teens. Due to the pandemic, the site had to shut down and the students did not complete their entire program of making. I made the decision to include the adult administrators and decision-makers in the study, which made a tremendous impact on my overall view of the important role of leadership. I discovered that IL was a significant factor in the success of the program, especially through the lens of social justice amid a pandemic.

As I reflected on the significance of leadership in perilous times, four questions arose: What does intentional leadership look like? What does social justice have to do with it? How do human capabilities as a social justice approach factor into outstanding leadership? Furthermore, can intentional leadership be taught? There are four themes I will explore—distributional justice, relational justice, capabilities approach, and intentional leadership within the framework of social justice theory.

Following, I will begin with a general discussion of intentional leadership and its relationship to educational practices because it connects to the succeeding human rights approaches. I then contrast this view with a more inclusive justice perspective. Using the ubuntu ethic of community and social justice, which focuses away from individual human rights, provides a more enlightened understanding of human rights through the idea of community care.

Pandemic Woes, Public Health, and Leadership

The COVID-19 virus opened the festering wounds of inequality, injustice, and unethical norms in many of our organizational leadership practices. Our society was woefully unprepared, and the lack of a rapid response inside and outside of the organizational edifices left thousands without jobs and their basic human needs unmet. Many youth and young adults who typically headed toward summer employment found themselves unable to help their families, further stressing an already anxiety-laden environment.

The urgency of this topic is represented in the numbers from the United States Bureau of Labor Statistics (2020, 2021). Unemployment dramatically increased over the previous year due to the human devastation created in the wake of the pandemic. It has been particularly pernicious for Black/African Americans and other people of color. The pandemic-induced economic downturn disrupted all sectors of society, and many are still floundering in 2021 despite the uptick in employment and lower unemployment rates. Data in July 2020 stated that the unemployment rates were 25.4% for young Blacks, 25.4% for Asians, and 21.7% for Hispanics, which signaled a sizable increase over 2019. While data from July 2021 showed improvement with young Blacks (13.6%), Asians (12.3%), and Hispanics (11.7%), the numbers remained in double digits. These societal concerns are social justice issues and require a reexamination of all pillars of our society.

When I reflect on youth workforce development, I recognize that it is the lifeblood to sustaining the continued growth and economic development of the United States. How we deal with these problems where jobs continue to go unfilled and family members continue to succumb to the virus will be critical to the United States' economic survival. At this juncture, our organizational and elected leaders must deconstruct the common organizational structures and reconstruct the notion of what it means to be a leader.

Intentional Leadership

I begin this section by asking, what does intentional leadership look like? My search for a definitive definition of intentional leadership was fruitless. However, my study revealed the praxis of intentional leadership (IL) as a critical conceptual finding. I learned that being intentional with our thoughts, beliefs, desires, and hopes puts into action leadership behaviors that are transformative. It means that when you become committed to the possibility of something, your actions become the purposeful operation of your behaviors.

I used IL as a descriptive term to identify the characteristics of a particular type of leader. Using IL is an approach that brings awareness to the "collective, boundaryless, and connected leadership" found across multiple stakeholder engagements (Swensen et al., 2016). In educational leadership, these stakeholders include parents/guardians, students, families, administrators, teachers, government officials, and others who make important decisions related to the operation and academics of a school's organization (The Glossary of Education

Reform, 2014). Furthermore, to move toward a more socially just leadership style that is decolonizing and inclusive, intentional leaders build upon their personal set of values and sense of integrity to foster trust among all stakeholders.

IL is purposeful and done with the understanding that the leader, whom I consider a manager of groups of people and/or operations, is aware of the human capabilities of collective action. For instance, through a leadership style based on trust and integrity, an educational leader can transform existing practices and cultures that are incongruent with the forward progression of teaching and learning in new ways, especially in times of uncertainty.

IL is not well-defined as an area of research and study. In mapping the connections with other leadership types, I found the space where IL is located. For example, Figure 7 displays the connections between leadership styles and outcomes.

Figure 7
Leadership Connectors

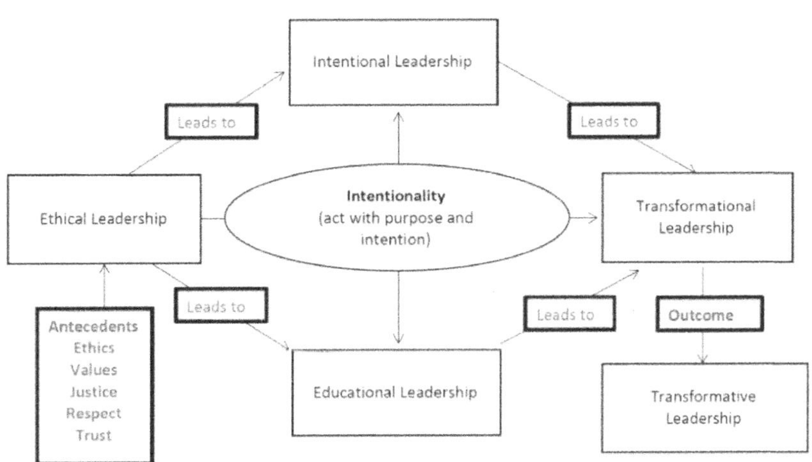

I have chosen to focus on ethical, transformational, and educational leadership because of their relationship to IL. What these leadership types have in common is that in every instance, relationships with others are at the center. Leaders at multiple levels within this framework play a role in developing strong leaders, whether they are young, seasoned, or reluctant. Leadership development can occur at any age and is needed, especially in current times where the next generation of leaders are key to the nation's future (McClellan, 2013). Thus, in answer to the question, can intentional leadership be taught? I believe it can.

As leaders pursue leadership development, transformational leadership should become a primary goal. It is rooted in an ethical foundation with intention, leading to a transformational and transformative outcome. Thus, intentional leadership is a descriptive term underpinning the identity of a leader who lives and works from an intrinsic set of values that can lead to lives of fulfillment and well-being for both leader and follower. IL is purposeful because it connotes that the leader understands the value and agency people bring to all interactions.

These types of leaders lead by example and understand the importance of nourishing personal and professional growth along the way for those whom they lead. For example, the leader's awareness of the social determinants of health and well-being and its implications on social justice informs their personal and professional code of ethics and values that underpin their actions. Although leading in times of turbulence is not easy, being grounded in the practice of ethical values and decision-making is essential.

Intentionality, as a connector to IL, is the overarching desire to do something and manifests through the purposeful operation of the leader's actions. It can be situated between ethical and transformational leadership. I view ethical leadership as core to IL and it drives the leadership behaviors of all the other types.

Ethical Leadership

Beginning with the ethical leadership connection, a leader's behavior (words and actions) is governed by their personal values, ethics, sense of justice, respect for others, and desire to develop trust. This type of leadership is discussed frequently in leadership theories because of its implications on behaviors (Avey et al., 2010). These authors suggested that ethical leadership is a desirable state because a leader's ethics is influential on both the followers' adherence to and deviance from ethical behaviors. It can play a moderating role in the relational aspects of person-to-person interactions and foster prosocial behaviors.

An excellent example of leadership excellence is German Chancellor Angela Merkel. Chancellor Merkel's "rock-solid" leadership style cannot be denied, having led Germany's helm for 16 years (van Esch, 2021). The author noted the secrets of the Chancellor's success included "strong leadership skills … high public trust, competence, care, trustworthiness." Germany preferred her "reasoned, compromising and fact-based approach to politics over sweeping statements." In many respects, Merkel exhibited the characteristics of intentional leadership. Her ethics, values, steadfastness, and intentions shaped her to be a transformational leader of her country. Figure 8 shows some of the many positive characteristics of exemplary leadership. Intentionality and ethics are the anchors of these prosocial behaviors

Figure 8
Descriptive Leadership Terms

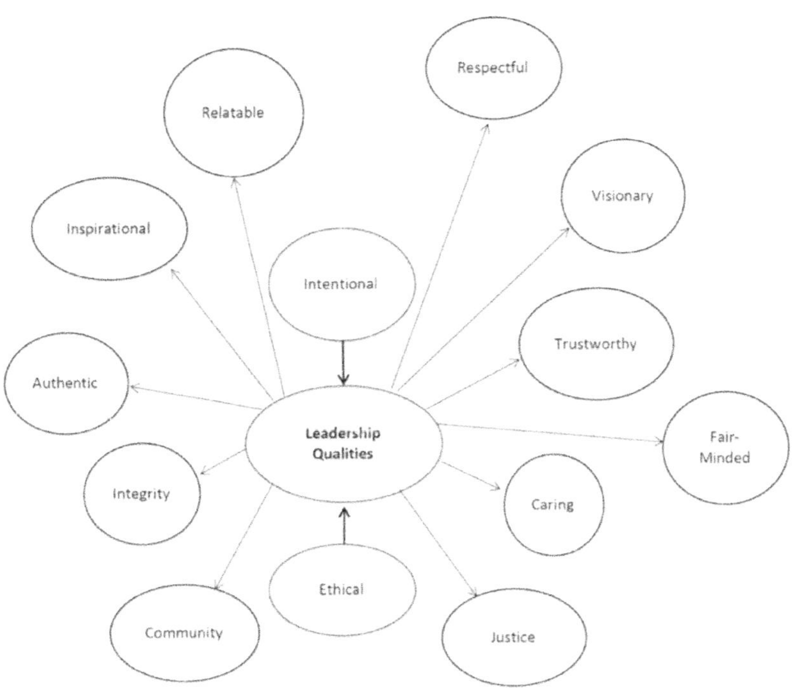

Many contemporary leaders' visions of what leadership needs to look like acknowledge the necessity for a more inclusive, diverse, and equitable workforce. Historically, there are examples of IL that support many transformational leadership characteristics. Bonaparte (2015) moved beyond transformational leadership and noted several historical figures who exemplified transformative leadership. She stated, "While history has documented the work of notable African American women such as Harriet Tubman, Sojourner Truth, and Mary McLeod Bethune, their contributions as leaders, particularly in the context of transformative leadership, has not been fully described" (p. 5). This leadership model focuses on the characteristics of ethics, values, empowerment, and societal interest in the greater good.

For example, Harriet Tubman supported other Blacks by providing housing and other supportive services for individuals. Her transformative leadership style can be located in her foundational roots (ethical and idealistic values), which guided her leadership decision-making. Whether leading enslaved African Americans to freedom or "concomitantly encouraging independence through self-sufficiency activities," Tubman made it "possible for these women not to have to rely on government assistance to support themselves" (Bonaparte, 2015, p. 3). Leading formerly enslaved people to freedom and securing safe havens are the hallmarks of her transformative leadership style.

One such contemporary leader who exhibits transformative leadership qualities is Michelle Obama. The former first lady is characterized as having a rock-solid character with the capacity to motivate, inspire, and call others to action (Inspiring Leadership Now, 2020). She is compassionate and shows empathy, self-confidence, and authenticity, and is relatable to others. I most appreciated her honesty and integrity. What makes her such an excellent leader is her ability to build trust with people regardless of their political affiliations (Huhman & Hedges, 2012). Furthermore, according to the final Gallup Poll, she consistently had high approval ratings. Her transformative leadership style was exhibited throughout her adult life by intentionally putting her time and education to use in community building. Her transformative style changed the lives of countless others during her 8 years in the White House–the People's House (Slevin, 2016). What is described here are all outcomes of transformative leadership where intention resides. It shows the qualities necessary for positive results. It is what intentional leadership looks like, and social justice has played a starring role in these extraordinary lives.

Intentional Leadership in the Field of Education

From my purview, IL begins with a state of mind. As a set of personal values, attitudes, and beliefs about ourselves and each other, the behavioral expression shows up in how we interact with the world around us. This leadership approach reflects those personal attributes.

The role of intentional leadership in education is vital to student achievement. Two aspects of educational leadership involve supporting teachers with their professional development and teaching students how to learn. However, a needed area of improvement is in the instruction of student learning. Carter G. Woodson (2009), in the *Mis-education of the Negro*, believed "No people can go forward when the majority of those who should know better have chosen to go backward, but this is exactly what most of our misleaders do" (p. 59). Furthermore, an adult participant from my study, Muhammad, stated:

> The educational system focuses on learning, but I'm not sure that they are teaching the youth how to learn in a very intentional way. As an educator, I may learn the three domains of learning; I may know them but do my students know them. So, we have to teach learning and make sure that [intentionality] is embedded into their approach to everything. (Wilson, 2021, pp. 66–67)

The excellence of education in some school systems in our nation is left wanting due to social justice inequality. To change this disparity, training and development of our workforce and leaders must be done intentionally, focused on all students achieving. So, how can IL be applied in practice, and what does social justice have to do with it?

Leadership studies in the United States are based on a Western Eurocentric worldview that encapsulates the ideas and approaches to economic and material wealth. These are the vestiges of colonialism that exist beyond post-colonialism. Economic empowerment in the workforce continues to exploit the power differential inherent in capitalism. The transformational leadership capabilities of our national political and educational organizations have become even more crucial today. The infusion of intentional leadership in our educational leaders

(Figure 7) can greatly enhance their capabilities to become transformative leaders. Additionally, our ability to "build back better" requires our leaders, in this case, educational leaders, to lead not just from a past understanding of how the world works but from the heart of social justice needs. Hence, to answer what does social justice have to do with intentional leadership, I contend that leaders who are grounded in social justice and human rights are more effective in their leadership capacity.

Social Justice and Human Rights

To understand the importance of distributional and relational justice, we must ask what social justice means. Examining social justice in this new pandemic threat, I needed to consider its interconnection with distributional and relational justice—two vital elements of social justice that I used to frame my study.

The concept of distributional justice refers to the principles by which goods and services are equitably distributed in society (Gewirtz, 1998). The United States has always had a vested interest in distributional justice (See Rawls' 1971, *A Theory of Justice*). In addition, Sen's (2004) theory of human rights proposed that economics and social rights are "broad class[es] of human rights." Being cognizant of social justice issues, intentional leaders who lead from an ethical way of knowing with intention can put into action equitable laws and policies for the greater good of society. How society distributes resources goes beyond having access to opportunities; rather, it includes the relational "human beliefs, attitudes, experiences, and ideologies about who should receive what resource (money, goods, services) and at what amount" (Wilson, 2021, p. 75).

Relational justice is the social and economic relations of power distribution. It can best be defined as a "bottom-up justice, or the justice produced through cooperative behavior, agreement, negotiation or dialogue among actors ..." whether during peacetime, a global pandemic, or a post-conflict situation (Casanovas & Poblet, 2008, p. 323). I view leaders as people who, through their words and actions, inspire and motivate others around a common goal, and their leadership is a social construct that is both relational and cultural (Ospina & Schall, 2001). This human connectedness becomes part of the systems of governance, education, and organizations. Miller (1986) emphasized growth-promoting relationships that are grounded in a mutuality that empowers all involved in an interaction. Comstock et al. (2008) identified how "growth-fostering relationships" are critical elements in understanding power and privilege in any system where human connectedness, belonging, and social inclusion are central. In other words, the relational view of distributional justice gave important context to understanding how the political and cultural relationships intertwine and shape the legal realities that create a just or unjust world (Wilson, 2021).

One factor critical to becoming an IL is how its qualities influence social justice and human rights issues. Our educational institutions have a foothold in all communities, and their leaders are tasked with the enormous responsibility for the care, education, and learning of generations of young people. These are relational justice issues. Our entire social existence is relational, encompassing relationships with other people, our environments, and the political and ecological systems that impact our lives. Ideally, these relationships should create ways to ensure fair and equal treatment for the well-being of everyone. However, when I look back over the past century, the same degree of inequality continues to exist. Therefore, IL plays a greater role here in identifying a leader's ability to motivate others to move toward a shared vision that is fair and equitable.

Lastly, social justice is a critical lens to view human rights and the central capabilities to which every individual is entitled. In essence, social justice means equal opportunity and equal treatment for all. It is built on four pillars: human rights, access, participation, and equity. Following are the central capabilities (Nussbaum, 2011), which refer to an approach to human rights that brought forward the idea of opportunities and freedoms created for the common good. These concepts are undergirded by the relationality of all human interactions (Comstock et al., 2008). The capabilities approach is another way to understand social justice.

Capabilities Approach to Justice

So, how do human capabilities as a social justice approach factor into outstanding leadership? As noted above, social justice can be conceptualized in terms of distributional and relational justice. Despite the various disciplinary definitions, meanings, and applications making it difficult to conceptualize social justice specifically, there are diverse approaches to meeting the goals set by national and international justice conventions.

Taking up the question of what social justice is, psychologists Thrift and Sugarman (2019) examined Fraser's (2009b) argument that there are three principles that provide answers to these fundamental questions: "What is the good of social justice? (principle of participational parity), Who is owed social justice? (all-affected principle), and how are we to make decisions related to all aspects of social justice? (all-subjected principle)" (p.12). Fraser (2009a) rightly asserted that an appropriately expanded public sphere requires "new transnational public powers, which can be made accountable to new democratic transnational circuits of public opinion" (p. 99), which is participational parity. Fraser (2005) also asserted that the "all-affected principle" should be applied to all affected people in the global community, rather than locating in a specific geopolitical environment. For example, economic parity cannot be reached when wealth distribution within capitalistic societies (participational parity) is undermined by corporate outsourcing of jobs overseas and the exploitation inherent in that economic system. Thrift and Sugarman considered Fraser's framework appropriate to evaluate social justice claims.

Taking a deeper look at distributional justice, Keddie's (2012) review essay explored Fraser's capabilities model in relation to the critique by other authors who disagreed with Fraser's core propositions (principles of economic, cultural, and political justice). Her critics contend that the challenges for schooling, equity, and social justice should be reframed to include political representation justice as it relates to the political structures and relational strategies in schools. Keddie examined the problems of distributive and representative justice through Fraser's model and believed that the approach "is one of many useful and powerful lenses to comprehend the complex manifestations of injustice that characterize current equity and schooling landscapes" (p. 14). In my view, Fraser's model, while not ideal, expands the understanding of social justice in an educational context.

Reisch (2001) viewed social justice as a means to hold the most vulnerable populations among society "harmless in the distribution of societal resources" (p.350), while Nussbaum's (2011) idea of rights "provides a valuable intensification, connecting the idea of capabilities to the idea of social and political urgency and human centrality" (p. 36). The central capabilities approach is another way to explore distributional and relational justice opportunities and options through its lens. I pose two questions here: How do we secure human rights, and how do we provide access, participation, and equity for all?

Nussbaum (2011) argued that "where humans are concerned, the basis of these entitlements lie not in rationality, nor is any other specific human property, but, rather, in the bare fact of being a living human being: being born from human parents and having a minimal level of agency or capacity for activity" (p. 25). Her alternative conception of social justice uses the fundamental human capabilities as the threshold for securing these entitlements (Nussbaum, 1997). This theoretical frame is based on human agency. She considers her concept of human rights "important human entitlements, inherent in the idea of basic social justice, and can be viewed as one species of a human rights approach" (Nussbaum, 2011, p. 23). Further, she believes that "they belong to humans just on account of their human dignity and would be there even if there were no political organization at all, although no doubt they would not be secured to people" (p. 25).

Nussbaum's capabilities approach is not without its critics as an approach to human rights. There has been some tension with other theorists who view capabilities broadly. Walker (2001) calls into question the theoretical usefulness and analogized that Nussbaum is correct in wanting individual flourishing, but "it should also be for collective solidarities, the one with the other" (pp. 168–169).

While I see the utility of each of the reasons mentioned above behind the different theories, their focus is on individual human rights. There is no discussion of how leaders will ultimately enact the laws and write the policies around these justice matters and lead ethically. In other words, how will they define social justice for the collective good? With that, I must consider, in contrast, the more holistic, ethical approach of the South African ethic of ubuntu. Gade (2011/2012) provided a different and potentially more useful framework for human rights and capabilities.

Ubuntu Philosophical Approach to Justice

As I reflect on social justice, human rights, and capabilities, there is much that can be said about human rights struggles. It was the decisive leadership that came out of the social justice struggles that was life changing. As another approach to justice, ubuntu comes to mind. Early use of the South African term ubuntu has been referenced as a human quality (human nature, humanity, goodness of nature, moral disposition) and later connected to philosophy or ethic of a people (Gade, 2011). It can best be understood in terms of social justice, human rights, dignity, and the idea that our humanity is tied with others (Gade, 2012).

For example, Desmond Tutu, a man from humble beginnings, rose to leadership from a foundation of ubuntu. Speaking at the Academy of Achievement, Bishop Tutu reflected on his early education, recalling that

> Many of the people who taught us were very dedicated and they inspired you to want to emulate them and really to become all that you could become. They gave you the impression that, in fact, yeah, the sky is the limit. You can, even with all of the obstacles that are placed in your way; you can reach out to the stars. (Biography.com, 2014).

Hoffmann and Metz (2017) also described this development theory as follows:

> We extend the relational critique by arguing that all intuitively valuable capabilities have relational properties, where such relational properties are best understood in terms of relations of care for and identification with others. An ubuntu ethic has a richer normative conception of relationship, which extends well beyond an individual's ability to be supported by others or a concern about the harm of isolation as but one dimension of poverty. Since an ubuntu ethic locates ethical value fundamentally in the relationship between individuals, and not just individuals themselves, it follows that individual freedom often takes the form of interdependence with others, as the ability to relate to them in appropriate ways. (p. 156)

The wisdom of this ethical approach was evident in the interdependence I witnessed among the group members I studied (teen makers and adults). I noted the comradery among the teens, their support of each other's work, the respect given and received, positively accepting feedback and critique of their work from peers and instructors, and the sharing of ideas on techniques. The freedom of expression (verbally and artistically) was essential to trust-building, care, and identification with others—belongingness. So, when social justice is discussed, we are talking about freedom in all its forms, and relationships are at the heart of those experiences.

Relationships at the Heart of Human Experience

The terms "relationship" and "intentionality" showed up at the beginning of my research. My first impression on my first day on-site was the established relationships between the teen makers and adults. In each instance, it was apparent that their engagement with each other and the projects they were creating were intentional. The program began in September 2019 and ended in March 2020 due to the pandemic. During my interactions, I heard comments such as "It's like family," and the instructors were "helpful and nice." Michelle (adult participant) believed in the value of relationships. She expressed it this way:

> Relationships are 100% at the center of why I do the work and how I do the work. If they don't have healthy relationships with their peers and the adults in the space, if they don't like being there, if it's not fun, I know that they won't come. Centering relationships [and having] love at the center of what we do … that's always been so important to me. (Wilson, 2021, p. 60)

The teens' skills acquisition through the program design was significant. Social-emotional learning was a developmental skill I observed. For example, during their presentations to the group and adults, one student acknowledged the error of her ways. Their instructor reminded them (as a group) of the necessity to "write down instructions … why, because you could break something" (Wilson, 2021). When it was the teen's turn to present, she assured the instructor that she would write instructions down, and her cohort acknowledged the same.

One teen maker expressed that her work was "real heart work." It was telling how all of the teen makers reflected on their projects. The work every member (adults and teens) performed were emblematic of their why, how, and to what end. For example, Maya (an adult participant) viewed her role as one who facilitated program design. Her way of getting to know the teens was through individual meetings. She stated:

> I have a format, and it's like, who are you? What are you interested in? Where do you want to be in six months? Where do you want to be in a year? Where do you want to be in five years, but what their weaknesses are, what their strengths are? And I can help build programming through just that, getting to know your face through a format that's a little bit more structured than just like, tell me about yourself, young people don't. (Wilson, 2021, p. 65)

On the other hand, Jessie saw his role as a guide. He said:

> Almost all of our students were Black and a lot of them were coming from a nearby high school, so they work and … high school focused a lot on specific crafts and so then coming to our makerspace helped them use the concepts that they were learning in school. We're kind of guiding them on a certain trajectory because a lot of them were incorporating art into what they wanted to do and their career goals, so we were trying to give them a little more room to structure that and just give them a taste of what that might look like for them in practice. (Wilson, 2021, p.64)

The teens' learning (specifically authentic learning modalities) was connected to the leadership style of the educator. The interpersonal relationship between instructor, facilitator, and learner was the conduit that bound their interaction. These leaders embraced the organization's vision of being accessible to everyone. Collectively, their actions were intentional, relational, and focused on developing the teens as future entrepreneurs and leaders of their communities. Enrichment programs such as those found in makerspaces can promote the forward progression of youth and young adults' place in society.

Leadership and Makerspaces

Intentional leadership plays a significant role in the development of students' self-identity, self-efficacy, and career outlook. Makerspaces can provide an out-of-school enrichment experience that enhances core developmental competencies they will need in the workforce. However, all makerspaces are not created equally, and neither are their leadership teams. I define makerspaces as gathering places for tinkering, creating, and exploring, and they function as centers for learning and sharing knowledge (Martin, 2015). The makerspace I chose for my doctoral study has as its mission to "make tools, technology, and the knowledge to use them **accessible to all** [emphasis mine]," which is a very inclusive statement. There is no ambiguity there. Within their doors is a multicultural and intergenerational board of directors, staff, instructors, and members who are reflective of the community they serve. It is an essential point because the relationality of people, places, and systems are all things to consider when opening a makerspace.

Makerspaces are found in various locations, such as libraries, schools, and other public or private facilities nationally and internationally (Barton et al., 2016). Learning is everywhere to be found and is at the heart of these places. Martin, an administrator at the makerspace, expressed learning in these terms:

> If you teach someone welding, the skills they're learning are super applicable outside of the world of welding. But when you put it in an entrepreneurial framework and teach people more of a mindset and a way of thinking, just like a skill, it's kind of the difference between that old proverb teach a person to fish versus giving them a fish. Workforce development, in general, is kind of give folks a fish approach. Whereas entrepreneurship development, learning a little bit about business planning, finances, marketing, staffing ... that teaches people a mindset that they can take to a wide variety of jobs. (Wilson, 2021, p. 66)

Today, we need to retool our educational and development systems in this new normal 21st century environment. For example, agile proesses must be utilized as our government and industries transition to system-wide transformations anchored in equity, inclusion, and justice. Leaders within these institutions will need to move beyond the "give folks a fish" idea. There is an urgent need to develop strategies and design a constantly forward-moving curriculum. In other words, teach a person to fish, so they have skills that apply to a wide variety of careers.

Educational leaders, whether in-school or outside of school, have a nearly insurmountable job to prepare our young people for the future of work. Unfortunately, many students living in specific zip codes do not have the resources afforded to others in higher-income neighborhoods. These disparities impact their education, health, and quality of life. Access to educational opportunities (distributional justice) in these communities may be the intermediary step toward social justice. Likewise, supportive adult and peer relationships (relational justice) are the necessary relational factors that enhance a leader's ability to lead intentionally.

From my research, it became evident that the teenagers seemed to thrive in this maker culture. They were given the "substantial freedoms" to create, explore, and express (Nussbaum, 2011), bringing their authentic selves to the makerspace while gaining workforce skills they could use immediately and in the future. They had access to tools, the freedom to use them, and the necessary relationships supporting their efforts (Gade, 2011, 2012). The combination of these freedoms created an environment where the teen makers were treated with dignity, respect, and learned there was power in their voices, not just to be heard but to see their requests in action. A democratic maker culture arose. Having access to community makerspaces led by intentional leadership may help ameliorate some of these barriers, especially during times of crisis.

Research, Policy, and Education

In times of high stress and uncertainty, leaders must be vigilant over the threats facing their organizations and create agile processes to lessen the impact on valued customers and stakeholders. When getting through a crisis, as a leader, it is imperative to consider your ability to "rally the troops" toward the next business, organizational, or societal challenges (Williams et al., 2020). The role of intentional leadership is vital to the process.

I propose prioritizing educational research around intentional leadership related to social justice, human rights, and community in the service of youth development. These social justice concerns must be part of everyday educational conversations and decision-making. It has implications for a new kind of educational programming, staff development, and public policy initiatives, especially for young people from underserved and marginalized communities.

Conclusion

Throughout this chapter I identified the critical need for educational leaders to lead with intentionality and that ethical leadership is core to intentional leadership, which drives the behaviors that support human rights, access, participation, and equity. I provided insights into the role of intentional leadership, specifically in makerspace program development, design, and execution. Fortunately, the teen makers had the opportunity to learn, explore, and grow before the state-mandated closures due to coronavirus. Despite the challenges, the teen makers were college-bound with marketable skills that they could use as young entrepreneurs, if so desired. The possibility of a bright future was expressed by one teen maker who said, "What excites me about the program, it allows you to tap into like being an entrepreneur because at first, I didn't intend on being an entrepreneur" (Wilson, 2021, p. 57). It also opened possibilities for another teen maker who was initially focused on an engineering path but articulated he planned to study political science in college. His intention upon completing a master's degree was to return to the city and revitalize downtown as a political leader and entrepreneur.

I am reminded why leadership matters and its importance to each new generation. The world is changing, and for marginalized, underserved communities, it is in many ways going backward. In this exploration of distributional and relational justice, the capabilities approach and intentional leadership within the social justice framework of ubuntu show that reaching the higher ideals of democracy is possible. As evidenced throughout this chapter, if our society is to thrive and not merely survive, this is the moment for ethical, intentional, and transformational leadership to come to the fore.

Finally, the four themes I have explored—distributional justice, relational justice, capabilities approach, and intentional leadership within the framework of social justice theory—when integrated together, form a more unified lens to understand human rights and capabilities. Therefore, leadership during times of precarity is best served by those leaders who practice ubuntu and are thoughtful, caring, fair-minded, and trustworthy—having intentional leadership qualities that transform their leadership behaviors. Consequently, leadership fueled by an ethical, intentional, and transformational outlook can produce extraordinary results. Under that type of leadership, our society and the nation will have a chance to grow and thrive into the future.

Meet the Author

Gail Wilson, PhD earned her master's and doctoral degrees in human development from Fielding Graduate University, School of Leadership Studies. She holds a B.S. in behavioral and social sciences from the University of Maryland University College. Her professional experience includes an internship and subsequent career counselor position at a non-profit in Baltimore, Maryland that changed the trajectory of her life. That experience awakened a life-long interest and passion for assisting marginalized youth and young adults in underserved communities as they seek to find their life and career direction. One surprising factor from the findings from her dissertation, *Makerspaces: Making STE(A)M work in urban spaces* (2021), was the role of intentional leadership throughout program design and rollout. It was authentic, participatory, and innovative. Currently, Dr. Wilson has taken on international work and is a virtual Transformational Leadership instructor for emerging leaders in a management certificate program in Nassau, Bahamas. gwilson@email.fielding.edu

References

Avey, J.B., Palanski, M.E. & Walumbwa, F.O. (2011). When leadership goes unnoticed: The moderating role of follower self-esteem on the relationship between ethical leadership and follower behavior. *Journal of Business Ethics, 98*, 573–582. https://doi.org/10.1007/s10551-010-0610-2

Barton, A. C., Tan, E., & Greenberg, D. (2016). The makerspace movement: Sites of possibilities for equitable opportunities to engage underrepresented youth in STEM. *Teachers College Record, 119*(6), 11–44. https://resources.informalscience.org/sites/default/files/Equity%26MS.CB_.Tan_.Greenberg.pdf

Biography.com Editors. (2021). *Desmond Tutu Biography*. A&E Television Networks. https://www.biography.com/political-figure/desmond-tutu

Bonaparte, Y. C. (2015). A perspective on transformative leadership and African American women in history. *The Journal of Values-Based Leadership, 8*(2), Article 4. https://scholar.valpo.edu/jvbl/vol8/iss2/4/

Casanovas, P. & Poblet, M. (2008). Concepts and fields of relational justice. In *Computable Models of the Law* (pp. 323-339). Springer, Berlin, Heidelberg.

Comstock, D. L., Hammer, T. R., Strentzsch, J., Cannon, K., Parsons, J., & Salazar, G.

(2008). Relational-cultural theory: A framework for bridging relational, multicultural, and social justice competencies. *Journal of Counseling & Development, 86*(3), 279–287. https://doi.org/10.1002/j.1556-6678.2008.tb00510.x

Fraser, N. (2005). Re-framing justice in a globalizing world. *New Left Review*, 36. London.

Fraser, N. (2009a). Social justice in the age of identity politics: Redistribution, recognition, participation. *Geographic thought: A praxis perspective, 72*, 91. https://www.gesis.org/ssoar/home

Fraser, N. (2009b). *Fraser, Nancy. Scales of justice: Reimagining political space in a globalizing world.* Vol. 31. Columbia University Press, 2009.

Gewirtz, S. (1998). Conceptualizing social justice in education: mapping the territory. *Journal of Education Policy, 13*(4), 469-484. https://doi.org/10.1080/0268093980130402

Gade, C. B. N. (2012). The historical development of the written discourses on Ubuntu. *South African Journal of Philosophy, 30*(3), 302–329. https://hdl.handle.net/10520/EJC96149

Gade, C. B. N. (2011). What is Ubuntu? Different interpretations among South Africans of African descent. *South African Journal of Philosophy, 31*(3), 484–503. https://hdl.handle.net/10520/EJC125037

Haber-Curran, P., & Owen, J. E. (2013). Engaging the whole student: Student affairs and the national leadership education research agenda. *Journal of Leadership Education,* 12(3), 38–50. https://doi.org/10.12806/V12/I3/TF2

Hoffmann, N., & Metz, T. (2017). What can the capabilities approach learn from an Ubuntu ethic? A relational approach to development theory. *World Development, 97,* 153–164. https://doi.org/10.1016/j.worlddev.2017.04.010

Huhman, H. & Hedges, K. (2012). *5 Leadership takeaways from Michelle Obama.* ForbesWomen.https://www.forbes.com/sites/work-in-progress/2012/09/24/5-leadership-takeaways-from-michelle-obama/

Inspiring Leadership Now (2020). *First lady or fearless leader? Michelle Obama's 10 most admirable leadership qualities.* https://www.inspiringleadershipnow.com/leadership-qualities-michelle-obama/

Keddie, A. (2012). Schooling and social justice through the lenses of Nancy Fraser. *Critical Studies in Education, 53*(3), 263–279. https://doi.org/10.1080/17508487.2012.709185

Martin, L. (2015). The promise of the maker movement for education. *Journal of Pre-College Engineering Education Research* (J-PEER), 5(1). https://doi.org/10.7771/2157-9288.1099

McClellan, J. L. (2013). Contributing to the development of student leadership through academic advising. *Journal of Leadership Education, 12*(1). https://www.researchgate.net/profile/Jeffrey-Mcclellan-2/publication/333442541_Contributing_to_the_Development_of_Student_Leadership_through_Academic_Advising/links/60736a5c299bf1c911c5c07f/Contributing-to-the-Development-of-Student-Leadership-through-Aca

Miller, J. B. (1986). *What do we mean by relationshps?* (Vol. 22). Stone Center for Developmental Services and Studies, Wesley College. http://wcwonline.org/pdf/previews/preview_22sc.pdf

Nussbaum, M. (1997). Capabilities and human rights. *Fordham Law Review, 273.* https://ir.lawnet.fordham.edu/flr

Nussbaum, M. (2011). Capabilities, entitlements, rights: Supplementation and critique. *Journal of Human Development and Capabilities, 12.* https://doi.org/10.1080/19452829.2011.541731

Open Works (2020). *Mission: A makerspace for all.* https://www.openworksbmore.org

Ospina, S., & Schall, E. (2001, November). Leadership (re) constructed: How lens matters. In *APPAM Research Conference* (pp. 1–21). https://wagner.nyu.edu/files/faculty/publications/Leader.pdf

Rawls, John, 1921-2002 author. (1971). *A theory of justice*. Cambridge, Massachusetts: The Belknap Press of Harvard University Press.

Reisch, M. (2002). Defining social justice in a socially unjust world. *Families in Society, 83*(4), 343–354. https://doi.org/10.1606/1044-3894.17

Sen, A. 2004. Elements of a theory of human rights. *Philosophy and Public Affairs,* 32(4): 315–356. http://www.jstor.org/stable/3557992

Slevin, P. (2016, December 12). How Michelle Obama became a singular American voice. *Washington Post.* https://www.washingtonpost.com/graphics/national/obama-legacy/michelle-obama-biography.html

Swensen, S., Gorringe, G., Caviness, J., & Peters, D. (2016). Leadership by design: intentional organization development of physician leaders. *Journal of Management Development*. https://doi.org/10.1108/JMD-08-2014-0080

The Glossary of Education Reform, 2014. *Stakeholder.* https://www.edglossary.org/stakeholder/

Thrift, E., & Sugarman, J. (2019). What is social justice? Implications for psychology. *Journal of Theoretical and Philosophical Psychology, 39*(1). https://doi.org/10.1037/teo0000097

United States Bureau of Labor Statistics. (2020). *Employment and unemployment among youth - summer 2020.* https://www.bls.gov/news.release/pdf/youth.pdf

United States Bureau of Labor Statistics. (2021). *Employment and unemployment among youth - summer 2021.* https://www.bls.gov/news.release/pdf/youth.pdf

Van Esch, F. (2021). The secret of Angela Merkel's extraordinary success: her understanding of the distinctive features of German politics. *The Loop, ECPR's Political Science Blog.* https://theloop.ecpr.eu/the-secret-of-angela-merkels-extraordinary-success-her-understanding-of-german-politics/

Walker, M. (2003) Framing social justice in education: What does the 'capabilities' approach offer? *British Journal of Educational Studies, 51*(2), 168–187. https://doi.org/10.1111/1467-8527.t01-2-00232

Williams, R., Holman, W. & Fuchs, J. (2020). A makerspace's rapid response to the COVID-19 pandemic: A case study of Open Works in Baltimore, Maryland. *Coppin State University, Center of Strategic Entrepreneurship (CSI).* https://www.

greaterspacesandplaces.com

Wilson, G. P. (2021). *Makerspaces: Making STE(A)M work in urban spaces* (Publication No. 28862405) [Doctoral dissertation, Fielding Graduate University]. ProQuest Dissertations & Theses Global.

Woodson, C. G. (2009). The mis-education of the Negro. *The Journal of Pan African Studies, e-book.* http://www.jpanafrican.org/ebooks/3.4eBookThe%20Mis-Education.pdf

CHAPTER 4

INDOOR AIR QUALITY: WHY LEADERSHIP ON THE ENVIRONMENT MATTERS IN EDUCATION–ATTRIBUTES OF ENVIRONMENTAL SUSTAINABILITY

Jeanlee Weeks Parker
Institute for Social Innovation Fellow

This chapter explores findings to further ensure that school accreditation agencies take responsibility for monitoring indoor environmental quality in the classroom. Parker (2020) argued that simply enhancing the AdvancED/Cognia educational leadership accreditation process would be overwhelming, posing barriers to monitoring for poor indoor air quality in schools as a safety and health solution to improve students' cognitive status. This mixed-method study utilized the Exploring Accreditation Priorities for Ecological Sustainability survey (Parker, 2018), along with qualitative interviews, to examine why the accreditation policies and procedures of the AdvancED/Cognia systematically limit health and safety concerns related to indoor air quality in classrooms. The vital question was: What are the current barriers and potential solutions that ultimately lead the way for AdvancED/Cognia, an accrediting agency, to make a significant impact on indoor air problems in our nation's schools? The interviews of external examiners and key stakeholders functioning at various junctures of the accreditation process helped provide information regarding evaluation perspectives on AdvancED/Cognia engagement (or the lack of it) related to indoor air quality in the teaching spaces of its accredited schools.

Two themes arose from the qualitative interview data analysis: (a) barriers to a healthy indoor environment, and (b) responsibility for addressing these barriers to monitoring air quality. The first theme contained four subthemes: (a) funding;

(b) lack of training related to indoor air quality; (c) standards and compliance regulations; and (d) lack of awareness about how air quality affects student learning/ performance. Participants perceived a need for more involvement and concern under the second theme's three subthemes: (a) air quality as part of the accreditation process; (b) participants' level of involvement; and (c) perceived need for more involvement and concern. The chapter is supported by exploring additional themes, including health indicators, ecological factors, and professional development as a practical capability.

Educational Leadership

Educational leadership must identify barriers to resolving environmental issues of poor indoor air quality. It is important to be aware that the health and comfort of students and teachers play a crucial role in the learning and productivity of the classroom, as that, in turn, affects students' performance and achievement (EPA, 2022). According to Petersen et al. (2016), the indoor environment—the classrooms—has a measurable impact on learners' academic performance, as reduced carbon dioxide (CO_2) concentration increased the number of correct answers and decreased errors in four different performance tests. In short, the researcher identified CO_2 as a barrier to academic performance. I believe that educational leaders must reference the results mentioned above to adjust the classroom's CO_2 levels applicable to positive learning performance. Under the theme, *responsibility for monitoring*, Parker (2020) found that 48% ($n = 32$) of AdvancED/Cognia respondents definitely agreed that it is essential to monitor CO_2 in the classroom (p. 75), and that, to some degree, indoor air quality must be evaluated. Additionally, the study revealed that the AdvancED/ Cognia external review team should evaluate further evidence regarding the effects of poor indoor air quality on children in school (p. 129).

According to Pavlakis and Kelley (2016), educational leaders at all levels of the system should be encouraged to "rethink accreditation design" (sec. 4) and promote a continuous improvement process. For example, under accreditation criteria, schools can create a relationship between a direction for indoor air quality improvements and the support of student learning. Additionally, educational leadership must deal with external pressure to change. Paying attention to the quality and impact of professional preparation is a key context factor that has encouraged innovation. External forces have already impacted the structure and focus of educational leadership accreditation, signaling a potential window of opportunity for the new design sign of an accreditation model (Pavlakis & Kelley, 2016).

AdvancED/Cognia

As reported by AdvancED, Measured Progress, which was formed by the merger of two leading education nonprofits in November 2018, changed its name to Cognia. "The new name comes from the Latin word COGNITIO, which means knowledge" (Cognia, 2019). The Cognia Global Commission group of premier education experts worldwide evaluates whether an institution has earned the distinction of accreditation by Cognia, based on the information provided in the team's report, and grants an accreditation status accordingly.

> As an accreditation institution with the readiness to evaluate and assess the institution's education documentation, we partner with 36,000 educational institutions – employing more than four million educators and enrolling more than 20 million students (about the population of New York) – across the United States and 70 other nations. AdvancED was formed through a 2006 merger of the Pre-K-12 divisions of the North Central Association Commission on Accreditation and School Improvement (NCA CASI) and the Association of Colleges and Schools Council on Accreditation and School Improvement (SACS CASI) – and expanded through the addition of the Northwest Accreditation Commission (NWAC) in 2012. (AdvancED, 2017, sec. 1; Parker's (2020) research used the name AdvancED.)

Within this chapter, I prefer the name AdvancED/Cognia. A reasonable assumption is that Cognia was hitherto not a widely used name referencing AdvancED due to the transitional period of recognizing and citing its new organizational name.

Education Enrollment Analysis

Targeting statistical advancements in education enrollment analysis in public schools is practical, as it provides evidence aligned to students' environmental risk, particularly where the at-risk population is most significant in the case of poor indoor air quality. One may suspect that the problem is significantly worse today than it used to be. For example, in the United States, according to the Institute of Education Sciences, National Center for Education (2018), in elementary and secondary schools through grade 12, enrollment was projected to increase by 3%, from 50.4 million to 52.1 million students (about twice the population of Texas). According to National Center for Educational Statistics (2019), the racial and ethnic profile of 50.7 million students for the year 2017-2018 included "24.1 million White students, 7.8 million Black students, 14.0 million Hispanic students, 2.6 million Asian students, 0.2 million Pacific Islander students, 0.5 million American Indian/Alaska Native students, and 1.6 million students (about the population of West Virginia) of two or more races" (para. 1). These statistical projections indicate that most students will have exposure early in life to toxic chemicals found inside school buildings.

The growing student enrollment population should inspire school professionals to promote safe and healthy environmental sustainability programs. For example, at the center of exploring organizational assessment values of shared decision-making, the study revealed that environmental indoor air quality seemed not to have been incorporated into the schools' accreditation recommendations (Parker, 2020). One of the intended benefits of addressing the accreditation process is that, according to Erlandson et al. (2019), a proportion of the United States has exposure to indoor environmental pollutants, and those educational institutions are increasingly being held accountable for efficient, sustainable practices of improving indoor air quality. According to Brown et al. (2016), inhalation is a significant route of exposure to environmental pollutants indoors, and indoor environmental exposure is associated with a variety of adverse health outcomes associated with learning engagement. Indoor air pollution breathed in by our children calls for a risk management approach. The solution requires assessing pollutant exposure and managing inhalation exposure in order to bring them to acceptable levels established by authorized organizations.

Thus, accrediting educational institutions can lead to the sustainability of a healthy and safe learning environment in the classroom. However, external examiners to-date have not recommended that schools address indoor air pollutants in the classrooms during their evaluation process, even though such pollutants affect cognitive development and ongoing improvement. The accreditation systems and institutions are socially lagging in investing in a sustainable engagement review (see Parker, 2020, for more information).

Background of Research Question

Overcoming the current barriers of the classroom environment relative to poor indoor air quality is vital to closing the practice gap. The challenge of acknowledging barriers projects the question, "What are the current barriers and potential solutions that ultimately lead the way for AdvancED/Cognia, an accrediting agency, to make a significant impact on indoor air problems in our nation's schools?" (Parker, 2020, p. 8). Moreover, I believe that educational leaders should enhance knowledge of the ever-changing findings that link poor indoor air quality to the students' learning environment. In this analysis, the research question aims to facilitate further understanding of indoor air quality assessment in classrooms, exploring research findings to engage further relevant literature, and noting barriers and solutions relating to the AdvancED/Cognia accreditation process and its influence on addressing poor indoor air quality in schools. The question structures the scope of exploratory mixed-method research to broaden Parker's (2020) study concerning additional interviewees' comments relative to considering guidelines for implementing sustainable actions in an educational institution, incorporating indoor air quality factors in the educational field to increase learning performance, and developing sustainable learning strategies significant to the accrediting body for educational facilities.

This research question helps to focus on a single methodological process that includes multiple techniques for both quantitative and qualitative study design and data analysis (May et al., 2017). Hong et al. (2017) suggested that methods research synthesis is a systematic review in which the researcher integrates the findings of qualitative and quantitative studies. Under the literature on a typology of synthesis, a *mixed-methods research synthesis model* was defined by Creswell (2014) as a representation of studies that involve recognizing both quantitative and qualitative evidence that serves to give perspectives to the organized data. However, according to Berman (2017), data for this study are also connected to social equity—removing barriers to healthy learning. It is the lens through which the data were interpreted, thus answering the research question.

School Accreditation Examiners and Their Importance

As an effective method of achieving organizational change for high-quality institutions, external quality assurance models of accrediting bodies have been critically important for many years (Hayward, 2017; Liu, 2016). With quality assurance at the forefront of their minds, school representatives under an accreditation system work closely with external examiners, transforming their culture into one that is accountability-centered (Liu, 2016). Within this culture of accountability, accreditors know that it is their responsibility to align with existing school initiatives individually and to use benchmarks for high-quality evaluations of schools. They also consult with their communities of interest and determine the appropriateness of change (AdvancED, 2017; Liu, 2016). The accreditation process is a "patience-inducing exercise," according to Oldham (2018, sec. 1). For example, the self-assessment is carried out in conjunction with external quality assurance by having volunteers serve on the evaluation teams, which document their visits to institutions that have completed a self-evaluation by their principals. Afterward, the accrediting organization engages the district staff in reflective dialogue to validate that the standards for accreditation pertain to future efforts to improve student performance and organizational effectiveness (AdvancED Accreditation, 2017).

Cogwell (2016, as cited in Parker, 2020, p. 12) noted that external reviewers are stakeholders who can influence the quality and equality of education. "They do what they think they ought to do" (p. 7). Essentially, they are representative of a "principal-agent" relationship (p. 151) to ensure that the school can capture the skills and knowledge of its stakeholders. Due to their power to accredit schools, examiners are likely to focus on or to ignore such an essential issue as poor indoor air quality. This means schools receive recognition based on Cogwell's (2016) assessment of "relationships between accreditors and the public interest" (p. 18).

The significance of this viewpoint cannot be overstated. The lack of specific policies and procedures means that external examiners are not responsible for ensuring that an educational environment is conducive to learning, although they *are* responsible for assessing school conditions in the light of social equity. According to Rubaii (2016), the responsibilities of examiners must include equity and ecological justice to be socially and ecologically fair. I have, therefore, focused on the social equity of external examiners, because this responsibility implicates the health of our children. In exploring the research question of indoor air quality as an assessment component, we seek to ensure that barriers to and potential solutions to indoor air quality are considered part of the school assessment and understand the sustainability and equity status of school accreditation. I call specific attention to an ecological system where accrediting bodies interact with education institutions to provide evidence of an unhealthy environment to help change societal structure. As part of the societal evaluation of accreditors, there are many standards related to quality assurance of ecological education that regulate types of programs connected to accreditation outcomes (Rubaii, 2016). Promoting accreditation to include the idea of embedding technical knowledge of indoor air quality as an assessment reflecting quality performance level would be an indicator of organizational improvement that contributes to organizational resilience (Rubaii, 2016).

External Examiner/Reviewer Closes the Gap

As a way of contributing knowledge to the field of education relative to school environmental conditions, this research draws stakeholders into the accreditation process by Parker's (2020) attention to a participant's/respondent's current position as an external examiner or other held position within an educational institution. For example, the most frequently identified participants in the research are teachers (n = 22, 44%), principals (n = 20, 40%), external examiners representative of AdvancED (n = 6, 12%), and counselor or social worker (n = 2, 4%).

Members of an accessible subset sample (n = 7) clearly identified themselves as being actively involved as external examiners/representatives of AdvancED during a school assessment period. The data show that a variety of volunteer participants have served as external examiners. In practical terms, the interchangeable use of an external examiner, such as being part of an external review team or accreditation team, allows examiners and evaluators to share concerns or problems about air quality in the classroom. The accreditation team must consider recommendations to the school or district to address the issue. As members of the AdvancED/Cognia's external review team, examiners review terms of their assessment and evaluation process and raise issues to the lead evaluator for support and guidance for continuous improvement in the accreditation process.

Why This Problem Is Especially Important to Me

In terms of environmental views on the effects of poor indoor air quality on school students, no previous study has focused on the integration of indoor air quality into the public schools' accreditation process (Parker, 2020). For example, there is no literature relating to external examiners' recommendations for improvements in schools' environmental conditions due to the association of poor indoor air quality with student performance. In the literature review, Bluyssen (2017) connected the ideas of "what do we already know and what do we need to know about short-term and long-term health effects that affect learning ability" (p. 2) with the impact of the indoor school environment on the health, comfort, and performance of children in classrooms and the need for related accreditation standards and monitoring. The author noted that the indoor environment in classrooms has been included in studies on diseases and disorders. However, in many parts of the world, a new direction of research is needed to generate knowledge on the interactions of children with the indoor classroom environment.

The perceptions of a new study focus on a holistic analysis of classrooms and student performance. For example, research on the association between a measured environmental factor identified as indoor air quality where children are involved has proceeded to meaningful CO_2 air exchange and individual health effects and performance, but findings concerning the effects of CO_2 (exhaled by the children) on their health seem inconclusive. However, Bluyssen (2017) correlated "parameters of the indoor environment with the noise level and CO_2 such that a higher noise level may be associated with a higher level of children's indoor activities" (p. 6). In other words, a student's attention is reduced due to poor indoor air quality increased by $C0_2$. These factors are now known to stimulate noise and patterns of behavior problems.

Precautionary Strategy

In the ever-changing environment prior to the COVID-19 pandemic, the learning environment at some point was densely populated in certain areas, after which it shifted to a low-density learning environment due to online learning. With history in the making, scholars will argue that, in March 2020, school districts across the United States took leadership responsibility in closing their doors due to the worldwide COVID-19 health crisis. According to the Centers for Disease Control (2019), health officials and school administrators collaborated on implementing multiple precautionary prevention strategies to reduce the spread of COVID-19. At the same time, it is important to mention that, before the onset of the COVID-19 pandemic in 2020, nearly all the leadership structures of educational accreditation institutions overlooked many measures demonstrating the unsustainability quality of the buildings' learning environment, in terms of ventilation and temperature. However, at the global height of the pandemic, schools closed, followed by teachers, parents, and students adjusting to functioning in online classrooms. Surprisingly, during this early 2020 period, my research (Parker, 2020) was addressing indoor air quality issues in the classroom, in terms of *Exploring Accreditation Priorities: A Study on Why a Major Accrediting Body for Public Schools is Ignoring Indoor Air Pollution in Classrooms*. In part, it helps to explain why accreditation agencies were ignoring indoor air quality as a factor in students' safety, health, and cognitive development. According to Parker (2020), the research indicated that assessing indoor air quality in the classrooms is an exceedingly arduous task, even more than challenging. At the same time, one respondent reminded readers that indoor air quality is a specific aspect of student health and learning (p. 80).

According to the Environmental Protection Agency, "there is no nationwide monitoring network that statistically measures valid samples of schools' indoor air quality" (EPA, 2021b). However, the collected data on the condition of public-school facilities' heating, ventilating, and air conditioning (HVAC) systems have been rated as being very unsatisfactory. Exposure to environmental pollutants is a tragedy, since we now know that indoor air pollutants are linked to reduced cognitive functioning (Petersen et al., 2016). In general, while students spend much of their time in a home environment, they also spend much of their time learning on school premises. According to Petersen et al. (2016), children who spend a substantial portion of their time in classrooms where the ventilation unit is poorly regulated tend to experience ill health effects. Broadly speaking, an appropriate ventilation rate in the school building places students in a quality environmental parameter that positively impacts health and learning (Hänninen et al., 2017). Moreover, the outcome analysis of indoor pollutants that adversely affect the health of school children recommends the deployment of counteractive measures to decrease respiratory illness (Chatzidiakou et al., 2015b).

Globally, leaders associated with educational institutions are increasingly prioritizing sustainable measures in schools to change the effects of poor internal air quality on students' scholarly performance (Thombs & Prindle, 2018). The rising concerns regarding sustainable practices based on the ecology of school buildings encompass many variables that overlap within one of the three pillars of sustainability: environmental, social, and economic (Dhahri & Omri, 2018; Purvis et al., 2019). These three pillars are indicators that provide information in detail about climate, health, education, and income. According to Rehr et al. (2015), indicators are composed of sustainable development "routes to improve children's environmental health efforts to reduce risk and to enhance well-being" (para. 5). Unfortunately, indoor air quality and its effects on the learning environment have been deemed less relevant to students' learning performance, given that assessing the quality of students' learning environment is traditionally associated with ventilation, class size, and types of activities.

Quantifying Learning Space

Lopez-Chao et al. (2019) asserted that students' perspectives on quantifying their educational space are viable to assess when known relationships affect student performance. Considering that we spend 90% of our lives indoors, and that both health and safety threats are encountered in our environment, Brink et al. (2021) pointed out that a positive indoor environment is essential for our health and well-being. These researchers insisted that indoor air quality conditions in the classroom must be optimized. Furthermore, there is an association among the actual indoor air conditions, students' perceptions and responses to these conditions, and their short-term academic performance. As reported, high concentrations of CO_2 were relative to material emissions' chemicals used indoors and other outdoor sources. As a justification to address the quality of the learning space, the evidence presents numerous aspects of educational leadership influencing student learning. For example, Cecilia et al. (2019) listed faulty teaching methods and lack of instructional resources as reasons for students' poor academic performances in science. However, the results indicated that academic performance is enhanced when students know their preferred learning styles, such as incorporating audio-visual materials presented during teaching and learning. Students' audio-visual seating positions align with their educational achievements, such that the quality of the teacher's voice or audio equipment conditions aligns with temperature and CO_2 in the space.

As knowledge is increased, students perceive the classroom as a social space for education regarding their seating arrangements and academic achievements. Keep in mind that there is a positive relationship between learning styles and space relative to students' academic achievements applicable to indoor air quality. As cited in Parker's (2020) research,

There is evidence that exposing children to poor indoor air quality during childhood is harmful to their health and development and negatively affects their school readiness (Cicutto et al., 2014; Clark-Reyna et al., 2016; Marcotte, 2017). Evidence indicates that in densely populated schools, where there are between 25-30 students per classroom, vulnerability is higher due to the poor environment inside. Low cognitive performance is one of the negative aspects of being in a densely populated classroom. (p. 36)

To support a space learning pathway, it is necessary to provide good indoor air quality interconnectedness to the learning space. According to School Space (2018), the components that should be linked involve providing air to breathe as an allocated element of good learning. For example, as teachers organize support and monitor the learning space, they must prepare students to lead in making decisions about an innovative learning environment without negatively impacting their present classroom. Approaching these specific concerns in terms of indoor air quality, learning space, and academic achievements assumes that school accreditors would need to have protocols describing the existing quality of the learning environment, establish a connection between the students and their environment, and initiate actions to increase student learning and possibly reduce absenteeism. This assumption is a "crucial factor to improvement in schools; it examines the level of influence the AdvancED/Cognia Standards have on the strategic planning process" (Gibbons, 2017, p. 65). As a potential sustainability solution for the learning space, Onyunde (personal communication, November 23, 2021) focused on considering guidelines for implementing sustainable actions in an educational institution:

> With a working background as a dean of curriculum and a qualified teacher of English/literature, I believe that teachers should come together to take sustainable actions to address setbacks for the educational system. For example, student teachers can communicate effectively with administrators for the students' equity in the learning environment.

Ecological Sustainability Factors

Indoor air pollutants increasingly become stressors in our schools. We must respond and emerge as a high-level resilient ecological system. Notably, in a functioning practice of resilience regarding building issues, the focus is on interventions central to addressing root causes of poor health learning environments (Sheffield et al., 2017). According to AdvancED (2019) findings, ecologically sustainable practices, specific to prescriptive recommendations, are not addressed by AdvancED/Cognia Accreditation Standards Policies and Procedures. Moreover, the personal communication from a participant in the Parker (2020) study acknowledged that the accreditation assessments were not vital for education quality assurance. The research noted a defeatist comment made by one participant, namely: "It is almost like we'll settle for evil because we need our schools, good or bad" (p. 76). A participant recognized that the practice of ecological sustainability is relevant only if such practices are required by state law. On the other hand, this participant also expressed that AdvancED/Cognia should look at ecologically sustainable practices when politics are removed, and the issues are clearly explained (p. 74).

There are additional applicable considerations for sustainable practices. One participant recognized that the practice of ecological sustainability is relevant only if such practices and products are required by state law: Recycling and the use of eco-friendly products might vary throughout the years between accreditation and review. However, a participant in Parker (2020) noted that the sustainability of indoor air quality criteria has a potential solution to health issues that could result in AdvancED/Cognia leading towards a significant impact on indoor air quality problems in our nation's schools (p. 84).

When organizations overlook features of indoor air problems, injustice is underlined. An unfair related experience prevails in moral exclusion, meaning that one is limited to a less-than-whole environmental experience. One respondent was quite bluntly opinionated, stating as follows: "The need to address most recycling programs is a waste of energy and tax dollars." Another stated, ''Bringing together Reduce, Reuse, Recycle develops recycling because it is the least efficient method of conservation'' (p. 75). Additionally, one participant stated that the impact of any type of ecology or sustainability program as part of the accreditation process would be a conflict of interest (p. 75).

This limitation is due to complex interactions generated by the decision-making process, whereby occupants of an indoor environment may perceive a discrepancy between reported illnesses acquired from being in a designated harmful environment and management not addressing the serious health effects by inspections or repairs of buildings (Finell & Seppälä, 2018). The understanding is that administrators "do not know how indoor air problems relate to the work or learning environment nor where the problems begin" (Finell & Seppälä, 2018, sec. 3). Therefore, decision-making discrepancies exist regarding whether to assume the responsibility for improving an environment that makes its occupants sick. Thus, when there is little knowledge about environmental issues, organizations such as accrediting agencies may fail to look at indoor air quality in the school evaluation process. Decision-making and communication can help solve indoor air problems (Finell & Seppälä, 2018) by applying more attention to the students' environmental experiences.

It turns out that findings related to ecologically sustainable practices, specific to prescriptive recommendations, are not addressed by AdvancED/Cognia Accreditation Standards Policies and Procedures (AdvancED, 2019). A personal communication from one participant acknowledged that the accreditation assessments were not reliable for education quality assurance. Yet, the participant noted that using criteria for sustainable indoor air quality might provide a potential solution to health issues that could result in AdvancED/

Cognia having a significant impact on indoor air quality problems in our nation's schools (Parker, 2020, p. 96). Andualem et al. (2019) claimed that key ecological factors hindering sustainable practices in the school environment, where there was poor indoor air quality due to a combination of insufficient outside air supply, dense population per classroom, lack of standards for indoor bacterial load, and allergens such as molds and cockroaches, were all triggers of asthma attacks.

In Andualem et al.'s (2019) study, the researchers noted that the concentration of indoor bacterial load and the physical school environment had positively correlated with environmental factors such as ventilation. They explained that the increased activity of occupants in an enclosed parameter caused higher room temperatures, thus favoring the growth and multiplication of indoor bacteria. To safeguard the occupants of the school from bacteria in indoor air pollutants, schools must assess the bacterial load and other obstacles to learning found in all public schools. Understandably, barriers—obstacles to addressing indoor air quality in the learning environment—must be overcome. In other words, we need to understand better how students interact with various indoor air particles. Other baseline factors to consider in setting up sustainable practices for the school environment are cluttered rooms, chipping paint, bus idling, and smoking (Nuss et al., 2016).

Research evidence regarding indoor environmental health disparities makes it clear that we must set sustainable strategies to reduce the negative factors affecting schools, health, and growth in the development and education of children. According to Rubin et al. (2017), "Disparities in educational opportunities, quality of teachers and even the school buildings and the surrounding built environment are major factors in the cycle of environmental health disparities" (p. 124). School assessments by accrediting agencies should deliver sustainable tactics to address disparities in educational opportunities. It is essential to acknowledge the problem of indoor air quality as an issue for sustainable initiatives, because accreditors' assessments tend to disregard the setting and actions for the improvement of indoor air quality in schools. Moreover, when educational professionals become aware of poor indoor air quality, they must improve it. The understanding is that, when poor indoor air quality is not addressed, it can harm student learning, reduce the effectiveness of teachers and staff, and increase absenteeism, generating negative publicity that damages a school's and administration's reputation. Schools can improve their indoor air quality by involving teachers. On the front line, teachers observe when indoor air quality changes affect students and themselves (EPA, 2021b).

There is a significant association among ventilation, water leakage, and health. These findings apply to indoor air quality, as they relate to the school environment and the use of accreditation agencies to monitor it. Accordingly, researchers have associated water leakage with dampness that causes mold growth, specifying several other problems causing inadequate ventilation and poor drainage-water leakage. For example, in an earlier 2018 study, Salthammer et al. noted that aerosols or gas-phase compounds derived from cleaning activities affect indoor air quality. These compounds can interact with airborne particles from the water leakage-settled dust in molds to produce secondary indoor air pollutants. Concentrations of indoor dust particles, influenced by temperature with phthalates (from cleaning solutions, toys, childcare articles, and cables) in the gas phase, have been introduced into the indoor environment (Salthammer et al., 2018; Al-Qasmi et al., 2019).

Environmental Sustainability

The Brundtland Report (1987) defined *environmental sustainability* as an "improvement that satisfies the desires of prevailing generations without compromising the ability of future generations to meet their own needs" (p. 1). According to the EPA (2021a), environmental sustainability is a long-range process of maintaining the environment in harmony with human behaviors, ambitions, and needs. For this reason, it is absurd to attempt to keep the environment separate from human concerns. Environmental sustainability entails measures of needs. For example, the number of people in a classroom clearly can affect the health benefits of natural ventilation. Subsequent to that report, an analysis of indoor pollutants that adversely affect health was performed, and counteractive measures were recommended (Chatzidiakou et al., 2015). When last reported, many K–12 school infrastructure conditions in the United States were crumbling, thus requiring sustainable environmental actions (Center of American Progress, 2019). Regarding the quality of the learning environment, it should be evident that educators and evaluators must be environmentally aware of the associations among poor indoor air quality (IAQ), schoolchildren's health, their learning performance, and how schools are accredited (Parker, 2020). Onyunde (personal communication, November 23, 2021), when asked, "What sustainable learning strategies do you think a significant accrediting body for educational facilities should acquire to develop a training awareness program to maximize learning equity?" responded:

> I am a forerunner with the tradition of sustainable actions. As a business person and educator, I understand that not addressing sustainability in schools is an education setback for kids that want to know everything. As I mentioned before, we must practice equity as identified for our small working system, no matter the general or the typical class. It draws dialogue to address the guidelines for implementing sustainable actions in an educational institution. I am most willing to help in any way that I can to bring awareness of learning equity.

Bajada et al. (2020) noted that the development of learning equity applicable to environmental sustainability thresholds accentuates guiding principles for reviewing students' learning experiences. It requires assessors to understand that sufficient knowledge of the subject matter is relative to the condition of the environment. According to Assefa (2020), "guidance documents can be used to record and communicate new performance benchmark values to practitioners the same way the normalization values and weighting factors are communicated" (p. 203).

Assuring Future Policies

Defining *indoor air quality* is considered a reasonable approach to subjective assessments of perceived air quality (Bahnfleth, 2017, p. 84). It is essential to underscore the impact of poor indoor air on students' health and performance. For example, to increase community involvement in a healthy school environment, professionals should discuss indoor air quality standards, which should be associated with scientific evidence of indoor exposure, followed by showing the effect of contaminants on the buildings' occupants.

According to Xu et al. (2018), the reactions between airborne particles and chemical constituents encompass the need for comprehensive indoor air evaluation on exposure to these substances. As an essential point, Xu et al. (2018) noted, "Efficient environmental protection should control pollution reduction policies and should be executed to suppress the health risks" (p. 860). Reasonably, accreditors like AdvancED/Cognia should hold schools accountable for doing such measurements of controlling the air quality in schools; it should be conducted according to Xu et al. (2018) to avoid concentrations of mutagenic and carcinogenic compounds inhaled by classroom occupants (teachers or students). Moreover, with indoor air quality being a major issue in the cases of COVID-19 and its variants rising and leveling off, we should be in a position to consider EPA precautions of ventilation-control of airflow requirements relevant to indoor climate conditions. Activities such as opening doors and windows and increasing vent size reduce the potential spread of the airborne transmission of COVID-19.

Educational stakeholders should examine indoor air quality factors concerning the importance of AdvancED/Cognia and their education community in heeding indoor air quality in future policies. Considering indoor air quality factors in the educational field to increase learning performance, M. Thomashow (personal communication, September 27, 2021) noted:

> I believe that indoor air quality is an important factor to improve student learning performance in the classroom. However, indoor air quality was not a priority for sustainable design during my tenure at Unity College. Still, it is an area that impacts, and it is good that you are researching indoor air quality in the classroom.

Numerous studies have stated that indoor air pollution in the physical school environment has a significant impact on the learning and productivity of the school's population. For example, Stafford (2015) studied the effects of indoor air quality on academic outcomes, reporting that children had significant health problems from inadequate indoor air quality (IAQ) in school classrooms. Stafford also found that participants' cognitive function scores decreased in domains with low ventilation rates. Allen et al. (2016) added that low ventilation rates and decreased cognitive function at schools needed investigation, because cognitive functions among workers and students in green environments were notably exceptional. These researchers voiced the belief that school authorities should take action to advocate for a better indoor learning environment with significantly decreased levels of pollutants.

Health Indicators

Children's environmental health risk is reduced by a sustainable and environmental health indicator that monitors changes in this area. The indicator for the economic pillar, for example, would assess the degree of compliance with the long-term cost of children exposed to ozone (Rehr et al., 2015), which aggravates respiratory conditions, leading to missed days in school and lessened learning performance. The results then add an economic stressor, namely, the cost for caretakers (Rehr et al., 2015). Moreover, the Environmental Protection Agency (EPA), the American Society of Heating, Refrigerating and Air-Conditioning Engineers (ASHRAE), and accreditation organizations are the significant barriers to improving indoor air quality in classrooms. According to World Health Organization (2021), global air quality guidelines can help organizations reduce air pollution and enhance children's safety and health. To achieve this, "organizations should secure investing in improvements" (p. 20). Practical guidance is optional, and few schools know about it; AdvancED/ Cognia does not refer to it. However, the EPA does have an Indoor Air Quality Tools for Schools Action Kit that offers technical solutions for managing such problems as moisture/mold and integrated pest control (EPA, 2021b). ASHRAE provides information for residential buildings as part of its IAQ management standard. To help educators improve indoor air quality in classrooms, ASHRAE should provide guidance specifications. Recognize that the learning spaces should not integrate teachers' storage spaces were by school supplies, resources materials- mainly cluster, are outdated and built up over the years. According to Bahnfleth (2017), to support the findings and make changes, professionals of diverse backgrounds must create a unique opportunity to consider the status of IAQ laws, consensus standards, and IAQ best practices, specifically those of high-performance buildings.

Professional Development: A Practical Capability

To improve leadership quality in the environment learning, I reference Nussbaum's (2011) capability approach that acknowledged ethics for social-ecological justice. In this manner, I express interest in sustainable evaluation methods prepared to increase social equity in schools by including environmentally sustainable awareness adapted for accreditation assessments. A sustainable learning environment is significant to practical reasoning structured as a capability approach that sets the totality of opportunities we have for choice and action in our specific contexts (Nussbaum, 2011, p. 22). Indeed, Nussbaum's capabilities approach seeks to analyze education and abilities in terms of the conditions of classroom interactions, whereby "the essentials," the needs or states of human capabilities, are influenced by goal formation. As an ethical learning sensitivity to others' nurturing thinking skills, Nussbaum's capability theory formulates ecological systems to discuss central human functional capabilities. An ethical approach to risk and uncertainty needs to measure the environmental quality (Peppin Vaughan, 2016), which involves the entire diverse environment, including building technology, design, economics, and social equity concerns. Accordingly, Nussbaum's capabilities approach seeks to analyze education and abilities in terms of classroom interactions whereby "the conditions or states of human capabilities are valuable expressions of relationships" (p. 157). More specifically, the phenomena of indoor environmental quality are fundamental to the life experiences in a classroom. They significantly affect how students feel or can perform activities in that space, as the ecological challenges of the indoor environmental quality affect the integrity of ecological ethics. In a sense, ethics acknowledges a capability approach to moral issues in a social-ecological system.

In sum, I have shared findings that ecologically sustainable practices, specific to prescriptive recommendations, are not being addressed by AdvancED/Cognia Accreditation Standards Policies and Procedures (AdvancED, 2019). Moreover, the personal communication from one participant has acknowledged (Parker, 2020) that current accreditation assessments do not guarantee education quality assurance. This participant further noted that insistence on indoor air quality criteria is a potential solution to health issues that could result in AdvancED/ Cognia having a significant impact on solving indoor air quality problems in our nation's schools.

Diverse View of an Ecological Factor

A diverse view of a sustainable ecological factor comes about when organizations overlook features of indoor air problems. Thus, injustice is underlined, as an unfair related experience prevails in moral exclusion, meaning that one is limited to a less-than-whole environmental experience. This limitation is due to complex interactions generated by the decision-making process, whereby occupants of an indoor environment may perceive a gap between reported illnesses acquired from being in a designated harmful environment and management not addressing the serious health effects by inspections or repairs of buildings (Finell & Seppälä, 2018). The understanding is that members of upper management "do not know how indoor air problems relate to the work or learning environment nor where the problems begin" (Finell & Seppälä, 2018, sec. 3); therefore, decision-making discrepancies exist regarding whether or not to assume the responsibility for improving an environment that makes occupants sick.

When there is little knowledge about environmental issues, organizations such as accrediting agencies may fail to look at indoor air quality in the school evaluation process. On the other hand, decision-making and communication can help solve indoor air problems (Finell & Seppälä, 2018) by applying more attention to the students' environmental experiences. For example, when presented with the question, "What sustainable learning strategies do you think a significant accrediting body for educational facilities should acquire to develop a training awareness program to maximize learning equity?" M. Thomashow (personal communication, September 27, 2021) noted as follows.

> Early in my years at Unity College, I reviewed the course offerings, majors, and programs and emphasized re-designing environmental studies and sustainability curriculum programs. For an extended period, I have thought about how to offer innovative ideas about learning components that embody life skills to academic constituencies that pursue the responsibility of energy efficiencies. I argue that accreditation bodies' regulation timelines and guidelines for evaluations of higher educational institutions are not inclusive of maximizing equity. The school accreditors need numerous justifications to align the students' accomplishments with the directives of their educational institution. For example, the authenticity of students' environmental discussions may entail their

> way of life, but an accreditor may not review it as not relevant to the pattern of environmental learning.

Moreover, F. Onyunde (personal communication, November 23, 2021) observed:

> I have experienced how the administrative committee often overlooks sustainable actions for specific human specialties. Often, I have observed that the education platform of student teachers was energetic toward attenuating status as a professional teacher. Their output holds them accountable to take actions that all students should have equity for their education, no matter their identifiable gender.

In the field of educational systems learning outcomes, AdvancED/Cognia acknowledges that the path to improvement has focused too much on standards and accountability, but not enough on equity and the conditions of learning in schools (Foster, 2016, as cited in Parker, 2020). In the broadest sense, AdvancED/Cognia's team of professionals is responsive to learning conditions in schools, as it is acknowledged that there are no specific federal accreditation requirements for schools at the K–12 levels; rather, they must meet state standards for performance (Oldham, 2018, sec.1) where air quality policies are concerned. According to Ulker and Bakioglu (2019) accreditation contributes less to student learning-related activities compared to varied improvement practices over a specified time.

Throughout this study, I delved into evidence around the indoor air environment associated with student health and learning outcomes as linked to accreditation processes. As mentioned earlier, there is indeed an association between the school environment relative to air quality and its significant impact on academic achievement. Thus, I want to close this section by emphasizing involvement in evaluating indoor air quality factors in the educational field to increase learning performance, notably when presented with the question of how one has been or not been involved in considering indoor air quality as a factor in increased learning performance. According to M. Thomashow (personal communication, September 27, 2021),

> I am very particular about the well-being of campus life, and I explored well-being primarily in terms of sustainability values. In many ways, our college recognized itself as an Environmental

> college. I have a professional sustainability interest in campus conscience for ecological resilience to inspire economic development, as partially mentioned before. It is crucial to market the sustainability field in higher education because sustainability enhances its economic capabilities. My leadership position was specific to discussing environmental education issues that amplify the means to learn about sustainability constantly. Our academic community had rebuilt buildings with low or zero carbon and utilized solar and wind power. I see the importance of indoor air quality factors to improve students' learning performance in the classroom. However, the indoor air quality was not emphasized as sustainable design during my tenure to enhance cognitive skills. Still, it is an area that affects students, and it is good that you are researching indoor air quality in the classroom.

Accreditation can be an exogenous force for improvements in the social equity of schools (Rubaii, 2016). In this research, the exploration of social equity has been fundamental to the social values and policies found in accreditation standards. External examiners in the accreditation agency do recognize forms of social equity in terms of social values (Rubaii, 2016); thus, aligning social equity within the schools' accreditation process with the use of standards helps address the external examiners' scope of improvements, by providing insights into the social relationships between themselves and society, and with the school as a part of society. This relationship, I believe, generates meaningful behavior in terms of knowledge and reasoning that affects quality accreditation, giving it relevance. In fact, with "relevance, there is a concern for 'applicability,' which refers to all the stakeholders that an educational institution serves" (Lalić, 2018, para. 9).

Rubaii (2016) wrote, "Accrediting bodies assert the value of social equity in their standards regarding learning outcomes, but their standards and reporting requirements on the national and international level suggest otherwise" (p. 541). In my experience, external examiners perpetuate social inequality due to the influence of access and opportunity in the education system; they also mask differences by omitting essential information. As a way of contributing knowledge in the field of approved accreditation of elementary schools with external examiners' experiences, I have hoped to encourage representatives of AdvancED, an accrediting organization, to focus on the area of continual improvements, suggesting that schools should not be accredited when there are environmental issues in terms of various forms of poor indoor air quality.

Literature on Environmental Practices in Schools

Haverinen-Shaughnessy and Shaughnessy (2015) considered the importance of indoor air quality in relationships between students' test scores and both classroom ventilation rate and temperature. The researchers mentioned that ventilation was correlated with health issues, and learning in school was diminished by poor indoor air quality. The noteworthy results indicated that a steady state of concentrated carbon dioxide was increasing in classrooms. The emphasis on sources that have caused this increase focused on CO2 in the schools, along with such variables as physical activity, surface area, and whether the windows were left open or closed.

It appears to date that students' socioeconomic backgrounds are the main variable influencing the outcome of students' test scores. However, the underlying results suggest that the threshold of asthma symptoms of school-aged children of the lowest and highest socioeconomic status has been less studied and more biased. Thus, less ventilation in energy-saving buildings is considered an example of a "modern living environment and lifestyle which is associated with increased prevalence of allergies among children" (Sun et al., 2019, p. 596). These findings suggest the need to assess the quality of the indoor environment. Whether the schools are underprivileged or wealthier, "psychosocial factors influence how indoor air quality is perceived" (Finell et al., 2017, p. 330). This conclusion indicates that indoor air quality observed in a school environment may reflect a "psychosocial environment" (Finell et al., 2017, p. 22), as the study showed that building-related and psychosocial factors influenced schools' indoor air quality.

Al-Hubail and Al-Temeemi (2015) presented data related to air pollutants in school buildings. The authors determined that there is a significant correlation between CO2 concentrations in schools and health problems incurred by the students. The study suggested that exposure to prominent levels of indoor air pollutants over time worsens students' learning ability. The authors also noted that the literature needs to provide qualitative data on students' health complaints inside classrooms. The authors' findings, along with the perceptions of study participants, indicated that more attention should be given to monitoring air quality. They are all making recommendations to stakeholders to control air quality problems in schools. Both the authors and the participants in this study have contributed to the future assessment of air quality in buildings by leading the way towards making a significant impact on indoor air problems in our nation's schools.

Modern societies view children's health and well-being as top priorities. But links between air pollution and children's school performance and health have received little attention and are not well understood in the U.S. This lack of focus and understanding on the part of the evaluation of the association between poor indoor air quality and academic performance represents a critical determinant for a change in environmental components of exposure to various pollutants. In terms of academic engagements, Thomashow (personal communication, September 27, 2021) noted, in answer to the question, "In what role have you collaborated in considering guidelines for implementing sustainable actions in an educational institution?" as follows:

> As college president and chair, I collaborated with faculty, team members, and people interested in environmental change, human relationships, and sustainable living to implement environmental practices in campus life. For example, to promote environmental practices and to stimulate diverse teaching and learning narratives, I emphasized the importance of perceiving environmental change, specifically within the campus habitat. The campus is ecological. The challenge is how to deepen that awareness while providing students, staff, and administrators with professional development opportunities to advance a sustainability agenda.
>
> To attract students to college life, I advocate for art as a campus academic engagement. Students' integration into the art program enhances the environmental message and allows awareness of sustainability. For example, emphasizing eating well or what is happening in our lives is projected as a mural on on-campus buildings. The art projects promote interactive expressions of

curricular initiatives.

Unity College reflected an awareness of sustainability to the campus food service department and the surrounding community. We transformed our campus landscape into wildflower gardens, grew food with the local NGO, and distributed food to the cafeteria and the local community.

Research Design

In the phases of this research process, weight was given equally to components throughout the data collection and analysis (Alsaleh, 2016). For example, the survey depicted the frequency distribution of characteristics of the demographic variables. Relative to being a member of a defined group, the respondents all had attributes of contributing knowledge to an educated population. This study of a quantitative web-based survey delivered an independent variable of a "participant's educational level of responsibilities." The dependent variable showed characteristics of the participant having an educational leadership role in assessing and improving an elementary school setting. The relation shown in this example gives a representation of the participant's current or previous level of responsibilities within an educational system that documented the descriptive statistical analysis. The apparent strategy was the key driver for choosing to use the mixed methods technique as an exploratory approach, as it provided summaries of the sample and measures of data. As described by several authors who support mixed methods (Creswell, 2017), the quantitative description was synthesized with the qualitative themes to explain the statistics associated with survey results and the statistical approach used for the interviews. Primarily, the study captured a trend; it leveled the integrating data across studies, synthesizing them, because no single method was sufficient.

Mixed Methods Synthesis Results

Data Analysis

This section presents research findings on barriers and solutions to the AdvancED accreditation process and its influence on addressing poor indoor air quality in schools. The information here describes the quantitative and qualitative data and analyses for this mixed-methods study. I begin with descriptive statistics used to assess frequencies of nominal level variables from the quantitative survey. In the quantitative phase, participants ($n = 66$) completed an online survey comprising 18 questions, which took approximately 10 minutes to complete. Of the 66 participants, a subpopulation ($n = 3$) participated in qualitative interviews. In this qualitative phase, participants responded to five open-ended questions. Following the description of the quantitative data is the thematic analysis (TA) of qualitative data used to contextualize responses from the interviews to obtain rich levels of themes. Participants' expertise in evaluation measures offered dedicated support for continuous improvement. However, most of the survey participants felt discomfort in participating in interviews and did not consent to that stage of the research. The assumption was that internal examiners who participated in this study had the disposition to judge schools' performance during the internal school self-assessment period. They had been indirectly or directly involved in their school's preparation for the visitation of AdvancED's External Examiners Team.

Respondents identified themselves as an internal school examiner or as an individual who had observed the roles of the internal and external examiners. All the participants acknowledged that they were in the field or at other junctures of the accreditation process, especially school health and safety. More importantly, participants in the study communicated a framework for understanding how to address indoor air quality in an educational environment.

Quantitative Descriptive Statistics Results

While all the questions from the survey whose results are listed below were part of a quantitative measure, each question offered respondents an option to comment. Many participants did make comments on the survey. These comments are incorporated into the quantitative, descriptive statistics because they were related to each of the questions, even though the comments themselves are qualitative data. If some of the sentences incorporating or relating those comments seem uncoordinated, it is because it is sometimes challenging to decide on the correct pronouns.

Result 1

How satisfied are you that the Accreditation Standards Policies and

Procedures of AdvancED comprehensively address health and safety issues? This was a way to ascertain the opinions of those who serve or have served as AdvancED external examiners about how satisfied they were with the accreditation process. The most frequent response was "Somewhat satisfied" (n = 38, 62.30%). The responses for "Very satisfied" (n = 17, 27.87%) showed it to be the second most observed category. The fewest number of respondents were "Not satisfied" (n = 6, 9.8%).

Result 2

Which safety or health issue do you think is most important for AdvancED to provide feedback on enriching the learning environment in the schools? This question was designed to focus on and identify respondents' roles in working with indoor air quality assessment. The highest-ranking category was "cleaning and maintenance" (n = 18, 29.03%), followed by "heating, ventilation, air conditioning (HVAC)" (n = 12, 19.35%). Several respondents (n = 8, 12.90%) felt that "playground safety" was practical for enriching the learning environment. Other respondents (n = 8, 12.90%) agreed that "securing doors" was important for AdvancED to mention in their assessments.

Based on the findings, the variables of playground safety and securing doors are equivalent. Fewer respondents (n = 6, 9.68%) tended to agree that "integrated pest management" should be represented to improve the schools' learning environments. Still other respondents (n = 5, 8.06%) suggested that feedback about "light/windows fixtures" during the evaluation period was important. The survey results identified the same number of respondents (n = 5, 8.06%) as having an awareness that "eliminating moisture and molds" was an effective means of enriching the learning environment.

Result 3

Do you believe that AdvancED/Cognia should look at ecologically sustainable practices at your school such as recycling and the use of ecofriendly products? This question was used to uncover respondents' familiarity with ecologically sustainable practices in schools, such as recycling and the use of eco-friendly products. The most frequent response to this question was "Yes, definitely" (n = 25, 37.88%). Then "Yes, to some extent" (n = 21, 31.82%), "Not sure" ($n = 18$, 27.27%), and "Do not know" ($n = 3$, 4.55%). It is worth mentioning that "No" was not scaled in this question. One participant ($n = 1$, 2%) clarified his or her response by saying, "Not sure, because 'no' was not an option."

These findings indicate that ecologically sustainable practices are explicit prescriptive recommendations that AdvancED accreditation standards do not specifically address, although they should. One participant recognized that the practice of ecological sustainability is relevant only if such practices and products are required by state law. On the other hand, this participant also expressed that AdvancED should look at ecologically sustainable practices, when policies are revised, and the issues are clearly explained.

One respondent acknowledged that some schools are presently practicing ecological sustainability, but it is not well-established in all the places they visited during the accreditation period. Another commenter noted, with reference to qualitative data analysis, that "Not all communities have the infrastructure to support schools in this endeavor," explaining why that person chose "No" as the answer to this question. One participant mentioned that his or her school has a PTA, with an internal committee that focuses on these issues.

Regarding the future views of ecologically sustainable practices within a school, a participant noted that recycling and the use of eco-friendly products might vary throughout the years between accreditation and review. This participant added that there may not be a way to monitor how consistent a school is in maintaining these practices. Focusing on this same question, another participant thought that schools should consider eliminating the need for such large buildings in the first place and repurpose buildings that have already been built.

One participant indicated "Not sure," followed by a comment of wanting to know what AdvancED is. This participant also mentioned that the curriculum in his or her school was the only part being assessed during the accreditation period. Another survey taker proposed that learning take place at home with the aid of technology.

Result 4

Should the External Review Team evaluate evidence for poor indoor air quality for children in school? With this question, I was interested in opinions on whether respondents were open to change to evaluate for poor indoor air quality for children in schools. The majority of survey respondents (*n* = 34, 51.52%) reported, "Yes, definitely," that the External Review Team should evaluate for poor indoor air quality in schools. The second most frequent response was "Yes, to some extent" (*n* = 17, 25.76%). Others stated they were not "Not sure" (*n* = 8, 12.12), followed by those who disagreed with the premise, choosing "No" (*n* – 7, 10.61%), that reviewers should evaluate evidence for poor indoor air quality in schools. This response aligns with the comment that evaluating indoor air quality is a difficult task, but it also suggests that evaluators would be willing to think more about assessing indoor air quality in the schools. As noted earlier, at least one respondent made the point that indoor air quality was a specific aspect of health and safety practices. When examiners have concerns or problems about air quality in the classroom, the accreditation team must consider recommendations to the school or district to address the issue.

In the survey, a respondent stated that the examiners have the power to include in their report health and safety issues if there is concern from the team. That person added that, if there is a noticeable problem, the team should highlight that in its report, with guidance for the school to consult qualified experts to evaluate the situation. Concerning instructions and training given to evaluators, one of the participants went on to note that instructions given by the agency for which external examiners assess safety and health issues in the schools do not align with what is evaluated regarding indoor air quality within the schools. Others commented that evaluators are not qualified for this task, nor are they compensated for it. One survey respondent reported feeling unsure, having a lack of knowledge about AdvancED, because that person was from New Zealand, where indoor air quality was not an issue for the schools.

Overview

Another point is that the data showed that many respondents did not even know whether AdvancED/Cognia's assessments included looking at schools' indoor air quality. In other words, even as part of the accreditors' ongoing accreditation process, participants were unaware of safety and health standards used to measure the schools' roles and responsibilities related to improving indoor air quality. The enumerated response asserts Collins' (2015) point that accreditation is a controversial topic when changing an institution's management or standards.

Qualitative Data Analysis

According to Parker (2020), limited funding, lack of training in improved indoor air quality, standards, and compliance were the four barriers to a healthy indoor environment. Unawareness that performance was affected by the indoor environment was the fifth barrier. Three subthemes were discussed related to air quality monitoring:

- the role of air quality in accreditation
- the level of involvement of participants
- the need for involvement and concern

Barriers to a Healthy Indoor Environment

Narratives from all participants contributed to the development of this theme, as they discussed the barriers that they believed led to unhealthy indoor air environments in schools. Participants observed that myriad factors contributed to poor indoor air quality in schools, with funding by far the biggest obstacle to clean indoor air quality. Participant 1 indicated that schools did not address indoor air pollutants because of the costs associated with doing so but added that "Accrediting agencies should focus on the fact that healthy and safe schools do not cost much more than regular maintenance projects." Participant 2, however, stated that the cost associated with managing indoor air quality in schools might be higher than other school maintenance and that this increased cost would cut across different areas.

Last but not least, Participant 3 said that addressing indoor air quality issues would require more funding, adding that budget cuts related to school maintenance also negatively affected the quality of air in schools. Participant 3 added, "I believe that schools don't prioritize indoor air quality due to frequent cuts in maintenance funds from state and local governments." Moreover, according to two of the participants, there appeared to be a significant lack of training and awareness related to indoor air quality. Participant 2 stated, "There is not a lot of concern for indoor air quality in the classroom, possibly due to lack of educational awareness programs within their organization," while Participant

3 offered a similar perspective, noting that "Many schools don't know of or have tools to learn how to address indoor air quality problems." Participant 3 added that school officials and accreditors likely had a "lack of training to identify a quality learning environment."

Standards and Compliance

Participants generally acknowledged problems with compliance related to indoor school air quality. According to Participant 3, "There is a decline in the enforcement of state health policies," and there are no overall formal standards for indoor air quality in schools, workplaces, and the like. On a broader scale, Participant 3 said that multiple organizations are responsible for maintaining clean air in schools, adding, "I know that there is a general disconnect at the federal and state-level education and public health agencies, to acknowledge the enforcement of tools needed to manage building conditions."

Lack of Awareness that Indoor Environment Affects Performance

Two participants believed that officials might be more inclined to focus on enhancing school indoor air quality if they knew how poor air quality impacts children's academic performance. As Participant 2 shared, "Schools need to increase awareness and involve stakeholders about how parents view the importance of high air quality as to how it affects the teachers and students and their ability to perform at a higher level." Participant 3 echoed this sentiment, stating, "On these levels, many are not aware that academic performance like low standard test scores can be due to building conditions, particularly inadequate ventilation."

Responsibility for Monitoring Air Quality

In this theme, the three participants discussed their beliefs about who should be responsible for monitoring school air quality, along with their own levels of responsibility for doing so. They also spoke about the need for more concern and increased involvement in ensuring decent quality indoor air for students. These three participants agreed that there was a growing need to address social-ecological legislation and classroom issues.

Air quality should be part of the accreditation process. Participant 2 thought that "The accreditation process should have some control in assessing the upkeep of playgrounds and restrooms." This statement was based on that person's involvement and experience with the accreditation process. Participant 3 suggested that one way to do this would be for accreditors to "filter research results about air quality in the classroom into their engagement with the schools," adding that there should be more concern for healthy indoor air quality and safe water quality. This participant believed that there was a lack of concern on the part of accreditors for school indoor environmental quality.

Participants' Level of Involvement

Participant 1 had very little interest in healthy air quality in the classroom, being "focused mostly on buildings' energy costs" at the expense of indoor air quality. Participant 2 noted the "gross oversight of assessing schools for a healthy learning environment "of AdvancED/Cognia's accreditors but was not directly involved in these accreditation practices. Finally, Participant 3 described using a different model to improve indoor environmental air quality, not that of AdvancED.

One aspect of indoor air quality in schools agreed upon by two participants was that more people should participate. There should be more involvement. Participant 1 suggested that organizations "take actions favorable to local and state policies relative to health in the workplace" to enhance indoor air quality. Participant 2 believed that "The school environment and children's learning should be a concern for the school and the communities" and that "Indoor air pollution problems in the classroom need to be addressed by all workers in the school systems." Participant 2 also suggested that organizations and communities have adopted an attitude of indifference toward improving indoor air quality in schools, thinking that they might not be able to do so successfully. In terms of improving the students' learning outcomes, participants did not consistently detail comments about using heating, ventilation, and air conditioning (HVAC) systems in schools to do so. They did, however, highly rate the proposition that AdvancED/Cognia should provide feedback about the HVAC system as a critical safety issue. According to the participants, this feedback aligned with enriching the learning environment.

In this study, participants were unsure if indoor air quality should be tied to school policy. The results conceptualized the responsibilities of environmental decision-makers and government policymakers to promote a better learning environment. Respondents seemed to agree that indoor air quality should be part of accreditation. The connection between indoor air quality and the accreditation system strengthens the link between air quality indicators of students' health and safety. For example, in this study, one aspect of indoor air quality in schools on which participants agreed was that more people should be more involved in safety and health issues to enrich the learning environment in schools. Similarly, according to Alves et al. (2016), various stakeholders involved in environmental planning and education policy are considered professionals who seek ways to influence the outcome of what may affect the quality of the school environment. Participants in this process are problem solvers. They offer short-term and permanent control measures for indoor air quality, such as mold protective measures that involve maintaining humidity between 30 and 60% with air conditioning and dehumidifiers (p. 15).

Results presented in this section indicate that barriers relating to indoor air quality during the accreditation process were central to participants' responses to the research question covered in this study. As a result of the research, it is evident that the external examiners/representatives of AdvancED/Cognia felt between somewhat satisfied and very satisfied with the Accreditation Standards Policies and Procedures of AdvancED. Despite differences in the feedback on the specific questions, participants' responses drew attention to data features that connected with other authors' studies on barriers to the assessment of indoor air quality in schools. The findings are consistent with the qualitative data found in this study, which revealed that organizations and communities have adopted an indifference toward improving indoor air quality in schools. They appear to have concluded that they might not be able to enhance air quality at all.

Analysis and Discussion

The data clearly revealed answers to the main research question: What are the current barriers and potential solutions that ultimately can result in AdvancED/Cognia leading the way towards making a significant impact on indoor air problems in our nation's schools? In this section, I attempt to analyze, interpret, and offer conclusions about the results described above.

HVAC systems are fundamental to addressing indoor air quality in the classroom. In this study, participants held the view that schools should have greater commitment to the importance of the HVAC systems in their buildings. In terms of minimizing the potential harm from classroom pollutants, they suggested that AdvancED/Cognia should provide feedback on schools' HVAC systems. However, a literature review showed no evidence of the reduction of poor air quality being evaluated by an accreditation process. Accepting AdvancED/Cognia's involvement in assessing air quality during its accreditation process is one way to fulfill responsibilities related to the indoor air quality problem in schools.

The call to educate the accrediting agency about health risks associated with exposure to the indoor emission of particles suggests that temporary, short-term solutions may decrease risks to children's health. For example, Madureira et al. (2016) indicated some remediation from air pollution by giving students more breaks and recesses between classes, decreasing the occupancy per room, increasing the exchange of indoor air with outdoor air, and improving the cleanliness of facilities. These appear to be pitiful fallbacks, but they may be necessary until state and federal education legislation addresses this significant problem in the school environment.

At this point, indoor air pollution breathed in by our children is a risk management task (Brown et al., 2016). The solution requires assessing pollutant exposure and managing inhalation exposure, bringing them to acceptable levels as established by competent organizations. However, I contend that if accreditation organizations (AdvancED/Cognia, in particular) say they are addressing safety and health issues in schools, they should not continue to give clean bills of health to a supportive learning environment while ignoring the seriousness of indoor air pollution and its consequences. Because the health of our children is at stake, the evaluations of educational institutions must inform our actions (Collins, 2015) and yield evidence in alignment with educational facilities and student performance.

According to Albader (2018), this could be a tactic used to encourage stakeholders' behavior towards preventive maintenance, which is essential to simple planning for a high-quality facility. Thus, to address indoor air quality to improve schools' environments, human actions by AdvancED/Cognia must be considered, even as I have done in this study. Admittedly, due to the small number of participants (66), my research does not present the most comprehensive data on this topic and its social justice aspects. However, I contend that the external examiner teams' representatives from accreditation agencies were clearly not always aware of schools' air quality. Their versions of the certification standards "have not formalized into preventing, identifying, and fixing indoor air quality problems for schools" (Parker, 2020).

There must be a concern for the indoor environmental factors associated with ventilation and temperature that affect indoor air quality and influence school measures for academic assessments. In their studies, Kwan et al. (2020) and Rai et al. (2021) argued that the built environment protects against unwanted and harmful pollutants. Additionally, Rai et al. (2021) noted that promoting a protective environment increases knowledge of indoor microbes that negatively affect human health. Again, as noted in the survey, evaluators should be willing to assess indoor air quality in the schools. At least one respondent pointed out that indoor air quality is a specific aspect of health and safety practices. When examiners have concerns or problems about air quality in the classroom, the accreditation team must consider recommendations to the school or district to address the issue.

Overall Summary

In this section, I presented the research problem in terms of the role of external examiners as representatives of AdvancED/Cognia, an accreditation organization. I have recognized this as a problem within the assessment process, through policies that do not offer insight or, as in the title of Parker's analysis (2020), ignore the regulation of indoor air quality relative to the learning environment. I reasoned that AdvancED/Cognia should play a significant role in communicating to schools about such environmental issues as poor indoor air quality in the classrooms. I discussed underexplored areas of research regarding external examiners' barriers to citing evidence of poor indoor air in schoolrooms. The study presented and explained the rationale, in terms of aspects of social equity, as a form of leadership for environmental change. I aligned social equity within the schools' accreditation process with the use of standards to address the external examiners' scope of improvements, providing insights into their social relationships.

Recommendations

To address AdvancED/Cognia, an organization that lacks a comprehensive understanding of indoor air pollution in its recommendations to educational institutions, I recommend that AdvancED/Cognia stop ignoring it. I have explained previously why the word "ignoring" is appropriate for this monograph. In short, my dissertation titled "Exploring Accreditation Priorities: A Study on Why a Major Accrediting Body for Public Schools is Ignoring Indoor Air Pollution in Classrooms" (Parker, 2020) remains a scholarly published paper. It is my adamant desire to lessen the adverse consequences that can potentially arise from not taking responsibility for a body's actions in servicing the world's vast educational community. For AdvancED/Cognia to undertake the task of addressing indoor air quality in schools, the affiliates of educational institutions should examine air quality regulatory procedures as part of a future accreditation process. The conclusion that accreditation agencies are not committed to regulating indoor air quality in the schools supports this recommendation.

According to Parker (2020), before COVID-19, I felt that AdvancED/Cognia, the school accreditor, would resist accepting my recommendations to assess and monitor factors of indoor air in their standards. Furthermore, I presented my paper to members of AdvancED/Cognia via a Zoom meeting. Their response was, "You presented a very respectable paper with positive ideas we never thought about." Furthermore, I have seen evidence that AdvancED/Cognia now includes some environmental factors in its standards—but in a rough draft. This predicted movement toward addressing indoor air aligns with comments by F. Onyunde (personal communication, November 23rd, 2021):

> In a way, I have been directly and indirectly involved with our government accrediting body for our school. In 2013-2014, our curriculum performances were improved by introducing Drama, Language, Religion, and books appropriate for levels of education. We were managing our bus areas to improve indoor air quality in the classrooms. Our schools were unifying building infrastructures – as, for example, sustainably designing schools' windows to provide better lighting for better learning performances, and we

> increased our learning spaces. We advocated for the school's plant areas, for example, gardening for school kitchens.

M. Thomashow (personal communication, September 27, 2021), noted similarly:

> Unity College emphasized campus gardens to promote awareness both on campus and in the surrounding community. We transformed our campus landscape by planting wildflower gardens, we grew food in partnership with local community organizations, and we distributed vegetables to the cafeteria and the local community.

Conclusions

When researching exploratory primary-level studies in this domain, I integrated and summarized criteria that could be used by a systemic review to compare and contrast "advantages and limitations" (Robinson & Hammitt, p. 969). I explored patterns of research in the areas of the quantitative and qualitative results to respond to the research question: What are the current barriers and potential solutions that ultimately can result in AdvancED/Cognia leading the way towards making a significant impact on indoor air problems in our nation's schools? As shown in the study, I explained the process of the three-phased mixed methods research synthesis, while revealing barriers and solutions relating to AdvancED/Cognia's accreditation and its influence on poor indoor air quality for children in school. I also observed that educational leadership on improving the learning environment matters. It interconnects accreditation opportunities, academic performance, and seating positions, quantifying space as mentioned in various previous studies. Indeed, it is clearly linked to methods of improvement in the student learning environment. However, since there are little to no data about the accreditation agencies' influence on addressing indoor air quality challenges, this analysis focused on building strategies related to personal training and awareness by feedback from external examiners as part of the accreditation review. An interviewee in Parker's (2020) research noted as follows:

> To reduce the barriers to addressing safety and health issues in the learning space, accrediting agencies needed to develop professional training and awareness of the health effects associated with poor indoor air quality and students' learning performance. Others, who

> opposed this view, believed that the design of training awareness did not need to link air quality with student health and safety or with students' learning performance (p. 91). In the opinion of another, who presented a different perspective, the design of training awareness does not need to link air quality to student health and safety or learning performance. (p. 36)

The conclusion that organizations and communities have adopted an indifference toward indoor air quality in schools is unacceptable. Similarly, the idea that they might not be able to improve indoor air quality significantly is also defeatist. This narrative points to the participants' way of saying, "Stop overlooking indoor air quality." The results of this study lead to the recommendation for schools and accreditation agencies to become increasingly aware of poor indoor air quality and its effect on children's learning. One participant's response indicating having no clue about indoor air quality in schools makes this recommendation essential. Another participant did not know how to acquire knowledge regarding what his or her school had done to pay attention to classroom air quality.

This analysis provides a research synthesis design for achieving a systematic review that integrates qualitative and quantitative data (Creswell & Creswell, 2017). For example, the study contributes to understanding the emerging narratives of external examiner representatives of AdvancED/Cognia pulled by assessing sustainability practices. As a result, the representatives were somewhat satisfied and pleased with the linkages of barriers to assessing indoor air quality (IAQ). To advance future sustainability knowledge, I assert that the accrediting bodies should establish environmental sustainability responsibilities linking awareness of schools' poor IAQ with accreditors' criteria. One participant emphasized focusing on this question; another participant thought that schools should consider eliminating the need for such large buildings in the first place and repurpose buildings that have already been built.

Because I saw this research question as an issue of social/ecological justice, I looked for data through the lens of a concerned activist. I explored evidence representing the relationships between the data and the authors of studies, forming a synthesis (Heyvaert et al., 2016). During this period of exploration, I understood and kept in mind that proper research includes comments by the researchers about their interpretation of the findings, and should not be limited by their backgrounds, such as their gender, culture, history, or socioeconomic origin (Creswell, 2017).

Preventive measures facilitate environmental equity reforms. One of the challenges is creating an environmentally sustainable awareness of the association between poor indoor air quality, schoolchildren's health, and the method of how schools are accredited. Environmental sustainability policies and solutions related to poor indoor environmental quality impact the learning ecology and assessment equity. Proposing environmental sustainability as an equity issue brings attention to effective educational outcomes.

Meet the Author

Jeanlee Weeks Parker, PhD is CEO/Owner of Teacher's Environmental Education Research Management LLC, which acts as a consultant to educational organizations and businesses involved in sustainability marketing management. A Fellow at Fielding's Institute for Social Innovation, she serves on Fielding's Sustainability Advisory Council. She is a member of the International Society of Indoor Air Quality and Climate and is a green classroom professional at The Center for Green Schools at the U.S. Green Building Council. Dr. Parker also actively volunteers at Franklin Park Conservatory and Botanical Gardens. She holds a doctorate in education (EdD), with a leadership for change concentration in sustainability leadership, from Fielding Graduate University. Working as a licensed K-12 substitute teacher, she has had direct knowledge of school systems learning equity. Previously, she worked as a secondary teacher in chemistry and physics, grades 5–8, at the Manarat Jeddah Girls' International School in Jeddah, Saudi Arabia.

References

AdvancED. (2017). *History and Overview of AdvancED.* https://advanced.instructure.com/courses/89/pages/history-and-overview-of-advanced

Al-Hubail, J., & Al-Temeemi, A. S. (2015). Assessment of school building air quality in a desert climate. *Building and Environment, 94*(2), 569–579. https://doi.org/10.1016/j.buildenv.2015.10.013

Allen, J. G., MacNaughton, P., Satish, U., Santanam, S., Vallarino, J., & Spengler, J. D. (2016). Associations of cognitive function scores with carbon dioxide, ventilation, and volatile organic compound exposures in office workers: A controlled exposure study of green and conventional office environments. *Environmental Health Perspectives, 124,* 805–812. https://doi.org/10.1289/ehp.1510037

Al-Qasmi, N. N., Al-Thaiban, H., & Helaleh, M. I. H. (2019). Indoor phthalates from household dust in Qatar: Implications for non-dietary human exposure. *Environmental Science and Pollution Research, 26*(1), 421-430. https://doi.org/10.1007/s11356-018-3604-8

Alsaleh, N. (2016). Qualitative data analysis: Step by step guidelines from collection to analysis. Paper presented at the 15th Qualitative Methods Conference, University of Glasgow, UK.

Andualem, Z., Gizaw, Z., Bogale, L., & Dagne, H. (2019). Indoor bacterial load and its correlation to physical indoor air quality parameters in public primary schools. *Multidisciplinary Respiratory Medicine, 14*(1), 2. https://doi.org/10.1186/s40248-018-0167-y

Assefa, G. (2020). Life-cycle assessment-based environmental performance targets for buildings: what is next?. In B. E. Brownell (Ed.), *Examining the Environmental Impacts of Materials and Buildings* (pp. 188–216). IGI Global.

Bahnfleth, W. P. (2017). Defining indoor air quality. *ASHRAE Journal, 59*(5), 84.

Bajada, C., Singh, S., Jarvis, W., & Trayler, R. (2020). The use of threshold concepts supports student learning through assessment – A case for renewing public trust in business education and qualifications. *Higher Education Research and Development,* 1–16. https://doi.org/10.1080/07294360.2020.1775558

Berman, E. A. (2017). An exploratory sequential mixed methods approach to understanding researchers' data management practices at UVM: Integrated findings to develop research data services. *Journal of eScience Librarianship 6*(1): e1104. https://doi.org/10.7191/jeslib.2017.1104

Bluyssen, P. M. (2017). Health, comfort and performance of children in classrooms – New directions for research. *Indoor and Built Environment.* 26(8), 1040–1050. https://doi.org/10.1177/1420326X16661866

Brink, H., Loomans, M. G. L. C., Mobach, M. P., & Kort, H. S. M. (2021). Classrooms' indoor environmental conditions affecting the academic achievement of students and teachers in higher education: A systematic literature review. *Indoor Air, 31*(2), 405–425.

Brown, K. W., Minegishi, T., Cummiskey, C. C., Fragala, M. A., Hartman, R., & MacIntosh, D. L. (2016). PCB remediation in schools: A review. *Environmental Science and Pollution Research, 23*(3), 1986–1997. https://doi.org/10.1007/s11356-015-4689-y

Brundtland, G. H. (1987). *Our Common Future: Report of the World Commission on Environment and Development.* Geneva: UN-Document A/42/427. http://www.un-documents.net/ocf-ov.htm

Cecilia, O. N., Cornelius-Ukpepi, B. U., Edoho, E. A., & Richard, E. O. (2019). The influence of learning styles on academic performance among science education undergraduates at the university of Calabar. *Educational Research and Reviews,*

14(17), 618–624.

Center of American Progress. (2019, February). The case for federal funding for school infrastructure. https://www.americanprogress.org/article/case-federal-funding-school-infrastructure/

Centers for Disease Control and Prevention. Operating schools during COVID-19: CDC's considerations. *National Center for Immunization and Respiratory Diseases (NCIRD), Division of Viral Diseases*. https://www.cdc.gov/coronavirus/2019-ncov/community/schools-childcare/schools.html

Chatzidiakou, L., Mumovic, D., & Summerfield, A. J. (2015). What do we know about indoor air quality in school classrooms? A critical review of the literature. *Intelligent Buildings International, 4*(4), 228–259.

Clarke, V., & Braun, V. (2017). Thematic analysis. *The Journal of Positive Psychology, 12*(3), 297–298. https://doi.org/10.1080/17439760.2016.1262613

Cognia|. (2019). *Measured Progress is changing its name to Cognia.* https://bit.ly/3AudgW9

Cognia. (2020). *Accreditation handbook*

Collins, I. (2015). Using international accreditation in higher education to effect changes in organizational culture: A case study from a Turkish university. *Journal of Research in International Education, 14*(2). https://doi.org/10.1177%2F1475240915592589

Creswell, J. W. (2014). *Research design: Qualitative, quantitative, and mixed methods approaches* (4th ed.). Sage.

Creswell, J. W & Creswell, J. D. (2017). Research design: Qualitative, quantitative, and mixed methods approaches. Sage Publications.

Environmental Protection Agency. (2021a). *Environmental Sustainability*. https://www.epa.gov/sustainability/learn-about-sustainability#care

Environmental Protection Agency. (2021b). *Take actions to improve indoor air quality.* https://www.epa.gov/iaq-schools/take-action-improve-indoor-air-quality-schools

Erlandson, G., Magzamen, S., Carter, E., Sharp, J. L., Reynolds, S. J., & Schaeffer, J. W. (2019). Characterization of indoor air quality on a college campus: A pilot study. *International Journal of Environmental Research and Public Health, 16*(15), 2721. https://doi.org/10.3390/ijerph16152721

Finell, E., Haverinen-Shaughnessy, U., Tolvanen, A., Laaksonen, S., Karvonen, S., Sund, R., Saarristo, V., Luopa, P., Ståhl, T., Putus, T., & Pekkanen, J. (2017). The associations of indoor environment and psychosocial factors on the subjective evaluation of indoor air quality among lower secondary school students: A multilevel analysis. Indoor Air, 27(2), 329–337. https://doi.org/10.1111/ina.12303

Finell, E., & Seppälä, T. (2018). Indoor air problems and experiences of injustice in the workplace: A quantitative and a qualitative study. *Indoor Air, 28*(1), 125-134. https://doi.org/10.1111/ina.12409

Gibbons, D. A. (2017). *Factors that influence accreditation in Nebraska public districts and schools* (Publication No. 10267888) [Doctoral dissertation, University of Nebraska]. ProQuest Dissertations and Theses Global.

Hayward, F. M. (2017). Reflections on two decades of quality assurance and accreditation in developing economies. *Planning for Higher Education, 46*(1), 21–31. https://www.proquest.com/scholarly-journals/reflections-on-two-decades-quality-assurance/docview/2008824298/se-2?accountid=33310

Heyvaert, M., Hannes, K., & Onghena, P. (2016). *Using mixed methods research synthesis for literature reviews.* SAGE.

Kwan, S. E., Shaughnessy, R., Haverinen-Shaughnessy, U., Kwan, T. A., & Peccia, J. (2020). The impact of ventilation rate on the fungal and bacterial ecology of home indoor air. *Building and Environment, 177.* https://www.sciencedirect.com/science/article/pii/ S036013232030158X

Lalić, A. B. (2018, September). Proceedings of the 26th CEEMAN Annual Conference: Redefining Management Education: Excellence and Relevance-Info Session on CEEMAN IQA-International Quality Accreditation. In *CEEMAN Conference Proceedings* (Vol. 26, pp. 32–37). CEEMAN-Central and East European Management Development Association.

Liu, Q. (2016). *The impact of external quality assurance policies and processes on curriculum development in Ontario postsecondary education* (Publication No. 10190926) [Doctoral dissertation, University of Toronto]. ProQuest Dissertations and Theses Global.

Lopez-Chao, V., Amado Lorenzo, A., & Martin-Gutierrez, J. (2019). Architectural indoor analysis: A holistic approach to understand the relation of higher education classrooms and academic performance. *Sustainability, 11*(23), 6558. https://doi.org/10.3390/su11236558

Madureira, J., Paciencia, I., Pereira, C., Teixeira, J., & Fernandes, E. (2016). Indoor air quality in Portuguese schools: Levels and sources of pollutants. *Indoor Air, 26*(4), 526–537. https://doi.org/10.1111/ina.12237

May, E. M., Hunter, B. A., & Jason, L. A. (2017). Methodological pluralism and mixed methodology to strengthen community psychology research: An example from Oxford House. *Journal of Community Psychology, 45*(1), 100–116.

National Center for Education Statistics. (2019). *Environment for learning, planning guide for maintaining school facilities.* (2019). https://nces.ed.gov/pubs2003/maintenance/chapter4.asp

Nuss, H. J., Hester, L. L., Perry, M. A., Stewart-Briley, C., Reagon, V. M., & Collins, P. (2016). Applying the social ecological model to creating asthma-friendly schools in Louisiana. *Journal of School Health, 86*(3), 225-232. https://doi.org/10.1111/josh.12369

Nussbaum, M. C. (2011). *Creating capabilities.* Harvard University Press.

Oldham,J. (2018). K-12 Accreditation's next move. *Education Next,18* (1), 24.

Parker, J. W. (2020). *Exploring accreditation priorities: A study on why a major accrediting body for public schools is ignoring indoor air pollution in classrooms* (Publication No. 27737645) [Doctoral dissertation, Fielding Graduate University]. ProQuest Dissertations and Theses Global.

Pavlakis, A., & Kelley, C. (2016). Accreditation in the professions: Implications for educational leadership preparation programs. *Journal of Research on Leadership*

Education, 11(1), 68–90. https://doi.org/10.1177/1942775116641663

Peppin Vaughan, R. (2016). Education, social justice and school diversity: Insights from the capability approach. *Journal of Human Development and Capabilities, 17*(2), 206–224. https://doi.org/10.1080/19452829.2015.1076775

Petersen, S., Jensen, K. L., Pedersen, A. L. S., & Rasmussen, H. S. (2016). The effect of increased classroom ventilation rate indicated by reduced CO2 concentration on the performance of schoolwork by children. *Indoor Air, 26*(3), 366–379. https://doi.org/10.1111/ina.12210

Purvis, B., Mao, Y. & Robinson, D. (2019) Three pillars of sustainability: In search of conceptual origins. Sustainability Science, 14(3), 681–695. https://doi.org/10.1007/s11625-018-0627-5

Rai, S., Singh, D. K., & Kumar, A. (2021). Microbial, environmental, and anthropogenic factors influencing the indoor microbiome of the built environment. *Journal of Basic Microbiology, 61*(4), 267–292. https://doi.org/10.1002/jobm.202000575

Rehr, R., Miller, G., & Foos, B. (2015). Children's environmental health indicators as tools to measure progress toward sustainability. *Sustainability: Science, Practice & Policy, 11*(1).

Robinson, L. A., & Hammitt, J. K. (2015). Introduction to the special series on research synthesis: A cross-disciplinary approach. *Risk Analysis, 35*(6), 963–970. https://doi.org/10.1111/risa.12437

Rubaii, N. (2016). Promoting social equity, diversity, and inclusion through accreditation: Comparing national and international standards for public affairs programs in Latin America. *Quality Assurance in Education: An International Perspective, 24*(4), 541–561. https://doi.org/10.1108/QAE-02-2016-0007

Rubin, I. L., Geller, R. J., Martinuzzi, K., Howett, M., Gitterman, B. A., Wells, L., Garfinkel, W., Coles, C., Merrick, J. (2017). Break the cycle of environmental health disparities: An ecological framework. *International Public Health Journal, 9*(2), 115.

Sheffield, P., Uijttewaal, S., Stewart, J., & Galvez, M. (2017). Climate change and schools: Environmental hazards and resiliency. *International Journal of Environmental Research and Public Health, 14*(11), 1397. https://doi.org/10.3390/ijerph14111397

Stafford, T. (2015). Indoor air quality and academic performance. *Journal of Environmental Economics and Management, 70*, 34–50. https://doi.org/10.1016/j.jeem.2014.11.002

Sun, Y., Hou, J., Sheng, Y., Kong, X., Weschler, L. B., & Sundell, J. (2019). Modern life makes children allergic. A cross-sectional study: Associations of home environment and lifestyles with asthma and allergy among children in Tianjin region, China. *International Archives of Occupational and Environmental Health, 92*(4), 587–598. https://doi.org/10.1007/s00420-018-1395-3

Thombs, R., & Prindle, A. (2018). Ohio LEED schools and academic performance: A panel study, 2006-2016. *Sustainability, 10*(10), 3783. https://doi.org10.3390/su10103783

Ulker, N., & Bakioglu, A. (2019). International research on the influence of accreditation on academic quality. *Studies in Higher Education, 44*(9), 1507–1518. https://doi.org/10.1080/03075079.2018.1445986

World Health Organization. (2021). *New WHO global air quality guidelines aim to save millions of lives from air pollution.* https://www.who.int/news/item/22-09-2021-new-who-global-air-quality-guidelines-aim-to-save-millions-of-lives-from-air-pollution

Xu, H., Guinot, B., Ho, S. S. H., Li, Y., Cao, J., Shen, Z., Niu, X., Zhao, Z., Liu, S., Lei, Y., Zhang, Q, & Sun, J. (2018). Evaluation on exposures to particulate matter at a junior secondary school: A comprehensive study on health risks and effective inflammatory responses in Northwestern China. *Environmental Geochemistry and Health, 40,* 849–863. https://doi.org/10.1007/s10653-017-0030-7

CHAPTER 5

WHERE DO FAMILIES TURN: ADULTS WITH DISABILITIES IN A CARE(LESS) CULTURE

Maggie Buckley
Institute for Social Innovation Fellow

This chapter offers a theoretical discussion of *precarity* as experienced by people who give and receive care, the author's personal story, a description of a call to social justice through servant leadership, and some concluding thoughts. The story of our own family is meant to give life to this important topic. The more generalized descriptions of precarity, neoliberalism, and care theories, as these concepts relate to people with disabilities and their caregivers in America, provide historical context as well as recommendations for how best to provide support for caregivers and those who receive care in a post-neoliberal state. A description of a local project designed to reduce precarity by creating communities of care demonstrates how an ethic of care can emerge more strongly.

There are several salient issues arising in this chapter including persistent ideologies that limit our willingness to see and address the needs of our vulnerable people, leading to failure to create public policy and funding that supports those who need and give care. The pandemic has laid bare the inequities in our culture. As Gregory Boyle (2021), in reference to systemic racism notes, "The fault lines have been revealed. We've come to see that inequalities are not a defect in the system. It is the system." This is likewise true for people with disabilities. It is estimated that people with disabilities comprise 26% of adults and 20% of children in the United States, cutting across all racial and ethnic subgroups (Lee et al., 2018). People who are marginalized through disability have suffered more acutely during the pandemic than those who have adequate financial and social resources. Though people with disabilities are afforded certain protections under laws such as the Americans with Disabilities Act, they remain a marginalized and largely invisible group. As McDonald et al. (2020) noted, there continues to be an institutional bias in Medicaid, the largest financier of care for people with disabilities. Inadequate funding of community-based resources, including housing and equitable pay for staff, has created conditions that structurally compel people to live in congregate settings. Young people with disabilities are living in nursing homes and congregate care settings rather than in their own or their families' homes, despite federal laws and supreme court cases that presumably protect the rights of persons to live independently with support. [1] We know that there are increased risks for infection and death in congregate care, made even more evident during the pandemic (Chidambaram, 2020). These risks could be reduced with increased access to quality home care. We need to promote systemic change in the social contract to permit people with disabilities to thrive in their homes and communities. It is possible that through acknowledging and learning from people with disabilities, we can see that vulnerability is not diminishing, but rather adds a refreshingly authentic dynamic to our relationships. Indeed, a sense of purpose and vitality arise from our life struggles.

Vulnerable People, Neoliberalism, and the Pandemic

In general, the lives of people with disabilities are characterized by more uncertainty that deeply impacts one's life socially, physically, economically, and psychologically. This leads to a sense of greater inequality and powerlessness—the result of insufficient solutions to experienced problems and the need to endure circumstances beyond their control (Baart, 2021). The pandemic has hit our vulnerable people hard. As Hole and Stainton (2020) noted, the fears about our vulnerable family members contracting COVID-19 are palpable. The threat of hospitalization for people who cannot communicate in standard ways is terrifying. If a family is fortunate enough to have staff to assist, they must worry about whether the staff will inadvertently infect family members with the virus. Our family fears for the future. Others are in more immediate crisis. In preparation for our project on creating communities of care we, the organizers, have been collecting stories to illustrate the impact of the care crisis on our vulnerable people. Martha Nussbaum (2010) argued for the development of narrative imagination, imagining what it is like to be in another's shoes, as a critical feature of democratic citizenship. Take a moment to imagine what these lives are telling us about the degree of carelessness that exists in our current culture.

A recent report on a local news station (Proia, 2021) divulged information regarding a 33-year-old, business-owning single mother born with a physical disability who is struggling to get assistance with basic activities of daily living that most of us take for granted. She has been receiving care from home health care aides for 14 years, and their pay has never increased. She remarked that now that so many people have left the industry, it's a challenge for her to find any help. She noted, "A salary of $12.50 an hour is not enough. It's not enough to take care of a family, it's not a living wage. (…) They can go to Tim Horton's or Burger King or anywhere like that and make $15–$17 an hour easily doing half of the work." A powerful self-advocate who works tirelessly campaigning for disability rights for others has been sleeping in his wheelchair for the last two years because he does not have staff to transfer him to bed at night. A man with extraordinary leadership skills tries to hire his own staff through advertising and phone interviews. When he quotes the currently established pay rate of $12.50 per hour to the potential candidate, the person laughs and hangs up. This man, confined to a wheelchair, humbly tells us that he cannot get dressed for his workday without staff. These glimpses into the lives of people who need care are representative of a much larger social issue affecting our vulnerable people.

A care deficit, meaning the inability to find enough care workers needed to provide care for a growing population of adults with disabilities and the aging, has been predicted for several years now (Benhold, 2011; Llana, 2006). This deficit is largely reflective of yet another political and economic shift—the rise of neoliberalism. Neoliberalism is the sociopolitical positioning of individualized, market-based competition as the preferred governing principle for shaping human action in all areas of life, both at the individual and collective, societal levels (Sharma, 2018). Neoliberalism, as Tronto (2015) noted, refers to a *market-foremost* democracy, producing substantial inequalities and an absence of the political process of caring. Neoliberalism fails to consider an equality of voices and promotes the notion that money and power have ultimate value (Brugere, 2020). The citizen is defined as an economic person, a homo economicus. In a neoliberal society, the government limits its responsibility for the well-being of its citizens and instead empowers individuals or complex organizations to be responsible for their welfare through enterprise and competition in a marketized society (Sharma, 2018). The "ideal citizen under neoliberalism is autonomous, entrepreneurial, and endlessly resilient, a self-sufficient figure whose active promotion helped to justify the dismantling of the welfare state and the unraveling of democratic institutions and civic engagement" (Chatzidakis et al., 2020, p. 12). This view refuses to acknowledge our vulnerabilities and discourages interconnectedness.

In our culture, there is much discussion about economic and social capital. While social capital is reduced for all of us, it is in particularly short supply for people with disabilities. Dependency needs to remain invisible in this culture. The sense of obligation to care for and look out for those who will never be able to assume independence has been fractured. An alternative view is that the true wealth of a country lies in the relationships, kindness, and creativity of its citizens. In this view, nurturing capital has currency. As Lynch (2007) noted, "The amount of nurturing capital available impacts on people's ability to relate to others on an intimate level, but also to flourish and contribute in other spheres of life" (p. 554). Affective bonds are important in society both in the private and public spheres; however, as love and care are part of the private sphere, they are not taken seriously in the public domain.

The COVID-19 pandemic has revealed our collective vulnerability. This vulnerability can only be addressed through a commitment to be responsive to each other. Our people with developmental and intellectual disabilities, and those who support them, were struggling before the pandemic. Now the struggle feels overwhelming. The marginalization of people with disabilities and those who care for them is well documented. Disabilities summon societal fears about difference and vulnerability; it is easier to make the disabled and their families invisible than it is to support them and view the vulnerability up close (Greenspan, 1998). As Nussbaum (2015) noted, every society has a list of stigmatized groups, and generally these lists include people with disabilities; ethnic, racial, and religious minorities; and direct care providers. Paid caregivers assume a secondary dependency, as Kittay (1999) referred to it, particularly by assuming economic vulnerability, as much of the lowest paid work in this country is caregiving. The stigmatization of people with disabilities and those who care for them is fueled by our cultural inclination to value autonomy over interdependence, which appears to have strengthened, judging by our nation's response to COVID. We have witnessed clear resistance to public health initiatives for masking and vaccination to protect our most vulnerable people. The current staffing crisis will deepen if not addressed through systemic change. The need for long-term care will substantially increase over the next twenty years.

The elements of successful caregiving require, first, that we as a culture acknowledge the precarity experienced by people who need and give care. Secondly, we need to establish pathways for critical public conversations regarding a vision for care. Most importantly, we need to recognize that all care is relational. As McKnight and Block (2012) noted, the institutions and market organizations that we rely on to serve our most vulnerable provide just that—a service. It is the community that cares or fails to care for its members.

Precariousness Becomes Precarity

Fueled by neoliberalism, the state of precarity will only be reversed if we move towards a post-neoliberal state, advancing a compelling narrative for the necessity of caring communities. This narrative, based on relational theories of development and an ethic of care, will be advanced in a project described in this chapter. Headed by two grassroots community groups in Buffalo, NY dedicated to promoting an understanding of the needs of caregivers and care recipients, the project will target local faith communities to garner support for advocacy in the short-term around the current staffing crisis and in the long-term to promote an ethic of care in our communities. We propose that as John McKnight and Peter Block (2012) suggested, we turn to our communities and the abundance that exists in them to make connections and to make known the needs of our most vulnerable.

Precariousness, depending on circumstances beyond one's control, is everywhere. No one is protected from this unpredictability. And yet for many, todays and tomorrows are planned as if they are guaranteed. Even amidst threats of accidents, terrorism, global climate change, potential illness, and political upheaval, we push forward as if nothing can stop us. This is the cultural ideal—invulnerability. We behave as if we are completely independent and self-sustaining. Then a submicroscopic organism emerges, upending our certainty. Suddenly there is an awareness of vulnerability. This awareness may be new to some, but not to the thousands of people living with disabilities. For these folks and their families, life doesn't hold the same promise. We live with an acute awareness of our vulnerability and interdependence. We also live with the fear and isolation that accompanies disability in the absence of the protective resources of care needed to experience a sense of well-being.

Our well-being depends on living interdependently, enmeshed in a web of care. Unlike precariousness, a condition common to all life, whether we choose to acknowledge it or not, precarity is a condition that is unnecessarily created through a combination of both human action and inaction. Judith Butler (2010) defined precarity as a "politically induced condition in which certain populations suffer from failing social and economic networks of support and become differentially exposed to injury, violence and death" (p. 25). We depend on an infrastructure of care that supports all of our people. When these systems of care and support are fractured, those who rely on them descend into a state of precarity.

The COVID-19 pandemic has intensified the already compromised system of support for our most vulnerable people. It has created a crisis that is likely to produce dramatic changes in service delivery systems. It has also created an acute sense of alarm for people with disabilities and their families who do not know what, if any, resources will be in place when they can no longer care for their loved ones. A 2021 report issued by PHI, an organization that works to ensure quality care for older adults and people with disabilities by creating quality jobs for direct care workers, substantiates that although there is an increasing demand for direct care workers, low wages persist. The average wage for the direct care workforce was $13.56 per hour in 2020. Low wages, coupled with the often part-time nature of this work, make it difficult for members of this workforce to sustain themselves and their families. Forty-four percent of direct care workers live in low-income housing, and 45% receive some form of public support such as Medicaid and/or nutrition assistance. These are primarily women or people of color who have long been subjected to substandard wages and working conditions.

COVID-19 has heightened our awareness of the vital role direct care workers play and at the same time increased the challenges they encounter. As the PHI report (2021) noted, direct care workers risked their health providing care for people, often without adequate personal protective equipment, hazard pay, paid time off, and availability of care for their own family members. The long-term impact of the pandemic on direct care services is unknown; however, it is known that the need for direct care staff will increase substantially over the next several years. Paul Osterman (2015) estimated that there will be a minimal shortfall of 151,201 workers in 2030 and 355,301 in 2040. This is considered an underestimate because there is an additional projected shortfall of unpaid family caregivers, who deliver a substantial amount of care. This shortage is quite often attributed to the low wages associated with care work—a clearly valid point. However, there are other significant issues that discourage people from entering this field, among them difficult working conditions and disrespect by the market and government systems that interface with caregivers. In *Who Will Care for Us*, Osterham (2015) reported interviews conducted with senior members of the Medicaid and Medicare systems who had responsibility for funding long-term care. Osterham found that the Medicare and Medicaid administrations had little understanding of the challenges faced by the workforce.

Kittay (2021) claimed,

> The increased precariousness people with disabilities face in achieving and holding onto a good quality of life, whatever their disabilities, and the precarity that marks a set of labor conditions that creates the economic insecurity and social and political marginalization of care workers are linked (1) by the issue of dependency and (2) by the needs of adequate supports for dependency related needs. (p. 42)

Both groups of people are joined in their experience of social and political marginalization. Placing people with disabilities in situations where their care is in the hands of overworked, underpaid, and unvalued care workers compromises the dignity and well-being of both caregivers and care receivers.

The conditions associated with the precarity of care workers are symptomatic of a much larger issue in our culture—the gradual but steady eroding of caring values and in some cases a prevailing carelessness. Miller (2021) stressed that the crisis of care is "as much a moral and relational crisis as it is a political and economic one" (p. 49). Moral precarity, according to Miller (2021), "arises in circumstances where fulfilling the responsibilities one takes to be central to one's sense of ethical identity proves circumstantially impossible without also incurring considerable and unavoidable harm" (p. 52). This leads to moral injury. Consider the impact on the care workers, families, and advocates who are witness to the constant care deficits they feel powerless to correct. What happens to the person who needs to leave a care position because they cannot sustain themselves and their families while recognizing that their departure places the people they cared for at increased risk? What happens to the family member who is aging and can't secure staff to help care for their loved one? Unfortunately, confronted with these moral dilemmas, Miller explained that people are made to feel that if they were morally better, they would be able to avoid the possibility of letting down the persons they care for. Worse yet, they begin to question their identity as a caring person.

We have people feeling morally injured when they realize they cannot do enough for others while, at the same time, people in a global pandemic refuse to mask and vaccinate when doing so can be harmful to themselves and the vulnerable people surrounding them. How did care become such a contentious, divisive political and social issue? This is best answered by examining the historical and ideological issues impacting our response to the need for care.

Our Evolving Story of Care

The way a society chooses to care for its people is informed by a multiplicity of factors that evolve over time. Care practices are strongly influenced by cultural and social complexities and are best understood within an historical framework. During the 19th century, caregiving was (and remains) a gendered practice, organized by women through a web of community obligation and reciprocity. Empathy was encouraged as caregivers drew on their personal experiences of suffering and spirituality to establish relationships with those who needed care. The intensity of these connections made institutionalization only a last resort. There was certainly economic disparity in the quality of care. Much of the information gleaned about historical care practices was from the diaries of women who represented the more economically privileged. Notwithstanding the hard work and instances of inequality of care at that time in history, there are two notable features of 19th-century accounts of care that are generally absent today—work that was valued and a shared communal practice that created robust ties among women caregivers (Abel, 2000). Looking at care practices from a historical perspective, it is evident that they were grounded in communal relationships.

A confluence of events occurred during the latter half of the 19th century that altered the structure, value, and location of caregiving. The model of communal care underwent a fundamental change that persisted into the 1960s (Rothman, 2004). Institutionalization took precedence over family care. Family obligations were redefined by significant ideological changes. The cultural worth of the three main components of caregiving—instrumental, emotional, and spiritual—was devalued from 1850 onward through the idealization of scientific rationality (Abel, 2000; Waerness, 1987). With the advent of the scientific approach to care, the spiritual and emotional dimensions of care were simultaneously devalued. Rationality, objectivity, and neutrality replaced relational values. Reliance on spirituality was considered a passive approach and thought to undermine the power of scientific knowledge. Scientific practitioners asserted that intense personal connections distorted understanding of patient needs and promoted overindulgence.

The regimentation and emotional distance of institutional care were antithetical to the relational care practices of the home. Institutions were often placed at a great distance from where families lived, so visiting was difficult and often impossible. Mothers distanced themselves from their institutionalized children for a multiplicity of reasons. Some mothers depleted their physical, emotional, and financial resources before agreeing to commitment. There was an increasing stigma attached to disability, prompting women to disengage in an effort to heal their family's reputation. For others, it was their only way to bear the pain of separation. Finally, once a person was institutionalized, he or she became a ward of the state, permitting facility administration to determine visitation and discharge procedures, further diminishing parental engagement in caregiving (Abel, 2000).

While the care of individuals with disabilities was shifted from the home to the institution, another major cultural transformation had taken place—the shift from an agricultural to an industrial society. The most distinctive feature of this cultural reorganization was the division of life into discrete functional sectors—the private sphere of the home and the public sphere of the workplace (Bellah et al., 1985). This resulted in strong boundaries between domestic and competitive work, in contrast to the less distinct boundaries of the earlier 19th century. The home increasingly was thought of as a moral and emotional sanctuary from the insensitivity of the marketplace. Women were expected to concentrate on the affective and moral roles of mother and caregiver and were dispossessed of an economic role. Male roles gained status in this new structure of society, while women's work was considered devoid of economic worth.

This cultural reorganization was also distinctive for the ways that it generated new images of the collective American character. This collective, or what Bellah et al. (1985) referred to as a representative character, was a way for people to organize their lives. More than abstract ideals, it encouraged people to merge their individual identities with the requirements of the social roles dictated by certain standards. Powerful societal myths accrued around the ideals of the self-reliant individual. Self-reliance and independence were ascribed to male roles and silently supported by the moral ecology maintained by women (Bellah et al., 1985). To maintain these ideals, rigid boundaries emerged between domains of home and work, giving rise to dualistic thinking. Values associated with masculinity in the public sphere gained dominance over those values associated with femininity in the private sphere. The elevation of reason over emotion, instrumental over affective work, individualism over interdependence, and capitalist over communitarian values further sharpened the distinction between the two worlds. Thus, public and private values were sharply contrasted and correlated with a split between the utilitarian approach of the workplace and the expressive style of the home.

Social distance means, at the most basic level, how much distance exists between people (Tronto, 1993). The institutionalization of people with disabilities created a social distance that continues to negatively impact caregiving, even today. According to Tronto (1993), as individuals interacted with increasing numbers of people, often living at great distances from each other, contextual morality was replaced with universalistic morality. Universalistic morality was grounded in reason, and since it was presumed that reason was the same everywhere, it followed that universalistic morality was a means of publicly coping with different people and varied ways of life. The problem here is that caregiving is particularistic, not universalistic, and trust develops when particular needs are understood, acknowledged, and satisfied.

Just as a confluence of factors shifted care of disabled individuals from families to institutions, a convergence of dynamics coalesced to relocate the care of persons who were developmentally disabled back to the communities. Past attempts to limit family and community involvement in the lives of the disabled through institutionalization were successful. In fact, families were so marginalized by personal and political constraints and disengagement that they were powerless to address the barbaric conditions at Willowbrook until a public exposé drew attention to the horrific conditions there (Rothman & Rothman, 1983).

Willowbrook was a New York State institution for the developmentally disabled. Its name is synonymous with neglect and abuse. Staff members such as William Bronston, Michael Wilkins, and Elizabeth Lee advocated for reform from the inside, leading to the famous exposé in January 1972 by television reporter Geraldo Rivera. This depiction of the conditions there mobilized a response from the public and policymakers, ultimately resulting in the closure of Willowbrook and other state institutions. Disclosure of abuses, coupled with the civil rights movement that extended legal recognition of civil rights to the disabled, guided a gradual reconfiguration of services for the disabled in the community, replacing institutions with group homes and day service options for residents. This settlement was not only supposed to rectify the wrongs done to these approximately 6,000 individuals, it was intended to become a yardstick of care and community placement that would eventually be applied throughout the state.

The public policy of deinstitutionalization emphasized community care for developmentally disabled and mentally ill individuals, expecting families to respond, particularly women in families, without adequate support and resources to do so (Hooyman & Gonyea, 1995). When care occurred primarily in institutional settings, the people needing and giving care became invisible.

Though the institutions for people with developmental disabilities have emptied, the impact of social distance and the removal of care practices from the mainstream remains.

Contemporary Care Theory

Current care theorists centralize relational practices in contemporary conceptions of care. Noddings (2002) developed a phenomenology of caring, a general description of "what we are like when we care" (p.13). She noted that care begins with receptivity, a special kind of attentiveness. Attentiveness is expressed through an emotionally based interactive pattern between the carer and the cared-for, during which the carer wants to understand what the cared-for is going through. The carer must then respond in some way, which Noddings referred to as *motivational displacement*, a process by which the carer's motive energy flows toward the cared-for. An integral part of the caring relation is reciprocity, not in the traditional sense of taking turns with caretaking work, but rather in relational terms of allowing the caretaker to know that their caring work has been received. Monitoring of care effects is critical when caretaking occurs over time. Noddings distinguished natural caring—the form of caring that arises from affection—from ethical caring, or care that arises from obligation. Ethical caring occurs because we choose to sustain an ideal of ourselves as carers. It facilitates the restoration of natural caring when lost through fatigue or frustration. According to Blustein (1991), a person who cares about caring and stops caring or feels at risk of becoming uncaring will act to find a means to attach to someone or something to care about. In Noddings's framework, care as a virtue is distinct from care as a relation. Caring as relation depends on the connection between the carer and cared-for.

Missing from Noddings's (2002) depiction of care is attention to the contexts where care occurs, the ideologies and values that define it, the material conditions and resources necessary for care, and the power relations that define the ways care has been structured (Fisher & Tronto, 1990). Noddings makes important observations about the motivation to care in one-to-one relationships. However, a singular focus on the personal motivation for caregiving makes it difficult to see the ways that it is a social and political process dependent on resource availability and successful interconnections among all parties involved in the process. Caregiving, as it occurs across locations, is best comprehended when seen as a part of the culture where it occurs.

In *The Care Manifesto*, Chatzidakis et al. (2020) argued that we are experiencing a pressing need for a policy that places care at the center of our awareness. Broader than a conception of hands-on care, care as they define it "is also a social capacity and activity involving the nurturing of all that is necessary for the welfare and flourishing of life" (p. 5). Authors of *The Care Manifesto*, who make up the Care Collective, noted that the ability of care workers to provide care is limited not only by poor pay but also by exploitation, understaffing, inadequate job security, and a lack of training and job support. The Care Collective advocates for a model of universal care, meaning that care in all its forms is prioritized, not only in the domestic sphere, but in all spheres of life. Prioritizing care in this way promotes it as a political, life-sustaining process.

Joan Tronto's theory captured the components elegantly, representing what is most salient to the care process. First, Tronto and Fischer (1990) broadly defined care as "a species activity that includes everything we do to maintain, continue, and repair our world so that we can live in it as well as possible" (p. 40). The first step, caring *about*, recognizes the level of need with a corresponding value of competence. The second is *taking care of*, that is, planning for care with a value of responsibility. The third, *caregiving*, involves the direct meeting of needs with the corresponding value of attentiveness. *Care-receiving*, with a value of responsiveness, refers to optimal interactions between caregiver and care receiver (Fisher & Tronto, 1990). Tronto has since added a fifth step in the process: *Caring-with*, with the corresponding values of plurality and solidarity, means that caring needs, and the way they are addressed, require alignment with democratic principles of justice, equality, and freedom for all (Tronto, 2013). This step heightens our awareness of the communal nature of care and reminds us that care is always relational and always involves an element of power. Caring acts transpire in a political context and are reflective of a society's values, customs, and institutions (Tronto, 2015). Tronto contends that if we are to have an inclusive citizenship, we need to realize that caring will lead us there. To this point, she offered a new definition of democracy as the "allocation of caring responsibilities and assuring that everyone can participate in those allocations of care as completely as possible" (Tronto, 2015, p.15). Furthermore, Tronto proposed that a functional democracy is composed of people who are attentive, responsible, competent, and responsive, in accord with the values of caring (Tronto, 2015). These traits are best transmitted through a relational orientation to development.

Relational Development

Contemporary theories of care agree that care is always relational. Relational theory is an alternate model of development that suggests that growth and development occur within a context of affiliation, involving the formation of increasingly complex relationships. In this way, it differs from the traditional theories of development that emphasize separation and individuation as optimal developmental outcomes. Autonomy and separateness are the standards by which we have been traditionally measured, and they are considered a confirmation of psychosocial adjustment and mental health. There is another path to psychosocial growth and maturation defined by connection rather than separation. Initially conceived by Jean Baker Miller (1976) as a new psychology of women, the model has been extended at the Stone Center, most notably by Alexandria Kaplan, Judith Jordan, Irene Stiver, and Janet Surrey. Relational theory is based on the premise that growth occurs in the context of relationships through particular types of interactions. Growth enhancing interactions involve mutual empathy and mutual empowerment. Individuals enter growth-promoting relationships aware of their vulnerabilities and with a sense of responsibility to the relationship. The work of the scholar/practitioners of the Stone Center has guided the development of a theory of *self-in-relation*, a model that maintains that aspects of the self, including such qualities as autonomy, creativity, and affirmation, become apparent in the context of relationship, and there is no apparent need to disengage from relationships for self-development to occur (Surrey, 1991). Psychological development has historically been assessed within models that either minimize or treat as weaknesses the characteristics such as empathy and mutuality that Miller redefined as strengths.

There are important practices inherent in growth that require elaboration to facilitate understanding of the distinction between self-in-relation and other long-established theories of development. The essential elements of the core self are summarized by Surrey (1991) as

> an interest in and attention to the other person(s), which form the base for emotional connection and the ability to empathize with the other(s); the expectation of a mutual empathic process where the sharing of experience leads to a heightened development of self and other; and the expectation of interaction and relationship as a process of mutual sensitivity and mutual responsibility that provides the stimulus for the growth of empowerment and self-knowledge. (p. 58).

The similarities between this developmental process and the interpersonal processes of care are remarkable and confirm the conception of care as a relational activity. This construction of development conveys the importance of affiliation necessary for all humanity. Relational theory, rather than focusing on developmental endpoints, illuminates the increasingly complex processes of self-development. It offers an alternative to the predominant and powerful models that fail to appreciate the significance of interdependence and emotional connectivity.

Mutual empathy and mutual empowerment in relationships are vital to psychological growth and caregiving. Mutuality does not mean equality or sameness; it refers to a way of relating where all people are participating as fully as possible (Miller & Stiver, 1997). In situations combining caregiving, it involves the recognition of mutual concerns and complementary strengths (Haigler et al., 1998). In a relational paradigm, power does not mean power over, but rather the power to act effectively in the world and the power to interact so that both benefit. According to Miller and Stiver (1997), mutually empowering and empathic connections lead to feelings of zest, empowerment, and worthiness.

Actualizing human capabilities is the goal of human development. The expansion of choices and opportunities paves the way for people to lead fulfilling, dignified lives. Viewing development through Martha Nussbaum's human capabilities approach is a constructive approach for people who are marginalized through disability. Nussbaum (2011) offered a list of central capabilities designed to address the conditions pivotal to a quality life. She made a particular point about cognitive disability that is critical to development. She noted that "the attitude towards people's basic capabilities is not a meritocratic one—more innately skilled people get better treatment—but, if anything, the opposite: those who need more help to get above the threshold get more help" (p. 24). Nussbaum suggested that, in the case of a person with a cognitive disability, the goal is to create conditions for the person to have the same capabilities as a person without a cognitive disability. This would be accomplished through the use of a surrogate to assist in care and decision-making. Our family's personal experience with caregiving is reflective of the cultural dynamics that impact care as well as the possibility for creating caring support systems that embody the elements of relational care.

Carly's Story

My story begins with my daughter, Carly. Carly is funny and forgiving. She loves fiercely. If you're feeling sad or anxious, she senses it. Carly loves the Beach Boys, swimming, and spaghetti. She is exceptionally grateful for small gifts, always recalling who they came from. Over the past few years, Carly has developed an impressive art portfolio. She paints from her heart and it shows. Her artwork is complex, full of emotional expression. She paints what she cannot say.

As a parent, I celebrate who Carly is and appreciate her accomplishments. However, she has undeniable needs and without substantial support she simply cannot live safely in this world. If I only tell you about why she is so valued by her family and friends, you may not understand the depth of her vulnerability or how we fear for the day when we can no longer care for her. This is the dilemma faced by so many parents of adult children with disabilities. We do not want to diminish who our children are, but we must ensure their future care. That means we are often placed in a position of defining our children by what they cannot do. Though Carly is strong in so many ways, she needs my voice to advocate for her support. My hope is that I represent her as authentically as possible. So, this is what I need to tell you.

Carly was born with Down syndrome. As a little girl I knew she was different from other children with this syndrome. While I was prepared for her to have developmental delays, Carly was inexplicably more delayed than her peers. Her attention span was extremely short. Her peers in early intervention classes began walking between eighteen and twenty-four months; Carly's first steps emerged at three years. She often sat gazing at her hand. Surrounded by her sister, three years older, and a cadre of neighborhood friends, Carly rarely engaged in the playfulness of her sister and peers the way we hoped she would. Social skills are often cited as an area of strength for people with Down syndrome, yet Carly struggled socially, often behaving unpredictably. When Down syndrome intersects with other conditions it creates confusion for parents and professionals alike. I blamed myself in ways too numerous to count for her "meltdowns," erratic behavior, and overreliance on routine.

Carly began accumulating diagnoses throughout childhood and adolescence. Beginning with attention deficit hyperactivity disorder, she acquired other labels as treatments for each diagnosis failed. These included anxiety disorder, depression, mood disorder, bipolar disorder, and obsessive-compulsive disorder. It now appears that Carly has a co-occurring autistic spectrum disorder, a subjective diagnosis often difficult to make given the complexity of symptoms of Down syndrome and autism. What adds to the difficulty of diagnosis is that people with Down syndrome have a relative strength in social skills, so that even when these skills are compromised by autism, they often appear more social than the typical individual with autistic spectrum characteristics. Research indicates that anywhere from 5–39% of people with Down syndrome may also have autism or autism spectrum disorder. (Moss, 2009; DiGuiseppi, 2010). Carly's behavioral challenges limited her ability to be fully included with typical peers in educational settings; however, we were blessed with compassionate family, friends, and neighbors. Throughout her childhood and adolescence, Carly enjoyed supportive relationships with extended family, teachers, and family friends that eased the daily difficulties created by her dual diagnosis.

When Carly exited the educational system at age 21, she entered day habilitation services, a program offering prevocational and social skills, personal care training, and recreation on a daily basis, funded through the home and community-based services Medicaid waiver. Generally, the services are provided in groups of 15 moderately to severely disabled individuals with three staff members. This was in stark contrast to the educational model where Carly was with five other students and two to three staff members. She spent her day in a room that was an amorphous, converted warehouse space—but converted into what? There were classes there, but it did not look or feel like a school. There were homemaking activities, but it did not look or feel like a home. The concrete block, windowless walls, painted a bright yellow, did not compensate for the absence of natural light. Steel support beams intermittently spaced throughout the room, the same bleak gray color of the steel ceiling, contributed to a feeling of cold, ill-defined space. The indeterminateness of these surroundings mirrors the experience of disabled adults in this culture, where no real sense of place or belonging exists. There was too much noise. Carly could not filter out the necessary from unnecessary information that came at her. Her confusion became noncompliance, leading to almost weekly phone calls during the middle of a workday to come and to pick her up. The calls were accompanied by a confusing medley of emotion—blame, exasperation, and regret. I was upset by the staff's frustration, but at the same time, I understood it. During times when Carly is better able to regulate her behavior, she endears herself to those around her through her exuberance, infectious laugh, and alternately, her look of concern, accompanied by her familiar question, "Are you okay?" I understood that the staff's best intentions were to respond caringly to her, but best intentions do not make up for poor staff ratios and ineffective program design.

At the time Carly attended this program, research indicated that an inability to respond effectively often results in a high rate of employee turnover. Frequent factors that contribute to staff burnout include emotional exhaustion, depersonalization, and reduced feelings of personal accomplishment (Geysen, 2001). Currently, direct support personnel (DSP) turnover rates approach 45% of the workforce, with average vacancy rates of 9%, leading to troubling inconsistencies of support in the lives of people with developmental disabilities (Smith et al., 2019). This inconsistency in the workforce has many implications, including a negative impact on the quality of support, potential increases in the occurrences of abuse, neglect, or mistreatment as well as increased administrative costs for recruiting, hiring, and training new DSPs. Congregate care settings have consistently been linked to poorer outcomes, from limited access to care, to lack of control and failure to meet essential needs, to abuse and neglect (McDonald et al., 2020).

Carly understood immediately that she was in the wrong environment in the day habilitation program. She attempted to leave during the first several days and needed to be physically stopped from walking out, while repeatedly saying "go home." She mounted a steadily intensifying campaign of resistance. Carly could not articulately name the problem, but she was relentless in expressing her displeasure. She often refused to enter the program room, remaining in the hallway, physically demonstrating her inability to participate. When she tried to participate, her insistence on routine, need for sameness, and tendency toward repetitive behaviors, characteristics of the autistic spectrum, interfered. If she entered the room and noticed someone in her accustomed seat, she responded frantically, crying and verbally demanding "get up, get up." Because she has multiple disabilities, it was difficult for staff, especially unfamiliar staff persons, to accurately assess her motivation. She was not willfully demanding to take charge, but rather responding to an internally driven neurobiological problem associated with autistic spectrum disorder, involving an excessive need for systematizing and assuming a rigid stance regarding the behavior of objects (Baron-Cohen & Belmonte, 2005).

In 2004, we established a *circle of support*—a group of family, friends, and paid caregivers who are asked to be the voice for an individual's hopes and dreams and the safeguards to make sure that services are addressing his or her needs in a safe and appropriate manner. The circle is a vital and mandated component of *self-direction,* a current model for service delivery, which is achieved and expressed through relationships, not simply a change in the material resources and circumstances of one's life (Dowson & Salisbury, 2000). Through this process we created an individualized budget and person-centered plan for Carly to receive services embedded in relationships in the community.

At 23, Carly left day habilitation and began learning to define what was important to her within the context of close supportive relationships. In the daily log kept by her DSP, Annie, we saw evidence of what matters to her. She participated in animal care, took long walks in the park, and went to the Springville farm auction every Wednesday where she thoroughly enjoyed walking amidst the animals up for auction. She was particularly enthusiastic about going to Annie's farm, where she loves to feed and help groom the animals. Though her attention to these activities is short, she is building a sense of competence in relationship with Annie. Most importantly, she is learning to make choices and negotiate in empowering, rather than disempowering, ways. While she continued to experience mood swings, they did not define her day or her sense of who she is. We saw Carly make tremendous personal growth in a short period of time. Her anxiety was reduced so that her energy has shifted, making it easier for her to engage in the moment. She was less apt to ask repetitive questions, such as "program tomorrow?" that reflected her worries about attending a program that was not working for her. She slept better and had more self-control. Her focus improved during her morning routine, positively impacting her ability to care for her personal needs. She was making meaningful choices and was in a caregiving relationship that she valued. In the everydayness of their experiences, Annie and Carly taught us about the importance of connection in paid care. People think that I conceived this arrangement for Carly's care but really, Carly did. She knew she could not survive in day habilitation. I simply gave voice to her needs and desires.

Our decision to care for Carly at home, to be in partnership with paid professional caregivers, was made first and foremost out of love and a deep commitment to help her create a meaningful life. It was also made out of fear that Carly's spirit, that which animates her, would be broken by the emotional turmoil she experienced in a setting where her needs could not be effectively met. We were encouraged by her response. She was less anxious; her mood was more stable. Yet I remained uneasy, knowing that it would be difficult to maintain what was started, given the complexity surrounding caregiving. I did not realize in the first years how enduring this care arrangement would be. In 2019, after 17 years, Annie was still with us, a rarity in the world of direct support care. Despite continued mood swings, angry outbursts, and resistance to complying with necessary boundaries, Carly has endeared herself to Annie. As a family, we accommodated Annie's needs, advocating for pay raises and always granting requests for time off. We did this out of respect and gratitude for her commitment and the work she does. Most importantly, we did it to do what we could to support this magnificent and complicated relationship. In *Love's Labor,* Kittay (1999) called the relationship between her significantly disabled daughter and her caregiver, "the relationship with no name (p. 166)"—a phrase invented by Kittay's son. It is an apt description. I have often hesitated over describing Annie as Carly's personal assistant. It sounds so businesslike. It does not nearly describe the dynamics between them, but there really is nothing that does. More often they look like friends or sisters, but that idea violates the cultural divide between work and home. We are continually processing, trying to make sense of what this relationship means in the context of a culture that presents us with confusing and contradictory images of what it means to work and care for others.

Prior to COVID-19, our participation in self-directed home care was far more ideal than what many families experience. We have been privileged with skills (from our chosen professions) and experience, as well as the support and encouragement of family and friends and dedicated professionals, which allowed us to navigate a system that is complicated and requires time and tenacity. To be clear, we were able to offer support to Carly and Annie's care relationship because we are at a point of having flexibility in our schedules. For families struggling with competing demands, it is much more difficult to accommodate the needs of both family members who need care and their caregivers. Also, Carly's care is funded through Medicaid's *Self Direction*, a program where budgets are configured to allow for higher pay rates for staff, while still being cost-effective for Medicaid. The pay rate eliminates the all-too-frequent problem of staff leaving to find more sustainable work.

Self Direction, also referred to as Self Determination, was advanced in the 1990's by Tom Nerney and a group of people with disabilities and their families. It was not conceived as a new program, but as a basic restructuring of existing services, designed so that a person with a disability can create a meaningful life in the community and experience lasting relationships. It was established with the vision that people with disabilities are vital members of our communities who will be supported as members of the community, rather than as clients of programs or consumers of services. They will be able to determine their own futures, with appropriate assistance from families and friends. Citizens will see themselves as competent and willing to become involved in the lives of people with disabilities (Nerney & Crowly, 1994). This program was also proposed as a fiscally conservative response to the increasing need for care amid dwindling economic resources (Nerney, 2003). It is a reform movement committed to placing control of resources for long-term support directly in the hands of people with disabilities and their families and allies. Self Determination is based on the following principles: the *freedom* to develop a personal life plan, deciding where and with whom to live and establish personal relationships, the *authority* to personally control (with assistance) a targeted amount of publicly funded long term care dollars, the support to arrange these resources in ways that are meaningful to the person receiving care, the responsibility to use these dollars in wise and cost effective ways, and the *confirmation* that people with disabilities and their families are to be included in public policy discussions and redesign issues (Nerney, 2003).

Currently, Self Direction is a service option funded through the Medicaid home and community-based waiver. It is available throughout the United States in variously designed configurations. Advocates for Self Determination questioned how one could have a good quality of life based primarily on short-term relationships with agency personnel. It was created, first and foremost, as a way to promote full community inclusion for individuals with disabilities and the establishment of long-term relationships. Self Direction begins with a planning process that consists of a circle of support convening to help the person with a disability and his or her family design supports that are both necessary and meaningful. Self Direction allows for significant control over by whom, where, and how services are delivered. It is a customized plan that is managed by the persons receiving services and their allies such as family members, friends, and care managers. In New York State a person/family who is self-directing works within a personal resource account (determined through an instrument that assesses the person's needs) to develop a self-directed budget that includes allocations for staffing, goods, and services. Self-directed services are often sought by people who, though disabled, have the capacity for considerable independence. It is also a highly effective approach for those who have more complex needs, due to the customization of services. For people with high support needs, such as my daughter, who cannot make decisions independently, it is imperative that they have relationships with family and/or friends who are available to assist in directing their services.

The Emergence of COVID-19

The COVID-19 pandemic added another layer of complexity to Carly's care previously unimagined. People with Down syndrome have an increased susceptibility to infections, particularly pneumonia. Carly was seriously ill with

Legionnaire's disease in October 2019, so we are very concerned about exposure to COVID-19. Carly does wear a mask, but not for long periods of time, nor does she understand the concept of social distancing. In March of 2019, we were forced to pause Carly's Self Direction plan in order to isolate her from exposure to the virus. Annie was in full agreement with our decision. We had no idea that this pause would continue into 2022. Initially, Carly adjusted well to the novelty of our isolation. As time goes on, she is becoming more frustrated, sad, and confused. Annie has not returned to work though we keep in touch through weekly Zoom calls and hope that she will return one day. Annie was initially advised not to get vaccinated by her health care provider due to a potential allergic reaction. Carly cannot socialize with unvaccinated people. Annie was eventually successfully vaccinated, but each time we began talks about her return to work, the COVID-19 numbers rose, making all of us uncomfortable. We worry that Annie will eventually need to move on to different work. Most direct care support workers would not be able to remain out of work for a substantial amount of time. Annie's profile differs from the many DSPs who are supporting their entire families on their wages. According to a PHI report on direct care workers released in 2021, one in six lives in a household below the federal poverty line and 45% live in a low-income household. Annie is married and her children are grown, so she has some financial flexibility that other DSPs do not have, yet she will need to return to work within the near future. We are trying to plan for how this will work with Carly's need for social isolation and the inevitable changes to her day this brings. If we cannot ensure a full-time position for Annie, we cannot expect her to remain. Her value to our family is incalculable, but we remain aware that for Annie this is a job. Anecdotally, we have learned that some people are losing their self-directed plans due to lack of available staff. We live in fear of losing Annie, who is irreplaceable at so many levels.

For now, at age 39, Carly is wholly dependent on us, her mother and stepfather, to make sure she is safe and thriving in her family home. Carly needs assistance with all her personal care needs. She cannot choose weather-appropriate clothing without aid. Though she enjoys helping in the kitchen, she cannot prepare food independently. Most significantly, Carly cannot keep herself safe. She cannot call 911 for help. She is impulsive and unable to fully comprehend danger, thus she must be very closely supervised in the community and at home. Carly needs consistent, reliable, loving support. We worry unceasingly about the day when we will no longer be able to provide the care Carly needs. With the looming cuts to existing services, we don't know how her future will look.

An Intentional Virtual Community of Care

We need community-people outside but alongside institutions to spark a commitment to an ethic of care. Communities of care offer the possibility of connecting people who hold a vision of care and a voice of influence in the broader culture. Relationships are central to care. As McKnight and Block (2012) noted—institutions provide services; care is given from the heart of an abundant community. Our ongoing project was designed to promote an ethic of care in our local communities. It provides evidence of what care, relational theory, and servant leadership look like in practice. The information presented here is taken from meeting notes and personal communication with people involved in this project. The persons quoted here have agreed to be represented in this chapter. In response to the constraints of the pandemic limiting in-person contact, the project was conceived as a virtual coffee hour experience. It is intended to promote awareness and connection, inviting people with and without disabilities to get to know people's stories. The plan is part of a joint effort involving Buffalo and Western New York Friends of L'Arche. L'Arche is an international organization that promotes a culture of shared lives between people with and without disabilities. Carefully crafted circles of support create relationships that grow in faith and friendship, leading to a sense of authentic belonging. There are currently over 154 L'Arche communities throughout the world. Some create networks of families, some concentrate on housing, some on social and creative initiatives. All share a fundamental dedication to service, community, spirituality, and outreach. Each L'Arche community in the United States establishes its own 501(c)(3) organization that reflects the values of L'Arche, while expressing the unique ethnic, cultural, and religious makeup of their own area. ARISE (Advocacy, Respect, Inclusion, Support, and Equality) is a self-advocacy group that is part of VOICE Buffalo, a community organizing association that trains people in faith communities and other community organizations to develop sustaining relationships that work towards a more equitable and prosperous community.

This project results from the dedicated leadership of ARISE, Voice Buffalo, and the Caring Majority. ARISE is particularly instrumental in catalyzing the efforts to promote awareness of the needs of people with disabilities. Observations and interviews suggest that the leadership in this organization represents servant leadership as described by Robert Greenleaf (1977). The following excerpts of conversations about the work of ARISE make evident the characteristics of servant leadership. Because care is relational, we cannot overlook the critical importance of what individuals bring to the movement. It is these people who show us what servant leadership and relational theory look like in practice. Here you will meet two such people who use their wisdom and experience to move us toward a more caring culture.

Mike Rogers is a self-advocate, a co-leader of ARISE, and a regional organizer for the Self Advocacy Association of New York State (SANYS). Born with a physical disability necessitating the use of a wheelchair, Mike never, even as a child, believed that he or anyone with a disability should be treated differently than anyone else. As an adult, Mike accepts his need for physical assistance with grace and dignity—he feels it's not important how we get to do something [meaning the support it takes], just that we can do it. He leads ARISE with a calm and soothing demeanor, taking great care to make sure everyone at this now-virtual table is heard. When praised for his manner, he humbly credits it to years of experience and the skills he learned at his first job. Before becoming an advocate, Mike worked at a call center, fielding calls from angry, frustrated customers who were dissatisfied with a product or experiencing tech issues. By necessity he learned anger management skills, but he offers so much more than that. This is interesting, coming from a person who never set out to be an advocate. Following his call center job, a friend mentioned an opening for a self-advocate with AmeriCorps. His response was, "I don't think I could ever speak to the public, but I'll try it." When younger, he believed that "nobody cares [about disability]." With experience he learned that "you have to push, if you work hard enough things will change." This man, who didn't believe that he could speak publicly, presents as a compelling, passionate, sincere, and sensitive person who easily captures the attention of his audience with his wisdom and wit.

When Mike was ten years old, he felt like a "regular" person, but he could see that having a disability meant that you were treated differently and often excluded from the mainstream. Sometimes he described feeling a "righteous anger" over the exclusion he witnessed in schools. Mike was inspired by his faith but perhaps not in a typical way. He says that he looked up at the sky one day and said to the devil, "I'm going to stop you from doing this to people." He meant segregating them but didn't have the word at that age. He laughs about this now, saying, "Never challenge the devil. He'll take you up on it."

Mike and the other volunteers at ARISE have recently achieved a major victory in advocacy. After years of steadfast work, they have just celebrated the opening of a satellite office in an accessible part of the community. This office, where determination for service eligibility for adult services occurs as well as employment for advocates with disabilities, now has a location that is accessible through public transportation. The main office is in an area unreachable through public transportation and offers limited specialized transportation for people who desire to work or attend meetings there. Encouraged by this recent success, ARISE is moving on to address the critical shortage in staffing. This is both personal and political for Mike. He acknowledges that he worries constantly about staffing. He saw this crisis coming. He has experience advertising, interviewing, and employing his own staff through a Medicaid Self Direction program. During one such interview, when he quoted the $12.50 an hour salary and the requirement that the position entailed applying to a local agency serving people with developmental disabilities, the applicant responded that he expected $25.00 an hour and would only agree to work independently. Mike also has the added worry of the pandemic now as he has had lung problems in the past and recognizes his increased vulnerability. Despite these worries associated with his need for care and the pandemic, Mike remains undaunted in his advocacy work. He enthusiastically says he experiences joy all the time through his opportunities to support people and help others learn to speak out. Mike says the best thing about ARISE is that we "empower each other." He adds, "Nothing I do will ever shut anyone out."

Sophia Roberts is the regional coordinator of SANYS and an active member of ARISE, where she sees her purpose as supporting others to advocate for themselves. Sophia has worked in the field of developmental disabilities for

26 years. Sophia sees people with disabilities as her spiritual mentors because she is witness to their great faith, joy, and acceptance of their vulnerability. She describes being in community with people and helping them as her saving grace, adding that that's where she sees mercy, grace, and love. She experiences a sense of God through people and feels we're like God's hands—part of the creative force which we can choose to add to or be destructive. When asked about joy in her work, Sophia responded first that she thinks grief is the flip side of joy, and she is grieved when she sees that people with disabilities are not seen, valued, or listened to. She experiences joy when people experience their own powerful voice and use it. Sophia recalls a time when she felt overwhelmed by witnessing the wrongs without being able to correct them. She couldn't meet all the needs, and there was so much that didn't make sense. She has learned to deal with the pain and stress, vulnerability, and helplessness. Her ability to cope with the perpetual need she sees has not diminished her compassion and responsiveness. At ARISE meetings, Sophia is always attentive to the needs of the self-advocates. She has the capacity to empower, encourage, and support all at once. Sophia has a way of providing informal leadership to the group, clarifying information and suggesting a direction while encouraging active participation from everyone. She has a sophisticated understanding of the service system that she conveys with sensitivity.

Sophia is devoted to the people she serves. In the midst of this staffing crisis, she assists the people who lack staff whenever she can. She has some thoughts on issues of dependency. Sophia said that though it may seem like an overwhelming responsibility to be a lifeline to someone's (with a disability) independence, she believes that the negative messaging about dependency needs has created unnecessary fear, discouraging people from entering or remaining in the field. She noted that it's actually a wonderful feeling to be that lifeline. Beyond salary, Sophia notes that there is an urgent need for reform. She noted that currently direct care staff are working excessively long shifts and without days off to compensate for staffing shortages. She would like to see a task force of direct care workers to advise on policy reforms. Sophia is looking forward to the virtual coffee hours when we can "invite people into relationship" with people with disabilities as a pathway to improving care.

Larry Spears, president and CEO of the Robert K. Greenleaf Center for

Servant-Leadership, discovered two previously unknown and unpublished writings, which spanned nearly 50 years. After examining Greenleaf's writings along with his published work (1970; 1977), Spears (1995) developed the 10 characteristics of servant leadership: (a) listening, (b) empathy, (c) healing, (d) awareness, (e) persuasion, (f) conceptualization, (g) foresight, (h) stewardship, (i) commitment to the growth of people, and (j) building community. Observations support that both Mike and Sophia are acting as servant leaders, particularly in these areas. *Listening well* is a strong component of ARISE meetings. There are mechanisms in place so that no one talks over anyone else. The meetings always start with a check-in and end with the opportunity for each attendee to offer a comment or observation about the process during the meeting. *Empathy* is obvious as one observes both Mike and Sophia listen to and comment on stories about care shared in meetings. There have been times when individuals have cried—primarily from being overwhelmed by life's difficulties. In those moments, both Mike and Sophia have set aside the agenda to offer concern, comfort, and *healing*. Mike and Sophia have an *awareness* of the local political structure and the workings of the Office for People with Developmental Disabilities and candidly share their insights. Each member of the group has grown in political awareness since joining. The members of this group have been encouraged to meet with local representatives and participate in press conferences as part of their *growth*. Finally, in terms of community building, ARISE is connected with other groups who support people with disabilities. The plans for a virtual coffee hour will extend these connections to groups beyond those composed of individuals with disabilities and their families. In this time of critical need for reform of caregiving, it is vital to involve the larger community. We need to actively engage members of our community in crucial conversation about the moral and social imperative to care for our most vulnerable people.

The Lunch and Learn Project

Members of ARISE and L'Arche Buffalo and Western New York began with a commitment to sponsor the work of the Caring Majority, who are in the midst of a major campaign to raise the minimum wage of direct care workers in New York State by 150%, bringing the starting salary from $12.50 to $22.50 per hour. This is an urgent call to action prompted by the critical shortage of home health care staff. The Caring Majority was seeking local sponsors for social media events to garner support from New York State Legislators. Following discussion with all stakeholders, it was determined that ARISE, Voice Buffalo, and Friends of L'Arche would sponsor this effort and concentrate on this work as the initial focus of our coffee hours.

We mobilized letter-writing campaigns, held Zoom meetings, and contacted local legislators. Within two months, two powerful members of the New York State Legislature committed to signing on to support the Fair Pay for Home Care bill from a region of the state that lacked sufficient support for the bill. It is anticipated that the influence of these two legislative members will garner the support of other legislators as well. Work continues through letter-writing campaigns and email blasts and will extend to the recruitment of community members through subsequent coffee hours.

Our coffee hours will begin with the congregations that are aligned with Voice Buffalo. We have chosen faith communities because, in the words of Victoria Loorz, co-founder of the Wild Church Network, "Religion's true purpose is to restore our relationships with each other and the earth."

> The word *religion*, at its roots, means *re*, "again," and *ligios*, "connection," like ligaments. Religion is meant to offer us support to *connect again* what has been separated. Apparently, we need constant reminders to continually reconnect with the fullness of life, the whole, the holy. What we've created is more like *disligion*: disconnection from people and species unlike us. When religion loses its purpose and colludes with the forces of separation instead, it becomes irrelevant and even irreverent. (Loorz, 2021, p. 19)

Each session will have a story of a person needing or giving care. Our culture is defined around stories, so we hope to build a larger story of caring communities based in kindness and competence. We will educate our participants about our service systems and how we can partner with these systems to create webs of support in our communities. Most importantly, we want to change the messaging around caregiving. We need new thinking about how to care so that we can reconstruct it as meaningful and life giving rather than burdensome and limiting. Each of us has gifts to give that can lead to inclusive, hospitable communities where we develop true awareness of the needs of all our people.

The people of ARISE and L'Arche are what McKnight and Block (2012) called *community connectors*. They believe in and value community, are active in inviting people to join them, and graciously contribute their time and talents. Both L'Arche and ARISE are subcultures trying to close the social distance described by Tronto (1993) that defines disability in our culture by creating small intentional communities of care. Yet little is known about these efforts. L'Arche was founded over 50 years ago and remains largely invisible. The work of these communities has been transformative for the people they touch, but their reach is too limited by dominant cultural voices that promote independence and disconnection. Our coffee hours hope to shine a light on the lens of looking at each other from a perspective of care and, furthermore, to insist that our public policies reflect our universal need for care. Nel Noddings (2002), a prominent contributor to discourse on caregiving, proposed that the values and behaviors that inform ideal caregiving in the home can be extended to guide social policy. She contends that these ideals are fluid except for one fixed element—every member of a caring home (and I would add, a caring society) can count on the response, "I am here," when he or she calls.

Book Study on the Spirituality of Care

Friends of L'Arche has designed a book study for the virtual coffee hour. In a letter to Robert Ellsberg (2020), Pope Francis presented a compelling rationale for using books as a tool of inspiration for social change.

> We never come out of any crisis the same: either we come out better or worse, but never the same; and that will depend, to a large extent, on our capacity to cultivate—especially in the younger generations—an imagination that would help them believe that another way of writing history is possible. We need to recover memory and give voice to those who made our history great, a history that is glorious because it was forged in sacrifices, in daily struggles, in the lives given that believed in the dream of God. How good it made me feel to remember the Servant of God Dorothy Day who found in the Gospels and in the lives of the saints the source of inspiration that marked all her life and mission.

> I believe that reading, in that sense, can have a powerful role and become a compass that points the way, guides and allows us to cultivate a spirit capable of moving toward great goals that embrace the good that awaits us all. In this sense, I encourage you to continue your work in that difficult but important and delicate task of creating accompanying volumes that give flight to the spirit and help reach the places where new narratives and paradigms are being formed (Evangelii Gaudium 74). The health of a culture is also measured by its capacity to pool its best resources and awaken the best talents to create networks of solidarity that allow us creatively to build new alternatives to what affects us today. (Pope Francis)

Conversations about how we care for one another are so important, especially at this time when so many people need care. In the absence of a commitment to care from our communities, we will enter a care deficit that will seriously jeopardize the well-being of our people. Care work has been ignored for a long time in our culture. The emphasis on materialism and independence in our country has resulted in a devaluation of the work that negatively affects both the people who need and the people who give care. Currently, there is a great deal of emphasis on raising the wages of direct care workers, which is clearly important, but not enough. We believe that creating a space for critical conversations about the spirituality of giving and receiving care that emphasizes the well-being of both caregivers and care receivers is essential to address this current crisis.

Our goals are

- to engage faith communities in discussion of the spirituality of care,
- to discuss the need for an Ethic of Care to inform our public policies,
- to inform the community of the staffing crisis impacting our most vulnerable people,
- to enlist faith community support in advocacy for caregivers and care receivers, and
- to create small intentional communities of care.

Our book selections are

- *The Spirituality of Caregiving* by Henri Nouwen,
- *Adam: God's Beloved* by Henri Nouwen,

- *The Age of Dignity* by Ai-Jen Poo, and
- *The Abundant Community* by John McKnight and Peter Block.

This book study will be initially offered to the faith communities that are part of Voice Buffalo. From there we will promote the study to other interested organizations. Our dependency on the marketplace for care has reduced our capacity for kindness, compassion, civility, and generosity. In our consumer-directed society, we have distanced ourselves from care-for others and our world. We hope to heighten the collective capacity for care by awakening what is dormant in our collective lives. Though we had hoped to hold in-person gatherings, promoting hospitality among participants, we can also generate the advantages of remote discussions. For persons with disabilities and those giving care, transportation issues and care responsibilities often isolate and create limits to participation. The opportunity for remote discussion has the potential to expand participation and broaden our reach.

Conclusion

In a democracy, we have the power to create a vision of a culture of connection and caring. "Just imagine: What if nine out of ten change initiatives, in our organizations or in our societies, were driven by excitement, by the idea that this would serve somebody in a different way, that this would give us a better way of living? This would be very different from crisis and fear, our current primary motivators for change" (Greenleaf, 1977, p. 348.) In the framework of relationship-based organizing suggested by McKnight and Block (2012), we are asking people to come together from a perspective of community abundance, focusing on possibility rather than scarcity.

We need support for our most vulnerable people. As Kittay (2021) noted, "We need political structures and social policies that make accommodating the needs of people with disabilities a nonnegotiable demand in a wealthy society" (p. 43). Living with disability will always have an element of precariousness. It does not need to result in a state of precarity. Likewise, there is absolutely no reason that choosing caregiving work or being a family caregiver should push anyone into a state of precarity. So, how do we get there?

The project envisioned by ARISE and Friends of L'Arche Buffalo and Western New York looks to faith communities as places to build support for the adoption of an ethic of care to guide the political process. While there are instances today where faith communities seem to be more aligned with neoliberal values, there are those who support actions that are consistent with the values described here.

L'Arche and ARISE manifest an ethic of care. Both communities illustrate the value of people with and without disabilities working together to create meaningful lives. They are small movements compared to the larger forces at play but are nevertheless important for the values they embody. L'Arche has been in existence for over 50 years. There are small communities scattered throughout this country and the world. There are currently more communities in formation that are bringing innovative partnerships and ideas about care to their communities. The work done by L'Arche and ARISE as well as the theories of care and compassionate relational development need to become more common in public discourse. Caring Across the Generations, an advocacy organization, has developed a policy paper for building a care infrastructure. *The Age of Dignity*, authored by Ai-Jen Poo, offers inspirational and exciting ideas for care options that benefit both caregivers and care receivers.

Within the past several years there has been a growing recognition that family and paid professionals need to form partnerships to improve the quality of life for care recipients and extend the resources available for caregiving (Nerney, 2003). This strategy is also a means of merging services and care for the common good. In essence, we are combining two distinct institutions with distinct cultures—that of the family and that of paid care providers. This new form of caregiving is freighted with complexity. It is gendered, and it is informed by a confluence of potent ideological structures that define our responses to those who need care. There are critical social justice issues regarding gendered, class-based inequalities that position caregivers in poorly compensated, devalued working conditions, negatively affecting the quality of care.

COVID-19 has laid bare the inequities in our system, particularly for the vulnerable, that include an ever-expanding swath of people in America. In fact, COVID-19 made us all vulnerable; however, some of us have the protective resources to minimize our vulnerability while others endure fear, isolation, and need. There is a particular concern for adults with disabilities in this time of profound uncertainty.

In the words of Jim Wallis (2014), founder of the Sojourner's ministry,

> I believe the moral prerequisite for solving the deepest problems this country and the world now face is a commitment to an ancient idea whose time has urgently come: the common good ... It is time to reclaim the neglected common good and learn how faith might help, instead of hurt, in that important task. Our public life could be made better, even transformed or healed, if our religious traditions practiced what they preached in our personal lives: in our families' decisions; in our work and vocations; in the ministry of our churches, synagogues and mosques; and in our collective witness. In all these ways we can put the faith's community's influence at the service of this radical neighbor-love that is both faithful to God and the common good. (p. 3)

Whitney Walker, the executive director of Voice Buffalo, once commented that "Advocacy is driven by love." This sentiment can turn us from desperation to aspiration. Nussbaum (2013) noted that even in stable democracies there are daily stories of many emotions expressed regularly—anger, fear, sympathy, envy, grief, and many forms of love. These emotions can add strength and intensity, or they can derail us on our path to an inclusive, equitable society. What if we were to adopt an attitude of "revolutionary love" as Valerie Kaur (2020. p) describes it? In her work, she likens this process to the labor of birth—in this case, giving birth to a new form of caring communities.

So, where do families turn? They turn to their communities. It will take time. If we can create small, virtual, intentional communities of care where we offer stories of people who give and need care and have crucial conversations about the spirituality of care and the importance of an ethic of care in forming our responses to our vulnerable people, perhaps we can infuse this process with excitement and the possibility of a better future for everyone.

End Note

[1] In a landmark court case in 1999, Olmstead v. L.C., the U. S. Supreme Court ruled that unnecessary institutionalization of people with disabilities constitutes discrimination and violates the Americans with Disabilities Act of 1990.

Meet the Author

Maggie Buckley, PhD is a Fellow at the Institute for Social Innovation at Fielding Graduate University where she earned a doctorate in human development. She currently serves as executive director of Transforming Care, a nonprofit organization dedicated to the creation of sustainable supports for individuals who need long term care as well as their families and caregivers, so they can access the critical spiritual, material, and social resources needed to thrive in their homes and communities. She is mobilizing community resources to found a L'Arche community in the Buffalo Western New York area. L'Arche is an international federation where people with and without disabilities share life and friendship in community. Maggie previously authored "From Risk to Resilience: Promoting Positive Family Adaptation through Self-Determination" in *Mental Health and Wellness Supports for Youth with IDD* (Baker & Bloomberg, 2013). transformcarenow@gmail.com

References

Abel, E. K. (2000). *Hearts of wisdom: American women caring for kin 1850-1940.* Harvard University Press.

Baart, Andries. 2021. Precariousness, precarity, precariat, precarization and social redundancy: A substantiated map for the ethics of care. In M. Hamington & M. Flower (Eds.), *Care ethics in the age of precarity,* (pp. 91–119). University of Minnesota Press.

Bellah, R. N., Madsen, R., Sullivan, W., Swidler, A., & Tipton, S. (1985). *Habits of the heart: Individualism and commitment in American life.* Harper & Row.

Bellah, R. N., Madsen, R., Sullivan, W. M., Swidler, A., & Tipton, S. (1991). *The good society.* Alfred Knopf.

Benhold, K. (2006, March 7). From afar, money maker and mother. *New York Times.*

Blustein, J. (1991). *Care and commitment.* Oxford University Press.

Boyle, G. (2021). *The whole language: The power of extravagant tenderness.* Avid Reader Press/Simon & Schuster.

Brugere, F. (2020). Caring democracy as a solution against neoliberalism and populism. In L. Ward & P. Urban (Eds.), *Care ethics, democratic citizenship and the state* (pp. 137–159). Springer International Publishing.

Butler, J. (2010). *Frames of war: When is life grievable.* Verso.

Chatzidakis, A., Rottenberg, C., Litter, J., Hakim, J., & The Care Collective. (2020). *The care manifesto: The politics of interdependence.* Verso Books.

Chidambaram, P. (2020, April 23). State reporting of cases and deaths due to Covid

19 in long-term care facilities. KFF. https://www.kff.org/coronavirus-covid-19/issue-brief/state-reporting-of-cases-and-deaths-due-to-covid-19-in-long-term-care-facilities/

Coleman, J. (1988). Social capital in the creation of human capital. *American Journal of Sociology, 94,* 95–120.

Fisher, B., & Tronto, J. C. (1990). Toward a feminist theory of caring. In E. K Abel & M. K. Nelson (Eds.), *Circles of Care* (pp. 35–62). SUNY Press.

Geysen, G. (2001). Burnout in the human services with developmentally disabled adults: An investigation of the role of social responsibility and adult attachment style. *Dissertation Abstracts International Section B: The Sciences and Engineering, 62*(1-B), 547.

Greenleaf, R. K. (1970). *The servant as leader*. The Robert K Greenleaf Center.

Greenleaf, R. K. (2002). *Servant leadership: A journey into the nature of legitimate power and greatness* (L. C. Spears, Ed.). Paulist Press.

Haigler, D., Mims, K., & Nottingham, J. (1998). *Caring for you: Caring for me*. Rosalynn Carter Institute.

Hooyman, N., R., & Gonyea, J. (1995). *Feminist perspectives on family care: Policies for gender justice*. Sage.

Hole, R & Stainton, T. (2020). COVID 19: The precarity of families and disability. *Child & Youth Services, 41*(3), 266–268, https://doi.org/10.1080/0145935X.2020.1834997

Kaur, V. (2020). *See no stranger: A memoir and manifesto of revolutionary love*. Random House Publishing Group.

Kittay, E. F. (2021). Precarity, precariousness and disability. In M. Hamington & M. Flower (Eds.), *Care Ethics in the Age of Precarity* (pp.19–47). University of Minnesota Press.

Llana, S. M. (2006, March 6). Global stopgap for US nurse deficit. *Christian Scientist Monitor.*

Loorz, Victoria. (2021). *Church of the Wild: How nature invites us into the sacred.* 1517 Media.

Lynch, K. (2007). Love labour as a distinct and non-commodifiable form of care labour. *The Sociological Review, 55*(3), 550–570.

McDonald, K., Fialka-Feldman, M., A. Barko, A., & Burgdorf, M. (2020). Legal, ethical, and social issues affecting the lives of people with intellectual and developmental disabilities. In L. M. Glidden, L. J. Abbeduto, L. L. McIntyre, & M. J. Tasse (Eds,), *American Psychological Association handbook on intellectual and developmental disabilities*. American Psychological Association.

McKnight, J., and Block, P. (2012). *The abundant community: Awakening the power of families and neighborhoods*. Berrett-Koehler,

Miller, J. B. (1976). *Toward a new psychology of women*. Beacon Press.

Miller, S. C. (2021). Neoliberalism, moral precarity and the crisis of care. In M. Hamington & M.Flower (Eds.), *Care ethics in the age of precarity* (pp. 48–67). University of Minnesota Press.

Miller, J. B., & Stiver, I. P. (1997). *The healing connection*. The Beacon Press.

Nerney, T. (2003). The system of the future. *TASH Connections, 29*(11/12), 6–10.

Nerney, T., & Crowley, R. (1994). *An affirmation of community*. University of New Hampshire Institute on Disability.

Noddings, N. (2002). *Starting at home: Caring and social policy*. University of California Press.

Nussbaum, M. C. (2011). *Creating capabilities: The human development approach.* Harvard University Press.

Nussbaum, M. C. (2013). *Political emotions: Why love matters for justice.* Harvard University Press.

PHI. (2021). *Direct care workers in the US: Key facts 2021*. PHInational.org. https://www.PHInational.org

Proia, O. (2021, December 2). *It's life or death: Need for more home health care workers increases.* WKBW. https://www.wkbw.com/news/local-news/its-life-or-death-need-for-more-home-health-care-workers-increases

Rothman, S. (2004). Family caregiving in New England. In C. Levine & T. Murray (Eds.), *The cultures of caregiving: Conflict and common ground among families, health professionals and policy makers* (pp. 57–69). Johns Hopkins University Press. http://neolib.uga.edu/neoliberalism-introduction.php

Spears, L. C. (1995). *Reflections on leadership: How Robert K. Greenleaf's theory of servant leadership influenced today's top management thinkers.* John Wiley & Sons.

Surrey, J. (1991). The self in relation. In J. Jordan, A. Kaplan, J. B. Miller, I. Stiver, & J. Surrey (Eds.), *Women's growth in connection* (pp. 51–66). The Guilford Press.

Tronto, J. C. (2013). *Caring democracy: Markets, equality and justice.* New York University Press.

Tronto, J. C. (2015). *Who cares*. Cornell University Press.

Waerness, K. (1987). On the rationality of caring. In A. S. Sasson (Ed.), *Women and the state: The shifting boundaries of public and private* (pp. 207–234). Century Hutchinson.

Wallis, J. (2014). *The (un)common Good: How the gospel brings hope to a world divided.* Brazos.

Yee, S., Breslin, M.L., Goode, T.D., Havercamp, S.M., Horner-Johnson, W., Iezzoni, L.I., & Krahn, G. (2018). *Compounded disparities: Health equity at the intersection of disability, race and ethnicity*. The National Academy of Sciences, Engineering and Medicine.

CHAPTER 6

LEADERSHIP IN SMALL COMMUNITIES

Laurence P. Gebhardt
Institute for Social Innovation Fellow

Uncertain and changing times in the 21st century bring various economic, social, political, environmental, and technical challenges—problems needing resources and issues needing research and deliberation. Chapters in this book share a range of scholarship applied to leadership imperatives to create new knowledge and solve problems. This chapter is a personal reflection that shares some experience about leading and facilitating change in a small American metro area over a 20-year span, along with descriptions of some community change initiatives and outcomes. Former House Speaker Tip O'Neil agreed with the phrase "All politics is local" commonly used in U.S. politics since the 1930s. The term "local politics" refers to needing community leadership skills to influence the allocation of resources (time, talent, money, land, etc.) to achieve social and economic justice and needed change. Leadership in these times can build greater participation, draw fresh ideas, and facilitate collaborative action.

The 2020 census reports that about 60% of the U.S. population lives in cities or towns with fewer than 50,000 people. Small towns can be in rural areas or suburbs of larger urban areas. Non-metro areas account for over 70% of the nation's land area. While some small towns are stable, most exhibit demographic and economic changes that affect diversity, equity, and inclusion. Figures 9 and 10 illustrate these population and land statistics.

My wife, Janie, and I bought our first house in Pocatello, Bannock County, Idaho in 1970, and then were nomads for 30 years with 19 submarine Navy and post-Navy moves in eight states and countries, and many communities. Most of these moves were not long enough for us to deeply engage in community

Figure 9

U.S. Rural and Urban Areas

Note. U.S. Department of Agriculture Economic Research Service [1]

Figure 10

U.S. Metro and Non-Metro Counties

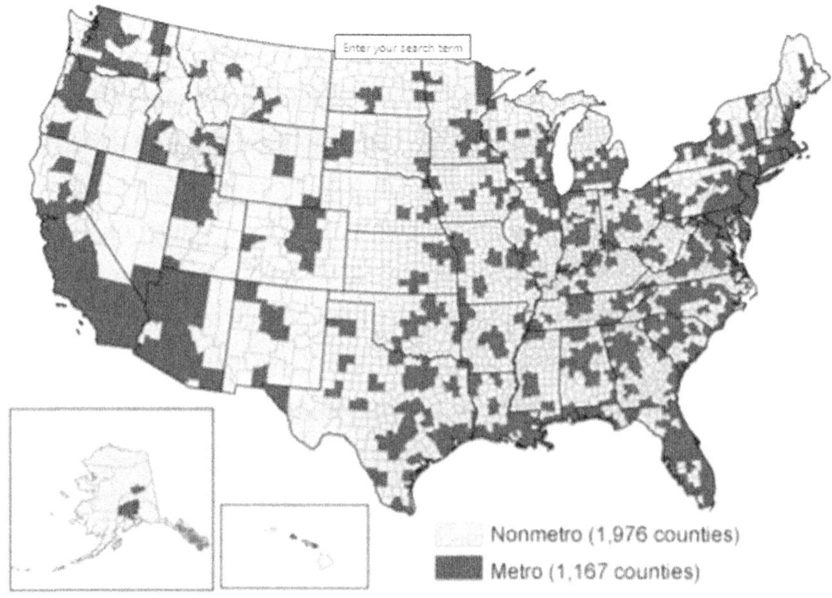

Note. U.S. Department of Agriculture Economic Research Service [1]

life. Our move before Pocatello was to North Kingstown, Rhode Island. Lasting a decade, it enabled bloom-where-you-are-planted opportunities for graduate studies, a transition from active Naval service, service in several United Church of Christ congregations (for Janie), community projects, and business development. We returned to be closer to aging parents, Janie's role as the local UCC Pastor, and my work as a periodic commuter. It also helped to start and expand commercial shipyards that were not in Idaho. Along the line, we learned of a range of injustices such as discrimination, inequity, bias, and exclusion that affected minority groups and members of non-majority social classes. This chapter summarizes our scholar-practitioner change initiatives and experiences in Pocatello, Idaho, between 2001and 2021. Our experience is that smaller towns are often defined by characteristics like a slower pace of life, family-oriented events, walkability, proximity to nature, and an authenticity (such as historical roots) that are not evident in larger places. Not only are more people choosing to move to these undersized enclaves, but more travelers are also coming. Some small towns have developed unique personalities that give them a cosmopolitan or an offbeat feel. We have lived in Utah, Mississippi, and Idaho. From experience and news coverage, we perceive that many small towns across America are in relatively conservative or red states where social change initiatives are resisted. I consider the term conservative to imply a belief that a better community preserves a status-quo culture valuing rights such as personal property and patriotism but a smaller government with little regulation, low taxes, and less diversity.

My engineering and business education focused mostly on quantitative data that led to explanatory knowledge. Bellah et al.'s 1985 book, *Habits of the Heart: Individualism and Commitment in American Life*, revealed how qualitative data adds understanding knowledge. Explanatory knowledge emphasizes facts; understanding knowledge includes beliefs, feelings, and emotions. My scholarship has blended cultures of inquiry into a systems approach strongly influenced by social science. The application of social science scholarship adds tools and methods to assist the would-be change agent in a small community.

I have practiced, studied, and taught continuous improvement in organizations. A quality process is plan, do, check (or study), and act, or PDCA. [2] For me, the research process goes in an iterative spiral manner through these (or similar) stages: observe, gather what is already known, and make logical but un-evaluated assumptions about initial conditions to get started. Search for underlying causes and logical corrective action; hypothesize a change process; test the hypothesis; analyze results; critically appraise them; apply the results; adjust or change the hypothesis assumptions; and repeat. In academic terminology, a hermeneutic spiral moves from text to context that spirals nearer and nearer toward explanation and understanding of significance for today. Can principles of organizational continuous improvement be adapted to social change in a small town?

My New England experience taught me that outsiders are not accepted as change agents. The rule of thumb was that a seven-year residence is needed before fresh ideas are even considered. Consultants often have this experience when their expert advice is left on the shelf with no real, lasting impact. Small town social change is then a marathon, not a sprint; however, change can be accelerated by building trust with constituencies of like-minded or like-activity-oriented people who can comprehend the improvement spiral process. Advocates for communities of diversity, equity and inclusion are both historic and contemporary.

Community and the Politics of Place

In about 430 BCE, Pericles' funeral oration, written by Thucydides, was to remember heroes of the Peloponnesian War and to praise democracy in the context of Athens as a great city. Pericles spoke that Athens is not conceivable as a great city without its citizens. Athens did not just exercise democratic principles in government but also in everyday life. Athenians not only enjoyed equality before the law; they were also equal when it came to opportunity. Being born poor or of low status did not prevent a talented man from getting ahead. Much of this freedom and opportunity was attributed to people obeying the law, but not just the formal, written laws. People also obeyed the unwritten polite conduct and tradition mores and were judged by their fellow citizens. The life Athenians enjoyed also rested on most citizens being knowledgeable about and involved in politics and a culture that sought to benefit all citizens, not just a select few. This system is a major point of pride for Pericles, and it is to protect this set of democratic virtues that he wishes his fellow Athenians to fight.

In his book *Community and the Politics of Place*, Daniel Kemmis (1992), a former Montana legislator and mayor of Missoula, Montana, advocated Pericles' understanding that strengthening of political culture must take place in the context of specific places and the people who struggle to live well in such places. In American colonial and frontier times, the need for neighbors' help in a rugged environment promoted community cooperation and tolerance. Since the nation's founding, our public life has been influenced by evolving special interest groups, education for citizenship shifting toward the American empire and corporate impact, the closing of new land frontiers, and the opening of new internet frontiers. Robert Putnam (2020) explored these trends in his book *Bowling Alone—The Collapse and Revival of American Community*. Might more public life, based on practices that renew the recognition and commitment of the community, develop in the arenas of economics and politics? This chapter reflects one small community's experience.

Social Science Concepts Aiding Change

A start point for leading small-town change is understanding the soil on which the new seeds of change are to be sown. U.S. counties are not simply red or blue politically; they have many differences. The Patchwork Nation project of the Jefferson Institute used demographic data to break the nation's 3,143 counties into 12 different types of voter/citizen communities (Chinni & Gimpel, 2010). Using Patchwork labels, Bannock County and the City of Pocatello have evolved into a blend of Mormon outpost, tractor country agriculture, and economic boomtown.

Pocatello, in rural Bannock County, is 160 miles north of Salt Lake City, Utah and 240 miles east of Boise, Idaho. The population grew from fur trapping, mining, agriculture, and the railroad beginning in about 1835. The town is built on land ceded from Shoshone-Bannock tribes in 1889. On the smaller Fort Hall reservation, Indigenous persons have sovereign land, separate from Pocatello, yet many are integrated into the community. Pocatello has grown to just over 50,000 people—a small metro area now more diverse than the state in general in part because of Idaho State University, founded in 1901. A lasting legacy monument celebrates late 1800s diversity including a dynamic population of African Americans, Mexicans, Chinese, Japanese, Italians, Greeks, French,

Irish, Indigenous persons, and other ethnic groups that provided labor to build Pocatello's infrastructure and the railroad that served growing mining and agriculture industries. The City of Pocatello is named after an Indigenous chief.

Idaho became a state in 1890. Boise Public Radio reported that Idaho's first 100 years resembled a wild-west, multi-party shootout where no one had a clear majority (Boise State Public Radio, 2014). The Idaho Women's Suffrage Amendment was on the ballot as a legislatively referred constitutional amendment in Idaho and passed on November 3, 1896. Idaho began its libertarian tilt toward the Republican party in the 1970s. Then the Church of Jesus Christ of Latter-Day Saints (LDS or Mormon) and other conservative faith groups left the Democratic party in opposition to liberal social issues like feminism, abortion rights, and environmentalism. Between 1990 and 2000, Idaho's population grew 28%. In 2001, Pocatello was majority LDS. Idaho's reputation as a conservative state attracted many from California, Oregon, Washington, and other states who were even more conservative than traditional Idaho Republicans. Since 2010, Republicans have held all congressional and statewide offices in Idaho. Since 2016, the state legislature has been 84% Republican, a super-majority. In 2001, Pocatello was 90% White. In 2021, Pocatello is 84% White, 9% Hispanic, 1.9% Indigenous persons, 0.8% African American, 2.5% mixed-race, and 1.5% Asian; 97% are U.S. citizens. Five thousand seven hundred sixty-two people live on the Fort Hall Reservation, out of which 1,826 (32%) identify themselves as non-Indigenous. The increase in non-White, non-Christian, non-heterosexual, and relatively poor populations raises White fears of status or privilege loss resulting in a range of aggression and discrimination. In 2001, the airport gift shop sold t-shirts labeled "Welcome to Pocatello. Set your clocks back 25 years." Those t-shirts are gone now, yet some status-quo thinking remains along with injustice such as discrimination, exclusion, inequality, disrespect, and even disgust that affect minorities and present opportunities for social change. Minorities (such as tribal members, LGBT, people of color, or non-Christians) have reported micro-aggressions such as negative comments or gestures. Their voices are often dismissed in politics and economic development, yet all people contribute to community vitality. Economic change that supports social change for justice can work in parallel.

A change agent can integrate into small-town constituencies to accelerate trust-building and understanding. Meeting and having conversations with one's neighbors can be a start. Moreover, attending organization meetings, listening, and volunteering (in churches, service clubs, arts enclaves, education groups, health and environmental groups, sports groups, and more) can help discern town values, build friendships, create networks, and build collaboration. Other thought leaders can be identified and invited to participate. In 2005, Rev. Gebhardt's church congregation encouraged her to engage more in community life. She was elected as a school district trustee, re-elected multiple times, and has served over 15 years. I joined Pocatello Centennial Rotary Club in 2001, served as club president, and have helped coordinate many community projects. Long-term committed participation gives authenticity to community change agents.

Small-town characteristics, including worldviews, morality, communications, and love are revealed through constituencies. In their book *Creating Paths of Change*, Will McWhinney et al. (1997) reminded us that initiating change produces imbalance and resistance to change in part because views of reality—our worldviews—are different as we ask: What is real? What causes the world (our town) to be as it is? What is the meaning of change? McWhinney et al. submitted that seeds of change begin to grow toward incrementally revitalizing and adapting an existing setting, or through renaissance (rebirthing) to something new. Change can be some combination of these two directions. The authors suggested that worldviews are a blend of beliefs, with some beliefs being more dominant than others:

- unitary beliefs such as policies, rules, creeds, principles
- sensory beliefs such as actions, behaviors, events, objects, data
- mythic beliefs such as ideas, visions, metaphors, dreams, inspirations, creations
- social beliefs such as values, feelings, preferences, motivations, attitudes

McWhinney et al. implied that the prospective change agent should learn what is most real to the community, learn how things usually happen, and learn what people's tendencies are regarding accepting change. Initial learning is helped by newspaper articles, letters and commentary, TV news and feature archives, and social media. Part of world view is morality—principles concerning the distinction between right and wrong or good and bad behavior.

Philosopher Jonathan Haidt categorized moral imperatives on a spectrum of liberal to conservative political thought in his book *The Righteous Mind* (2012). Haidt's data suggested that moral values of caring and fairness are important to those politically liberal, while conservatives endorse loyalty, authority, and sanctity. Haidt's Moral Foundations Questionnaire data from 130,000 participants yielded a set of curves (shown in Figure 11) that lead to convergence of moral values, a phenomenon that implies opportunity for civil discourse in Pocatello, a community that feels somewhat conservative. Pocatello faith groups, service clubs, and kindness organizations have given a greater voice to the more liberal morality of caring and fairness, using specific examples in ways that help inform then change more conservative hearts and minds toward justice. Examples of moral awareness are described later in this chapter.

Figure 11

Scores on the Moral Foundations Questionnaire (Haidt, 2012)

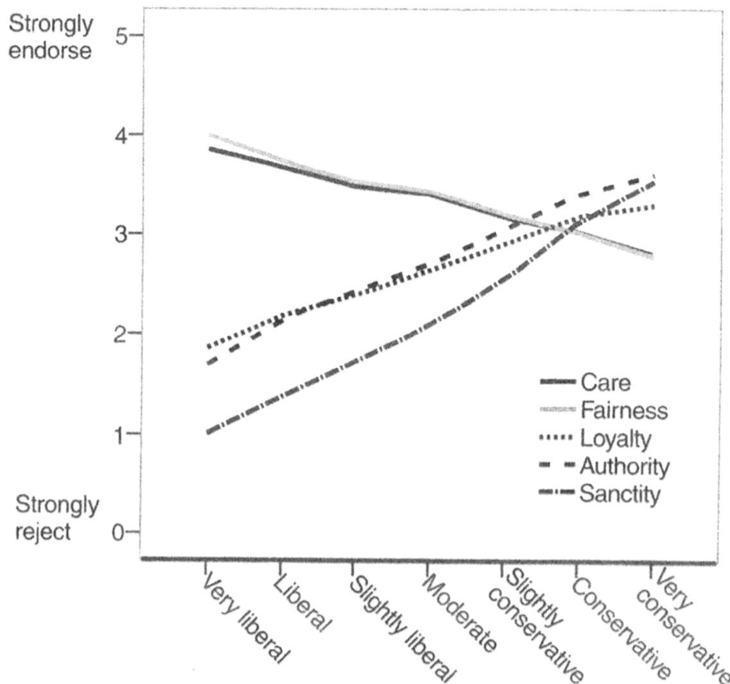

Source: Jonathan Haidt. [3] Used with permission.

James O'Toole, in his book *Leading Change* (1995), suggested that change agents must find ways to overcome the ideology of comfort and the tyranny of custom, which are the status-quo of the community's haves (wealthy, powerful, etc.) and key roadblocks to change. Overcoming status-quo thinking and habits can lift up those who are poor, marginalized, and so forth. O'Toole suggested that natural conservatism of groups can only be overcome by appeal to moral necessity where proposed change is perceived by the haves as righteous and a necessary step toward progress within an accepted moral framework. An integrity model shields against criticism around change matters. A change agent must learn community realities and struggle to discern, along with other community members, what are the just things to do and how to do them justly. Changes for justice can include elements of moral foundations including care, fairness, loyalty, authority, and sanctity. The change agent must articulate publicly the struggle to learn and do just, right, and common-good things using terminology that is change-oriented but not offensive. For example, O'Toole's words "comfort" and "custom" are easier for some to hear than White privilege or racism.

A related process is to help make sense of current conditions and possible changes. Sense-making can lead to meaning-making then to change action planning (Weick, 1995). For this chapter, sense-making is about making sense or having awareness of the external world of the community, while meaning-making is about relating it to our inner world. Sense-making may ask objective questions such as, "How does this idea affect the economy or environment?" Meaning-making may ask subjective questions like, "What does this situation mean to me," "How do I feel about it," and "What should I do?" In real-world practice, problems do not present themselves to prospective change agents as givens. They must be constructed from the materials of complex and problematic situations which are puzzling, troubling, and uncertain. To convert a problematic situation to a solvable problem, a change agent must help people make sense of an uncertain situation that initially makes no sense. When professionals consider what road to build, for example, they usually deal with a complex and ill-defined situation in which geographic, topological, financial, economic, social, and political issues are all mixed up together. Pocatello's non-discrimination ordinance development had economic, moral, and world-view complexity that required leadership change to help citizens and the City Council to make sense of it and then take meaningful action. Senior citizens can add years of experience to the sense and meaning-making process.

The JoHari window (Figure 12) reminds that much of individual-group communication is categorized into information that is known and shared by all, information that is kept hidden or secret by individuals, information that is blind or unconscious to some, and information that is unknown to anyone. A process of small-town change helps shrink the secret, hidden, and unknown so that all feel included and informed. An example of the JoHari ask-tell process is discussion by members of faith groups dealing with complex questions such as racism and LGBT issues. A short tutorial about the Johari window enables more open telling of hidden or secret personal biases, then shares how the biases were learned from relatives or authority figures. The goal of moving more information into an open and shared region can help a friend gently reveal how other friends have been blind to their biases, micro-aggressions, or attitudes of disgust of others. When hidden and blind information become open and shared, unknown information such as learning about the groups and individuals previously held in bias can become more familiar and appreciated. Storytelling provides a way to open and make information that has been hidden, blind, or unknown more accessible.

Martha C. Nussbaum, professor of law and ethics at the University of Chicago, argued in her book *Creating Capabilities: The Human Development Approach* (2011) that traditional economic and political change strategies ignore our most basic human needs for dignity and self-respect. Nussbaum suggests ten capabilities involved in a good human life. This chapter considers two of these capabilities to be most important in small community change for social justice:

- being able to imagine, think, and reason, use the senses and have the educational opportunities necessary to realize these capacities; and
- being able to live for and to others; to recognize and show concern for other human beings.

In a following book exploring emotions and the nature of social justice, *Political Emotions: Why Love Matters for Justice* (2013), Nussbaum asked: "How can we achieve and sustain a decent liberal society, one that aspires to

Figure 12
The Johari Window

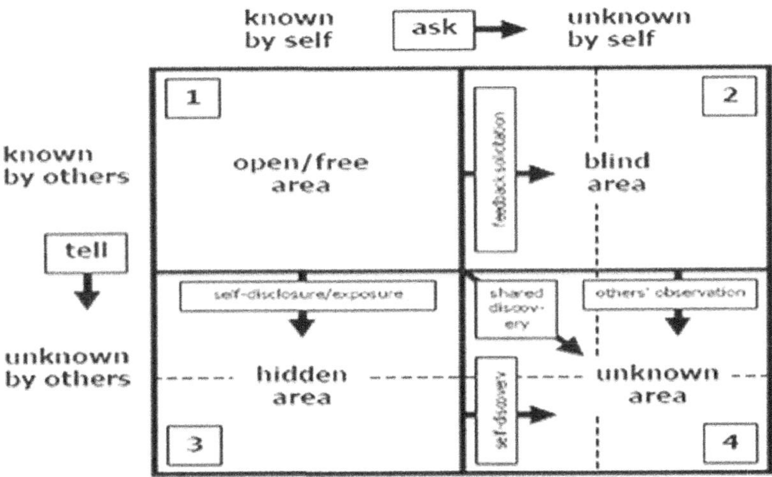

Note. Adapted from J. Luft and H. Ingham (1961). [4]

justice and equal opportunity for all and inspires individuals to sacrifice for the common good" (hardback cover)? One of her conclusions makes the case for love, where political emotions rooted in love—in attachments to things outside our control—can foster commitment to shared goals and keep the forces of envy, comfort, and disgust at bay. The word *love* is not in the general lexicon of Pocatello political and business leaders, but the related terms kindness, care, and fairness are often heard. For this chapter, the term love is more about affection based on admiration, benevolence, or common interests.

Application of Principles

The work of a scholar-practitioner is interplay between learning theory and principles, then applying those in initiatives and projects aimed at social change for justice. Can synthesizing worldviews, status-quo realities, moral values, and communications encourage a transition across a spectrum of emotions and feelings toward love as fairness, kindness, and caring that motivates and sustains change? For this chapter, emotion is a natural instinctive state of mind deriving from one's circumstances, mood, or relationships with others that can result in physiological sensation or feeling. Think of your physical feelings after helping another, or after being intensely angry with another. The least love-oriented emotions in a small town are ignorance and apathy—"I don't know, and I don't care"—along with self-interest. Most people can exhibit some sympathy—pity or sorrow—toward people with misfortune. Good storytelling can help move cognitive sympathy toward felt empathy, the emotional component of really feeling what the other person is feeling. Transitioning from self-interest to proactive respect and caring for others means experiencing emotions and prompting thought and action in compassion. Legend has it that Congressman Willard Duncan Vandiver said, "I am from Missouri. You have got to show me." [5] Showing and telling about justice or injustice may not be enough. It is also said that some will not recognize injustice, or justice, until they believe it exists. For example, micro-aggression against LGBTQ persons or people of color may be unnoticed by people who don't believe it exists. Action to encourage compassion in a small town includes helping people see and believe in the injustice, inequity, or lack of inclusion in their midst so they can take compassionate action. Actions that help people see and believe in justice as principles of diversity, equity, and inclusion can sustain compassionate action.

Moving into Action

The leadership frameworks that effect change in a small community are principally distributed, inclusive, and participative. Change leadership trajectory is toward developing organizational power with members as opposed to power over them, toward collaboration between organizations rather than competition, and toward understanding driven by shared stories, hard data, and common-good initiatives as opposed to special interests. Unexpected leadership in a small community can help citizens make sense of the current realities and facilitate a better vision acceptable to most of the population.

The domains of precarity (with its uncertainty and stresses) and need for change apply to public and higher education, law enforcement, faith groups, kinship groups experiencing discrimination/caste dynamics, and citizens with relatively low incomes, along with impacts of mental health, drugs, and COVID-19. Seven examples of projects or initiatives are described to illustrate application of leadership for social change and justice in this small metro community. Each of these descriptions implies a broader, deeper, and more complex story. Public information about these short descriptions can be found through the Pocatello newspaper, *Idaho State Journal*, whose tagline is "empowering the community" (Idaho State Journal, 2021), and other sources listed in the end notes.

Faith Groups

Many small towns have religious or faith organizations with relatively high participation. Most of the world's faith groups state a belief in fairness and reciprocity sometimes named the Golden Rule. Most congregations represent a vertical and horizontal slice of the community—from poor to rich, young to old, singles and families, disabled and abled-bodied, professional, crafts, and service jobs. There is often mutual respect within congregations where pastors and thought leaders can inspire people to learn about injustice then move toward compassionate kindness that stems from a love of humankind rather than from a fear of God. In Pocatello, several outreach organizations emerged from committed action by leaders supported by congregations. Examples included YWCA childcare, Family Services Alliance for victims of domestic violence, Aid for Friends homeless shelter, and Bannock House for estranged teens. Collaboration by faith groups can engage with larger and more complex issues. The Portneuf Valley Interfaith fellowship [6] expanded to include more than 20 groups, including non-Christian minorities such as Bahai, Jewish, Muslim, and atheist groups. Faith groups here operate a long-running food drive, Feeding the 5000 Families, and bringing the community together for Thanksgiving and Rev. Dr. Martin Luther King celebration. Church collaboration helped develop Peace Village, a multi-cultural spring break day camp for 8–12-year-olds involving stories, music, crafts, and games from other cultures. International students, Shoshone-Bannock tribe members, and others participated in Peace Village. Similar collaboration has continued an Alternative Gift Market that collects donations for humanitarian initiatives in lieu of traditional holiday gifts. Church groups have organized large scale public help such as cleanup after an urban-wildland fire that destroyed 66 homes. The stories of sympathy, empathy, and compassion by church people are modern parables shared through commercial media, social media, and organization newsletters that influence community emotions. Leaders in religious organizations often share stories and inspirations through membership in other constituencies. Faith group leaders fill some elected positions on the City Council and on the School District Board of Trustees, serve on various advisory committees, and as service club members.

In 2001, the LDS President Gordon Hinkley preached a sermon to the entire denomination advocating collaboration between faith groups. [7] He said, "But we shall go forward, returning good for evil, being helpful and kind and generous. I remind you of the teachings of our Lord concerning these matters. You are all acquainted with them. Let us be good people. Let us be friendly people. Let us be neighborly people. Let us be what members of The Church of Jesus Christ of Latter-day Saints ought to be." This outreach helped build collegiality within the Portneuf Valley Interfaith Fellowship with increasing participation in common-good activities. An example is that the annual exclusive LDS Pioneer Day Parade celebrated in July was expanded to become a community-wide Independence Day event.

Service Organizations

Small towns like Pocatello have service clubs. Most service clubs have mottoes that imply functional alliance with social and economic justice principles. [8] Service clubs have high ethical standards. Zonta's slogan is empowering women through service and advocacy. Rotarians say service above self. Kiwanis' motto is serving children of the world. Civitans are builders of good citizenship. Lions club members strive to be leaders in community and offer humanitarian service. In a small metro area, hundreds of community business and organization leaders meet regularly for acquaintance and fun along with gathering talent and funds to accomplish service projects. Like churches, there is a spirit of mutual respect which opens opportunities for thought leaders to propose service-type action and liaison with like-minded people or groups. The Pocatello Chamber of Commerce [9] strengthens our local economy, promotes the community, connects local businesses, advocates in the interest of business with government, and develops community leaders. Faith group and service club members form many of the chamber board of directors. Service clubs in small towns steer clear from overt political activities yet influence community culture.

Service organizations and service-oriented businesses have a strong voice in commercial media which in turn has influence with public government. Specific focus service groups can be formed by thought leaders who collaborate in small towns perceptions and government. In 2010, White supremacy groups spread hostile literature, CDs, and burning lawn crosses in Pocatello. Faith group and service club leaders formed the Pocatello 2Great4Hate organization [10] to help combat hateful activities, build organization responses, and engage local government and law enforcement. This effort, along with school district surveys led to public support for a non-discrimination ordinance described in the following local politics section.

School District and University

The Idaho constitution Article IX recognizes that the stability of a republican form of government depends mainly upon the intelligence of the people, so requires the legislature of Idaho to establish and maintain a general, uniform, and thorough system of public, free common schools. For 20 years, citizen-leaders have been elected as school district trustees who are forward-thinking, advocating learning today for the possibilities of tomorrow. For many years, residents have voted to increase their taxes for public education through supplemental levies. Opponents of taxes or public education have been unable to thwart local leadership. The district vision is that the community of children, parents, educators, and patrons work collectively, so learners have the skills to be successful contributors in a changing diverse world. As in other states, Idaho has challenges teaching history and principles of diversity, equity, and inclusion in secondary and higher education, yet many examples of principled leadership are on record. Some examples of marathon vs. sprint leadership help illustrate opportunity.

In the early 2000s, community leaders became more aware of bullying and the traumatic impact on evolving young lives. Leaders formed Healthy Pocatello, Healthy Youth using survey tools from the Search Institute aimed at positive youth development and stemming from the notion that understanding systems of access, opportunity, justice, and power is necessary to eliminate barriers. Conservative voices opposed survey questions about sexuality and religion. Survey work revealed that discrimination affected LGBTQ youths and youths in non-dominant religions. Over time, leaders organized two parallel actions. The first was groundwork leading to a non-discrimination ordinance described in the politics section below. The second was an education program facilitated by Steve Wessler, a human rights educator and trainer [11] specializing in conflict resolution. Wessler's work resulted in additional community, public school, and university surveys that included sexuality and religion topics, which informed thought leaders and led to a series of participatory seminars aimed at asking hard questions, such as, "What does your faith group teach about LGBTQ people or about people of different religions?" In Idaho, public funds will not cover community surveys or consultants for conflict resolution. This fact resulted in church and service club members obtaining a grant from The Pride Foundation, whose mission is building a better, safer, and more equitable world for LGBTQ+ people and our families in the Northwest. Multiple copies of books with lessons on dealing with diversity and bias were purchased. An example is Sondra Thierderman's *Making Diversity Work: 7 Steps for Defeating Bias in the Workplace* (2003). These initiatives must be repeated, refreshed, and reminded to avoid backsliding to biased or prejudiced ways.

Bad behavior in schools impacts learning and educators' morale. Conservative thinking in Idaho tended to move misbehaving youth into a pipeline of suspension and expulsion and a path from school to prison through the criminal justice system. Community leaders became aware of the evolving principles and practices of restorative justice that focus on rehabilitating offenders through reconciliation with victims and the community. Thus, training for school administrators, teachers, and law enforcement was approved by school district trustees. Success in schools also resulted in community application through the juvenile court system. Communication of restorative justice successes through schools, media stories, and service clubs has helped sustain and expand the program.

The Shoshone-Bannock tribes had for years asked for the Pocatello High School mascot, Indians, to be changed in part because other school sports fans often used derogatory or violent terms like redskins and scalping at pep rallies and games. Despite strong status-quo voices to retain Indians, the Board of Trustees adopted a school-recommended new mascot, Bison Thunder. [12]

Arts and Music Community

Pocatello has been a magnet for cultural refugees who have added leadership to the city, university, and schools' rich history of music, drama, art, sculpture, and more. Over two decades, significant investment has created a world-class performing arts center at the university and an 11,000-seat amphitheater funded and sustained with no tax dollars and coordinated by community leaders. A wide range of distributed arts are found here.

In the early 2000s, acoustic musician groups were growing but had no clear listening audience venue. A local church set up a recurring First Friday Coffeehouse in their gym in the historic downtown area, set small tables with red and white checked tablecloths and a candle, and invited the public and performers of music, poetry, and stories. The financial model split a small entry fee between performers and non-profit groups such as the Free Clinic and a shelter for persons without homes. Restaurant and bar owners invited performers to their locations. The First Friday event evolved into a historic downtown First Friday Art Walk featuring the growing number of galleries and antique dealers. More people spending time in the historic downtown has led to several innovative brew pubs, a robust farmer's market, and a weekly Revive at Five music and dance event. The feeling at these events is welcoming and inclusive. Acoustic music has long been associated with protest movements. In the 2000s, themes of protest music in Idaho focused on preserving the environment, wildlife, and, more recently, social justice.

Outdoor public sculpture is included in many public park areas, funded by the efforts of service clubs. Sculptures recognize historical icons such as Chief Pocatello, early railroad hobos, early pioneers, and trappers. A companion to sculpture is found in large public murals that depict human conditions, the environment, wildlife, and more. The Pocatello Arts Council believes that the arts create and unite vibrant cultures. [13]

Sports and Outdoors

Pocatello is a high mountain valley in a region with national recognition for mountain biking, running, fly fishing, skiing, and more. Local leaders from service clubs fostered collaboration to design and begin community trails and walking and bike paths—a greenway. This initiative had a slow start in the early 2000s, opposed by some who wanted no tax money spent and by some property owners who refused rights of way. Leaders formed the non-profit Portneuf Greenway Foundation, [14] attracted a community-wide board, worked on publicity, and steadily expanded the system toward 27 miles of ADA-compliant, 10-foot-wide paved trails, nature areas, fishing ponds, and Portneuf River revitalization in the greater Pocatello area. A spirit of intergenerational friendliness and inclusion is felt here.

A resident whose daughter had spinal bifida noted that she had no safe place to play outside of home property. He told the story in service clubs and church, which built awareness resulting in a community project to build Brooklyn's Playground, [15] an all-inclusive playground specifically designed so that the 11% of disabled students in the school district had a place. The community has raised over $500,000 of non-tax money and celebrated the playground's 10th anniversary in September 2021.

A young couple who are baseball fans conceived a Pocatello semi-pro team that could compete in the Northern Utah Baseball League. This initiative revitalized a strong history of community baseball to use a city-owned field with bleachers. Now in its seventh season, the Gate City Grays attracts young players and inter-generational fans. This venture has stayed financially solvent through sponsorship by businesses and service clubs. American Legion sells food and Centennial Rotary Club sells beer. Teenage youth buy photos of local sports heroes; octogenarians say that for $10 they get to see a great game and buy a hamburger and beverage.

Older and Kind Women

Part of the unexpected leadership for social change and justice in Pocatello came from senior women, referred to as crones by Theresa Southam in Chapter 2. Older women in faith groups, the arts community, service clubs, and political organizations have wisdom from living life. They often became voices for making sense of complex situations where conflicting moral differences, competing worldviews, and misinformation blocked deliberation and progress toward consensus. Wise women, perhaps perceived as community grandmothers or elders, had strong and confident voices in groups to challenge negativity and move the conversation back on track toward solutions. Wise women could recount personal experiences from Pocatello history that helped put current issues in the context of similar issue resolution in the past—a process that helped the community continue to grow.

Kind and caring voices, often women's voices, have helped move Pocatello toward a more loving spirit. In 2004, a grant from Robert Wood Johnson Foundation funded the Pocatello Called to Care organization. A director coordinated youth and adults to assist frail elderly, chronically ill, or disabled people to remain in their homes by doing routine chores such as yard and housework, help paying bills, and running errands. Subsequently, the Kind Community organization [16] was started by women from Pocatello service clubs with goals and objectives for a vision of the greater, kinder good of our community, particularly uplifting community youth. Kind Community organizes events, campaigns, projects, and relationships for our diverse yet collaborative city. Kind and caring voices generate community publicity in commercial and social media, which contribute to attitudes that are alternatives to violence, loneliness, gangs, and criminal activity. The impact of kind and caring attitudes is seen in community men who regularly volunteer to help one another in neighborhoods and on projects, such as rebuilding bicycles for youth.

Small Community Politics

Small community politics often deal with city infrastructure, development initiatives, and taxes. Issues do emerge that present opportunities for leaders to reveal emotions and take steps toward kindness and justice.

Add The Words, Idaho is an LGBTQ+ activist group and political action committee extant since 2010 that advocates adding the words "sexual orientation" and "gender identity" to the state's human rights act. After 10 years, however, Add The Words activists had been unable to achieve legislative support. The Pocatello surveys done by Steve Wessler in the early 2000s had revealed that LGBTQ+ discrimination exists in Pocatello. Advocates in Pocatello became aware that a city non-discrimination ordinance could be developed to protect city LGBTQ+ people and did not require state legislative action. An informal coalition of citizens began an education effort with youth, families, faith groups, and service clubs that evolved into the Fair Pocatello campaign. Understanding the sources of biases helped some change. Awareness of the impact of all citizens fully participating in the economy changed some minds. A proposed non-discrimination ordinance, aided by the city's legal officer, was brought to the city council in the Spring of 2013, with dozens of citizens testifying support against vocal opposition. The draft ordinance was voted down. Additional efforts and lobbying led to the ordinance narrowly passing in July 2013, after a council member had a change of heart and mind. Ordinance opponents petitioned to repeal, but voters upheld it in 2014. [17] LGBTQ+ residents' experiences in 2021 indicate the ordinance effort has had a lasting positive impact on quality of life.

Immigrants and refugees became an Idaho political issue in 2016 as Syrian refugees began resettlement. Evidence from the United Nations High Commission on Refugees revealed some 80 million people were displaced from their homes, and of these at least 26 million were refugees who could not return home because of natural disasters, economic failure, war, or discrimination. Pocatello's history of faith groups resettling refugees began in the 1970s but shifted mostly to Federal coordination in 1980. Anti-immigrant voices opposed to Syrians and Muslims raised fears and disinformation about refugee legality, health, morality, religion, and capabilities. A group of Pocatello residents became aware of the refugee situation through media reports [18] and contacted the director of the Federal refugee resettlement center hosted by the Community College of Southern Idaho in Twin Falls, about 115 miles west of Pocatello. Field trips revealed refugees were working hard to become new Americans, moving toward economic independence and social integration. Some refugees sought academic and technical education at Idaho State University in Pocatello. The support group BRIDGES Idaho was formed to help provide immediate needs such as clothing and furniture and long-term support, including job and education connections along with issue advocacy. BRIDGES helped refugees, often shy or worried about publicity that could harm family members still in dangerous homelands, to tell their stories. Commercial and social media interviews were arranged. Refugees spoke to faith groups, service clubs, and affinity groups such as sports and arts. Feedback from conservative community members told BRIDGES that learning about refugee realities and positive contributions changed their hearts and minds. In 2019, the Trump administration required states and communities to certify their willingness to accept refugees in writing to the U.S. State Department. BRIDGES lobbied the Pocatello City Council members and the mayor, who passed a unanimous resolution supporting refugee resettlement. Some negativity toward immigrants and refugees was felt by international students at Idaho State University, who partnered with BRIDGES volunteers to draft a welcoming city resolution, which was unanimously voted in 2020. The Pocatello mayor recounted that he received significant negative feedback about refugees yet had the political courage to continue support even as Afghan refugees began arriving in Pocatello in late 2021. The work of BRIDGES volunteers, who are part of local faith groups and service clubs, has influenced an attitude accepting diversity, equity, and inclusion.

In 2019, university students and others formed an advocacy group patterned after Black Lives Matter, naming their group Pocatello People of Color United (PPOCU). Students included Indigenous persons, Asians, Arabs, Middle East groups, and others. Some group members called for demilitarizing police and protests against law enforcement. Service club members' interaction with law enforcement, PPOCU, the local NAACP Chapter, 2Great4Hate, the city mayor, and other leaders created a forum to continually review and educate around human and civil rights concerns in ways that has built mutual respect and helped achieve justice goals while precluding most protest activity.

In 2017, a new city flag emerged from hundreds of design submissions. Central to this design are the three mountain peaks most prominent to Pocatello, which symbolize industry, recreation, and education. The compass rose is a directional emblem symbolizing Pocatello's central role as a transportation and trade hub for rail, road, and air. The design points to our past, present, and future. Its colors represent the region's agricultural ties and prosperity of the city; the snowy peaks show our mountain views. The form also creates an abstract arrowhead to acknowledge the area's Indigenous history. The design conveys upward motion, signifying positive hope for the future. The blue symbolizes the sky, and the blue line near the bottom of the flag symbolizes the Portneuf River.

In 2021, a process for an updated 20-year comprehensive plan, "Our Valley, Our Vision," began. The plan will reflect the voice of residents and will be the guiding document for shaping Pocatello's future. The planning survey asks six questions: What do you love about Pocatello? What are some of the biggest challenges facing Pocatello? What would you be most excited to show an out-of-town visitor? What do you find least appealing about Pocatello? What do you do for fun in Pocatello? What would you want to improve about Pocatello? The vision and corresponding action steps can provide a common language to connect various city plans, policies, and programs to the community's identified values. The plan will take nearly two years to complete and will include a wide variety of community outreach methods and collaboration between city leaders and community members. In 2022, Pocatello's political culture feels like a convergence of its geography and its citizens toward a community of place.

Summary and Lessons Learned

Smaller communities present needs and opportunities for change to improve quality of life and elements of justice. Those communities face uncertain or unpredictable reasons to substantially transform themselves or make adaptive adjustments to sustain life and relationships. Unexpected leaders can become influencers or agents for change. Unexpected leaders may be former residents returning to a hometown, persons transferred into a new town, longer-term or older residents becoming aware of community problems and issues, or young adults experiencing injustices personally. Unexpected leaders with a bloom-where-you-are-planted philosophy can achieve social change results.

Unexpected leaders often have little voice in a small community because they do not have experience or a network of colleagues to validate their trustworthiness. Building trust and associations can be accelerated. Archives of community newspapers, historic museums and monuments, and conversations with senior citizens can provide facts and understanding. Unexpected leaders who see and believe that injustice exists can learn about the community culture, dominant worldviews, most prevalent morality factors, and terminology that makes sense to residents to accept or resist change.

A small community often has several overlapping constituencies where sympathetic and compassionate people can be found. Faith groups often promote a golden rule of fairness and reciprocity. Service clubs advocate good citizenship. Music and arts organizations are usually diverse and inclusive. Public and higher education serve all. Sports and outdoor activities bring intergenerational people together. Business leaders who regularly donate to common-good causes can be valuable allies. Many older women possess great wisdom along with kind and caring outlooks on life and great political and public connections. Some elected officials in city government, school boards, or advisory committees believe that kindness and caring matters for justice.

Change in a small community is typically a slow process—a marathon and not a sprint. It takes time to find community colleagues who see injustice. It takes more time to overcome the resistance of people who do not believe that injustice exists in their town through discrimination, bias, or inequality. When constituencies of people begin to see and believe that injustice exists, pathways toward political or public action can move ahead. When a problem needing resources becomes more apparent, then collaboration to gather resources occurs. Small communities have issues, such as homelessness, where sustainable solutions require extensive research and deliberation.

The unexpected leader can add effective tools and methods to facilitate and sustain change for justice. Authoritative information is in the literature and case studies of social sciences. Examples are oral, written, and visual storytelling; exercises to understand personal morality and worldviews; strategies to explore sources of bias and overcome biases including unconscious or blind bias; group communications; innovations to promote learning; and celebrating successes.

This chapter highlights a scholar-practitioner model of a husband-wife team who returned to Pocatello, Idaho, adopted a bloom-where-we-are-planted philosophy, and worked to achieve changes for a political culture of justice not apart from the place itself. Other chapters in this book provide additional insights and strategies, such as building caring communities, further employing crone wisdom, team and public leadership, and technology application.

End Notes

[1] Source: U.S. Department of Agriculture Economic Research Service, in the public domain. See: https://www.ers.usda.gov/topics/rural-economy-population/rural-classifications/what-is-rural/

[2] PDCA (plan–do–check–act or plan–do–check–adjust) is an iterative design and management method used in business for the control and continuous improvement of processes and products. It is also known as the Deming circle/cycle/wheel, the Shewhart cycle, the control circle/cycle, or plan–do–study–act (PDSA). Another version of this PDCA cycle is OPDCA. The added "O" stands for observation or as some versions say: "Observe the current condition." This

emphasis on observation and current condition has currency with the literature on lean manufacturing

[3] Data from https://yourmorals.org/ . Figure 3 is replication of Figure 8.2 of (Haidt, 2012) Figure used by personal permission (email) from Dr. Jonathan Haidt.

[4] The Johari window is a model used to evaluate the extent of open and authentic communication between individuals and groups. The goal is to increase the amount of information about the self that is known both to the self and to others. The model was devised in the 1950s by U.S. psychologist Joseph Luft and U.S. psychiatrist Harrington V. Ingham. The Johari window is a term in the APA Dictionary of Psychology. See: https://dictionary.apa.org/johari-window

[5] Willard Duncan Vandiver (March 30, 1854–May 30, 1932) was a Democratic member of the United States House of Representatives from the state of Missouri. He is popularly credited with the authorship of the famous expression: "I'm from Missouri, you've got to show me," which led to the state's famous nickname, "The Show Me State."

[6] Faith groups in Pocatello collaborate through the Portneuf Valley Interfaith Fellowship. See: https://portneufinterfaith.org/

[7] Church of Jesus Christ of Latter Day Saints President Gordon Hinkley sermon and call to be neighborly at General Conference 2001. See: https://abn.churchofjesuschrist.org/study/general-conference/2001/04/the-work-goes-on?lang=eng

[8] For an article describing service clubs and their mottoes, see: https://www.britannica.com/topic/service-club

[9] The Pocatello-Chubbuck Chamber of Commerce promotes and fosters a favorable business climate through networking, advocacy, and educational opportunities for the benefit of Chamber members and our community. See: https://www.pocatelloidaho.com/

[10] Pocatello 2 Great 4 Hate has 400 community members https://www.facebook.com/groups/209581025729888 The group has completed a decade of activism. See: https://www.idahostatejournal.com/news/local/2great4hate-celebrates-a-decade-of-activism/article_0a2077ad-a5a6-52c8-9e4b-a19fa27b858c.html

[11] Steve Wessler is a human rights educator, trainer, and advocate specializing in conflict resolution. He works with schools, colleges, non-profit organizations,

healthcare institutions, law enforcement agencies, workplaces, and communities to prevent bias, harassment, discrimination, and violence. See: http://www.stevewessler.com/

[12] Thunder the Bison replaced Indians as Pocatello High School mascot. See: https://www.idahostatejournal.com/news/local/thunder-the-bison-mascot-makes-debut-at-pocatello-high-school/article_62e2a69b-22da-52c4-abaa-e128fe3e0d6e.html

[13} The Pocatello Arts Council mission is to foster an inclusive arts community that empowers artists and audiences to strengthen artistic ventures, expression, and community participation throughout the city. See: https://www.pocatelloartscouncil.org/

[14] The Pocatello Greenway Foundation works to develop walking and bicycle trails in Pocatello See: https://portneufgreenway.org/ Related work is developing a vision to clean and restore the Portneuf River in Pocatello. See: https://river.pocatello.us/

[15] Brooklyn's Playground is an all-inclusive facility created by community collaboration. See: https://www.brooklynsplayground.org/

[16] The Kind Community organization was formed by women from Pocatello service clubs and others. See: http://kindcom.org/

[17] News account following voter affirmation of Pocatello's non-discrimination ordinance. See: https://www.idahostatejournal.com/members/the-people-have-spoken-pocatello-s-lgbt-non-discrimination-rules-will-remain-in-place-officials/article_58f76e94-e177-11e3-9f4c-001a4bcf887a.html

[18] Media reports of refugee problems influenced public opinion in Twin Falls. See: https://www.nytimes.com/2017/09/26/magazine/how-fake-news-turned-a-small-town-upside-down.html BRIDGES Idaho formed as a refugee support organization aligned with the Federal resettlement center in Twin Falls and now assisting with resettling Afghan refugees. See: https://www.facebook.com/bridgesidaho

Meet the Author

Laurence Gebhardt, PhD earned a BS electrical engineering degree then served 26 years as a Navy nuclear submarine officer, retiring as a Navy captain. Following active duty, he earned a Master's in adult education and began a second career focused on defense conversion manufacturing. He completed his PhD degree in human and organization systems while starting up a commercial shipyard in Rhode Island. Dr. Gebhardt has helped expand and improve commercial shipyards in Massachusetts, Alaska, and other states. He led the National Shipbuilding Research Program technical panel for workforce development. His service activities in Idaho include being adjunct faculty at Idaho State University, past president of Pocatello Centennial Rotary Club; president, BRIDGES Idaho refugee support organization, and board member of Pilgrim Cove Foundation. He is a Fellow, Institute for Social Innovation, Fielding Graduate University. Dr. Gebhardt has received Rotary and community awards for service. lpgebhardt@gmail.com

References

Bellah, R. N., Madsen, R., Sullivan, W. M., Swidler, A., & Tipton, S. M. (1985). *Habits of the heart: Individualism and commitment in American life*. University of California Press.

Boise State Public Radio (2014). "How Idaho became a one-party state". https://www.boisestatepublicradio.org/politics-government/2014-05-13/how-idaho-became-a-one-party-state

Chinni, D., & Gimpel, J. (2010). *Our patchwork nation: The surprising truth about the "real" America.* Gotham Books.

Haidt, J. (2012). *The righteous mind: Why good people are divided by politics and religion.* Pantheon Books.

Idaho State Journal. (2021). Adams Publishing Group. https://www.idahostatejournal.com/

Kemmis, D. (1992) *Community and the politics of place*. University of Oklahoma Press.

Luft, J., & Ingham, H. (1961).The johari window. *Human Relations Training News, 5*(1), 6–7.

McWhinney, W., Webber, J. B, Smith, D. M., & Novokowsky, B. J. (1997). *Creating paths of change: Managing issues and resolving problems in organizations* (2nd ed.). Sage Publications.

Nussbaum, M. C. (2011). *Creating capabilities: The human development approach.* Harvard University Press.

Nussbaum, M. C. (2013). *Political emotions: Why love matters for justice.* Belknap Press.

O'Toole, J. (1995). *Leading change: Overcoming the ideology of comfort and the tyranny of custom.* Jossey-Bass.

Putnam, R. D. (2020). *Bowling alone: The collapse and revival of American community.* Simon & Schuster.

Thiederman, S. (2003). *Making diversity work: 7 steps for defeating bias in the workplace*. Kaplan.

Weick, K. E. (1995). *Sense-making in organizations.* Sage Publications.

Chapter 7

Ujasiri As Leadership Capacity: Enhancing People's Power to Protect Women and Children from Violence

Kate McAlpine
Institute for Social Innovation Fellow

This chapter bridges the early chapters where precarity, social justice, and leadership are examined in community and educational settings and the later chapters where theory is set into action. In the early chapters the reader will have seen how unexpected leaders are railing against and resisting neoliberal systems and the institutions therein. In this chapter, the reader will learn of this same railing and resisting in Tanzania, as well as learning about the theory of *doing the right thing* and how that might be put into action.

Globally, around 1.7 billion children experience some form of abuse over the course of a year, inhibiting their lifelong well-being (Know Violence in Childhood, 2017). This chapter presents the concept of *Ujasiri*, a construct that emerged from Dr McAlpine's narrative research with Tanzanian citizens who protect children. Ujasiri is a core concept in her explanatory theory. It is the basic psychological process of doing the right thing (McAlpine, 2014) and is potentially key to transforming people into citizen protectors who prevent and respond to violence. The chapter also describes the first stage of a multi-stage action research project that extends the theory of doing the right thing and is currently being undertaken in Shinyanga district, Tanzania by the author and collaborators Raphael Denis, Mathias Mkude, and Janeth Semwene, all of whom are experienced community facilitators.

The action research seeks to identify, engage with, and learn from individuals who feel an urgency to end violence against women and children—drawing on a facilitation process called Theory U (Figure 13). This process enables groups to shift patterns of behavior by helping them to see the system in which they operate, to envision their desired future, to embody new behaviors, and then to explore that future through action (Scharmer, 2009). Cooperation, personal transformation, and collective action are built into the Theory U process and are key to its success. Theory U is an emergent strategy that draws on antecedent authors such as Paulo Freire, Myles Horton, Grace Lee Boggs, and Angela Davis. Our application of Theory U to prevent violence in Tanzania has global implications; for example, for the Sarvodaya work of the Gandhian movement in India, for Black Lives Matter in the United States, for aboriginal rights work in Australia, and ecoactivists in Honduras—all of which are united in their pursuit of peace and equality.

Figure 13
Theory U

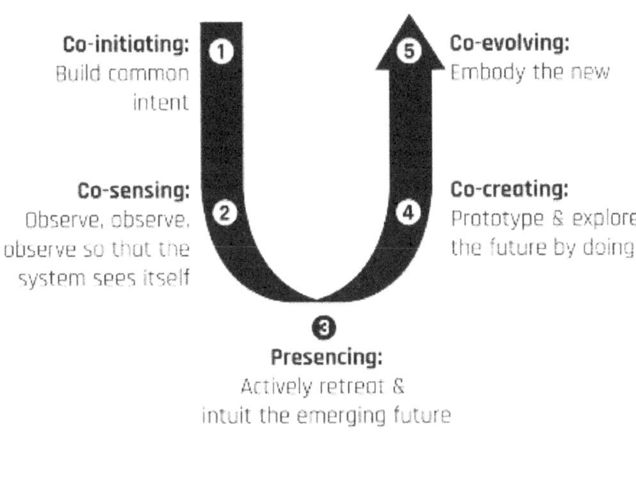

Note. Designed by Dr. McAlpine, Citizens 4 Change. Original artwork.

The action research process seeks to resolve the collective action problem of violence against women and children by cultivating the Ujasiri mindset. This will be described in depth later in the chapter and is an emotional capability whereby people attach to and love others (Nussbaum, 2015). The research process cultivates research participants' emotional, practical, associational, and affiliation capabilities (Nussbaum, 2011). Space is created for people to come together, to recognize and show concern for other human beings, and to engage in social interaction. People use their senses, imagination, thoughts, and reason; connect to their own experience; and empathize with others. They work together to engage in critical reflection as they conceive of a good life.

Nussbaum's capabilities theory is now a staple of human rights advocacy (Aviv, 2016), but it has been critiqued for being entrenched in liberalism and failing to take account of third world/postmodern feminist critiques (Vasbist, 2010). Nussbaum's high regard for individualism fails to grapple with the complexities of situations where agency is denied and where rights and laws are insufficient to drive well-being. This action research project is underpinned by a transformative feminist, intersectional, and integral stance that demands understanding of the whole system in which violence arises; the centering of power as a practical and analytic concept; and the scrutiny of power and violence from different perspectives (Atewologun, 2018; McAlpine, 2014; Wakefield, 2017; Wilber, 1996). We hope to counter Nussbaum's deficits by centering participatory strategies, explicitly engaging with voice and power, and in doing so demonstrating a decolonized approach to addressing violence against women and children.

This chapter describes the activities that we undertook in the co-initiating stage between June and September 2021. We started by conducting a household survey across Shinyanga district, asking people about their help-seeking behaviors. We conducted a social network analysis of these data and identified potential change agents. Finally, we facilitated a workshop with the most centrally connected individuals, where they explored their blind spots and determined the fundamental social problems that they want to resolve with the action research (Figure 14). These are the people that we call *The Backbone*. The group of 54 people consists of a mix of citizens who represent the government, holding as they do positions as village leaders or employment as public servants, and others who have no formal position in their communities but who are respected by their peers. Men and women are equally represented within the group, but there is no participation by children or young adults.

Figure 14
The Backbone at the Co-Initiating Workshop

Source: Kate McAlpine, Citizens 4 Change. Used with permission.

The Context for Ujasiri

Tanzania is an anocracy where power is not vested in public institutions but is instead spread amongst elite groups who compete for power (Marshall et al., 2012). In Tanzania, life is precarious. "The better-off solve their livelihood problems privately, while for the majority, life remains harsh, troubled and short" (Booth, 2011, p.1). In Shinyanga, the Sukuma tribe is dominant, practicing small-scale agriculture, livestock keeping, and rice cultivation as their main livelihood strategy. Universal education is a recent phenomenon; most elders have never gone to school, but in the last 10 years most young boys, if not girls, attend primary school. Opportunities to continue with higher education are limited. People value and adhere to their traditions, and the region has one of the highest rates of early marriage and female genital mutilation in the country (United Republic of Tanzania, 2016).

Across Tanzania, women and children are exposed to chronic levels of violence, and the circle of care around them is precarious. Sixty-four percent of children and youth in East African countries report experiencing physical violence; 22% report experiencing sexual violence; and 26% report experiencing emotional violence (Ministry of Gender Labor and Social Development, 2015; UNICEF, U.S. Centers for Disease Control and Prevention, & Muhumbili University of Health and Allied Sciences, 2011; United Nations Children's Fund Kenya Country Office, Division of Violence Prevention National Center for Injury Prevention and Control, U.S. Centers for Disease Control and Prevention, Kenya National Bureau of Statistics, 2012; Rwanda Ministry of Health, 2017). Close authority figures such as teachers and parents are often perpetrators of harm, even though they claim to disapprove of such punitive behavior (McAlpine et al., 2021).

Leveraging Ujasiri to Effect Change in Complex Systems

To initiate the action research, we conducted a household survey and social network analysis of 1,264 individuals in 18 communities in Shinyanga District Council in June 2021. Our intent was to identify individuals who are respected and highly connected to others in their community. We think that these people may be unexpected leaders within their community. If their energy and wisdom is harnessed, they may be the key people who act as vital connections within the system, ensuring that information about efforts to end violence reaches everyone in the community.

In the household survey, each adult participant was asked to name the people with whom they share a particular type of social relationship—the people that they go to for advice and information, whose opinions are important to them, who they trust, and to whom they report violence. For each relationship, they were asked about the person's age, gender, relationship, and what they considered to motivate that person—empathy, faith, hope, knowledge, love, morality, or something else.

The social network analysis identified 54 individuals who are centrally connected. This means that they have a high number of connections to others who see them as sources of support [1]. In September 2021, we invited this group to form The Backbone of the action research. They are the individuals who will provide the structure and energy to hold the change effort together on the ground. They are the unexpected leaders discussed throughout this chapter.

In this chapter, we present the concept of Ujasiri, which originated from narrative interviews that Kate and Mathias conducted with individuals who protect children in Tanzania in 2014 (McAlpine, 2014). Ujasiri is the Swahili word for confidence or bravery. Possession of Ujasiri differentiates people who protect women and children from those who say, "It's none of my business" when they see suffering. We learned that protectors' Ujasiri mindset is founded in a set of values about taking a stand as a responsible citizen. This chapter presents the toolbox of capacities that people who prevent or respond to violence—Protectors—draw upon when they navigate the dilemmas that arise. Given the challenges in mobilizing Tanzanians into collective action, the chapter concludes with reflections on how the Ujasiri mindset, which is currently understood to be an individual disposition, could be leveraged via The Backbone and the action research project in Shinyanga to catalyze collective action to combat violence against women and children.

Tanzania—A Country Where the Masses Live Precariously and Are Unable to Mobilize in Their Own Interests

Tanzania is a youth-bulge state where more than 50% of citizens are under the age of eighteen (Government of the United Republic of Tanzania, 2012). In 1986, Tanzania effectively abandoned the idea of socialism and self-reliance (*Ujamaa na kujitegemea*) that was enshrined in the 1967 Arusha Declaration. Instead, it moved towards a model of accumulation that hinges on increased foreign investment and exports, primarily in natural resource exploitation (Kelsall, 2003). The economy has shifted rapidly from a moral economy to a market economy (Manjolo et al., 2008) based on subsistence and cash crop farming, pastoralism, and a small number of urban service industries. A manufacturing base has never developed.

In Tanzania, the elite consists of a dominant coalition of the ruling party, *Chama cha Mapinduzi*, which is at the core of politics, business, and state bureaucracy. The ruling party espouses a contradiction. They claim the values of the open access state, such as institution building, accountability, and open governance, whilst behaving in ways that are typical of a natural state. In a natural state, the elite manipulates the economic system to secure the political order (North et al., 2009). In Tanzania, corruption takes four forms: privileging status, regulatory capture where special interests are prioritized over the general interests of the public, rent seeking where the elite obtain benefits for themselves through the political arena, and patronage. The rise of politics that is driven by money is systemic within the ruling party, motivated by a combination of need, greed, and accumulation (Cooksey & Kelsall, 2011). The state apparatus is characterized by little broad-based taxation, poor execution of policies, and poor provision of public goods. State institutions are inefficient and fail to generate loyalty. Parliament and the opposition are largely ineffective as a check. Civil society is weak, and the courts tend to be corrupt and do not constrain the executive branch. Yunus (2009) complained that in many countries people power has been replaced by money power, muscle power, and even firepower; and that is the case in Tanzania. Citizens in Shinyanga perceive good governance to be a joke, believing that they do not have any power over how decisions are reached and projects are implemented (Mesaki & Matotay, 2014).

Many Tanzanians are left out, with 26.4% living below the nationally defined poverty line (World Bank, 2021). Poverty remains an overwhelmingly rural phenomenon. The majority of Tanzanians are smallholder farmers, but agriculture is the least remunerative sector in the economy. Tanzania is classified as a poor to very poor performer in the provision of the elementary public goods that are preconditions for progress. The state seems unable to turn taxes, foreign aid, and investment into public goods in an efficient and effective manner (Booth, 2011; Cooksey & Kelsall, 2011). Mesaki and Matotay (2014) speak of a wall of silence that arises amongst citizens who fear the iron hand of the government machinery. People do not generally understand their rights and feel they have no say in matters concerning them. The fear stems from a belief that, given their economic situation, they won't be heard, and that if they do speak, they will not be taken seriously. This fear is often based on experience, because when they have tried to engage with formal channels, they have found them frightening. These factors combine to create a situation where the masses are unable to mobilize even though they recognize that their leaders do not have the interests of national development at heart. Shivji (2007) argued that civil society organizations have undermined and denuded traditional people's organizations, substituting themselves for the people. Associational life, the web of social relationships through which people pursue joint endeavours, is focused on small networks of friends that build on existing relations of trust.

Tanzanians do not habitually engage in collective action with others who do not share the same ethnic or religious background but may have secular or material interests in common. Hydén (2002) found only two associations of commercial farmers that indicated a readiness to organize and protest. Participants in Hydén's research explained that government officials are sensitive to open criticism and protest manifestations can backfire. Many villagers say that they have lost their faith in the merits of participation and collective action. Instead, they rely on individual initiatives to meet their needs, such as petty bribery of leaders and officials and working within their own social networks of relatives and friends (Rabe & Kamanzi, 2012). The elite continue to misappropriate national resources and allocate funds in self-serving ways. The masses continue to be left out of their own communities' development. Instead, individualism is on the increase and creates a situation where people do not stop to help when they see a woman or child suffering.

Violence Against Women and Children is Chronic, Normalized, and May Be Maintained by Social Norms

Searching for the conditions that describes a complete and flourishing life, Nussbaum called for "a society of citizens who admit that they are needy and vulnerable" (Aviv, 2016). Her capabilities approach is a theoretical framework for measuring and comparing the well-being of nations, listing ten essential capabilities that all societies should nourish (Nussbaum, 2011). Of particular pertinence to the core problem that this action research seeks to solve is the capability related to bodily integrity—to be secure against violent assault, including sexual assault and domestic violence. Violence in childhood inhibits people's ability to thrive in later years, and the effects of violence and toxic stress undermine the effectiveness of other social investments in education, health, and infrastructure.

Globally, one in three women have been subjected to physical and/or sexual violence during their lifetimes (World Health Organization, 2021). Violence and maltreatment of children costs East Africa over $20 billion annually and inhibits aspirations for inclusive development (Fang et al., 2012; Institute for Economics and Peace, 2015; Korir et al., 2016; Pereznieto et al., 2014; Save the Children South Africa, 2017). Inclusively developed societies involve people in the process of their own development and take seriously the question, "Does the system work for the many?" (McAlpine, 2020). The system does not work for the many when 73.5 million children in East Africa report experiencing physical violence, 26.5 million children report experiencing sexual violence, and 30.8 million children report experiencing emotional violence (Ministry of Gender Labor and Social Development, 2015; Ministry of Community Development Gender et al., 2011; Rwanda Ministry of Health, 2017; HakiElimu, 2020). Tanzanian children are chronically exposed to violence at the hands of close authority figures such as teachers and parents. In a recent study with children about their experience of violence in schools, 39% of students had experienced or witnessed corporal punishment and associated emotional harms (McAlpine et al., 2021). Thirty-three percent said that they felt like they were not important, 30% that their feelings were hurt, 30% said that they did not feel cared for, and 24% said that coercion force or threat had occurred. Children are often experiencing chronic exposure to harm, indicated by 53% saying that the harms they experienced or witnessed occurred more than once.

The circle of care around children is worryingly small. Children know violence when they see it, but 35% think that adults either approve of the harmful behavior, criticize it but do nothing, or just do nothing. Overwhelmingly, 87% of children know that many of the harms they experience are a form of violence. Girls seem to be more attuned to the existence of various harms but do not always problematize them as violent practices. They are also more attuned to the existence of emotional violence than boys, who are attuned to the physical forms of violence (McAlpine et al, 2021).

Violent behavior in school settings may not necessarily be caused by social norms. There may be many non-social reasons why teachers and parents are so punitive towards children, and our action research will explore those reasons in more depth as the project unfolds. However, the punitive behaviors that characterize children's experiences of school are maintained by social norms. Students' reference groups, the people whose views they value, are their parents and teachers. These adults are also perpetrators of harm. Students believe, from their lived experience, that harm is perpetrated frequently by parents and teachers, whose violence counters these adults' claims to disapprove of such punitive behavior. Students see that there are no real social sanctions taken against adults who are violent towards them.

Leadership in Precarious Times Requires an Appreciation of Our Collective Blind Spots

A blind spot is an area where a person's view is obstructed because they are physically and/or emotionally unable to go to that place and are consequently uncomfortable speaking about that issue. During the first stage of the Theory U process in September 2021, which Scharmer called the co-initiating phase, The Backbone mapped the problems in their communities, identifying those issues that members themselves were reluctant to acknowledge as being problematic. These blind spots need to be named, problematized, and resolved if the action research is to enhance power with and within women and children, as well as challenge others' power over them.

The Backbone used an integral framework (Wilber, 1996) to map their blind spots and to identify lines of inquiry that they wish to pursue in the co-sensing stage. In the domain of individuals' subjective interior—their emotions, faith, and sense of self—the question is whether women and children can identify and step into their own power. Nussbaum (2011) argued that emotions embody judgments about the world, and this research seeks to understand participants' emotional response to their own power and experience of violence. The Backbone believe that in their communities too many women and children's fundamental human need for love and self-expression are unfulfilled. The Backbone acknowledged that there is a risk that they ignore the agency of women and children and their potential to influence the behavior of others.

In the domain of behavior, the line of inquiry is what actions do individuals take? The Backbone explains that, in their communities, violent actions manifest in four ways: poor parenting and punitive treatment of women and children; a tendency to say, "It's none of our business" when people hear of instances of violence; a failure to adequately name different types of violence—gang rape, grooming—for what they are; and insufficient attention being paid to family bonding and togetherness. When violences are not named, they cannot be sufficiently problematized by the community and thus become resistant to change. This stalls any form of individual or collective action to prevent or respond to violence.

In the domain of institutions, including home and school as places where authority is exercised over children, the question is: How is the state's power used over citizens? The Backbone argues that corruption and poor implementation of the law undermines children and women's rights to safety. The needs of women and children are not centered as drivers of economic and social development and thus are given insufficient attention in governance processes. The absence of a circle of care and safety nets for people who are socially excluded exposes them to multiple harms. The blind spot that was owned by The Backbone was their own failure to empathize with fellow citizens who are economically and socially excluded.

Finally, in the domain of collective relationships, the question lies in how our collective power is used to oppress or emancipate others. The Backbone conceded that patriarchal authority in the home and society sustains oppression. But the blind spot persists; namely, a belief that violence is something that happens to others. Both perpetrators and victims are considered by their peers to be in some ways socially deviant.

In the last 10 years, anti-violence work in East Africa has been underpinned by a social ecological model that looks at people's risk and protective factors. Pease (2019) argued that framing violence against women and children from a public health perspective, using the social ecological model, exacerbates the existence of blind spots because it de-politicizes anti-violence work. He drew on his experience studying masculinities in Australia and the North and argued that violence is an inevitable consequence of patriarchy, of which there are five pillars: men's structural power over women, patriarchal ideologies, men's peer relationships, the exercise of coercive control in family life, and patriarchal subjectivities of individual men (Pease, 2019). The sponsor of this action research, Women Fund Tanzania Trust, is an indigenous organization that also believes that patriarchy and violence intersect. The co-sensing stage of this project, which kicked off in October 2022 and will run for 6 months, will explore if this framing of patriarchy and violence as inter-dependent is valid in the context of the Shinyanga district. We will facilitate dialogue with groups of women, men, government actors, and children, asking them about the nature and source of their inner confidence—their power within. We will ask also about their ability and experience influencing others and taking action based on uniting with them—their power with. This is about the form that inequality takes in their community, about social expectations on men's behavior and forms that male privilege take in the home, and finally about how men as individuals experience patriarchy in their lives.

Unexpected Leaders Do the Right Thing

Tanzania's nascent and ineffective formal child protection system requires that individuals take personal action to protect women and children. But only a few do so. Most walk past, trying to ignore the situation. They say, "It's none of my business" (McAlpine, 2014). The citizens who do identify as protectors face the dilemma of how to respond to suffering in the face of others' opposition and in the absence of a formal child protection system. They are required to answer the question, "What can I do?" Walsh (2006) argued that striving to answer this question becomes a value and a life assumption and "is a sturdy basis for a life well lived" (p. 152). He described how, when faced with suffering, we can respond in one of two ways. We can defend ourselves against recognizing the challenges and their implications, or we can face these twin challenges openly and live appropriately.

The core dilemma faced by people who take action to prevent or respond to violence is that they see the impacts of suffering but know that they will incur personal costs if they act. They face obstacles that include interactions with people who block their efforts, potential exposure to danger, challenges accessing support, and financial expense. Nonetheless, they intervene when they see a woman or child suffering because they feel an urgency for change, which stems from their Ujasiri mindset. Nussbaum places considerable value on the role of emotions (2015) as a driver of social justice. At its essence Ujasiri is an emotional response to others' suffering, and as such has relevance to similar upstander movements such as those inspired by Black Lives Matter and Generations Against Bullying, that draw on their members courage and strength. Figure 15 presents the genesis of the Ujasiri mindset.

The construct of the Ujasiri mindset emerged from the narrative research that Kate and Mathias conducted with child protectors as part of Kate's PhD study (McAlpine, 2014). The mindset explains why some individuals respond when they witness suffering and others walk by. Ujasiri is the Swahili word for bravery, but the mindset is more than the possession of courage. The Ujasiri mindset consists of protectors' moral codes. These manifest in three ways: as a feeling that "I can't close my eyes and do nothing," as a drive to do the right thing, and an aspiration to do one's best. The mindset is characterized by attitudes of

Figure 15

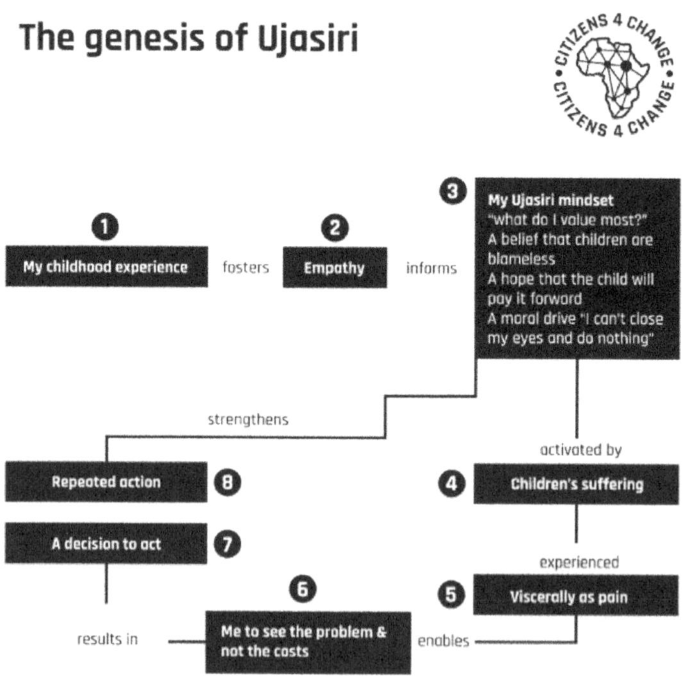

Source: Dr. McAlpine, Citizens 4 Change. Original artwork.

compassion, fearlessness, humility, and enthusiasm to jump in and give things a go. Protectors who have this mindset believe that education has inherent value and that children are a blessing and a national resource. They hope that the recipient of their help will pay that help forward to others. Ujasiri is latent until the protector is exposed to suffering, which they experience viscerally as spiritual pain. Upon witnessing suffering the mindset triggers action, despite the potential obstacles and costs that the protector may incur.

Empathy is a precondition for Ujasiri and is fostered in the protectors' own childhoods. In narrative interviews, they described their own childhoods in two ways: a childhood of love or a childhood of pain. As far as protectors are concerned, there is no middle state. Those who had childhoods of love explain that they saw others help their peers, they were cared for in spite of their parents' struggles, and they were demonstrably loved. Protectors who describe the pain of their childhoods speak of carrying its impact as adults. Both positive and negative childhood experiences foster an empathetic resonance with others. Protectors explain that their childhood experiences taught them the centrality of love. They have become sensitized to the struggles of others, and this can build an automatic desire to help (McAlpine, 2014).

Taking Protective Action Requires Improvisation

Because they cannot call upon the support of the authorities, protectors are forced to improvise as they act. Protectors deal with complex situations without always possessing the knowledge and skills that would help them make decisions that are in the child or woman's best interests. Protectors face obstacles that require them to answer these questions: Am I primed to hear a suffering child? Does my intuition tell me to get involved? How do I calm overheated emotions? How can I discover the truth? How do I tap into the help of the willing and persuade the blockers to support? What is in this person's best interests? In what role can I be of most help? (McAlpine, 2014).

Dilemmas emerge from the obstacles and questions that protectors face. A dilemma is a problem that offers only uncomfortable responses. In deciding how to respond, protectors draw on different strengths. And as they resolve the dilemmas, protectors build an improvisational toolbox. The toolbox consists of positive emotions of love and compassion; inner capacities of patience, persistence, hope, and trust; a positive attitude towards embracing action and the opportunity of being an involved citizen; knowledge of who to call upon; and skills that help the protector to navigate obstacles. In resolving these dilemmas, protectors draw on their cognition, spiritual development, interpersonal skills, and moral wisdom. As they repeatedly take action to prevent or respond to violence, they start to self-identify as protectors and build a toolbox of emotions, inner capacities, attitudes, knowledge, and skills that enable them to improvise more effectively.

Humans possess at least a dozen major developmental lines or intelligences. These include the cognitive, moral, interpersonal, emotional, self-identity, and values lines (Wilber, 2000; Gardener, 1983). All can be conceived of as strengths. Protectors draw on four developmental lines as they resolve the dilemmas that they face. They think. They tap into their faith. They use interpersonal skills. They draw on their knowledge and moral wisdom (McAlpine, 2014).

The cognitive line represents the types of answers that people give to the question, "What is?" It is the line that is drawn upon when protectors are asked to answer the question, "What is going on?" Protectors use rational, data-seeking, and analytic skills when they seek to understand the core problem facing the child or woman. But they do so without being conscious that they are seeking out different perspectives, weighing them and using the emerging picture to inform the action that they take. Protectors draw on their cognition because people cannot draw on a moral line without having the cognitive appreciation that one's actions have consequences. In answering the question "What should I do?" protectors draw on both their cognitive knowledge and their moral wisdom. Some consciously think about how to resolve the dilemma and draw on their intellectual resources. Others use their professional knowledge. Some draw on the tacit knowledge that they accumulated by listening to the stories of the elders through childhood. Others draw on their own wisdom.

Protectors draw on their faith and spiritual intelligence when responding to the question, "Does my intuition tell me to get involved?" They speak of how God builds their conviction that they will be successful, how they are using God-given talents, and how God helps them more broadly. Protectors use their networks to access advice, resources, and connections. They use their interpersonal skills to influence people within those networks (McAlpine, 2014).

As protectors intervene to protect others, they experience positive emotions that prime them to take more action. Love is supplemented by the protectors' inner capacities of patience and persistence, hope that someone will assist, and trust in their own abilities. As protectors act, they start to cultivate a positive attitude that embraces being an involved citizen. They possess a drive whereby they feel that they must take responsibility.

Protectors Transform as They Repeatedly Do the Right Thing

When a protector acts, faces obstacles, and confronts dilemmas, they start to build their improvisational toolbox. Protectors resolve dilemmas by drawing on their developmental strengths. As protectors repeatedly intervene to prevent or respond to violence, a positive feedback loop is created whereby they become more attuned to people's suffering, take more protective actions, expand their toolbox, and become increasingly competent. As a result, they are more successful and see positive outcomes from their actions. Their motivation to continue protecting increases and intervening in situations of suffering becomes habitual. Eventually, protecting others becomes the protector's identity and they start to answer the developmental line that asks, "What am I?" Interviewees in the 2014 study described themselves as *Warrior Activists for Children* (McAlpine, 2014).

Leveraging Ujasiri to Effect Change in Complex Systems

Given the documented challenges to mobilizing Tanzanians to take collective action, this final section explores how the Ujasiri mindset, which is currently framed as a disposition possessed by individual protectors, could be leveraged to support a broader social change process that resolves the complex problem of violence against women and children.

A complex situation is characterized by the involvement of multiple parties, ideas, and interests. The solution is not obvious; thus, a creative and emergent approach must be adopted. The issue of violence is complex in two ways. Almost every actor has been personally touched by violence, the legacy of which many still carry. The second area of complexity is in the nature of the stakeholders. Most citizen protectors, children, perpetrators, government representatives, and faith communities claim a commitment to ending violence but struggle to cooperate and to action the pledges they make toward resolving violence. The complexity navigator is a tool developed by Perspectivity (2020) that draws on complexity theory and provides a framework to inform the facilitation of processes in complex situations. The framework includes eight elements that need to be managed in complex situations. These are the backbone, urgency for change, shared ambition, responsive leadership, involvement of all, reinforcing actions, adaptive learning, and vital connections. More information about each can be found in Figure 16.

One element of the complexity navigator that particularly resonated with us is the idea of urgency for change. Part of the challenge in addressing violence is that everybody claims to disapprove of violence, but their values in action are often quite a different matter. After using the social network analysis to identify the most centrally connected individuals in the communities, we felt the need to better understand individuals' interests towards addressing violence. Government representatives and volunteers have recently been given formal oversight on child protection in the communities and we were particularly keen to understand more about their urgency for change. With this in mind, one of our team spent three weeks meeting individually with the formal representatives of each community asking them about their personal beliefs in relation to violence, their beliefs about others, their anticipation of social approval and disapproval, their own sense of responsibility, and their ideas for action. With over 1,300 responses, we are now analyzing the data to better understand (a) the prevalence of violence, (b) if violence is driven by social or non-social factors, (c) the motivation of people who have a mandate to prevent and/or respond to violence, and (d) people's ideas for action to address violence.

This analysis shifts the action research project into the second stage—co-sensing—where representatives of the system in which violence arises come together to observe the phenomena and make sense of it in a way that seeds actionable change. We facilitate separate dialogues with public servants, local leaders, women, men, and children about the form that patriarchy and violence take in their lives, and the intersection between the two. Five dialogues take place in each of the 18 communities in Shinyanga, concluding with a mixed session where representatives of each group come together to make meaning

Figure 16

The Co-sensing Stage of Theory U

The Line of Inquiry

- Given victims have the lived experience and motivation to affect change, how can their agency be meaningfully engaged?
- What harms are occurring, where, perpetrated by whom? Which of these types of violence are being normalized?
- What can be learned from peace studies and applied to educating people about peaceful and skillful parenting?
- What do the formal and informal system look like? Who are the actors?
- What is the motivation of different individuals? Who is responsible for what?
- What is the social return on investing in the national plan of action to end violence?
- How to transform masculinities and socialize boys to spread peace?

Co-sensing Outcomes

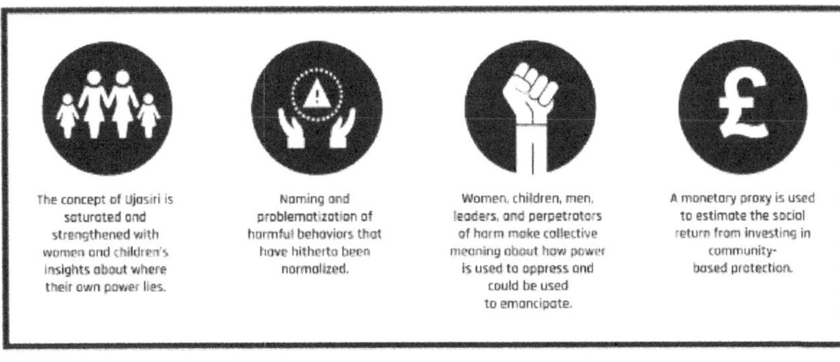

Source: Dr. McAlpine, Citizens 4 Change. Original artwork.

of the insights that they have had in their separate groups. Figure 17 shows representatives in dialogue.

Once participants have observed the system in which violence arises, the Theory U process requires these same participants to actively withdraw into a meditative space where they connect with their hearts and spirit, before then intuiting what solutions they would like to put into action to address violence. This is the prototyping phase and will be led by The Backbone. The social value created by each solution will be quantified using a social return on investment approach (Durie et al, 2012). Solutions that have a demonstrable impact in preventing or responding to violence will be integrated into the district council's plan to end violence toward women and children. This plan advances the Tanzanian government's national plan to end violence, advancing its commitment to Sustainable Development Goal 16: Promote just, peaceful, and inclusive societies.

The eight elements of the complexity navigator (Figure 3) are lenses that The Backbone will take up as they inquire into the system in which violence occurs. We anticipate four broad outcomes that will inform the prototypes that The Backbone group go on to develop and test as home-grown solutions to violence.

The only certainty in life is uncertainty. This is true even in traditional settings such as Shinyanga, where communal practices, such as early marriage and female genital mutilation, that were considered legitimate are now coming under pressure as young people are being formally educated and as communities are exposed to different social expectations. Change is a constant, but facilitating change processes in ways that do not alienate those who have an interest in the status quo demands sensitivity. In combination, Theory U and the complexity navigator remind us to find those individuals who feel an urgency for change, to understand the perspectives of those who do not, and to involve them all. The process creates space for non-judgemental conversations among both groups and provides them with an opportunity to create a shared ambition for change that they can both buy into. Seeking understanding of individuals' deep-seated motivations enables us to identify unexpected leaders who can champion change. When the time comes for taking action, we will need to ensure that actions reinforce rather than undermine each other. We will need to re-visit our

Figure 17
Dialogue with Women During the Co-Sensing Stage

Source: Dr. McAlpine, Citizens 4 Change. Used with permission.

social network analysis and tap into the vital connections that are embodied by The Backbone—the key unexpected leaders who support information to flow in their community. We will need to continue learning adaptively about what works, under what conditions, and why.

Our belief is that by following these principles we will identify many hundreds of individuals in Shinyanga who possess the Ujasiri mindset and who take action to protect women and children. Learning from their lived experience provides an opportunity to saturate Ujasiri and to integrate a more comprehensive and nuanced analysis of power into the concept. In doing so, we anticipate that the Ujasiri mindset may evolve into a mindset that characterizes not just citizen protectors, but also other unexpected leaders in complex systems. These include the courageous forest protectors who defend trees and the landscape from violence, the brave women who protect the streets for others, and the upstanders who speak out when people are being attacked or bullied. They all draw on deep wells of love, empathy, and courage when they strive to do the right thing.

End Notes

[1] The research in Shinyanga is being funded by Women Fund Tanzania Trust, which is Tanzania's only indigenous funder of community-based feminist activists. I would like to recognize and appreciate Raphael Denis, Mathias Mkude, and Janeth Semwene's contribution to facilitating this research process.

[2]https://public.tableau.com/app/profile/kate.mcalpine/viz PotentialchangeagentsinShinyangaSOCIALNETWORKANALYSIS

Meet the Author

Kate McAlpine, PhD has 25 years as a scholar practitioner in East Africa. Her multidisciplinary approach is informed by her PhD in human and organizational systems and her theory of doing the right thing—how people resolve the dilemma of being responsible citizens in uncertain times. Her research and consultancy practice builds a critical mass of child protectors in East Africa and uses mobile technology to learn from them how to resolve violence against women and children. kate@citizens4change.net

References

Atewologun, D. (2018, August 28). Intersectionality theory and practice. *Business and Management.* https://doi.org/10.1093/acrefore/9780190224851.013.48

Aviv, R. (2016, July). The philosopher of feelings. *The New Yorker.* https://www.newyorker.com/magazine/2016/07/25/martha-nussbaums-moral-philosophies

Booth, D. (2011). Working with the grain? The Africa power and politics programme. *IDS Bulletin, 42.* https://doi.org/10.1111/j.1759-5436.2011.00206.x

Cooksey, B., & Kelsall, T. (2011). *The political economy of the investment climate in Tanzania.* Overseas Development Institute. https://www.researchgate.net/publication/228817301_The_Political_Economy_of_the_Investment_Climate_in_Tanzania

Durie, S., Inglis, J., Leathem, K., Lumley, T., & Piper, R. (2012). *A guide to social return on investment.* https://www.theleapco.com/resource/knowledge-hub/toolkits/a-guide-to-social-return-on-investment-2015

Fang, X., Brown, D. S., Florence, C. S., & Mercy, J. A. (2012). The economic burden of child maltreatment in the United States and implications for prevention. *Child Abuse and Neglect, 36*(2), 156–165. https://doi.org/10.1016/j.chiabu.2011.10.006

Gardner, H. (1983). *Frames of mind: Theory of multiple intelligences.* Basic Books.

Government of the United Republic of Tanzania. (2012). *Census of Tanzania.* United Republic of Tanzania Government Portal. http://www.tanzania.go.tz/census/index.html

HakiElimu. (2020). *The state of violence against school children in Tanzania Mainland.* https://www.hakielimu.or.tz/download/the-state-of-violence-against-school-children-in-tanzania-mainland-2/

Hydén, G. (2002). *Divergent social capital and the problems of building civil society: Evidence from Tanzania.* American Political Science Association 98th Annual Meeting, Boston, MA, United States.

Institute for Economics and Peace. (2015). *Global peace index: Measuring peace, its causes and its economic value.* https://www.economicsandpeace.org/wp-content/uploads/2015/06/Global-Peace-Index-Report-2015_0.pdf

Kelsall, T. (2003). Governance, democracy and recent political struggles in Mainland Tanzania. *Commonwealth & Comparative Politics, 41*(2), 55–82. https://doi.org/10.1080/14662040412331310101

Know Violence in Childhood. (2017). *Ending Violence in Childhood. Global Report 2017. Know Violence in Childhood.* New Delhi, India. http://globalreport.knowviolenceinchildhood.org

Korir, J., Mohamedali, F., Makokha, J., & Asienwa, B. (2016). *Gender-based violence in Kenya: The economic burden on survivors.* United Nations Kenya. http://genderinkenya.org/wp-content/uploads/2017/12/GBV-Costing-Study-1-Nov-5.pdf

Manjolo, I., Likwelie, S. B., Kamagenge, A. M., Mesik, J., Owen, D., & World Bank. (2008). Community foundations - The relevance of social funds in urban areas: The Tanzania Social Action Fund experience. *Social Funds Innovation Notes, 5*(1). https://openknowledge.worldbank.org/handle/10986/11154

Marshall, M., Gurr, T. R., & Jaggers, K. (2012). *POLITY IV PROJECT: Political regime characteristics and transitions, 1800-2012 Dataset Users' Manual.* Center for Systemic Peace and Societal-Systems Research Inc. https://www.systemicpeace.org/polityproject.html

McAlpine, K. (2014). Integral activist epistemology: A model for researchers to act on personal values. *Journal of Integral Theory and Practice, 9*(1), 113–123.

McAlpine, K. (2015). *Doing the right thing to protect children in Tanzania. An explanatory theory of the basic psychological process of doing the right thing and a practical theory to enable more and better protection of children.* (Publication No. 3688840) [Doctoral dissertation, Fielding Graduate University]. ProQuest Dissertations and Theses Global. https://drkatemcalpine.co.uk/wp-content/uploads/2021/10/McAlpine_2015_PhD_

Doingtherightthing.pdf

McAlpine, K. (2020). *The preconditions for inclusive development in Tanzania.* Institutions for inclusive development; Dar es Salaam, Tanzania. https://drkatemcalpine.co.uk/wp-content/uploads/2021/10/McAlpine_2020_InclusiveDev.KM_.pdf

McAlpine, K., Dennis, R., & Semwene, J. (2021). *Tanzanian students' experience of safety and inclusion in school.* Citizens 4 Change, London, UK. https://rejuvenate.global/project/tanzanian-students-experience-of-safety-and-inclusion-in-school/

Mesaki, S., & Matotay, E. (2014). Levels, causes and consequences of the fear phenomena: Findings from a pilot study in Tanzania. *Global Journal of Human Social Science, 14*(1). https://socialscienceresearch.org/index.php/GJHSS/article/view/974

Ministry of Community Development Gender & Children. (2011). *Violence against children in Tanzania: Findings from a national survey 2009.* United Nations Children's Fund, U.S. Centers for Disease Control and Prevention, and Muhimbili University of Health and Allied Sciences. https://www.togetherforgirls.org/wp-content/uploads/2017/09/2009_Tanzania_Findings-from-a-Violence-Against-Children-Survey.pdf

Ministry of Gender Labour and Social Development. (2015). *Uganda violence against children survey: Findings from a national survey.* UNICEF. https://www.unicef.org/uganda/media/2156/file/Violence%20Against%20Children%20Survey%202018.pdf

North, D. C., Wallis, J. J., & Weingast, B. R. (2009). *Violence and social orders: A conceptual framework for interpreting recorded human history* (Kindle edition). Cambridge University Press.

Nussbaum, M. C. (2011). *Creating capabilities: The human development approach.* Harvard University Press. https://www.hup.harvard.edu/catalog.php?isbn=9780674072350

Nussbaum, M. (2015) *Political emotions. Why love matters for justice.* Belknap Press.

Pease, B. (2019). *Facing patriarchy: From a violent gender order to a culture of peace.* Zed Books.

Pereznieto, P., Montes, A., Langston, L., & Routier, S. (2014). *Shaping policy for development: The costs* https://childfundalliance.org/wp-content/uploads/2014/10/ODI-Policy-Brief.-The-cost-and-economic-impact-of-violence-against-children.pdf

Rabe, P., & Kamanzi, A. (2012). Power analysis: A study of participation at the local level in Tanzania. *An ASC Working Paper, 105*/2012. https://www.researchgate.net/publication/261550429_Power_Analysis_A_Study_of_Participation_at_the_Local_Level_in_Tanzania

Rwanda Ministry of Health. (2017). *Violence Against Children and Youth Survey: Findings from a National Survey, 2015-2016.* UNICEF. https://www.unicef.org/rwanda/reports/violence-against-children-and-youth-survey

Save the Children South Africa. (2017). Violence against children: The cost of inaction to our society and economy. *BMJ Global Health*. http://dx.doi.org/10.1136/bmjgh-2017-000573

Scharmer, O. (2009). *Theory U: Leading from the future as it emerges* (Kindle Edition). Berrett-Koehler.

Shivji, G. (2007). Reflections on NGOs in Tanzania: What we are, what we are not, and what we ought to be. *Development in Practice, 14*(5). https://doi.org/10.1080/0961452042000239832

United Nations Children's Fund Kenya Country Office, Division of Violence Prevention National Center for Injury Prevention and Control, U.S. Centers for Disease Control and Prevention, & Kenya National Bureau of Statistics. (2012). *Violence against children in Kenya. Findings from a 2010 National Survey.* https://resourcecentre.savethechildren.net/pdf/vac_in_kenya.pdf

United Republic of Tanzania. (2016). *Tanzania Demographic and Health Survey and Malaria Indicator Survey (TDHS-MS) 2015-2016.* https://dhsprogram.com/pubs/pdf/fr321/fr321.pdf

Vasbist, L. (2010). Martha Nussbaum's Capabilities Approach: Perils and Promises. *Journal of the Indian Law Institute, 52*(2), 230–66. http://www.jstor.org/stable/43953495

Wakefield, S. (2017) *Transformative and feminist leadership for women's rights.* Oxfam America Research Backgrounder Series.https://www.oxfamamerica.org/explore/research-publications/transformative-feminist-leadership-womens-rights

Walsh, R. (2006). Responding to suffering and evil: Integral principles. *Journal of Integral Theory and Practice, 1*(4), 151-158.https://drrogerwalsh.com/wp-content/uploads/2009/07/1061_100_Articles_Responding-to-suffering-and-evil-Integral-principl....pdf

Wilber, K. (1996). *A brief history of everything*. Gill & Macmillan.

Wilber, K. (2000). *Integral psychology: Consciousness, spirit, psychology, therapy.* Shambhala.

World Bank, Global Poverty Working Group. (2021). *World bank data.* https://data.worldbank.org/country/tanzania?view=chart

World Health Organization, on behalf of the United Nations Inter-Agency Working Group on Violence Against Women Estimation and Data. (2021). *Violence against women prevalence estimates, 2018. Global, regional, and national prevalence estimates for intimate partner violence against women and global and regional prevalence estimates for non-partner sexual violence against women.* https://www.who.int/publications/i/item/9789240022256

Yunus, M. (2009). *Creating a world without poverty: Social business and the future of capitalism.* Public Affairs.

Section Two

Challenging How to Lead During Precarity

CHAPTER 8

FROM UNCERTAINTY TO TRANSFORMATION: EMERGENT GENERATIVE TEAM LEADERSHIP FROM THE VOID

Kathleen A. Curran
Institute for Social Innovation Fellow

Randal J. Thompson
Institute for Social Innovation Fellow

The coronavirus pandemic gave rise to more than a crisis. It catalyzed a cataclysm demanding a different approach to leadership than leaders generally employ to mount a response. Conventionally, leaders *react* to external events thrust upon them. They may recognize a crisis and begin to act by using plans drawn up in advance with the aim of mitigating impact and rebuilding infrastructure, processes, and supply chains so that people in the crisis area can resume previous lives and livelihoods, and the affected region can rejoin the rest of the still functioning world. In some cases, self-selected *extremis leaders* willingly step into the leadership role as needed without request or requirement. Such leaders give "purpose, motivation and direction to people when there is imminent physical danger and where followers believe that leader behavior will influence their well-being or survival" (Kolditz, 2007, p. xvi).

The global pandemic, however, proved different in many ways. Although people "waited for the strong leader to emerge" (Keränen, 2019, p. 3), positional and authoritarian leaders proved to be impotent and abandoned the people in their charge, and while extremis leaders may have contributed greater clarity and hope, their approach was simply no match for the extreme multidimensional, open-ended disruption brought by the pandemic. As effective as either leadership response might have been in a routine crisis, neither could match the challenge of COVID-19. It became evident that in such a cataclysm, there is no returning to normal, a reality that became obvious as the pandemic shattered our conceived notions of normalcy. Instead, a state of uncertainty, confusion, and fear persisted globally, exposing a *void* in individual leader capacity.

The aim of this chapter is to elaborate a kind of leadership salient to the pandemic-imposed amplified uncertainty in the world, namely *emergent generative team leadership.* The chapter unfolds by first defining the void, then constructing the theoretically grounded construct of generative leadership that emerged worldwide to fill that void. A description of the distinguishing four forces igniting generative team leadership follows with real-time, real-life illustrations of the emergent process—from teens, to communities to corporate contexts—that filled urgent needs of the moment and continued. Finally, we consider questions of the sustainability of this new form of team leadership that converts access to socio-emotional resources into assets, forming a new social fabric going forward.

The Void, Emergence of Generative Teams, and Generativity

The Void

The *Online Etymology Dictionary* (Harper, 2000) cites the noun "void" as derived from Anglo-French and Old French, circa 1300. As a verb, void refers to unoccupied, vacuum, vacant; as a verb, it means to abandon (Harper, 2000). The meaning extended from the early 15th century to include the sense of "lacking or wanting." In 2020, the leadership void left an opening that filled with turbulence, "a state of unpredictable change that was not foreseen," and chaos, that is, "extreme turbulence" (Lane & Down, 2010). Turbulence and chaos occurred on multiple layers: externally in society, comparable to what the rest of the world was experiencing, and internally in people's organizations, communities, and teams. Working conditions changed almost overnight. Working from home became the norm for many. Similarly, as many teams in organizations became virtual, many of them became self-led as the distance between leaders and teams militated against traditional leader-follower relations. Teams were suddenly forced to adapt their comfortable processes for communication, decision-making, and servicing clients, even though no one knew exactly what they were adapting to.

Chaos produces increasingly complex problems that are (a) *dynamically complex*, which means that cause and effect are far apart in space and time, (b) *generatively complex*, which means they are unfolding in unfamiliar and unpredictable ways, and (c) *socially complex*, which means that the people involved see things very differently and so problems become polarized and stuck (Kahane, 2007, pp. 1–2). Such complex problems pose adaptive rather than technical challenges, namely challenges of meaning, values, emotions, worldview, and relationships (Heifetz et al., 2009).

Within the void churning in chaos, leaders offered no clear solution or way forward. In many cases, turbulence took the form of divisive animosity, a frequent outcome of fear. Yet, that same void also created conditions for inspiring the emergence of a different kind of leadership, built from spirit, attitude, emotions, and behaviors that transformed uncertainty to a new way of collective thriving. Senge et al. (1999), Senge (2017), and Surgi et al. (2016) suggested that focusing on the individual heroic leader misses the opportunity to allow for this new kind of team leadership to emerge. This chapter offers a construct of such leadership, emergent generative team leadership, which supplants the hero archetype with a more dynamic, empowered leadership approach better suited for the inevitable environment of uncertainty our future holds. Emergent generative team leadership is ignited by the four forces of intent, hope, care, and love. Such leadership enhances the dignity of team members by facilitating their capability to take control of and make decisions that affect their lives and hence furthers social justice as conceptualized by Nussbaum (2011). The following sections will illuminate the theoretical bases on which this construct rests, and operationally describe the four forces fueling generative team leadership.

Emergence of Generative Teams

March 2020. COVID-19 held the world's attention. Reactions to the unknown ranged from minimizing its gravity and likely impact to communities going into lockdown and self-quarantine in defense against the insidious virus. Like mushrooms, more than 1,000 volunteer groups in the United Kingdom spontaneously formed to help those self-isolating during the COVID outbreak.

The groups picked up laundry, delivered food, made a friendly phone call, and undertook many other helpful acts. A theater group set up an umbrella organization to coordinate the many community aid groups across the country. In the words of a co-founder of one of the groups, "The response from the public is overwhelming … It shows us what is possible when we prioritize simple compassion. People are self-organizing with incredible efficiency, respect, and creativity" (Lynch & Khoo, 2020, para. 4).

At the same time, people throughout the United States began establishing informal networks and mutual aid teams to meet the new needs of those around them. A group of librarians in Aurora, Colorado assembled kits of essentials for both the elderly and children who would not be able to access the meals they normally received at home or school. In the Bay Area, disabled people organized mutual aid for one another. In Seattle, a collective began helping "Undocumented, LGBTQI, Black, Indigenous, People of Color, Elderly, and Disabled, folks who are bearing the brunt of this social crisis" (Tolentino, 2020, para. 2). Undergrads helped other undergrads who had been barred from dorms and cut off from meal plans. Prison abolitionists raised money so that incarcerated people could purchase commissary soap. In New York City, scores of groups from all five boroughs organized volunteers to provide child and pet care, deliver medicine and groceries, and raise money for food and rent. Relief funds were organized for movie-theatre employees, sex workers, and street vendors. University of Minnesota medical students assembled a group called the Minnesota COVIDSitters to help their professors cope with the fact that they had been pulled out of university teaching to work on the front lines, as well as to help other front-line workers meet family needs. The group matched nearly 300 volunteers with 150 or so hospital workers, including physicians, nurses, custodians, cooks, and other essential employees. The students established rotations of three to five volunteers for each family in need to carry out family duties frontline workers no longer had the time to take care of. On March 16, 2020, restaurants in New York closed, leaving nearly a quarter of a million people out of work. Three restaurant employees started the Service Workers Coalition, quickly raising thousands of dollars to distribute as weekly stipends (Tolentino, 2020).

March 2021. In just one year, a vaccination against COVID-19 was approved for emergency use and available to high priority and high-risk groups such as older adults. While good news, limited COVID vaccine appointments proved challenging to locate and land. The appointment-making system was convoluted, fluid and changing, and online, which made the process almost impossible for those of the high-risk groups who generally had limited computer skills. Rescue came in the form of spontaneous support groups launched by tech-savvy teens. Seeing the need, teens banded together and stepped up to help seniors and others in their communities who needed a hand accessing the online system. Keeping up with schoolwork meant that the teens recruited, inspired, and mobilized others to join. They trained fellow teens in the required technology and created a Google Voice phone number that seniors could call for aid. Others jumped in to provide a catalog of all sites with available vaccines. Their overall implicit vision was simple: Help until it is not needed. As one volunteer shared, "You can just help with skills that a lot of people have and come together to make something better" (Broadfoot, 2021, para. 4).

With COVID restrictions, the work context was suddenly in chaos as work from home became the survival method of the times. Questions without solutions were abundant: How could teams stay productive? How could the sales force continue to meet customer needs? How could teams communicate and stay aligned? Squadify™, a team effectiveness assessment used in our consulting practice, offered a quantitative means to discern COVID-induced shifts in corporate teamwork. The tool measures team members' rating of attitudes and behaviors considered *important* for team effectiveness and their perceptions of the *presence* of those elements in their teams. The comparison of the two ratings thus reveals the gap between what is ideal and real. Pre-COVID assessments from 23 teams across diverse industries and sectors collected before the pandemic and compared with mid-COVID data, where most if not all teams were then remote, showed significant shifts in their assessment of what had become important for team performance and what they felt was now present on their teams. As will be discussed in more depth later in this chapter, the greatest shifts were in the psycho-emotional and social aspects of teamwork, not the task-related ones. Teams reported feeling happier at work, being more open to and receptive of feedback, being more motivated to achieve goals, and feeling part of a more cohesive and purposeful team. While clarity of goal was still ranked most important, the collective caring and collaborative means for reaching the goal took on greater importance and relevance.

These examples illustrate that spontaneously formed or strengthened teams, groups, and communities joined forces with an intuitively shared vision (Nussbaum, 2011) and a readiness to step up to deploy their skills for the good of all. These and many more examples illustrate how community groups quickly formed to help people negatively impacted by the pandemic and provided food, housing, and health support. As the Squadify™ data showed, a similar phenomenon was discerned in the already existing teams in the corporate context as they appeared to coalesce into stronger more focused and caring teams.

These examples shine the light on the ignited power of community, the increased communal relationships on teams, and the need to organize locally in order to take the provision of our basic needs into our own hands. Social critic Jeremy Lent (2020) posited that "this rediscovery of the value of community has the potential to be the most important factor of all in shaping the trajectory of the next era" (para. 33). As one member of a spontaneously formed care community explained, "The day-to-day practice of mutual aid is ... a matter of 'prefiguring the world in which you want to live'" (Tolentino, 2020, para. 20).

While some people went into denial during the coronavirus, even denying its existence, others, as indicated above, took action. These action-oriented people resisted the pressure in chaotic spaces to rush back to the so-called "rational space," a move that does not work. Instead, they moved toward the "creative space" of new discovery (Lane & Down, 2010). These examples illustrate generativity, which highlights that from the void created by extreme uncertainty, communities and teams stepped up and self-organized to lead themselves in support of a shared vision and purpose. Most noteworthy, however, is that the greatest team changes reflected the sources of their power to adapt and flourish, namely, intent, love, care and hope, the igniting forces of emergent generative team leadership.

Generativity

The void, chaos, and the adaptive challenges of the pandemic catalyzed a process of generativity. The examples provided above suggest that the kind of leadership that rises up and fills the void left by conventional leaders is based on generativity. Generativity emerged in organizations and teams. Clearly, no one acted alone. Rather, in each case, groups self-organized and self-managed. They were driven by love, care, and hope and with the intent to help in the way needed in the moment. The capacity to step up emerged from within each individual. Individuals became collectives; collectives emerged to fill the void.

Generativity can be defined as the creation of new images, metaphors, and physical representations that have two qualities: "They change how people think so that new options for decisions and/or actions become available to them, and they are compelling images that people want to act on … Generativity includes the processes and capacities that help people see old things in new ways" (Bushe, 2019, p. 142). Generativity transmutes uncertainty into a resource, creating an opportunity to invent new frames, structures, processes, and relationships. Generativity also means becoming less focused on proving ourselves and advancing our individual interests and more concerned about enabling others to find their voice, to stretch and discover their potential to contribute. A generative approach is well-suited for highly uncertain environments where there is very little information available (Steinbruner, 2002). Such an approach transcends analysis and rationality out of necessity because there are no relevant empirical data to analyze. Like an "alchemist, such an approach transmutes uncertainty into a resource, an opportunity to invent new frames, structures, processes and relationships" (Castillo & Trinh, 2019, p. 370).

In organizations, generativity occurs when a group of people discover, create, and/or are presented with an image that allows them to experience their work and organization differently (Bushe, 2013, 2019). Such a generative image influences both how people think and the decisions and actions they take. Over time, as people notice themselves and each other making different decisions and taking different actions, a new normative order arises of shared assumptions. In this way, the culture is changed, which in turn influences what people think (Bushe, 2019, p. 144).

Organizations and teams that emerged during the pandemic developed "generative capacity, the … capacity to challenge the guiding assumptions of the culture, to raise fundamental questions regarding contemporary social life, to foster reconsideration of that which is 'taken for granted' and thereby furnish new alternatives for social actions" (Gergen, 1978, p. 1346). To embrace the path of generativity requires that we cultivate an ethic of care and focus our concern on the good of the whole (Macaux, 2012). We argue, as the stories of generative teams show, that such a path also requires intent, hope, and love.

Generativity in Creating a Post-Pandemic World

Communities also formed around the world that viewed the pandemic as the opportune time to reinvent society based on a generative image of a more equitable, ethical, and just society where individuals would be freed to develop the capabilities that underlie a life of dignity and social justice (Nussbaum, 2011). Otto Scharmer's GAIA journey united over 10,000 people globally in an online "impromptu global infrastructure for sensemaking, for leaning into our current moment of disruption and letting this moment move us toward civilizational renewal" (Pendle, 2020, para. 1). Through the practice of presencing, community members opened their minds, hearts, and wills and allowed the future to reveal itself through a process of social emergence until what arose was crystallized, prototyped, embodied, and then performed. The GAIA journey continues as global, self-organized topic- or place-based groups begin to implement their projects to create positive system changes in areas such as sustainable architecture, health and well-being, and presencing practices for educators, all aimed toward reinventing ecosystems and societies (Scharmer, 2006).

Leadership scholar-activist Kathleen Allen organized a global group to develop a whole systems approach to implementing regenerative leadership in their own organizations based on *active hope*. The group defines active hope as resilient individuals and groups who are actively working to create the society and the environment to promote collective well-being (Macy & Johnstone, 2012). Allen argued that the first steppingstone toward generating active hope is "intent" as they solidify their determination and grit by building their muscle to try to create something better. Practicing gratitude and cultivating one's imagination and self-efficacy help to build active hope in oneself, Allen contended, and dreaming together through circles of engagement builds active hope and confidence that change is possible in one's group or team. Active hope says, "We are persistent and we are determined to make the future a thriving place" (Allen, 2021). This is the heart of intent.

Sikh Activist Valerie Kaur gathered thousands of people around the world to join in the *revolutionary love* movement to work for social change. Her meetings throughout the pandemic included ceremonies of dedication to the movement, prayers, meditations, music, and actions to be take based on the power of love as a weapon to counter the evil reflected in hate crimes on the rise in the United States and build a new world based on love.

Many other groups self-organized to redefine the post-pandemic world after viewing the cataclysm of the pandemic as a liminal space that opened the possibility to create a better world for all. All of these groups began with the clear *intent* to change the world and employed a highly participatory approach in which everyone in the community was a leader whose perspectives blended together to move the world forward. Values of transparency, creativity, and collaborative dialogue were infused in the various groups' processes (Lane & Down, 2010). As Kahane (2007) wrote, "Complex problems [...] [defined as having a low level of agreement and certainty] can only be solved using processes that are 'systemic, emergent and participatory'" (p. 32). Powerful conversations through which possibilities emerge create dynamic stability in unstable systems (Bushe, 2013, 2019). This dynamic stability is maintained by focusing collective attention on the intangible and symbolic layers of reality such as values, mission, patterns, processes, learning, and relationships (Castillo & Trahn, 2019). What we posit as the fundamental rationale for generative leadership is this: The relational and social-emotional factors that have taken a back seat in the past are absolutely critical now.

Emergent Generative Team Leadership

Generative leadership is a form of leadership that creates a context which stimulates innovation within complex systems such as organizations, communities, and teams (Surie & Hazy, 2006). In the complex systems approach, "leadership" is not limited to an individual. Rather, leadership is a system comprised of recognizable patterns of social and relational organizing among autonomous, heterogeneous individuals as they form and develop into a system of action (Hazy & Uhl Bien, 2015). The system of action, therefore, is equal to a system of shared behaviors among aligned individuals, that is, a team, who collectively takes on the responsibilities of creating the conditions for team effectiveness.

Notably, the system of action does not develop from formal deliberation as much as it emerges to meet and adapt to needs. This approach means that the team recognizes the potential of each individual's leadership capacity and capability, not as an individual contributor but as a contributing part to a greater whole. Generative team leadership emphasizes the importance of broader, nonlinear organizing that operates and grows iteratively, building on both individual practices and complex system effects. Simply put, generative team leadership multiplies individual value in service to the greater good and overarching purpose.

We argue that emergent generative team leadership is what occurred in many community support groups and some corporations around the world in response to the turbulence and chaos swirling in the void. We also propose that this form of leadership is what is needed in future inevitable situations characterized by increasing complexity, uncertainty, ambiguity, and flux, and requiring continual adaptation, regardless of context or level of position. Our premise is that generative team leadership emerges as a result of conventional leadership void when the four igniting forces of intent, hope, care, and love are present. The relationship among individuals creates a coherent collective that organically fills the void with what is needed at the moment of need.

Characteristics of Generative Team Leadership

A generative approach to emergent team leadership in the void, therefore, includes shared vision, interdependence, and organic organizational infrastructure.

Shared Vision

In conditions of chaos, actions speak louder than words and there is a greater focus on intangibles (Castillo & Trinh, 2019, p. 367). The community support groups and the VaxConnect and VaxHunters, for example, aligned naturally, selflessly, and seamlessly around the straightforward vision of *help until it is not needed anymore*. Even when initially not explicitly stated, the teams' purpose and measurement of success were focused on the time when people would be safe and whole again. Importantly, the shared vision worked to inspire and mobilize individuals to join initiatives as well as to cohere individuals to the cause driving their efforts.

Interdependence

Author of *Disasterology*, Samantha Montano (2021), found that individuals at the specific site of a disaster are the first and immediate source of support to those in need. Not relying on formal roles or rank, individuals step in and form an interdependent collective, held together by the common vision and purpose. Even though instantaneously mobilized by one, it is clear that one can do nothing alone; the power is in the team and team leadership.

Interdependence includes sharing leadership and holding genuine concern for others, fostering a process of mutual influence that further supports knowledge creation (Rai & Prakash, 2012) as well as deepens trust. Individuals learn from each other and teach each other, embodying a multiplier effect on process improvement. The global pandemic produced thousands of such interdependent teams around the world. Covid Mutual Aid has created a map of these group to facilitate connections. [1]

Interdependence among the emergent generative teams extended multidimensionally. Not only were individuals cognizant of roles and responsibilities, morphing according to need, they developed interdependence critical to achieving their desired outcome. They provided each other __- the emotional support needed to sustain energy and efforts, especially in the uncertain times when the goal line was unknown. In sum, thousands of examples, many of which we have provided, showed that team members relied on each other, supported each other, and achieved together.

Organic Organizational Infrastructure

Emergent team formations do not enjoy the luxury of advance planning. Rather, organizational infrastructure consisting of internal systems, processes, and structures which facilitate broader meaningful interaction across team members and execution of their shared aim is organically built and self-managed (Ramezan, 2011). In systems terms, process structures, for example, provide paths for feedback loops that accommodate recursive influences and reflexive causation, promoting information flow between internal and external boundaries at multiple scales (Todorova & Durisin, 2007). Emergent generative teams developed internal communication plans and external information gathering processes, allowing for adaptation to services as needed. Illustratively, social aid groups in the United Kingdom developed a system for learning the types of needs of community members, from grocery deliver to loneliness care. The teen vaccine support groups organically developed a system for mobilizing and deploying classmates when the need for their service expanded.

Organizational infrastructure provides the network that facilitates the coordinated positive intentions of all those who join the initiative, smoothing operations and leveraging skills, especially critical in the state of uncertainty imposed by the global pandemic. Without such process structure, time and energy are lost or lessened in effectiveness. A core characteristic of generative leadership, the organic infrastructure of the emergent generative team enables teams to maintain flexibility in order to accommodate changing conditions (Cicchetti & Rogosch, 1996). The infrastructure that organically emerged from the void was clearly both adaptive and enabling, expediting what needed to be accomplished at the moment and accelerating the system of action improvements as they arose.

"The capacity to achieve a shared future through the development of multiple pathways to reach success" provides operational underpinning (Castillo & Trinh, 2019, p. 367) crucial to generative team leadership in the void, summarized by the three core enablers listed above. Not a problem-solving leadership approach, emergent generative team leadership derives from a purpose that team members care about, reflected in a powerful image, according to Bushe (2013, 2019). Bushe (2019) cited how the image of sustainable development transformed global dialog and generated a new way of doing and acting in the world. The image of the "new post-pandemic world" has now served as such a powerful image, motivating self-organized teams and groups around to world to shift into a generative change-oriented mode. This leadership is driven by conversations that respond to disruptions of previous repetitive and limiting patterns that are so severe that the "people involved believe that the way things have been no longer works and they cannot go back" to business as usual (Bushe, 2013, p. 11). Resonant with our examples of emergent generative team leadership, such conversations comprise emergent bottom-up approaches that catalyze new more adaptive patterns and complex order to emerge from the current disorder.

Emergent Generative Team Leadership Depends upon Relational and Social-Emotional Forces

Thus far, emergent generative team leadership appears to be grounded in structure and processes that facilitate adaptation to emergent needs. Yet, it is important to emphasize that emergent generative team leadership rests firmly on a relational approach to organizing (Macaux, 2012). Further, it depends largely on "the connective tissue of relationships and the social-emotional forces that bind us to one another and to a cause" (Macaux, 2012, p. 4). As Macaux (2012) emphasized,

> Relational dynamics and social-emotional forces will have their effects, often decisively, on how the rational engine of achievement works and whether it thrives. The relational and social-emotional factors that have taken a back seat in the past are absolutely critical now … without the capacity for forming relationships of trust, common purpose, mutual respect, and cooperation, the whole will never become greater than the sum of its parts. Social-emotional resources are vital. (p. 4)

Intent, care, hope, and love provide these relational and social-emotional forces that ignite emergent generative team leadership. Macaux (2012) argued that generative leadership as "the spontaneous unfolding interactions of a group" is an emergent action that often arises as a consequence of circumstances in the surrounding environment. He posited that as challenges associated with complexity or novelty stimulate a team up until a point at which the team is virtually overwhelmed, the team needs to use moderating resources such as joint problem solving, dialoging, or other group practices to move forward. Such moderating factors work by stimulating reflection, reframing the problem, and providing a fresh perspective, which facilitates adaptive adjustment when facing challenging situations. The beneficial effects of these moderating variables are mediated by psychosocial competencies, such as a practiced capacity for reflection, openness to self-examination and personal change, and a capacity to talk openly and repair ruptures in relationships. Development that affects these mediating variables thereby catalyzes the positive effects of the moderating variables (Macaux, 2012, p. 7).

In their study of an organization in crisis, Sommer et al. (2015) found that individuals who had or were able to draw on emotional, cognitive, social, and instrumental resources generate "positive psychological capital" and "core confidence" comprised of factors such as hope, optimism, efficacy, and resilience were better able to cope with crisis. As the authors concluded,

> Insights into the mechanisms for positive emotions strengthening one's resilience in a crisis can be gained from Fredrickson's (2001) broaden-and-build theory, which suggests that positive affect increases cognitive flexibility, or the thought–action repertoires of individuals, which has been shown to increase the problem-solving efficacy and creativity of individuals ... In a crisis, such mental fluidity is essential because, by definition, such events involve unexpected and potentially traumatic situations that require new modes of operating and understanding. Embracing the path of generativity thus requires that we cultivate an ethic of care and focus our concern on the good of the whole. Doing so allows for acts of aligned leadership to arise more frequently at all levels. (Sommer, et al., 2015, p. 175)

The Four Forces Igniting Emergent Generative Team Leadership

Often, how leaders contend with turbulence and uncertainty in the external world is partly a function of how they deal with uncertainty within themselves (Lane & Down, 2010). The outcome may amplify the tendency to avoid, vacate, or step up with care and courage. The same can be said for a team. What is nurtured inside individuals manifests outside. Emerging from the void, generative team leadership has shown a greater tendency for what is inside of individuals in terms of intent, hope, care, and love to both compel and propel team members as a collective to face and fully engage the perceived need with care and courage.

While operational capabilities are requisite to support team leadership, we contend that the emotional, cognitive, social, and instrumental resources that catalyze generative team leadership and comprise "positive psychological capital" and "core confidence" are the vital signs, without which a team falters and reverts to seeking conventional leaders to rescue them. Intent, love, care, and hope are what convert thought to action. These igniting forces transform our will (intent), emotion (love), accountability (care), and spirit (hope) to generative team leadership.

Figure 18 illustrates the four igniting forces of emergent generative team leadership and graphically represents the interrelationships among the four social-emotional elements. The woven, integrated nature of the four forces is what lends the comprehensive power to our conception. No element is present in isolation. Inherently, each force is relational. Each force is carried out in coordination with others and impacts the nature of the relation and the outcome of the collective energy. Despite the manifestation of each force and the form in which agreement of definitions of love, care, hope, and intent exist, their sources in emotion, accountability, spirit, and will cannot exist alone. This has proven to be true in all cited stories of generative team leadership that arose throughout the global pandemic. Love, care, and hope guided by intent, within

Figure 18
The Four Igniting Forces of Emergent Generative Team Leadership

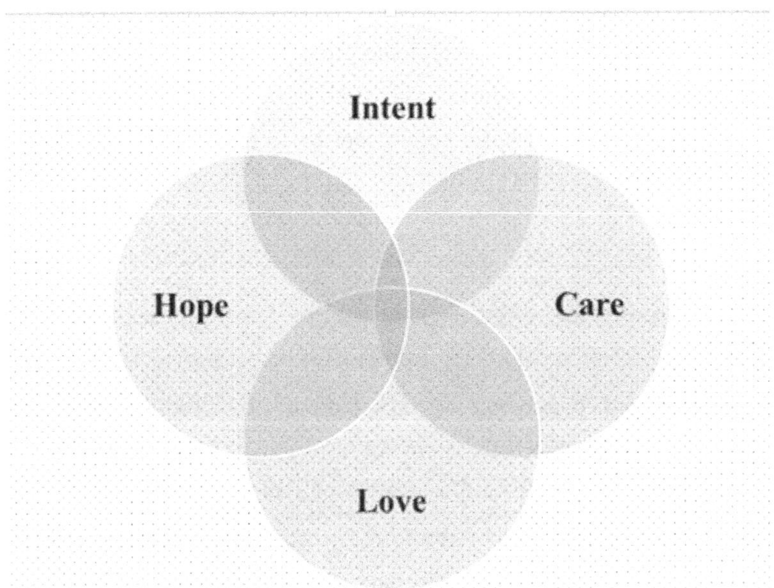

an ecosystemic perspective, provide the solid foundation for the conditions we need to cultivate for an equitable and sustainable future. In the next section, each element of the model is illuminated in light of the emergent generative team leadership that arose throughout the global pandemic.

Intent

Intent can be understood as the will to reach a different place of shared understanding that declutters the space of preconceived notions, judgments, and personal agendas, and clears the way for exploration, innovation, and co-creation. Intent begins from a place of conscious receptivity, not only accepting difference but expecting and inviting the possibility to be changed by the interaction with another. Not *if*, not *hopefully*, but *will* as both a capacity of being, thus identity, and as a process of connection from which co-creation and advocacy grow.

I-intend-it fuels a potent force, according to the principle of intentionality (Turner, 2017), which "not only guides all voluntary thought and behavior, but is also implicated in all meaning, value and purpose" (Turner, 2017, p. 2). Intent gives agency to individuals as well as to collectives, as they coalesce around a vision, given what is understood of interests and the situation.

Choices of action and degree of motivation reflect the mental model of the collective's *intent*, the intellect that creates the purpose and clarity of direction, sans personal agendas yet open to necessary adaptations. In the case of the teams, communities, and organizations that stepped up during the pandemic, intent was reflected in their spontaneous action to meet the needs of others and to employ the cataclysm as a liminal space to redesign the future.

Care

Care is relational and emotional, as well as a form of accountability. Care encompasses "feelings of concern, responsibility, and affection, as well as the work of attending to a person's needs" (Cancian & Oliker, 2000, p. 2). Care flow is a multilevel work process through which caring feelings and actions are generated and spread throughout an organization to address the needs of its members at dyadic, collective, and organizational system levels (Cancian & Oliker, 2000; Stiehl, 2018). As such, care is a disposition that ensures ethical responsibility, balanced with vulnerability.

Compassion is a type of care. Author Jen Groover noted that compassion forms the root of all empathetic habits. "True compassion exists when you give your strength, guidance and wisdom to empower another so that you can see who you really are and live in a greater capacity and expect nothing in return" (Groover, 2013, para. 7). Psychologist Sherry Campbell emphasized that "compassionate leaders seek influence, not authority. They don't demand, they encourage. They lead with hope. They guide, acknowledge, and support team members to combine their efforts, skills, talents, insights, passion, enthusiasm and commitment to work together for the greater good" (Campbell, 2018, para 8). Compassion and care drove the generative teams, communities, and organizations who spontaneously took action to care for others' needs, whether physical or emotional. Even the groups who joined together to redesign the post-pandemic world were meeting each other's emotional needs and thrived on care.

Hope

The spirit that is hope is a generative force characterized by lifting our gaze to the future (Jones-Shenk, 2020). Hope helps teams see the humanity and the thoughtfulness that the practice of hope requires. The definition of hope in emergent generative team leadership draws from the agency-oriented construct offered by Snyder (2010), which consists of a desired goal, the self-perception that the individual or team has the capabilities to achieve the goal, and the courage and will to reach the destination.

Advocacy and passion are copilots of hope (Jones-Shenk, 2020), which make hope much more than a distant aspiration. Rather, hope is a valuable asset that generative teams possess and continuously develop and convey to others to lift and improve the experiences of teams who may be reeling from external impacts. In other words, hope is a navigational tool fueled by strong beliefs and self-efficacy.

Jones-Schenk (2020) added a future-oriented focus to hope, making this force extra salient to emergent generative team leadership and the expected unpredictability and challenge to see around the corner. Emergent generative teams such as the teens supporting elderly groups seeking COVID vaccination appointments and the worldwide aid groups naturally looked to the horizon to continually assess incoming data in order to navigate the "now" while keeping abreast of the "new," simultaneously focusing on both so as not to become overwhelmed by current circumstances and to be ready for the unexpected. Hope is a way of getting "from the now to the next," a concurrent viewing of the now and the horizon of the future.

Hope requires leaders to be intentional in evaluating their own hopefulness and being transparent in conveying how they came to have hope while immersed in similarly despairing circumstances (Jones-Schenk, 2020). The generative teams, communities, and organizations who viewed the cataclysm as the opportunity to show the best in humanity and to look forward to a more positive future were driven by the hope that their actions made a difference and that a better world was possible and largely in the hands of those who would make it.

Love

Love is the generative force that has created and sustains the universe. Love is the greatest power we can possess, and it is the opposite of fear. As Maturana (1999) wrote "Love is the domain of those relational behaviors through which another (a person, being, or thing) arises as a legitimate other in coexistence with oneself" (p. 2). He added that "love is the only emotion that expands intelligence and learning," (p. 1) which makes love a strong partner to intent.

Equated to connection, sharing, and a mutual investment in other's well-being that brings mutual care, "love energizes a whole system and sets it in motion" (Fredrickson, 2013, p. 8). Love is a force that moves people above themselves. It is a political force that can make it possible for people to rule themselves. It extends beyond rationality and involves transformation (Hardt & Negri, 2009). "Love is what gives respect for humanity its life, making it more than a shell" (Nussbaum, 2015, p. 25). As William O-Brien contended (Taylor, 2016, para.1), "It's simple. Love is about helping another to complete him[her] self."

Love abounded as the emotional force that ignited generative teams, communities, and organizations during COVID as people "moved beyond themselves" and took actions they never took before and envisioned a future they never before were in a position to believe they could help to create. They were driven by the positive power in the universe, in others, and in themselves.

In practice, love inspires unity and the capacity to embrace imperfections (Nussbaum, 2015) and to see the humanity behind mistakes without blame. Importantly, love nourishes the choice to take responsibility for the brilliance and success of every collective endeavor, again emphasizing the agency of the collective, impelled by the four igniting forces of emergent generative team leadership.

A Corporate Example of Emergent Generative Team Leadership Ignited by the Four Forces

As previously mentioned, Squadify™ is an online assessment that is designed to reveal teams' perceptions of 37 factors deemed critical to team effectiveness. Teams are asked which of these 37 factors are important to their teams' effectiveness and the extent to which the same 37 factors are actually present in their own teams. Twenty-three corporate teams in approximately five countries and multiple geographic locations completed Squadify™ under pre-COVID conditions, then again during the period between March 2020 and March 2021, that is, after the pandemic had begun, or mid-COVID. We coded the 37 factors according to how they illustrated our definitions of the four igniting forces of intent, hope, care, and love and analyzed the results of the surveys to discern the extent to which the teams shifted their perceptions of (a) which factors were important conditions for their teams' effectiveness and (b) which factors were actively present within their teams.

Overall, a comparison of pre-COVID and mid-COVID data showed that teams re-ranked items. We found that (a) teams considered 99% of the 37 factors teams *important* for their teams' effectiveness and (b) 100% of the same 37 factors actually *present* on their teams. All changes in ranking suggested that teams reconsidered what was both *important* to team effectiveness and *present* on their team after the pandemic disrupted their work reality. We categorized the factors that changed in importance and presence into the four igniting forces of generative team leadership to determine whether this leadership approach may have emerged in these surveyed teams.

Table 10 and Table 11 identify the top 10 changes in importance and in presence the teams reported after the pandemic disruption. Changes in both the importance and presence of the 37 factors highlight a tendency for the teams to (a) take a more collective perspective and experience a stronger sense of cohesiveness, (b) place a greater focus on the importance of their internal organizational infrastructure as facilitating their work together during this time of turbulence, and (c) increase the open and active communication among team members. Most significantly, from being ranked 30th in pre-COVID times,

Table 10
Squadify™: Top 10 Changes in Perceptions of Importance—Pre/Mid-COVID

Ranking	Top 10 Changes in Perceptions of Importance
1	Coach each other to help
2	Happy at work
3	Effective processes to run the squad
4	Effective processes for decision-making
5	Clear measures for success
6	Support others in the organization
7	Open to new ideas and approaches
8	Listen to each other
9	Short term priorities deliver long term plan
10	Clear goal

Table 11
Squadify™: Top 10 Changes in Perceptions of Presence—Pre/ Mid-COVID

Ranking	Top 10 Changes in Perceptions of Presence
1	Squad speaks with one voice
2	Straight talking without offense
3	Disciplined execution
4	Clear plan to achieve goals
5	Effective processes to run the squad
6	Happy at work
7	Squad interests above the individual
8	Give each other feedback to help
9	Short term priorities deliver long term plan
10	Effective processes for decision-making

being happy at work moved to among the top six ranked items on both the importance (Table 10) and presence (Table 11) scales of the Squadify™ survey components, a result that one would not intuitively expect due to the severity of the pandemic and its repercussions.

Results from the Squadify™ survey reveal significant findings in regard to the four igniting forces of emergent generative team leadership, as discussed below.

Survey Findings: Intent

Intent impels the will and capacity of teams to reach a different place of shared understanding and purpose that may not have inspired the teams until a crisis or other disruption. Generatively, intent becomes a consciously held goal to connect with others and to co-create possibilities together, as individuals are in a place of conscious receptivity, not only accepting difference but expecting and inviting the possibility to be changed by the interaction with another (Curran, 2018). Intent is not a pre-planned place but a state of being open to possibilities, referred to as "open will" (Scharmer & Kaufer, 2013).

Intent was reflected in teams' changes in their ranking of perceptions of importance, as illustrated in Table 10. For example, *coach each other to help, support others in the organization*, and *open to new ideas and approaches* showed the greatest change in perception when comparing pre-COVID and mid-COVID Squadify™ results. Together, these examples suggest that teams increased their consciousness of the importance, thus impact, that intent can have on team success.

Shared intent, therefore, gave a more collective perspective to teams' membership, illustrated by a mid-COVID significant shift in perceptions of factors present (Table 11), expressed as teams *speak with one voice*. The teams became a potent force, driving *disciplined execution* through the teams' intent to accomplish their tasks, despite the chaos and uncertainty that they functioned within. When a team shares an intent, grounded in purpose, values, and beliefs, it naturally generates a cleared space for exploration and innovation. There is an openness to new possibilities for ways to accomplish tasks that keep work flowing, based as well on the belief that team members bring brilliance that supports team success.

Survey Findings: Love

The most powerful emotion, love fuses unity among a collective and on the Squadify™ teams. As a unifying force, love expands teams' intelligence, the only emotion that provides such impetus (Maturana, 1998). Intelligence suggests the capacity to see beyond oneself. Besides speaking with one voice, teams made a significant shift towards *placing squad interests above the individual*, a factor they identified as being present on their teams (Table 11). Relatedly, teams' efforts appeared to reconsider the efficacy of their previous decision-making processes and opted for a stronger collective approach that may not have been what they followed pre-COVID, but which made more sense during the pandemic.

In light of risking new processes, teams also tended to embrace imperfections, highlighted by Nussbaum as an essential aspect of love (Wilder, 2017). As an illustration, mid-COVID, teams identified *straight talking without offense* as a significantly more important present factor than pre-COVID (Table 11). This result suggests a greater acceptance of learning from mistakes and a greater tendency to create a non-blaming climate. Eric Fromm (2000) spoke of love as a form of taking responsibility without request or direction. In this sense, love is the act of will or intent that inspires the choice to be supportive and protective of the team and mission. Squadify™ mid-COVID findings appear to reflect this perspective in both perceptions of importance and perceptions of active presence on the team.

Survey Findings: Care

As defined here, care is an action, disposition, and an ethical responsibility to consider needs and vulnerabilities. Most importantly, care connotes accountability for making conscious, collective choices. On a generative team, there are no individual heroes; there are only interdependent and aligned internal and external relational resources. Team members are responsible to the collective and there is a high degree of other-awareness and inclusivity. Squadify™ results highlighted manifestations of care in statements such as *give each other feedback to help,* and again, emphasis on *effective processes as needed for decision making and running the team as a whole*, especially crucial in the time of uncertainty and dramatically disrupted working conditions. As illustrated by Tables 10 and 11, teams highlighted the increased importance of a community perspective mid-COVID and actually put into practice such a perspective in their decision-making processes. That is, mid-COVID, teams' words and actions reflected "We."

Survey Findings: Hope

The spirit of hope, operationalized by Snyder (1994), is more than an intangible wish. Rather, hope is a clear goal that includes the self-perception that teams possess the capacities and capabilities needed to reach the desired goal. Snyder's definition implies agency, which was manifest in how Squadify™ teams, mid-COVID, increased their consciousness of the importance of their *clear measures of success* and prioritized *clear plans in practice to achieve their goals.*

While both elements cited are generally common to effective teams, the significant shifts in the rank of those elements, as shown in Tables 1 and 2, highlight the emergent generative team leadership evoked and provoked by the void. Frequently, without a formal leader present and while they were reeling from the external impacts of COVID, the teams appear to have generated a spirit of hope to help sustain them. Clearly, that spirit served to improve their overall team experience.

Jones-Schenk (2020) viewed hope as a future orientation. Squadify™ results showed that these teams adopted a pragmatic perspective as they reported a significant shift in *short term priorities deliver on the long-term plan.* Clearly, the teams remained resourceful, despite the circumstances and acted on the present in adaptive ways as needed.

In conclusion, we propose that intent, love, care, and hope provided an unanticipated shift in values and perspectives of the corporate teams who completed the Squadify™ survey, as well as in the care communities that rose up from the void to provide unsolicited help during the pandemic. As a whole, the examples clearly demonstrate that emergent generative team leadership has taken charge with heart to serve the good of the collective, whatever the context.

From Capacity to Capability

The practice of emergent generative team leadership moves people from the

Figure 19

Iterative/Integrative Processes of Emergent Generative Team Leadership: Capacity to Capability

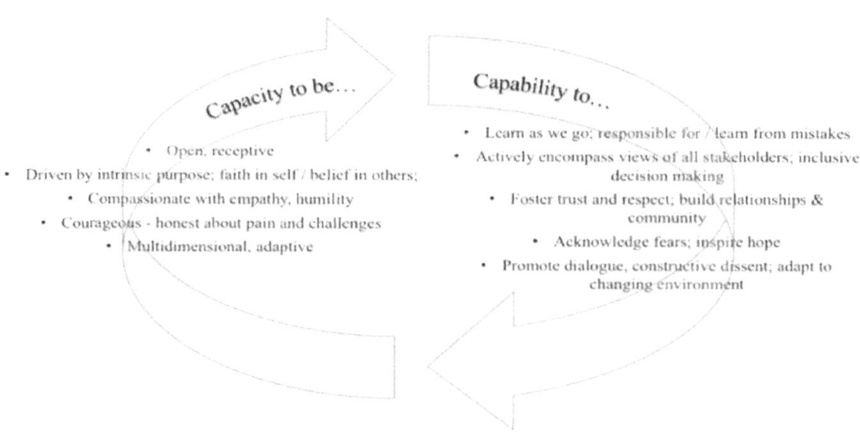

capacity that exists inside individuals to individuals' capability vis-à-vis others and toward a life of dignity with enhanced social justice (Nussbaum, 2011). This movement is shown in Figure 19.

Nussbaum (2011) considered capabilities as freedoms and choices. In the case of the chaos created by the void of positional, more authoritarian leaders, the lid was taken off, so to speak, allowing individuals the freedom to spontaneously choose to act in the face of necessity and possibility. Individuals in care communities and some corporate teams were able to express their internal capacity for openness as the capability to learn while taking more responsibility for being leaders themselves. They shifted from their internal capacity for purpose and belief in self and others to an active capability to be inclusive and make communal decisions.

Transforming their capacity for compassion into their capability to form relationships and community, individuals fostered trust and respect. In the face of great challenges, individuals moved from their internal capacity for courage to the capability to openly acknowledge fears and inspire hope. Finally, from their capacity to see across time and adapt, they were able to express their adaptive capability by engaging in dialogue, deliberation, and constructive dissent and together achieve their goals in a spirit of openness and humility.

In terms of Nussbaum's (2011) capabilities required for a life of dignity and social justice, teams, communities, and organizations enhanced their capabilities to express (a) emotions, (b) affiliation, (c) senses, imagination, and thought, and (d) political influence. As we have argued, the emotion of love, disposition of care, spirit of hope, and will of intent serve as critical catalysts of emergent generative team leadership and enhance individuals' ability to form attachments outside of themselves (Nussbaum, 2011). Individuals practicing this leadership also strengthened their freedom for affiliation. As Nussbaum argued (2011), affiliation includes recognizing and showing concern for other human beings, being able to imagine the situation of another, and engaging in social interaction. In expressing their enhanced senses, imagination, and thought, participants in care teams and some corporate teams were able to use their imagination and thought in carving out new ways of leading and being together. They also strengthened their political capability to play a significant role in society often played by the government by "taking matters into their own hands" and solving challenges that remained unsolved because of the leadership void. Individuals were thus able to move from their internal capacities to socially expressed capabilities. Likewise, learning from their capabilities enhanced the capacities in an iterative and integrative process. Such a process, summarized in Figure 2, is critical for the practice and nourishment of emergent generative team leadership.

Conclusion: Converting Access to Assets

We have argued that emergent generative team leadership is ignited by the four forces of intent, hope, care, and love, which, when spontaneously fused in the moment of crisis, transform the void, as we have defined it, into a creative, self-organized, self-managed, and self-directed team, community, or organization. The cataclysm of the coronavirus pandemic served to open the door to empower individuals to form strong teams and communities to undertake what needed to be done. Yet the coronavirus pandemic may be only the beginning of increased complexity and disruptions in our society due to further crises and cataclysms. The question arises therefore regarding whether communities of care and corporate teams will continue playing a significant role in filling future leadership voids and in making emergent generative team leadership a predominant leadership approach.

In past crises when communities of care have emerged, scholars have debated whether such communities of care would continue filling leadership voids and serve to strengthen civil society (Thompson, 2018). In her 2020 New Yorker article, Jia Tolentino (2020) reported on her interview with Harvard political scientist Nancy L. Rosenblum, whose research showed that such groups that arise during crisis do not endure nor build a stronger civic sector. Rosenblum admitted that what was happening during the pandemic appeared somewhat different than during other crises, opening the possibility that such spontaneous care communities may become part of the future social fabric. What is significant about Tolentino's article, whose subtitle is "A Radical Practice is Suddenly Gaining Mainstream Attention," is that it posed the possibility of the lasting significance of such groups as a sign of deeply rooted social change.

The question regarding the future roles of communities of care and small communities is also taken up by other authors in this volume. In her chapter "Where Do Families Turn: Adults with Disabilities in a Care(less) Culture?" Maggie Buckley, for example, explored whether community care for the disabled can become a viable permanent social model. Laurence P. Gebhardt, in his chapter "Leadership in Small Communities," argued that small community constituencies such as faith groups, service clubs, public and higher education, locally owned and managed businesses, arts and music, sports, and local government entities have overlapping values and ethics that can be persuaded and motivated to overcome biases to achieve kindness, caring, and inclusion-oriented social change. Unexpected leadership can influence public and political emotions in small communities leading to increased kindness, caring, and justice.

We consider that such unexpected leadership may well be emergent generative team leadership. Further, we contend that such a model can be not only sustainably rooted but also resourcefully strong, thus of lasting significance, profoundly due to the forces "promoting discovery of novel and creative actions, ideas and social bonds, which in turn build [individuals'] enduring personal resources; ranging from physical and intellectual resources, to social and psychological resources … not just within the present, pleasant moment, but over the long term as well" (Fredrickson, 2013, p. 1367).

An unexpected advantage, the dynamic complexity surrounding the pandemic also offered time and space for emergent generative team leadership as a new model of leadership to become rooted and accepted as a viable alternative to conventional leadership, especially in environments of chaos and turbulence. Mobilizing, aligning, supporting, and executing in self-organized, innovative ways takes time and space, resources that the persistent pandemic granted to the emergent generative team leadership practicing communities, both social and corporate. Allowing a new way of being, becoming, and doing to take hold and become established, the opportunity to prove the validity of their self-organized and organically developed infrastructure, and importantly to demonstrate the power of the force of intent, love, care and hope, worked to begin a mindset shift from uncertainty to receptivity. This is noteworthy because mindsets naturally tend toward rigidity, particularly in contexts of stress, such as experienced during the pandemic.

The likelihood that mindsets will undergo any change largely depends on how explicitly self-conscious we are of our current mindsets and the extent to which we have access to the limitless emotional resources required for a mindset shift (Gupta & Govindarajan, 2002). The key that unlocks their potency is held by our very access to them. Access implies awareness and articulation of emotions that are already present in every individual, but often dormant or suppressed. Often, such social-emotional resources are deprioritized, taken for granted, or seen as peripheral to task execution, particularly in a work setting. Yet, without them, outcomes tend toward the instrumental more than the transformational, more tactical and short-term focused than strategically conscious and sustainable.

Access must be transformed into *assets* in order to become a normal part of individuals' repertoire of acting and relating. What kind of asset can having access to the forces of love, care, hope and intent become? Spurred by the global pandemic, the void unintentionally yet fortuitously revealed the leadership chasm to which community collectives and corporate teams spontaneously responded. Frequently unknown to each other, and unaware of the personal resources they had access to, individuals came together, compelled, determined, and inspired by an implicit purpose, and fueled their shared initiatives by love, care, hope, and intent. Drawing on the four forces, they gained access to a previously unarticulated power that proved so strong that countless enterprises sprouted and spread globally, critical needs were effectively met and creatively served, and self-empowered generative teams successfully elevated their productivity.

The imperative for us now is to determine what kind of consciousness we need to have to increase our access to these personal resources, the fuel that increases our viability to flourish in these new conditions we have created or must experience (Personal conversation, M. Bennett, November 3, 2021, during his webinar "Re-imagining the Future of the Workplace: Constructing Interculturally Viable Organizations"). Concurring with Marie Sonnet and Reid Spearman in their chapter, "Leading from the Edge: Precarity, Resilience, and Success in an Informal Academic Support Community," leadership can arise unexpectedly, from anywhere.

Clearly, what transforms uncertainty is nurturing increased awareness of the forces that fuel the consciousness of our new reality, enabling us to discover, understand and harness our own forces of love, care, hope and intent in order to embody the leadership needed in the inevitably turbulent future—in other words, the capacity and capability to convert access into assets that support "human flourishing … a state of optimal human functioning that simultaneously implies growth and longevity, beauty and goodness, robustness and resilience, and generativity and complexity" (Frederickson, 2013, p. 1373).

End Note

[1] See https://covidmutualaid.org/local-groups/

Meet the Authors

Kathleen Curran, PhD, is a global leadership development researcher, coach, facilitator and consultant, and experience designer; plus principal of Intercultural Systems Consulting, established in Singapore in 1996 and active worldwide. As an Institute for Social Innovation Fellow, Fielding Graduate University, she focuses her praxis on global leader identity, global talent development, and developing globally responsible strategies and outcomes. Recent publications include the co-edited volume, *Leadership on the Commons: Shifting Paradigms for a more Ethical, Equitable and Just World* (2022); "Developing Global Resonance for Global Leadership" in *Leadership and Power in International Development* (2018), "Global Identity Tensions for Global Leaders" in *Advances in Global Leadership* (2019), and "Global Identity and Global Leadership: Becoming, Knowing and Doing – Differently" in *The Study and Practice of Global Leadership* (2022). kathleen@intercultural-systems.com

Randal Joy Thompson, PhD is a scholar-practitioner who works in international development and researches leadership, the commons, and gender. She co-edited *Reimagining Leadership on the Commons: Shifting the Paradigm for a more Ethical, Equitable, and Just World* (2021) with Devin Singh and Kathleen Curran. Her 2021 book, *Proleptic Leadership on the Commons: Ushering in a New Global Order* proposed a novel leadership model for the post-capitalist transition. She co-edited *Leadership and Power in International Development: Navigating the Intersections of Gender, Culture, Context, and Sustainability* (2020) with Julia Storberg-Walker, which won the Human Resource Development R. Wayne Pace HRD Book of the Year Award. She holds a BA in philosophy from the University of California, Berkeley, an MA in philosophy and an MBA from the University of Chicago, an MA in biblical exposition from Capitol Seminary and Graduate School, and a PhD in human and organizational systems from Fielding Graduate University. rjoythompson@yahoo.com

References

Allen, K. (2021, November 2). *Leading from the roots. Regenerative leadership session October 2021* [Video]. YouTube. https://www.youtube.com/watch?v=A__Vm_9V5ns&t=1931s

Broadfoot, M. (2021, March 3). Teens and other volunteers help seniors find scarce COVID shots. *Scientific American.* https://www.scientificamerican.com/article/teens-and-other-volunteers-help-seniors-find-scarce-covid-shots/

Bushe, G. R. (2013). Generative process, generative outcome: The transformational potential of appreciative inquiry. In D.L. Cooperrider, D.P. Zandee, L.N. Godwin, M. Avital, & B. Boland (Eds.). *Organizational generativity: The appreciative inquiry summit and a scholarship of transformation* (pp. 89–113). Emerald Publishing.

Bushe, G. R. (2019). Generative leadership. *Canadian Journal of Physician Leadership.*

5(3), 141–147. https://bit.ly/3xta8IJ

Campbell, S. (2018). 7 Inspiring Traits of Compassionate Leaders. *Entrepreneur*. https://www.entrepreneur.com/article/310391

Cancian, F. M., & Oliker, S. J. (2000). *Caring and gender*. Alta Mira Press.

Castillo, E. A., & Trinh, M.P. (2019). Catalyzing capacity: Absorptive, adaptive, and generative leadership. *Journal of Organizational Change Management,32*(3), 356–376. https://doi.org/10.1108/JOCM-04-2017-0100

Cicchetti, D., & Rogosch, F. (1996). Equifinality and multifinality in developmental psychopathology. *Development and Psychopathology, 8*(04), 597–600. https://doi.org/10.1017/S0954579400007318

Curran, K. (2018). Global resonance. In R.J. Thompson, & J. Storberg-Walker (Eds.), *Leadership and power in international development: Navigating the intersections of gender, culture, context, and sustainability* (pp. 311–330). Emerald Publishers.

Fredrickson, B. L. (2001) The role of positive emotions in positive psychology: The broaden-and-build theory of positive emotions. *American Psychology, 56*(3), 218–226. https://psycnet.apa.org/doi/10.1037/0003-066X.56.3.218

Fredrickson, B. L. (2013). *Love 2.0: How our supreme emotion affects everything we feel, think, do, and become*. Hudson Street Press.

Fromm, E. (2006). *The art of loving*. Harper Press.

Gergen, K. J. (1978). Toward generative theory. *Journal of Personality and Social Psychology,36*(11),1344–1360.https://psycnet.apa.org/doi/10.1037/0022-3514.36.11.1344

Groover, J. (2013, September 12). 7 habits for an empowered life. *Huffington Post.* https://www.huffpost.com/entry/positive-habits_b_3551912

Gupta, A. K., & Govindarajan, V. (2002). Cultivating a global mindset. *Academy of Management Executive, 16*(1), 116–126. https://doi.org/10.5465/ame.2002.6640211

Hardt, M., & Negri, A. (2009). *Commonwealth*. Harvard University Press.

Harper, D. (2000). *Online etymology dictionary*. https://www.etymonline.com

Hazy, J. K., & Uhl Bien, M. (2015). Towards operationalizing complexity leadership: How generative, administrative and community-building leadership practices enact organizational outcomes. *Leadership. 11*(1),79–104. https://doi.org/10.1177%2F1742715013511483

Heifetz, R., Grashow, A., & Linsky, M. (2009). *The practice of adaptive leadership: Tools and tactics for changing your organization and the world.* Harvard Business Review Press.

Jones-Schenk, J. (2020). Hope as a generative force: Lifting our gaze to the future. *Journal of Continuing Education in Nursing. 51*(5), 203–204. https://doi.org/10.3928/00220124-20200415-03

Kahane, A. (2007). *Solving tough problems: An open way of talking, listening, and creating new realities*. Berrett-Koehler.

Keränen, A. (2019). *Exploring a new understanding of responsible leadership.* https://responsibility.global/exploring-a-new-understanding-of-responsible-leadership-part-1-830df82ce108

Kolditz, T. A. (2017). *In extremis leadership: Leading as if your life depended upon it.* Jossey-Bass.

Lane, D. A., & Down, M. (2010). The art of managing for the future: Leadership of turbulence. *ManagementDecision,48*(4),512–527.https://doi.org/10.1108/00251741011041328

Lynch, P., & Khoo, A. (2020, March 22). Coronavirus: Volunteers flock to join community support groups. *BBS News.* https://www.bbc.com/news/uk-england-51978388

Macaux, W. P. (2012). Generative leadership: responding to the call for responsibility. The *Journal of Management Development, 31*(5), 449–469. https://doi.org/10.1108/02621711211226042

Macy, J., & Johnstone, C. (2010). *Active hope: How to face the mess we're in without going crazy.* New World Library.

Maturana, H. & Punnell, B. (1999). The biology of business: Love expands intelligence. *Reflections, 1*(2), 58–66. https://bit.ly/3GZ7KMH

Nussbaum, M. (2011). *Creating capabilities: The human development approach.* Belknap Press.

Nussbaum, M. (2015). *Political emotions: Why love matters for justice.* Harvard University Press.

Pendle, D. (2020). GAIA journey and the healing potential of the social field. *Presencing Institute.* https://medium.com/presencing-institute-blog/gaia-journey-and-the-healing-potential-of-the-social-field-1e779dc1c588

Ramezan, M. (2011) Intellectual capital and organizational organic structure in knowledge society: How are these concepts related? *International Journal of Information Management, 31*(1), 88–95. https://doi.org/10.1016/j.ijinfomgt.2010.10.004

Scharmer, O. (2006). *Presencing Institute.* https://www.presencing.org/community/hubs

Scharmer, O., & Kaufer, K. (2013). *Leading from the emerging future: From ego-system to ecosystem economies.* Berrett-Koehler.

Senge, P., Kleiner, A., Roberts, C., Ross, R., Roth, G., & Smith, B. (1999). *The dance of change: The challenges of sustaining momentum in learning organizations.* Nicholas Brealey Publishing.

Senge, P. (2017). There are no heroes: Peter Senge on system leadership. *Massachusetts Institute of Technology Education.* http://leadership.mit.edu/no-heroes-peter-senge-system-leadership/

Snyder, C. R. (1994). *The psychology of hope.* Free Press.

Sommer, S. Amy, Howell, Jane M., & Hadley, C. N. (2015). Keeping positive and building strength: The role of affect and team leadership in developing resilience during an organizational crisis. *Group & Organization Management, 41*(2), 172–202. https://doi.org/10.1177%2F1059601115578027

Steinbruner, J. D. (2002). *The cybernetic theory of decision: New dimensions of political analysis.* Princeton University Press.

Stiehl, E., Kossek, E. E., Leana, C., & Keller, Q. (2018). A multilevel model of care flow: Examining the generation and spread of care in organizations. *Organizational Psychology Review, 8*(1), 31–69. https://doi.org/10.1177%2F2041386617740371

Surie, G., & Hazy, J. (2006). *Generative leadership: Nurturing innovation in complex systems.* Emergent Publication.

Taylor, S. (2016). *Generative leadership*. What is Dialogue? https://www.whatisdialogue.com/tag/generative-leadership/

Thompson, R. J. (2018). *Proleptic leadership on the commons: Ushering in a new global order.* Emerald Publishing.

Tolentino, J. (2020, May 11). What mutual aid can do during a pandemic: A radical practice is now gaining mainstream attention. Will it change how we help each other? *New Yorker*. https://www.newyorker.com/magazine/2020/05/18/what-mutual-aid-can-do-during-a-pandemic

Todorova, G., & Durisin, B. (2007). Absorptive capacity: Valuing a reconceptualization. *The Academy of Management Review, 32*(3), 774–786. https://doi.org/10.5465/amr.2007.25275513

Wilde, L. (2017). Embracing imperfection: Plato vs. Nussbaum on love. *Philosophy Now.* https://philosophynow.org/issues/122/Embracing_Imperfection_Plato_vs_Nussbaum_On_Love

Chapter 9

Psychology and Social Change: Challenging Ourselves and Systems

Dominique Eugene
Institute for Social Innovation Fellow

Myisha Driver-Woods
Institute for Social Innovation Fellow

La Tonya Lawrence
Institute for Social Innovation Fellow

In 2020, the coronavirus pandemic (COVID-19) had a global impact on many people, which yielded unprecedented economic, emotional, and social stressors. Specifically, in the United States, 2020 was a year with increased social unrest in cities across the nation because of the publicly documented homicides of African Americans, including Breonna Taylor, George Floyd, Ahmaud Arbery, and Daunte Wright, to name just a few. Their deaths brought heightened awareness of racial injustices and the need for dramatic social change. This *dramatic social change*, as described by de la Sablonnière (2017), is a body of theory and research that aims to understand the psychology of social change. Dramatic social change is characterized as a "rapid pace of change, a rupture in social structure, a rupture in normative structure, and threat to cultural identity" (de la Sablonnière, 2017, p. 2). The need for dramatic social change requires psychologists to prioritize their efforts to critically assess systems, practices, and definitions of leadership (Schedlitzki & Edwards, 2018) that continue to marginalize Black, Indigenous, and people of color (BIPOC).

As American society continues to grapple with the short- and unknown long-term effects of the COVID-19 pandemic and long-standing issues of disparities and discrimination on the mental health and overall social functioning of its citizens, psychologists are challenged with finding more effective approaches to address the psychological consequences of socio-economic division and injustices that exist amongst the masses. The BIPOC communities struggle with systems that keep them in metaphorical, and often literal shackles. Oppressive systems embedded in colonial views about healing makes thriving towards optimal well-being almost an impossibility for most. Borrowing from the West African [Ghanaian] concept of Sankofa—to reach back and gather the best of what the past can teach so that humanity can achieve full potential for moving forward (Gyekye, 1997; Quarcoo, 1972; Temple, 2010)—may provide insight into how psychologists might look back, pre-colonization, to identify more efficacious approaches for the confluence of issues emerging due to the pandemic. New approaches such as Hardy's (2016) privilege and subjugated task (PAST) model may provide psychologists, as transformational leaders, additional tools to effectively engage in racial discussions by limiting polarization and shifting the focus towards strategies for change and exploring change that is needed across various systems put in place by laws and policies rooted in White supremacy. Therefore, this chapter focuses on how psychologists can promote the development of transformational and change leaders by leveraging their individual and organizational influence to address inequities that prevent more optimal life. These inequities are described by Nussbaum (2011) as social capabilities of life, which she defined as society's capacity to provide the opportunity to live a life uninterrupted by premature death. This chapter will explore the role of psychologists, as part of institutional infrastructures, in positively impacting these systems to improve social justice issues that negatively impact one's capacity for life.

Dramatic Social Change

According to de la Sablonnière (2017), there are four categories of social change: stability, inertia, incremental social change, and dramatic social change (p. 2). Stability describes an event that does not affect societal norms or structures, even if this event negatively impacts a particular group of people. Inertia reflects a series of events that impact many people, and although change may be desired, the group does not have the capacity to implement the desired changes. Incremental social change is defined as a period where social transformation occurs slowly over time that changes social and normative structures (p. 2). Throughout history, ruling powers have been willing to concede to movements related to social justice and civil rights issues that took this path, with decades and sometimes centuries worth of political, social, and legislative actions leading up to milestones of significant change. In contrast, dramatic social change is defined as "a situation where a rapid event leads to a profound societal transformation and produces a rupture in the equilibrium for the social and normative structures, and changes/threatens the cultural identity of group members" (p. 12).

Historically, significant social change within the United States has been marked by specific social, political, and economic events that have garnered national and international attention. For example, technological advances in the mass production of goods marked the beginning of the industrial revolution in the late 1800s through the early 1900s (Mohajan, 2020). This shift moved masses of people from rural areas into cities and towns, thereby creating significant social changes in American society. Similarly, collective experiences and activities related to social justice can impact movements leading up to events (Harris, 2006) such as the March on Washington, which occurred on August 28, 1963, followed by President Johnson's signing of the Civil Rights Act of 1964. The March on Washington's focus on voting and civil rights was an impetus for the Civil Rights Act, which prohibited unequal voter registration requirements and desegregated public places (Aiken et al., 2013). These events and how they are documented create a collective memory of the past and can impact the ongoing struggle for civil rights and full citizenship for people of African descent, which began centuries ago and continues for BIPOC and other marginalized groups today (Jackson, 2021).

The global impact of COVID-19, civil protests, and social unrest in 2020 also motivated people to join efforts for change and engage in more meaningful dialogue about ongoing issues of inequity and social justice by questioning ideas, policies, and practices that contribute to inequities. The field of psychology and individual psychologists were not absent from this conversation. In 2021, the American Psychological Association (APA) issued a formal apology statement (APA, 2021a) and a plan for resolution. These statements and proposed activities address social inequities to reflect a shift and movement towards social change. An opposing perspective presented by the Association of Black Psychologists (ABPsi) was a rebuke of APA's apology. ABPsi is an association that was founded in San Francisco in 1968 after major disagreements with how APA viewed Black communities. The association set out to address the magnitude of problems Black psychologists and Black communities faced. The association prospered through the guided principle of self-determination to address mental health disparities, social problems the community faced, and to organize skills and abilities needed to influence much needed change (ABPsi, 1968). ABPsi (2021) stated APA has a long history of insidious promotion of racial hierarchy. The history of Euro-American psychology cannot easily be dismissed with an apology; therefore, this apology falls short and must empower BIPOC communities through APA "abdicating their unjustifiable claim to be the arbiter of universal human functioning (ABPsi, 2021, p. 1). The alternate standpoint presented by ABPsi speaks to an underlying need for dramatic social change.

In 2020 the emergence of the COVID-19 pandemic and its social and economic impacts created a dramatic change in most Americans' lives and magnified long-standing disparities in health (Bassett et al., 2020) and economics (Montenovo et al., 2020). The combined timing of the COVID-19 pandemic with the public murder of George Floyd and widely circulated videos of brutality and discrimination against BIPOC and other marginalized groups resulted in widespread efforts of people nationwide to create social change, with the potential to challenge systems to move from incremental to dramatic social change. According to de la Sablonnière (2017), dramatic social change has four characteristics: the pace of change, a rupture in social structure, a rupture in the normative structure, and change or threat in the cultural identity of group members. When applying de la Sablonnière's characteristics of dramatic social change to the events of 2020, the social conditions reflect (a) an increase in the pace at which people are impacted (COVID-19 illness, deaths, mental illness, negative economic impact, health disparities), (b) a rupture in social structure (negative impact on medical systems, social safety nets, polarized distrust of governmental intervention), (c) a rupture in normative structure (challenging habitual behaviors of discrimination, requiring new behaviors), and (d) a threat to cultural identity (social justice movements challenging the ideal American culture and values of equity and justice versus the experience of marginalized groups).

Since dramatic change can affect one's mental outlook, psychologists must be prepared to clarify the biological, psychological, and social influences that impact day-to-day functioning. Psychologists must reflect on their role in constructing societal change on micro and macro levels. As leaders in clinical, research, and organizational settings, psychologists seem uniquely positioned to support needed change related to issues of change and social justice. Other professional domains, such as architects involved with building a better operating room, are looking at how their infrastructure caters to racist environments and are taking steps to dismantling the system (Ibrahim et al., 2017). Psychologists would do well with taking heed of such necessary changes.

Theoretical Framework

The concept of *Sankofa* originates from the Akan people of West Africa and is expressed in the Akan language as *"se wo were fina wo sankofa a yenkyi"* (Gyekye, 1997; Osei, 2020; Quarcoo, 1972; Temple, 2010; Willis, 1998). This phrase translates to, "It is not taboo to return to the past to fetch what you have forgotten or lost" (Temple, 2010; Willis, 1998). Sankofa teaches that society must go back to its roots to move forward. There is a need for social concepts to return to what has been lost, forgotten, forgone, or even been stripped of to reclaim its dignity (Osei, 2020; Temple, 2010). Sankofa exemplifies the importance of reaching back to knowledge gained in the past and bringing it into the present to make positive progress (Gyekye, 1997; Osei, 2020; Quarcoo, 1972; Temple, 2010; Willis, 1998).

In discussing the concept of Sankofa, one must also address the Euro-American-centric character of the modern global order (Suffla et al., 2019) by exploring Nussbaum's (2011) concept of life. This exploration should be conducted through the lens of decolonial theory to highlight the need for re-imagined leadership for addressing dramatic social change. Decolonial theory provides a framework for understanding racialized violence inherent in the modern world (Maldonado-Torres, 2017; Ndlovu-Gatsheni, 2013). A central concept of decolonial perspectives is "*coloniality*: habits of mind and ways of being" such as colonial mentality and racial privilege (David & Okazaki, 2006; Phillips &

Lowery, 2018; Suffla et al., 2019, p. 1) that have roots in the colonial period but persist long after the end of colonial rule. Whereas mainstream accounts typically portray modernity and its individualist psychological manifestations as the leading edge of progress, decolonial theorists use the phrase "*modernity/coloniality* to emphasize the extent to which colonial violence constitutes the modern global order" (Suffla et al., 2019, p. 1). This phrase *modernity/coloniality* positions coloniality as the "darker side of modernity" (Mignolo, 2011)—the typically obscured shadow of racialized violence inseparable from the shiny project of modern individualist growth and development (Suffla et al., 2019).

Racialized violence, as described by Nicolas and Thompson (2019), is the ongoing occurrence of the harming and killing of Black people. It is also that which keeps Black people from being able to obtain psychological and physical safety because of the continued systemic separation, degradation, and inequalities imposed through "histories of exploitation and differential allocations of power across social, political, economic spheres … and ultimately compromises the collective pursuit of emancipation from racism" (Nicolas & Thompson, 2019, p. 587). The presumed superior stance of Whiteness casts Black peoples as inferior, less deserving, and inhuman, thereby perpetuating a wide range of disparities (political, social, and economic) that can lead to death (Helms et al., 2012; Nicolas & Thompson, 2019).

Modernity/coloniality sustains the nature of how colonialism continues to have an impact through brutal and structural violence on BIPOC communities (Mignolo, 2011; Helms et al., 2012; Nicolas & Thompson, 2019). The deprivation of psychological and physical safety strips communities of the ability to imagine a quality of life filled with capabilities. The inability to have any control over one's environment due to political infrastructures or material rights supports systemic separation, degradations, and inequalities. Nussbaum discusses having control over one's environment as the ability to effectively participate in politics and being protected in doing so. The material aspect consists of having equal property rights and equal employment as well as "having freedom from unwarranted search and seizure" (Nussbaum, 2011, p. 34). Such luxuries are not afforded to the BIPOC communities at large because of racialized views stemming from colonial models of governance. By delving deeper into the colonial darker past, an opportunity to transform into more just and equitable ways of being and leading can be possible.

Transformational Leadership

Burns (1978) first introduced the concepts of transformational and transactional leadership by describing transformational leaders as leaders whose behaviors uplift and motivate their followers towards a common good. He described transactional leaders as using followers' self-interests to motivate (Burns, 1978). Transactional leaders engage in contingent-based interactions focused on modifying or controlling the subordinate's behavior and reducing problems impacting designated outcomes or goals (Bass, 1985, 1999). In contrast, transformational leaders use shared vision to inspire subordinates and align their followers' individual goals with aspirations for the group's good (Bass, 1999). Bass (1985) applied these concepts to leadership and operationalized Burns' (1978) original model. According to Bass (1985, 1999), transformational leadership fosters autonomy and challenging work.

Although most leaders use transactional and transformational leadership behaviors, they typically lean towards a dominant style that reflects four dimensions: idealized influence, inspiration, individual consideration, and intellectual stimulation (Bass, 1985, 1999). Idealized influence (initially referred to by Bass as charisma) is described as the leaders' influence and model of high standards and the ability to communicate vision (Bass, 1999). Inspiration refers to the leaders' use of nonintellectual, emotional qualities to influence the process (Bass, 1985). Individualized consideration refers to leaders' ability to take a developmental approach of individuals by taking into consideration specific goals and personal needs (Bass, 1985). Finally, Bass (1999) described intellectual stimulation as actions that increase followers' awareness and interest in identifying and analyzing problems in innovative ways and the development of solutions. In essence, transformational leaders are aware of the needs of their followers and motivate them to move towards more collective good and goals.

An integral component of transformational leadership is its relationship with high moral reasoning. Transformational leaders aspire to and inspire others to elevate beyond their self-interest toward higher moral reasoning (Bass, 1999). In order to motivate others towards a higher moral good, effective transformational leaders exhibit higher moral maturity (Harkness et al., 1981; Turner et al., 2002).

In this sense, moral maturity is conceptualized through the lens of Kohlberg's (1976) proposed theory of cognitive moral development which theorizes that a person's moral capacity is connected to problem solving strategies developed in earlier stages. Kohlberg's (1976) theory described three levels of development including (a) preconventional, which is characterized by obedience to accepted authority, (b) conventional, which depends on established laws and rules to guide moral behavior, and (c) postconventional, during which a person relies more on universal principles to guide moral decisions. Researchers have expanded upon Kohlberg's (1976) work to include the development of moral reasoning across generations (Weber & Elm, 2018) and within the context of culture (Goldschmidt et al., 2021). Turner et al. (2002) described morally mature leaders as those who have more complex reasoning and relational skills and can draw upon a variety of possible solutions. Additionally, leaders high in moral reasoning are more likely to engage in behaviors associated with transformational leadership (Dukerich et al., 1990).

If the characteristics of transformational leadership as described by Bass (1985, 1999) are applied to working towards social justice, then psychologists as leaders must work to understand the collective goal of social justice movements and the ability to share this in a way that inspires others to move towards this goal. Therefore, psychologists who desire to truly embrace transformational leadership must be willing to examine their role in issues of social justice on individual and societal levels. Psychologists, thus inspired, must be willing to critically examine the complexities of social justice and how it relates to the psychological safety and well-being of marginalized people and develop solutions that positively contribute to improving the quality of life, as described by Nussbaum (2011), of people in our society.

Transformational Leadership & Social Justice

Research has demonstrated that utilization of a transformation leadership approach is effective in inspiring people towards goals that benefit the collective (Dappa et al., 2019). Psychologists and other professionals have contributed to the vast body of literature exploring transformational leadership's dimensions, applications, and benefits. Bass (1985, 1999) suggested that transformational leadership can be expanded as a paradigm to describe groups within organizations, larger socio-political systems, and international relationships. Research has demonstrated the positive impact of transformational leadership on organizational tensions and performance (Bass & Riggio, 2006), as well as performance at the managerial (Waldman et al., 2011), staff (Dvir et al., 2002; Zohar, 2002), and team levels (Bass et al., 2003). Research has also demonstrated the effect of transformational leadership on change and implementation (Farahnak et al., 2020).

Although transformational leadership has demonstrated positive impact on change (Bass et al., 2003; Bass & Riggio, 2006; Farahnak et al., 2020; Waldman et al., 2011; Zohar, 2002), this approach falls short of dramatic social change if an anti-racist lens is not integrated (Kendi, 2019). According to Kendi (2019), racism is a combination of racist policies and ideas that normalize racial inequities, and anti-racist policies are measures that sustain or produce equity among racial groups. Based on these definitions, psychologists who embrace transformational leadership as a model to support change and are guided by movement towards higher moral good must consider taking an anti-racist stance. An anti-racist actively moves beyond neutral and non-racist stances. An anti-racist actively and intentionally moves from fear into self-evaluation of ways that may be unintentionally reinforcing racist ideas and systems into challenging and transforming these systems, as well as magnifying the voices of those most affected. Psychologists as transformational leaders in their work with individuals, corporations, and as a collective group of professionals, can use this approach to support a movement towards a more just and equitable society. From this perspective, psychologists must operate with higher moral reasoning and work towards equity by contributing to the psychological and overall health and well-being of members of society.

Nussbaum's (2011) capabilities approach offers an assessment of quality of life by examining aspects of life and a person's opportunities within each of those facets. According to Nussbaum (2011), a socially just society should provide opportunities for choice within these categories for individuals. Within these ten capabilities, she describes the ability to "live to the end of a human life of normal length: not dying prematurely or before one's life is so reduced as not be worth living" (Nussbaum, 2011, p. 35). The challenge posed to psychologists as transformational leaders is to engage in the process of transforming, identifying, and aligning the goals of organizations and institutions to work beyond that of their individual self-interest to that of the higher moral good of social justice. This work includes the capability to live life without premature disruption, free from emotional and psychological oppression resulting in better overall health and quality of life for individuals and society. By examining the role of psychologists in making positive contributions towards reducing the psychological pain and suffering of others, the field can expand its lens of the role of psychologists in movements of social justice and dramatic social change. This can be accomplished, not only through interventions, but through research to increase the understanding of the human condition and psychological threats, such as racism and oppression, of any kind, and promote advocacy to reduce the negative impact of these oppressive forces.

New Approaches

Psychologists play a pivotal role in the areas of research, assessment, and treatment intervention that can broadly influence the larger society. As transformational leaders, they have an opportunity to critically evaluate current practices and re-imagine their role in contributing to an anti-racist society. However, they are often reluctant to challenge well-established theories on which these practices are based. The *Ethical Principles of Psychologists and Code of Conduct,* authored by the APA (2017), aimed to provide guidance for the dedicated action of psychologists and serve as standards of professional conduct. The preamble and general principles designated "aspirational goals to guide psychologists toward the highest ideals of psychology" (p. 2), and they are to be considered when resolving ethical dilemmas. Among these general principles are *Principle A*: Beneficence and nonmaleficence, *Principle B*: Fidelity and responsibility, *Principle C*: Integrity, *Principle D*: Justice, and *Principle E*: Respect for people's rights and dignity (APA, 2017).

Moreover, the APA offers a number of guidelines to advance health equity and cultural sensitivity, such as *APA Guidelines for Psychological Practice for People with Low-Income and Economic Marginalization* (APA, 2019a), *Guidelines for Providers of Psychological Services to Ethnic, Linguistic, and Culturally Diverse Populations* (APA, 2020), *Multicultural Guidelines* (APA, 2017), *APA Guidelines on Race and Ethnicity in Psychology: Promoting*

Responsiveness and Equity (APA, 2019b), as well as tools for guiding the gathering of data as in the *Cultural Formation Interview* (APA, 2013). While the preamble, general principles, and various guidelines are likely well-intentioned, there has been a dereliction of duty regarding equity, diversity, and inclusion (EDI) since the inception of American psychology as a scientific discipline in the mid-19th century. APA recently acknowledged this as a failure of their leadership (APA, 2021a).

Specifically, APA's board of trustees issued an apology to people of color for positing and promulgating racist ideology that undergirds American psychology. In their *Apology to People of Color for APA's Role in Promoting, Perpetuating, and Failing to Challenge Racism, Racial Discrimination, and Human Hierarchy in U.S.* (APA, 2021a), the APA acknowledged its participation in disparaging communities of color, which contributed to systemic injustices that fell short of its mission to "benefit society and improve lives" (p. 1). APA indicated the apology was constructed utilizing data from historical findings, surveys, listening sessions, and reports. One noted report was written by APA Division 45, the Society for the Psychological Study of Culture, Ethnicity, and Race, titled *Protecting and Defending Our People: Nakni tushka anowa* (Aiello et al., 2021) that proposed the need for an anti-racist discipline of psychology through the eradication of racist and colonial roots. APA acknowledged its complicity in conducting and publishing pseudo-research that falsely promoted White racial hierarchy, contributing to racial stereotypes and prejudices against communities of color. Furthermore, APA called for implementation of the EDI framework and asked psychologists and trainees to "consider the limitations of White Western-oriented clinical practice" (APA, 2021a, p. 1). Moreover, APA acknowledged failure to previously accept responsibility for promoting racial discrimination and expressed contrition for long-term impact. Though APA deemed their apology to communities of color long overdue, they are hopeful it will lead to a path toward atonement for racism and be a catalyst for "healing and reconciliation" (APA, 2021a, p. 1).

In addition to the apology, APA recognized the need for accompanying action and endeavored to expose, understand, and help dismantle racism operating in our society. Consequently, APA proposed a resolution in *Role of Psychology and APA in Dismantling Systemic Racism Against People of*

Color in U.S. (APA, 2021b) that explores the role psychological science may play in ameliorating the harms perpetrated by APA upon communities of color across systems, including early childhood development, health care, education, work, economic opportunities, criminal justice, public policy, government, and science. Included in the resolution is a call to all psychologists to actively engage in anti-racist efforts to address the causes and effects of all levels of racism in the education system, advocate for changes to policies and procedures that contribute to racist practices and outcomes, engage in anti-racist practice through an intersectional lens, develop preventive and intervention efforts to promote racial justice, and promote racial justice through their research, teaching, practice, and advocacy (APA, 2021b, p. 8).

APA (2021b) also encouraged psychologists to "seek further education and training on implicit bias, microaggressions, and the necessity of a developmentally, culturally sensitive and race-conscious, trauma-informed, and lifespan approach to treatment when working with populations with histories of oppression and intergenerational trauma" (p. 16). Overall, APA suggested this resolution will assist in committing them to an ongoing effort of dismantling the very racism they helped to legitimize.

Along with calling for psychologists to engage in anti-racist practice, APA acknowledged the "complexity of ethnoracial dialogues" in the United States (APA, 2021b, p. 2). Similarly, Hardy (2016) previously acknowledged the history of strained race relationships in the United States and noted the two prevailing approaches of engaging in racial discussions were spontaneity and avoidance. Both approaches are problematic in that the former usually involves strong emotional outbursts that strengthen divisiveness, while the latter contributes to underlying racial tensions that maintain the status quo. The overwhelming prevalence of these two approaches highlights the need for a structured approach to engaging in discussion about race.

PAST Model

Hardy's (2016) privilege and subjugated task (PAST) model offers psychologists, as transformational leaders, tools to effectively engage in racial discussion by limiting polarization and shifting the focus towards strategies for change. Underpinning the PAST model are two factors, power and privilege, which interlock, overlap, and mediate the construction and implementation of racial discussion (Hardy, 2016). Adherence to this power/privilege framework is essential to helping defuse combative discussion and facilitate constructive discussion. Therefore, implementation of the PAST model requires participants to engage in "racial self-analysis" to determine one's racial identity as either privileged or subjugated (p. 126). While recognizing that parts of oneself may align with privilege and parts with subjugation (Hardy, 2015), it is essential that race be the singular focus of this determination to prevent the discussion from devolving into a comparison of one's suffering (Hardy, 2016). Additionally, Hardy (2016) espoused that U.S. society was established with a White supremacist ideology; hence, for the purpose of progressive racial discussion, the PAST model assumes persons of White racial identity hold privileged positions and persons of color hold subjugated positions.

The PAST model (Hardy, 2016) proposes that racial discussion can be less polarizing and lead to meaningful transformation if discussions with participants, those with privileged and subjugated positions, rigidly adhere to certain tasks during intense discussion. The tasks of each group are listed.

Tasks of the Privileged

1. Differentiate between intentions and consequences and always start with an acknowledgment of the latter: *Focus conversations on the consequences experienced by the subjugated person.*

2. Avoid the overt and covert negation of subjugated conversations and disclosures: *Practice the art and skill of validation.*

3. Avoid reactive reflexes: Acts of relational retrenchment, rebuttal, and retribution. *Develop a thick skin.*

4. Avoid the issuance of prescriptions: *Supplant prescriptions with vulnerable disclosures about one's self.*

5. Avoid speaking from the KNOE (knowledgeable, neutral, objective, expert) position: *Always locate one's racial self in the conversation.*

Tasks of the Subjugated

1. Challenge silencing and voicelessness: *Use "I" messages and embed all statements within the framework of, "I think, I feel, and I wish." Practice and*

take risks in making just one comment more than you are comfortable making.

2. Regulate and re-channel rage: *Use rage as an energy source to foster and reinforce your voice and self-advocacy. Resolve to stay engaged in difficult conversations. Attack ideas, not people.*

3. Engage in a process of exhaling: *Focus on being congruent and communicating accordingly. Say what you mean and mean what you say.*

4. Cease and desist caretaking of the privileged: *Stay intimately engaged, but grant uninterrupted emotional space to [the privileged] to explore, understand, and experience the myriad of complex thoughts and feelings that race conversations are likely to provoke. Be caring without caretaking.*

5. Maintain investment in the conversation: *Refrain from analyzing "the other" while simultaneously speaking from the core of one's thoughts, feelings, and experiences.*

Hardy (2016) indicated the *Tasks of the Privileged* and *Tasks of the Subjugated* might have the most positive impact when utilized concurrently during race discussion; however, the tasks are not intended to be a solution for racial injustice. Notwithstanding, psychologists are challenged to review and implement the structured tasks of the PAST model and initiate productive racial discussion in professional and personal spaces alike. Actively engaging in anti-racist practice, whether a psychologist identifies with the privileged or subjugated, will not only begin to challenge well-established theories by confronting colonial mentality and other impediments to progressive race discussions, but it will also reveal the deleterious effects of racist practices (APA, 2021b, p. 8) and empower survivors of White supremacy toward a liberated existence (ABPsi, 2021). As psychologists are held to a higher standard of serving as transformational leaders in this capacity, they align individual goals with the greater goal and higher moral good (Bass, 1985).

As society faces a new world order, the culmination of the COVID-19 pandemic, ongoing social injustice, and social inequity, changes are needed for the sustainability of society. Part of that change requires dismantling the social construct that keeps individuals disenfranchised through White supremacy and perspectives of colonization. The denial or misguided perception of systemic racism points to a need for reforms that take a critical look at historical events that continue to contribute to the division among individuals because of the color of their skin. Members of the colonizer communities are beneficiaries of over 400 years of intergenerational systemic racial discrimination (Rothberg, 2020). It is imperative for the powers that be to acknowledge the shared ethical responsibility for becoming anti-racist.

Several professions are making attempts at shifting to an anti-racist environment at the workplace. Specific changes are needed to truly see how the systems have perpetrated a multitude of infractions against people considered outside the dominant race in the United States. Figure 20 is a world envisioned by Ibrahim et al. (2017) used for discussing health and healthcare through the lens of anti-racist approaches. It is their personal journey towards a transformation that they share freely with society to know better to do better.

This becoming anti-racist model can be applied to psychologists as transformational leaders working towards dramatic social change. Psychologists, as individuals and collectively, need to navigate past the "fear zone" and acknowledge that there has been an avoidance and denial of uncomfortable conversations, interventions, and standards of practice related to inequities. Psychologists should then move into the "learning zone" by participating in honest self-reflection related to individual and collective contributions of such inequities that prevent people from obtaining Nussbaum's (2011) capabilities, specifically her description of life free from unnecessary pain and suffering, which contribute to shortening the lifespan. Once in the "growth zone," psychologists embracing the characteristics of transformational leadership must use their influence to advocate for policies and practices that move towards the greater good of equity and anti-racism.

It is imperative for psychologists to actively work towards dramatic social change but through the stance of a transformational leader in order to deconstruct traditional approaches using decolonial theory (Maldonado-Torres, 2017; Ndlovu-Gatsheni, 2013). Learning and incorporating the concept of Sankofa to emphasize that using Nussbaum's social justice model and psychologists as transformational leaders utilizing approaches such as the PAST model (Hardy, 2016), psychologists can assist individuals and systems with engaging in meaningful dialogue to move the field forward in this important area. The

Figure 20
Becoming Anti-Racist

Note. Graphic is "free to use, copy, and share" at [1]. Ibrahim, A. M., Dimick, J. B., & Joseph, A. (2017). Building a better operating room: Views from surgery and architecture. *Annals of Surgery, 265*(1), 34–36.

use of guiding tools such as the becoming anti-racist approach (Ibrahim et al., 2017; Kendi, 2019) can be instrumental, not just for psychologists, in evaluating institutional practices and combating racial and social injustices.

Summary

Psychologists cannot continue to sit idly while so many travesties take place in society, with the field contributing to those disparities. For the field to be better, it must do better, not just talk about doing better. Equal rights and justice should not be just rhetoric for leaders to hang their shingles on. The psychological field, as with all other disciplines, must find new tools to dismantle the master's house (Lorde, 1983, 2018). In the wake of the murders and homicides of BIPOC communities, particularly George Floyd, a global reckoning occurred that included changes with popular advertisements and children's books: Aunt Jemima, cream of wheat, Dreyer's Eskimo Pie, Dr. Seuss, to name a few. Although a step in the right direction, that is not enough. These changes are only window dressing that do not go to the root of systemic oppression. Cross disciplinary, interdisciplinary, intersection of social justice movements can build for a better tomorrow. Dramatic social change asks for making things better, but transformational leadership requires solving, not just patchwork, but a true willingness to make changes and create capabilities for all to thrive despite the color of their skin.

End Note

[1] https://www.surgeryredesign.com/

Meet the Authors

Dominique Eugene, PhD is a Haitian American alumna of Fielding Graduate University's clinical psychology program. She is a licensed marriage and family therapist, a registered play therapist, a certified trauma specialist, and an infant-family and early childhood mental health specialist in California. She is a recipient of the Harvard University, Boston University, Northwestern University, and University of New Mexico (HBNU) Consortium Fogarty Global Health Fellowship and is an Institute for Social Innovation Fellow at Fielding. As an HBNU Fellow residing in Cape Town, she conducted research at Stellenbosch University on women offenders of intimate partner violence with history of childhood maltreatment and PTSD. She is an APA Division 52 Global Citizen Psychologist Citation awardee. She serves on the board of the California Mental Health Advocates for Children & Youth and the Association of Traumatic Stress Specialists and chairs the California Association of Infant Mental Health social justice committee. deugene@email.fielding.edu

Myisha Driver-Woods, PhD is a licensed clinical psychologist and earned her doctorate in clinical psychology from Fielding Graduate University. She completed her internship and post-doctoral fellowship training at Children's Hospital Los Angeles. Dr. Driver-Woods earned her BS in psychology from Howard University and MA in counseling psychology from National University. She is a California- endorsed, infant family early childhood mental health specialist and reflective practice facilitator II and a graduate of the leadership education in neurodevelopmental disabilities training program. She is a proud native of Compton, California and uses her personal and professional experiences to educate others and advocate for social and racial justice. She is a recipient of the Diane Kipnes Endowed Fund for Social Innovation Award and serves as a co-chair on the CalAIHM social justice committee. She also serves as a board member for PSYCHES of COLOR, a non-profit organization focused on supporting Black and Latinx youth. myjoidriver@gmail.com

La Tonya F. Lawrence, PhD is a waivered clinical psychologist with Monterey County Health Department. She studied at the Arizona School of Professional Psychology at Argosy University, earning a Master of Arts in sport-exercise psychology in 2010 and a Master of Arts in mental health counseling in 2011, and maintains a licensed professional counselor certification with the Arizona Board of Behavioral Health Examiners. Dr. Lawrence attended an APA-accredited, doctoral clinical psychology program at Midwestern University, earning a Master of Arts in clinical psychology in 2017. Additionally, she created *"Mindfulness Inclusion Training: Promoting Healthy Racial Socialization Within the Workplace,"* completed the dissertation, *"Eradicating Race-based and Subjugation Effects: Group Treatment for African Americans Who Endure Racial Trauma"* and earned a doctorate of clinical psychology in August 2019. With approximately 14 years of experience in behavioral health, Dr. Lawrence endeavors to facilitate healing conversations that mitigate physical and psychological manifestations of white supremacy. lafae33@gmail.com

References

Aiello, M., Bismar, D., Casanova, S., Casas, J. M., Chang, D., Chin, J. L., Comas-Diaz, L., Crane, L. S., Demir, Z., Garcia, M. A., Hita, L., Leverett, P., Mendez, K., Morse, G. S., Shodiya-Zeumault, S., Sloan, M. O., Weil, M. C., & Blume, A. W. (2021). Protecting and defending our people: Nakni tushka anowa (The Warrior's Path). Final report- APA Division 45 Warrior's Path Presidential Task Force. *Journal of Indigenous Research, 9*(2021), 8. https://doi.org/10.26077/2en0-6610

Aiken, J.R., Salmon, E.D., & Hanges, P.J. (2013). The origins and legacy of the Civil Rights Act of 1964. *Journal of Business and Psychology, 28*(4), 383-399. DOI 10.1007/s10869-013-9291-z

American Psychiatric Association. (2013). *Cultural formulation interview*. http://www.psychiatry.org/File Library/Psychiatrists/Practice/DSM/APA_DSM5_Cultural-Formulation-Interview.pdf

American Psychological Association. (2017). *Multicultural guidelines: An ecological approachto context, identity, and intersectionality.* https://www.apa.org/about/policy/multicultural-guidelines

American Psychological Association. (2019a). *Guidelines for psychological practice for people with low-income and economic marginalization.* http://www.apa.org/about/policy/guidelines-lowincome.pdf

American Psychological Association. (2019b). *Race and ethnicity guidelines in psychology: Promoting responsiveness and equity.* https://www.apa.org/about/policy/guidelines-race-ethnicity.pdf

American Psychological Association. (2020). *Guidelines for providers of psychological services to ethnic, linguistic, and culturally diverse populations*. https://www.apa.org/pi/oema/resources/policy/provider-guidelines

American Psychological Association. (2021a). *Apology to people of color for APA's role in promoting, perpetuating, and failing to challenge racism, racial discrimination, and human hierarchy in U.S.* https://www.apa.org/about/policy/racism-apology

American Psychological Association. (2021b). *Resolution on harnessing psychology to combat racism: Adopting a uniform definition and understanding.* https://www.apa.org/about/policy/resolution-combat-racism.pdf

Association of Black Psychologists (ABPsi). (1968). *Making a positive impact on black mental wealth!* https://abpsi.site-ym.com/

Association of Black Psychologists (ABPsi). (2021). *Why the APA's apology for promoting white supremacy falls short.* https://www.nbcnews.com/think/opinion/why-apa-s-apology-promoting-white-supremacy-falls-short-ncna1284229

Bass, B. M. (1985). *Leadership and performance beyond expectations*. Free Press

Bass, B. M. (1999). Two decades of research and development in transformational leadership. *European Journal of Work and Organizational Psychology, 8*(1), 9–32. https://doi.org/10.1080/135943299398410

Bass, B. M., Avolio, B. J., Jung, D. I., & Berson, Y. (2003). Predicting unit performance by assessing transformational and transactional leadership. *Journal of Applied Psychology, 88*(2), 207–218. https://doi.org/10.1037/0021-9010.88.2.207

Bass, B. M., & Riggio, R. E. (2006). *Transformational leadership* (2nd ed.) Lawrence Erlbaum.

Bassett, M. T., Chen, J.T., & Krieger, N. (2020). Variation in racial/ethnic disparities in COVID-19 mortality by age in the United States: A cross sectional study. *PLos medicine, 18*(2). https://doi.org/10.1371/journal.pmed.1003402

Burns, J. M. (1978). *Leadership*. Harper & Row.

Dappa, K., Bhatti, F., & Aliarah, A. (2019). A study on the effect of transformational leadership on job satisfaction: The role of gender perceived organizational politics and perceived organizational commitment. *Management Science Letters, 9*(6), 823–834. https://doi.org/10.5267/j.msl.2019.3.006

David, E. J. R., & Okazaki, S. (2006). Colonial mentality: A review and recommendation for Filipino American psychology. *Cultural Diversity and Ethnic Minority Psychology, 12*(1), 1–16. https://doi.org/10.1037/1099-9809.12.1.1

de la Sablonnière, R. (2017). Toward a psychology of social change: A typology of social change. *Frontiers in Psychology, 8*, 397. https://doi.org/10.3389/fpsyg.2017.00397

Dukerich, J. M., Nichols, M. L., Elm, D. R., & Vollrath, D. A. (1990). Moral reasoning in groups: Leaders make a difference. *Human relations, 43*(5), 473–493. https://doi.org/10.1177/001872679004300505

Dvir, T., Eden, D., Avolio, B. J., & Shamir, B. (2002). Impact of transformational leadership on follower development and performance: A field experiment. *Academy of Management Journal, 45*(4), 735–744. https://doi.org/10.2307/3069307

Farahnak, L. R., Ehrhart, M.G., Torres, E.M., & Aarons, G.A. (2020). The influence of transformational leadership and leaders' attitudes on subordinate attitudes and implementation success. *Journal of Leadership & Organizational Studies, 27*(1), 98–111. https://doi.org/10.1177/1548051818824529

Goldschmidt, L., Langa, M., Alexander, D., & Canham, H. (2021). A review of Kohlberg's theory and its applicability in the South African context through the lens of early childhood development and violence. *Early Child Development and Care, 191*(7–8), 1066–1078. https://doi.org/10.1080/03004430.2021.1897583

Gyekye, K. (1997). *Tradition and modernity: Philosophical reflections on the African experience.* Oxford University Press.

Hardy, K. (2015). *Race inside and outside of therapy room*. Psychotherapy Network Symposium.

Hardy, K. V. (2016). Anti-racist approaches for shaping theoretical and practice paradigms. In M. Pender-Greene & A. Siskin (Eds.), *Anti-racist strategies for the health and human services* (pp. 125–139). Oxford University Press.

Harkness, S., Edwards, C. P., & Super, C. M. (1981). Social roles and moral reasoning: A case study in a rural African community. *Developmental Psychology, 17*(5), 595–603. https://doi.org/10.1037/0012-1649.17.5.595

Harris, F.C. (2006). It takes a tragedy to arouse them: Collective memory and collective action during the civil rights movement. *Social Movement Studies*, 5(1), 19–43. https://doi.org/10.1080/14742830600621159

Helms, J. E., Nicolas, G., & Green, C. E. (2012). Racism and ethnoviolence as trauma:

Enhancing professional and research training. *Traumatology, 18*, 65–74. https://doi.org/10.1177%2F1534765610396728

Ibrahim, A. M., Dimick, J. B., & Joseph, A. (2017). Building a better operating room: Views from surgery and architecture. *Annals of Surgery, 265*(1), 34–36. https://www.surgeryredesign.com/

Jackson, S. J. (2021). Making# BlackLivesMatter in the shadow of Selma: Collective memory and racial justice activism in US News. *Communication, Culture and Critique*. https://doi.org/10.1093/ccc/tcab007

Kendi, I. X. (2019). *How to be an antiracist*. One World.

Kohlberg, L. (1976). Moral stages and moralization: The cognitive-development approach. In T. Lickona (Ed.), *Moral Development and Behavior: Theory and Research and Social Issues* (pp. 31–53). Holt, Rienhart, and Winston.

Lorde, A. (1983). The master's tools will never dismantle the master's house. In C. Moraga and G. Alzandua (Eds.), *This bridge called my back*, pp. 94–101. Kitchen Table Press.

Lorde, A. (2018). *The master's tools will never dismantle the master's house*. Penguin UK.

Maldonado-Torres, N. (2017). Frantz Fanon and the decolonial turn in psychology: From modern/colonial methods to the decolonial attitude. *South African Journal of Psychology, 47*(4), 432–441. https://doi.org/10.1177/0081246317737918

Mignolo, W. (2011). *The darker side of western modernity: Global futures, decolonial options*. Duke University Press.

Mohajan, H. (2020). The second industrial revolution has brought modern social and economic developments. *Journal of Social Science and Humanities, 6*(1), 1–14. https://mpra.ub.uni-muenchen.de/98209/1/MPRA_paper_98209.pdf

Montenovo, L., Jiang, X., Rojas, F. L., Schmutte, I. M., Simon, K. I., Weinberg, B. A., & Wing, C. (2020). *Determinants of disparities in covid-19 job losses* (No. w27132). National Bureau of Economic Research. https://www.nber.org/system/files/working_papers/w27132/w27132.pdf

Ndlovu-Gatsheni, S. J. (2013). *Empire, global coloniality and African subjectivity*. Berghahn Books.

Nicolas, G., & Thompson, C. E. (2019). Racialized violence in the lives of Black people: Illustrations from Haiti (Ayiti) and the United States. *American Psychologist, 74*(5), 587. https://psycnet.apa.org/doi/10.1037/amp0000453

Nussbaum, M. C. (2011). *Creating capabilities: The human development approach*. Harvard University Press.

Osei, E. A. (2020). Wakanda Africa do you see? Reading Black Panther as a decolonial film through the lens of the Sankofa theory. *Critical Studies in Media Communication, 37*(4), 378–390. https://doi.org/10.1080/15295036.2020.1820538

Phillips, L. T., & Lowery, B. S. (2018). Herd invisibility: The psychology of racial privilege. *Current Directions in Psychological Science, 27*(3), 156–162. https://doi.org/10.1177/0963721417753600

Quarcoo, A. K. (1972). *The language of Adinkra symbols*. Sebewie Ventures.

Rothberg, M. (2020). Introduction. From victims and perpetrators to implicated subjects. *The Implicated Subject* (pp. 1–28). Stanford University Press.

Schedlitzki, D., & Edwards, G. (2018). *Studying leadership: Traditional and critical approaches* (2nd ed.). Sage.

Suffla, S., Ratele, K., Reddy, G., & Adams, G. (2019). Decolonial approaches to the psychological study of social issues. *Society for the Psychological Study of Social Issues.* https://www.spssi.org/index.cfm?fuseaction=page.viewPage&pageID=2527&nodeID=1

Temple, C. N. (2010). The emergence of Sankofa practice in the United States: A modern history. *Journal of Black Studies, 41*(1), 127–150. https://doi.org/10.1177/0021934709332464

Turner, N., Barling, J., Epitropaki, O., Butcher, V., & Milner, C. (2002). Transformational leadership and moral reasoning. *Journal of Applied Psychology, 87*(2), 304–311. https://doi.org/10.1037/0021-9010.87.2.304

Waldman, D. A., Bass, B. M., & Einstein, W. O. (2011). Leadership and outcomes of performance appraisal processes. *Journal of Occupational and Organizational Psychology, 60* (3), 177–186. https://doi.org/10.1111/j.2044-8325.1987.tb00251.x

Weber, J., & Elm, D. R. (2018). Exploring and comparing cognitive moral reasoning of millennials and across multiple generations. *Business and Society Review, 12s*(3), 415–458. https://doi.org/10.1111/basr.12151

Willis, W. B. (1998). *The Adinkra dictionary: A visual primer on the language of Adinkra*. Pyramid Complex.

Zohar, D. (2002). Modifying supervisory practices to improve subunit safety: A leadership-based intervention model. *Journal of Applied Psychology, 87*(1), 156–163. https://doi.org/10.1037/0021-9010.87.1.156

Chapter 10

The Well-Informed Leader: Superior Decision-Making through Essence-based Mentoring™

David B. Haddad
Institute for Social Innovation Fellow

James Marlatt
Institute for Social Innovation Fellow

A New Leadership Framework

In this chapter, we present essence-based leadership addressed to high-level leaders. An example of innovative participatory action research (PAR) "changes the mind" of apex leaders responsible for critical, complex, decision-making. Apex leaders are accountable for decisions that have outsized economic, social, and environmental impacts. They include national and international leaders, public and private, and their close advisors. Such are heads of nations and major corporations responsible for executive decisions that relieve (or inflict) pain and suffering for thousands or millions of people.

Essence-based leadership is grounded in a new mentoring program based on transformative phenomenology originated by David Rehorick and Valerie Malhotra Bentz. It is inspired by the over-century long phenomenological tradition (Husserl, 1954,1970; Schutz & Wagner, 1970). Transformative phenomenology, combined with related robust models leveraged into Essence-based Mentoring™, addresses intractable complex sets of issues confronting apex leaders. The result is (a) increased self-awareness (consciousness-raising), (b) amplified action logic and superior decision-making, and (c) transformational change. We integrate stocks of knowledge, an array of methods, and summon expertise from related disciplines to form novel frameworks as catalysts leading to fresh discoveries and innovative solutions supporting apex leaders. (See Bentz et al, 2021; Marlatt et al, 2020; Rehorick & Bentz, 2017, 2008).

The Domain of Precarity

Framing apex leader decision-making within our emerging concept of *deathworlds* (Bentz et al, 2018; Bentz & Marlatt, 2021), we view apex leaders who greatly influence deathworld-making activities through the quality of their decision-making. Deathworlds are places on planet Earth that no longer sustain life. Valerie Bentz claims that every community is arrayed along a continuum of life-sustaining and deathworld-making elements. We experience deathworlds as we become increasingly aware of, for example, the climate crisis, pandemics, militarization, politics, and economic, social, and ecological destruction. Deathworld-making activities contribute to degradation and sickness: the death of places and persons, cultures and histories, inflicting collateral damage on other creatures. These are spaces in the world where the forces that work against life lead to physical, mental, social, and ecological decline. While deathworld-making may produce monetary wealth for some, it is ultimately a destructive process. Such processes are increasing rapidly. We are aware of them due to global, lightning-fast communications. This is a wake-up call to raise consciousness about our shared responsibility and to reverse these planetary death-making processes being expedited through apex leader decision-making.

We introduce transformative phenomenology (TP) as our core mentoring methodology. TP can bring vital support to apex leaders. In it, transformative learning takes place through a "leregogic" relationship—one where mentor and mentee relate as equals, as partners co-managing their learning dynamics (see Rehorick & Taylor, 1995). As apex mentors, we possess qualities that facilitate the acquisition of keen self-awareness, transformative learning, and robust leadership. As such we can monitor and reinforce developmental shifts. Essence-based mentoring grew out of years of our independent professional histories and research, ultimately taking form as our scholarly partnership took root.

Being mentored in transformative learning, apex leaders gain markedly increased cognizance, which enables them to make better-informed decisions. Their sharpened judgment turns on a newly acquired sensitivity to what at first seemed negligible details. Unseen, prior, latent dynamics were bound up in those taken-for-granted details—details that may derail even the most exacting calculations.

Transformation is a permanent stretching of the natural capabilities of the mind to reach fullness. Transformation is acquired insight to perceive the essence of relationships, people, objects, and complex states of affairs. Transformation means newfound respect for the depth and variety of social conditions we all must live in. We turn to a detailed examination of transformative phenomenology.

Transformative Phenomenology

The following description of transformative phenomenology reproduced in part from Marlatt, Rehorick, and Bentz (2020), depicts transformative phenomenology as a somatic-hermeneutic-phenomenology that is put into action in the lifeworld. It is an application of phenomenology—the study of consciousness and phenomena—that can lead to positive personal, professional, organizational, and social transformations. Founded on the essence-based phenomenology of Edmund Husserl, the social phenomenology of Alfred Schütz, the embodied phenomenology of Maurice Merleau-Ponty, the ontologic-existential phenomenology of Martin Heidegger, and the reflective interpretive hermeneutic methods of Hans-Georg Gadamer, it forms a kaleidoscopic or transdisciplinary model.

Phenomenology is a way of knowing that incorporates enriched, embodied awareness. A person's view of the world of everyday life, understandings, and situations of others can become clouded by preconceptions, scientific and popular constructs, media images, and distortions. Over time, these may blind us to what stands out to the unclouded phenomenological eye. Phenomenology directs us to the fullness of experience rather than a remote or pro forma accumulation of information and facts.

The aim of the study of phenomena (objects of consciousness) is to bring about full awareness and understanding of the essence of direct experience. Unlike traditional methods of inquiry, phenomenology provides a path to enrich awareness of our own consciousness. It challenges one to let phenomena reveal themselves, rather than predetermining what phenomena are. Phenomenology seeks to elicit and portray essence as the necessary structures of phenomena and to uncover the meaning of lived experience within the world of everyday life. Phenomenology combines two additional instruments in its cache. The first is somatics. Somatics is an approach with a long scholarly tradition. Transformative phenomenologists emphasize somatics as a philosophical tradition and also as healing practices found in yoga, meditation, and mindfulness that consider the interconnected nature of the body, mind, and spirit. Somatics promotes whole-bodied awareness and free-flowing internal communication where the capacity for knowing from within becomes the primary instrument of change. As Wordsworth said, "The eye, it cannot choose but see; We cannot bid the ear be still; Our bodies feel, where'er they be, against or with our will" (Taylor, 1998, p. 112).

The second method, hermeneutics, entails a thoroughly reflective search for meaning through the interpretation of texts and life experiences. Subjects might include conversations and relationships, histories, and social interaction. The interpreter seeks to reveal biasing effects of personal, cultural, and historically sculpted prejudgments and prejudices, making them visible and explicit. See Figure 21.

Phenomenologists use the term "lived experience" to connote the direct feelings, thoughts, and bodily awareness of actual life. The founder of phenomenology, Edmund Husserl (1954, 1970), explained phenomenological inquiry as a way of being, as well as a way of knowing. It involves the practice of *bracketing*, through which prior judgments and categorizations are suspended so that one's vision opens to what is actually occurring. A further phenomenological strategy is to change one or more elements of the phenomenon using imagination, so that one may see a wider variety of how things may be different, thus freeing the mind's preemptive grip on perceptions and feelings.

From Alfred Schütz, social phenomenology is a way of looking beyond one's natural attitude, the taken-for-granted that fills the world of everyday life—the lifeworld. Social phenomenology offers approaches to connect with social and cultural worlds from the perspectives of an individuals' motivation, sense of topical relevance, the typification of others, and relationships.

Writing rich descriptions of lived experiences (protocols) and collaboratively interpreting meaning is a foundational activity that increases self-awareness and enhances the understanding of the everyday world in which we practice.

Figure 21
Exploring Lived Experience Through Transformative Phenomenology (Marlatt & Noronha, 2021)

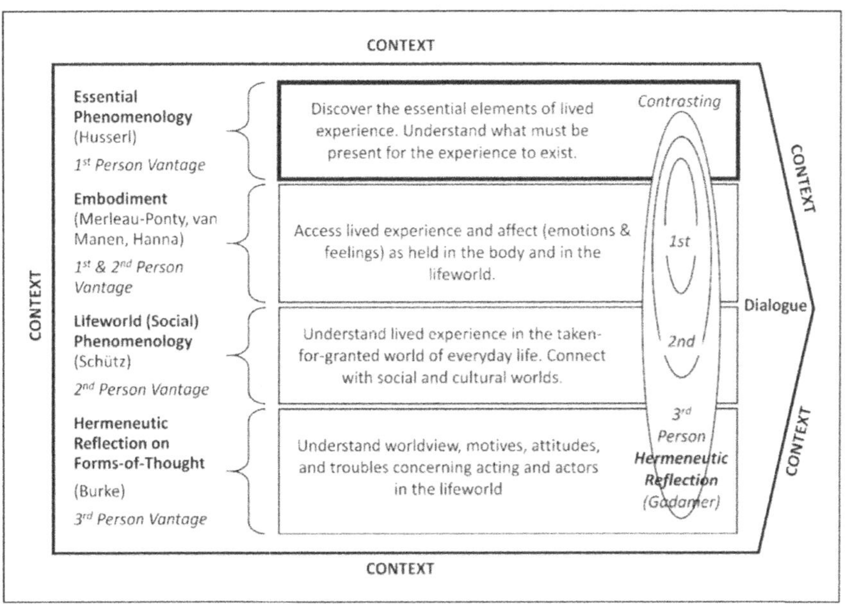

Source: James Marlatt and João Noronha. Used with permission. Original artwork.

Learners become immersed in their dilemmas from a first-person perspective. Phenomenological-based coaching offers a unique alternative avenue that builds self-awareness (Marlatt & Bentz, 2020; Marlatt & Noronha, 2021). Clients often experience a thoughtful, disorienting incoherence at the start of phenomenological writing. But deep mentored conversations, engaging hermeneutic explorations, and reflecting on lived experience may lead to a transformed mind. The veiled nature of the taken-for-granted is acknowledged and released; the unclouded phenomenological eye sees.

Engaging others from a somatic phenomenological foundation acknowledges one's *being* as the primary instrument of change through communicative-embodied-awareness. Somatics promotes whole-bodied communication, and phenomenology and hermeneutics increase self-awareness through a reflective understanding of the world of everyday life. The mentor's capacity for guiding the communicative construction of meaning creates a sense of collaborative action for change. Put together, communicative-embodied-awareness processes offer new avenues for improving the well-being and effectiveness of participants to be transformed.

Doing Phenomenology

A series of steps making up the phenomenological protocol is illustrated in Figure 22. Being new to the protocol, we recognize that our clients are blind to its inner workings. In the end, they are cognizant. Our approach begins with the apex leader first imagining a compelling concrete state of affairs anticipated to arrive in the not-too-distant future. A time horizon of 6–9 months would be suitable. We walk the client through the development of a rich description of that state of affairs using only the future perfect tense. The value of this linguistic technique is that it puts the leader ahead, as it were, of an event that has not yet occurred, affording the leader deep rational and emotional perspectives otherwise unavailable.

Major processes (Moustakas, 1994) of the protocol begin from that starting point. Mentor and mentee continue the journey by turning their attention to the epoché process, a process where prejudgments and biases are intentionally set aside. This allows the mentee to make a new beginning, starting from a clean slate of perception. The third is phenomenological reduction. It requires repeated cycles of looking carefully at the coming event before richly, textually describing it. Look again and describe. Repeating this dyadic exercise, the event is eventually thrown into full relief where the descriptions yield insight into elements previously out of view. Included here is the notion of horizonalization, where possibilities become unlimited. One may see a horizon and describe it in greater and greater detail, but one never actually reaches it. This describes a beautiful and robust aspect of knowledge creation on many levels.

At this point, a complete textual description is performed to set forth everything the phenomenological reduction yielded. This is a satisfying moment in the process and ought to be reflected on to obtain its full richness.

From there we continue by applying imaginative variations, enabling the mentee to derive structural themes. Last, a synthesis is developed through recombining epistemic themes drawn from the structures of time, space, others, causality, our bodies, and material reality. Final synthesis completes the process.

Figure 22
Developing Self-Awareness Through the Phenomenological Protocol

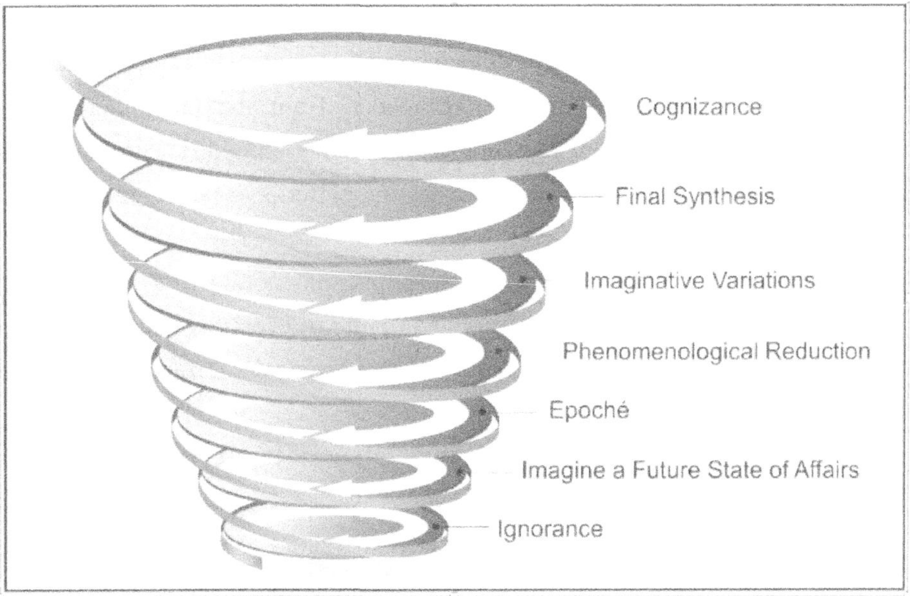

Source: David B. Haddad and James Marlatt. Used with permission. Original artwork.

Deep and time-consuming, engaging the phenomenological protocol while staying focused on a future state of affairs takes significant sustained effort. Thus, there is a need for qualified mentors to prompt and guide the writing process. As the client regularly engages with this method of discovery, anticipation builds. The skills of a phenomenological mentor must therefore be multi-disciplinary, sensitive, and highly developed. What sort of qualities are possessed by good phenomenological mentors?

Qualities of Apex Mentors

David Rehorick and Valerie Malhotra Bentz (2017) identified qualities of transformative phenomenologists based on their analysis of applied phenomenological research. (See Figure 3.) Qualities of transformative phenomenologists (apex mentors) include adopting phenomenology as a way of being, embracing embodied consciousness, and finding the "whatness" of experience. Phenomenological scholar-practitioners focus on looking beyond the taken-for-granted, with an awareness that lifeworlds are constructed through rich textual descriptions and patterns of communication.

Depicted as a wheel in Figure 23, offering multiple entry points, transformative phenomenology engages both mentor and mentee at the deepest levels of meaning-making. Extended from the phenomenological protocol, transformative phenomenology highlights embodied consciousness, authenticity, wonderment, and communication patterns as active constructs of the lifeworld.

Transformative phenomenologists adopt phenomenology as a way of being, seeking to transcend the taken-for-granted reality of everyday lived experience in service of generating deeper insight and empowerment through more robust understanding.

Learning in Relationship

Learning through transformative phenomenology occurs in a *leregogic* relationship—one where mentor and mentee relate as equals and partners as they manage their learning dynamics (Rehorick & Taylor, 1995). David Rehorick (Rehorick & Marlatt, 2020) described *leregogy* as

> a new conception for adult learning theory, one that arises as an extension of the rich developments in the fields of pedagogy and andragogy. In a leregogical relationship, dualistic distinctions such as teacher-learner and mentor-mentee are replaced by learning as fluid, open-ended, with everyone leading, teaching, and learning together. (para. 1)

As described in detail in the *Handbook of Transformative Phenomenology* (Bentz et al., 2021), "The qualities that are developed through engagement with applied somatic-hermeneutic-phenomenology are inherently transformative, both personally and professionally. Transformative Phenomenology leads to an embodied way of knowing and being that has the potential to change ourselves, our lifeworlds, and professional practice" (p. 88). The accessibility of TP has been well demonstrated (Haddad, 2002; Rehorick & Bentz, 2008). In addition to TP, secondary models bring a wealth of added support to the leregogic mentoring relationship.

Figure 23
Qualities of Transformative Phenomenologists after Rehorick and Bentz (2017)

Source: Valerie Malhotra Bentz and James Marlatt. Used with permission. Original artwork.

To capture the many dimensions of the mentoring context leading to transformative learning, we take a deeper look using three of James Marlatt's "21 meaning structures" described in his research on the nature of executive coaching (Marlatt, 2012). Here are six of his overarching thematic patterns tied to a deep learning coaching relationship:

- as a catalyst for transformative learning
- the foundation of the executive coaching relationship
- the nature of the executive coaching relationship
- the nature of the executive coaching dialogue
- the ineffable influence of the executive coaching relationship
- the transformative learning and the executive coaching relationship

Located under the heading, as a catalyst for transformative learning, the first meaning structure is labeled "enduring disorientation at the core of the client's dilemma." Marlatt (2012) explained:

> The client's emotional angst that stems from disorienting encounters with other people in the organization can remain unknown and inaccessible to the coach. Unresolved psychological issues in the client's lifeworld, combined with disorienting encounters with people in positions of power in the world of work, can lead to ensuing anxiety and enduring disorientation. The executive coach can help the client to surface the rational from the emotional ground, and to help the client come to terms with his or her disorientation. Enduring disorientation is at the core of the client's dilemma. At the same time, it is the catalyst for transformative learning. Disorientation is necessary, but not sufficient, for transformative learning to occur. (p. 160)

When mentoring apex leaders, disorientation is anticipated. Apex leaders are at the crossroads of muscular social, economic, and political currents, not a few of which appear suddenly, coming from off the radar screen. Examples include sudden devastating storms or earthquakes, social uprisings testing civil authority, and challenges to sovereignty and political stability by more powerful adventuresome neighbors. Dealing with disorientation is an art and an acquired skill. The apex mentor is essential to assist leaders in seeing the issues for what they are as well as facilitating the leader's return to equilibrium and sound judgment.

Staying with the client's perspective a bit further, we consider the foundation of the executive coaching relationship and its pivotal element, "Evolving trust: Cornerstone to the leadership coaching relationship." Marlatt (2012) laid out critical results of his research experience in the following passage:

> Every client involved in my study indicated that trust was key to our executive coaching relationship. A three-part model of trust will be helpful here. In this model, trust is a sociological phenomenon and consists of an expectation that a person will realize a favorable outcome via the bond of trust. Second, this expectation is based on interpreting one's own experience. That becomes the basis for

> believing there are good reasons for holding a sound expectation. A third element relates to what happens between interpretation and the favorable outcome of a certain expectation. This in-between zone takes an ineffable leap of faith involving the process of trust where "there is no automatic logic connecting interpretation ('good reasons') to trustful favorable expectation." This leap is also called suspension, "the bracketing of the unknowable which represents a defining aspect of the nature of trust." (p. 164)

Mentoring apex leaders heavily depends on the development of sincere confidence and unbroken trust for the relationship to get off the ground. People in power often find trusting their advisors problematic, so gaining and holding that trust is paramount to the success of the relationship.

Marlatt takes up the coach's perspective under the heading, "The nature of the executive coaching relationship: Performance anxiety hinders and deprives the leader of learning opportunities." In a highly reflective passage, Marlatt (2012) described the difficulty in maintaining a catalytic stance, that is, one where the mentor consistently evokes reflection in the mind of the client:

> Free-flowing dialogue is a demanding form of executive coaching that can lead to performance anxiety for the coach. It is not unusual to experience performance anxiety in response to an apparent lack of progress in catalyzing the client's reflective experience. When this happens, one's response is to move to a telling or advising mode or to transition to a more diagnostic mode of evidence-based coaching that relies on generalized theories based on psychology or human development. The tendency to move away from the essence-based coaching agenda and focus on the client's more immediate agenda might reduce the opportunity for dialogic openings to appear and reduce any potential for transformative learning. (p. 166)

Marlatt's work outlines the demands placed on both mentor and mentee required to spark and sustain transformative change. The essence of his work hits paydirt when the client comes to terms with his poignant disorientation under the umbrella of a safe, trusting, and collaborative relationship. Two essential components, indispensable personal attributes leading to a successful relationship, are genuine authenticity and expertly applying proven methods.

Human Capability Framework

The most precarious balance to be struck by key leaders is what Nussbaum (2011) defined as "living concern for and relation to other species." It appears that the majority of major political, social, and economic decisions are made from short-sighted, self-centered concerns. To adequately take into account

all species, inclusive of humanity, demands a system-based approach undertaken through a dexterous melding of both calculative and meditative mindsets.

Through the practice of essence-based leadership, apex leaders are coached (a daily practical approach) and mentored (a deepening reflective stance) to learn how to counter ossified inadequate mental habits of decision making, habits already proved counterproductive, and to do it just long enough to envision a better way, a better more elevated set of decisions to choose from, possessing superior guiding dynamics. Developing the ability to see, in a new light, vital issues faced every day promotes reconciliation of subtle built-in conflicts. Shedding light on one's biases allows the suspension of prejudgments, enabling the capacity to see each issue on its terms, discerning its governing dynamics as each, in fact, is. The ultimate goal is to surface new options to positive lasting social change, empowering leaders to make decisions that are best for all, bearing faithfully the weight of social justice, tilting from creating deathworlds to supporting lifeworlds.

Developing Self-Awareness

At the core of apex mentoring is the opportunity for leaders to develop deep self-awareness to support more broad-based and effective decision-making. Carden et al. (2021) defined self-awareness as integrating intrapersonal (self-conscious) and interpersonal (self-knowledge) perspectives developed through a process:

> Self-awareness consists of a range of components, which can be developed through focus, evaluation and feedback, and provide an individual with an awareness of their internal state (emotions, cognitions, physiological responses), that drives their behaviors (beliefs, values and motivations) and an awareness of how this impacts and influences others. (p. 25)

Transformative learning theory depicts one way of developing self-awareness (Dirkx, 2000; Mezirow, 2009). Transformative learning invokes change in one's underlying perception, the unconscious framework controlling the way we make meaning in the world—our worldview. This type of deep learning is often catalyzed by a disorienting event, understood through reflection, validated through dialogue with others, and consequently acted upon in the world. Such epistemic shifts in meaning-making can be mapped to patterns of human development that lead to more aware, inclusive, and encompassing ways of knowing. As we see it, this offers the potential for better decision-making (Kegan, 1982; Torbert, 2004). The promotion of critical reflection through mentoring is one modality at the center of developing self-awareness.

Not everyone is disposed to the development of self-awareness. The development of self-awareness involves being open to reflective inquiry, receptivity, and feedback. If the mentee is not willing to engage in the development of self-awareness, the intervention will be at a standstill. Eschenbacher explores resistance to learning as immunity to change (Eschenbacher, 2020; Kegan & Lahey, 2009).

Despite the extant theories highlighting processes for developing self-awareness, human development, and deep learning—where individuals can go on their life journey, and what happens when they do—less is understood about how to facilitate such movements. (See Patricia Cranton, 2016.) Apex mentoring offers a powerful array of combined methods to support such change.

Overview of Essence-based Leadership Lenses

Next, we turn to methodologies with properties similar to and symbiotic with transformative phenomenology. Each gets at essential leadership issues in distinct ways. See Figure 24.

Deep transformative learning is accomplished by lending the hand of essence-based mentorship to apex leaders as they clear away accumulated debris of everyday mental life, finally arriving at their inmost intention in support of vigorous decision-making. The leader's objectives are reached, behavior changed, and a general re-invigoration is experienced. At the core, we rely on phenomenology, described as "a style of thinking and an attitude of reflective attentiveness to the primordialities of human existence, to what it is that makes

Figure 24

Essence-based Mentoring™ Support and Selected Methods

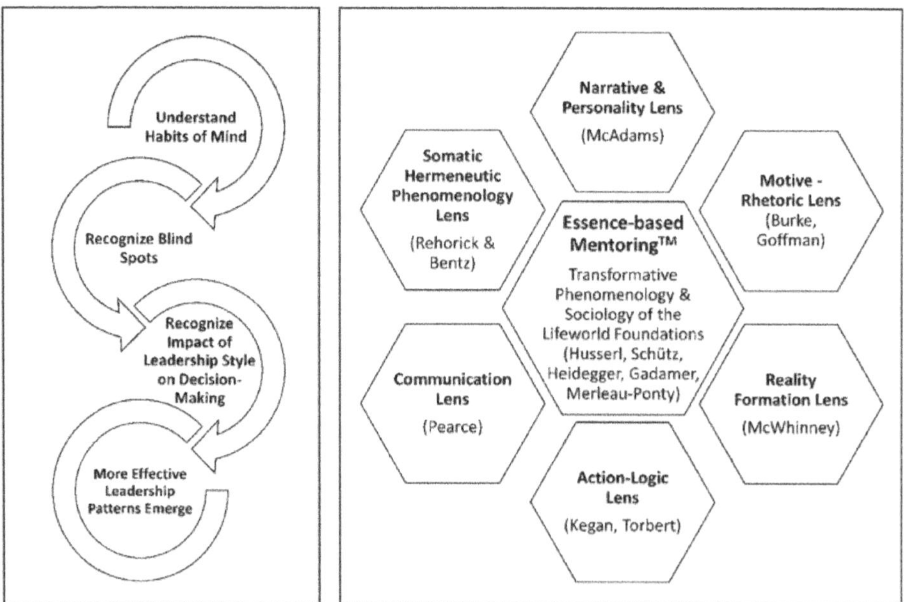

Source: James Marlatt and David B. Haddad. Used with permission. Original artwork.

life intelligible and meaningful to us" (van Manen, 2019, p. 911).

Each lens depicted in Table 12 extracts distinct essences of human experience. Using these innovations in essence-based leadership brings forward more completeness in the client experience and ultimately in their decision making than would be possible using only one, thus assuring greater success. Investigatory tools in the human realm are designed to observe the nature of human experience, uncovering paths leading to beneficial enduring transformation. Each is a particular model (lens) formed out of clustered essential insights. We briefly sample a few in this table: somatics, action-logic (the subject-object interview), narrative identity, reality formation, motive-rhetoric (pentadic analysis), and communication (coordinated management of meaning).

Table 12
Essence-based Mentoring™ Selected Methods, Scholarship, and Practice

Lens	Focus	Method	Scholarship & Practice
Somatic Hermeneutic Phenomenology	Developing self-awareness through phenomenological writing, coaching, and mentoring. Reflecting on lived experience.	Transformative Phenomenology: Guided protocol writing, reflection, and collaborative interpretation. Phenomenological coaching.	Rehorick & Bentz (2008, 2017); van Manen (1997, 2016), Wagner (1983), Hanna (1988), Marlatt & Noronha (2021), Marlatt & Bentz (2020)
Personality	Identifying characteristic embedded patterns of thinking, feeling, and behaving.	Psychology, psychometric assessments. Structured journaling.	McAdams (2016), Progoff (1975)
Action-Logic (Habits-of-Mind & Body)	Understanding thought processes that are used to construct reality.	Subject Object Interview. Constructive Development stage assessment. Action Inquiry. Immunity-to-Change. Dialectics.	Kegan (1982, 1994), Kegan-Lahey (2009), Torbert (2004), Laske (2015)
Narrative Identity	Understanding narrative identity and meaning-making authorship through autobiographical life storytelling.	Life Story Interview and others.	McAdams (2016)
Reality Formation	Understanding conflict and paths of change from the perspective of differing worldviews.	Change path heuristics.	McWhinney (1992, 1996)
Motive - Rhetoric	Understanding motivations behind decision-making.	Pentadic analysis. Impression management.	Burke (1969), Duncan (1984), Goffman (1956)
Communication	Understanding the process of communication and how meaning makes social worlds.	Coordinated Management of Meaning heuristics.	Pearce (2007)
Learning	Understanding the process and catalyst for Transformative Learning; developing self-awareness.	Transformative Learning processes (cognitive, affective, social, environmental, holistic, others).	Mezirow (2009), Dirkx (2000), Cranton (2016), Heron (1992)

Source: James Marlatt and David B. Haddad. Used with permission. Original tabulation.

Somatics

Developed by Thomas Hanna (1988), and touched on above, somatics is the practice of mind-body awareness in order to become more deeply informed. It describes a complex inner connection comprised of mental and physical health, intuitive balance, deep peace, and authenticity. (See Bentz, 2016).

The essence of somatics is in locating the *weighted nexus* of meaning-making sourced in the dynamic mind-body interface. Designed to help the client survey his internal self, he listens intently to and interprets even the minutest signals his body receives from the surrounding world, social and physical, and sends to him a synthesis of signals about wonder and curiosity, areas of pain and pleasure, ease and discomfort, peace and disruption, equilibrium and imbalance.

Somatics illuminates the supple resilient unity of body and mind. When made a daily practice, somatics allows one to access significantly more information about the structure of one's thinking and action in terms of how one experiences one's body and comportment in a wide variety of complex social settings.

Action Logic: Subject-Object Interview

This powerful lens of object relations was developed by Lahey et al. (2011). Based on a human development theory of multiple cumulative levels of consciousness distinguished by increasing complexity, remarkable findings arose. According to Kegan, there are five distinct levels of consciousness in play in the Western world. Incessant demands by the United States' culture pressure adults to reach and function at the self-authoring level four. But, as Kegan opines, "At the moment, fully one-half to two-thirds of the adult population appear not to have fully reached the fourth-order of consciousness" (1994, p. 191).

Yet, complex cultural demands are unrelenting, leaving those who do not reach level four under a ` great deal of pressure to sink or swim, sociologically speaking, or to either acquire additional cognitive and emotional capacity or remain frustrated when, in their hampered understanding, things just don't come together.

High-level decision-making demanded of leaders who still have not mastered the fourth-order of consciousness leaves their archaic action logic in the dust. Examples will help (Kegan, 1994, pp. 302–303). The fourth-order demands

- of parents, for instance, that they "institute a vision and induct family members into it,"
- that as intimate partners one has "a well-differentiated and clearly defined sense of self,"
- that at work one becomes "the inventor or owner of [one's] work,"
- that when confronting a diverse society, we "resist our tendencies to make 'right' or 'true' that which is merely familiar, and 'wrong' or 'false' that which is only strange," and
- that in psychotherapy we "transform our energies from manipulating the environment for support into developing greater and greater self-support."

All too often apex leaders bump up against their inadequacy to address the full context out of which problems arise. Using the subject-object interview, and similar approaches, essence-based mentorship stretches one's learning capacity to carry the client to level four, and beyond, as they master the essence of subject-object relations found in complexity.

Narrative Identity

Narrative identity theory has a strong field of outstanding authors (See McAdams, 2016). It is ubiquitous in the fields of psychology, sociology, and education. Of its many vigorous qualities, the one that may be most valuable is narrative theory's ability to reveal a leader's unconscious inner conflicts to himself, conflicts that prove a pattern of counter-productivity or outright self-sabotage.

Apex leadership is a white-hot crucible. In it, the leader's limitations quickly boil to the surface. It is here that self-sabotage appears on the world stage in full public view. By engaging an apex leader in narrative mentorship, the essence of one's self-authored, cross-purposed, self-destructive patterns is revealed privately in fine-grained relief. Using that insight as a new starting point, a leader gains new frames of mind, where one acquires the prerogative to re-author one's story and neutralize unwanted unhealthy patterns of thought and action.

Reality Formation

Will McWhinney (1992), a noted organizational theorist, invented the *reality inquiry*, a third-loop learning instrument that reveals the unconscious cognitive-emotional parameters by which an apex leader frames the world. Falling within one of four quadrants—unitary, social, sensory, and mythic—McWhinney described how individuals are rooted in a preferred reality. Reality can be depicted as a sliding matrix formed on the axes of plurality and agency. From that "base" one acts to influence others whose base may well be sourced in one of the other three realities. According to McWhinney, "Nothing happens 'where one is'; there is no action within a single reality for one's actions come from the interface of one view of reality with another" (p. 29). See Figure 25 and McWhinney et al. (1997).

McWhinney (1992) goes on to elucidate the nub of the problem. "Every human action, every attempt to change what is, involves us in logical contradictions because the logics of the realities are not compatible; the logic

Figure 25
Dimensions of Reality

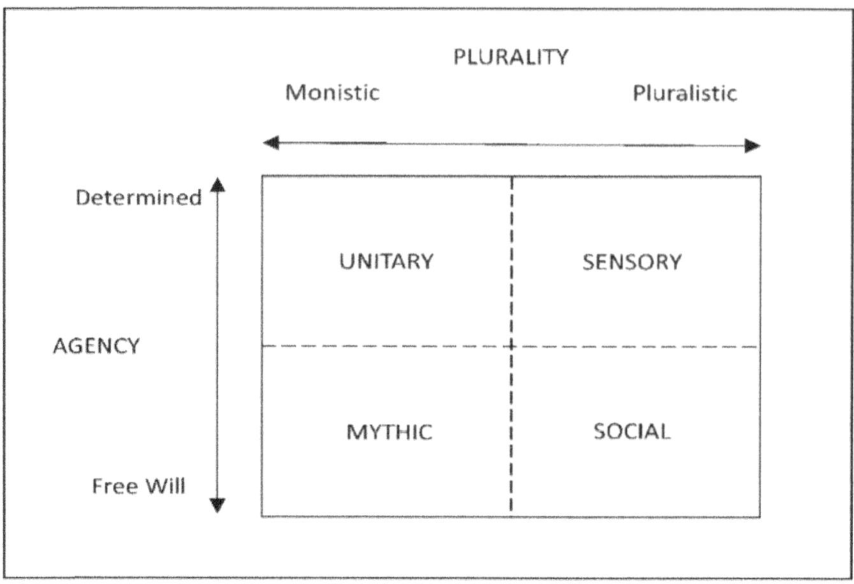

Note. Adapted from McWhinney et al., 1997, p. 28.

of one is outside the logic of another. Thus the *[essence of] paths of change are alogical* or paradoxical" (p. 29).

Some apex leaders are lauded for their consistency. But when logical consistency proves to create more conflict than it resolves, a new path of decision-making is demanded. Incorporating the reality inquiry in essence-based mentoring, leaders gain access to new ways of seeing that completely reframe the limits of their logic.

Motive-Rhetoric: Burke's Pentad

Kenneth Burke (1969) developed a hermeneutic heuristic approach to deciphering the motivations actors bring to the scenes they find themselves in and the roles they play. Based on a simple five-point analysis of interrelationships, the onlooker can interpret the essence of motive. The elements of Burke's dramatistic pentad are act, scene, agent, agency, and purpose. We extend the pentad to a hexad with the addition of the leader's attitude. See Figure 26

Figure 26
Burke's Dramatistic Pentad Extended to a Hexad with the Addition of "Attitude"

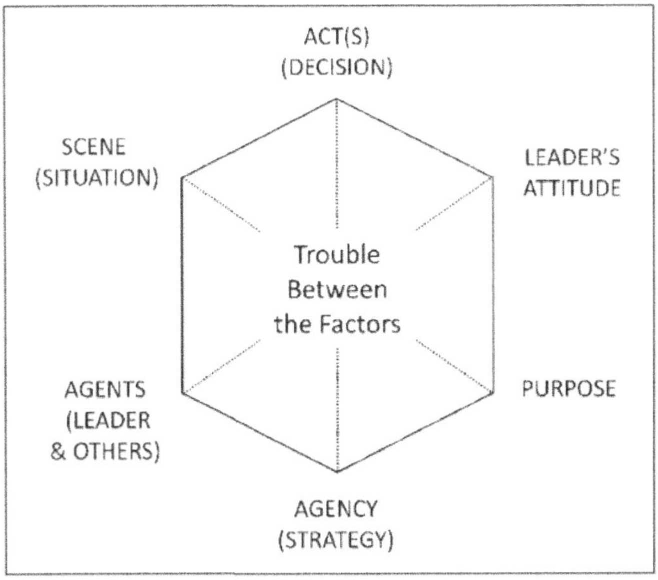

ACT(S)
(DECISION)
SCENE
(SITUATION)
LEADER'S
ATTITUDE
Trouble
Between
the Factors
AGENTS
(LEADER
& OTHERS)
PURPOSE
AGENCY
(STRATEGY)

Source: James Marlatt and David B. Haddad. Used with permission. Original artwork.

and Anderson and Althouse (2010). It is not the points themselves that reveal motives, but the relationships (ratios) between them that reveal the essence of motivation by accounting for all the elements of a scene. It allows us to discern the causes of action taking place.

What are the motivations of the actors? What are the various motivational priorities of interpreters observing the scene? These are not simple matters, but Burke's pentad is a key to unlocking their underlying meanings. Using the pentad stimulates more complex, comprehensive, and, in the end, more satisfying explanations of motivation. Burke's pentad, properly applied, offers the potential for adroitly navigating tempestuous social upheaval.

Communication: Coordinated Management of Meaning (CMM)

Developed by W. Barnett Pearce (2007), CMM posits as its essence the observable fact that our understanding of our worlds is a construction, something actively made by each of us each day. (See Berger & Luckmann, 1967). Our social worlds are not simply given. They are created, consciously and unconsciously, by the patterns of communication that we engage in. Pearce described how to recognize and modify one's communication and social meaning-making as a thing-in-itself. This objectification allows us to avoid self-sabotage and instead to reach desired goals.

CMM at its core is based around coordination, coherence, and mystery. Coordination "names those practices in which persons attempt to call into being ... their visions of the good, the desirable, and the expedient [...] 'Coherence' refers to the practices by which we tell ourselves (and others) stories in order to interpret the world around us and our place in it" (Pearce, 1989, pp. 20–21). Mystery is the "essence of that 'cosmopolitan' attitude that views one's own life and that of local society as a manifestation or part of something greater; it is a reminder of what is 'beyond' the immediate, present moment" (p. 23).

One of Pearce's (2007) useful heuristics is the LUUUUT model. LUUUUT is an acronym for (a) stories lived, (b) unknown stories, (c) untold stories, (d) unheard stories, (e) untellable stories, (6) stories told, and (7) story telling" (pp. 211-212). Pearce explained, "The tension between stories lived and told is also affected by the manner of our storytelling. There are many ways of telling the stories in which we make meaning of our lives, and each carries with it some consequences.... [Are they] accurate descriptions of an unchanging reality?" From here, the fullness of a story's various components can be thoroughly investigated with the goal of making a coherent and meaningful relationship. The essence of CMM is the realization that people are, like it or not, self-authoring individuals responsible for their speech patterns. Through those patterns, people make their social worlds.

Pearce's CMM is distinct from narrative identity theory discussed above. Narrative theory elicits the body of knowledge and interpretive analysis of how one tells oneself one's own story at both conscious and unconscious levels. Pearce's CMM investigates how we actively and outwardly create social worlds among us via the use of speech.

This brief survey of methodologies used in essence-based mentorship opens onto an appreciation of the depth of learning, motivation, and personal change we embark on with apex leaders. Transformative learning is our stated goal with clients. Once acquired it continues as a progressive enduring personal attribute.

Whether the mentor's approach is communication or narrative, third-order learning, or fourth-order consciousness, this very brief introduction sketches robust and generative paths of change.

Essence-based mentoring reliably yields transformation at deep levels. Each approach possesses such a nature that the mentor, too, is affected by applying its robustness as much as the client/leader is in learning it. In the hands of skilled mentors, the deep reflexive qualities of essence-based leadership methods unavoidably touch, challenge, and strengthen both parties.

Summary

In this chapter, we outlined a constellation of deep learning approaches to the theory and practice of Essence-based Mentoring™ as an innovative participatory action research theory and transformative practice supporting apex leaders responsible for critical, complex decision-making. Our premise is based on the ubiquitous, unavoidable, indisputably persistent, and pressing needs among apex leaders to dig deeper into their awareness before they take action. The preeminent augur used to excavate their awareness is transformative phenomenology.

We add to that supporting robust interlocking methodologies proven to disclose hidden dimensions of the essence of a leader's action logic. In precarious times, where power is shifting at a breakneck pace, the need for our leaders to act wisely in critical situations is never greater. Here we demonstrated how they can gain new vision and enrich their powers of perception fused to action for the greater good.

Meet the Authors

David Benjamin Haddad, PhD graduated from Michigan State University (BA, communications) and from Fielding Graduate University (MA, organizational development; PhD, human and organizational systems). Dean of academic affairs at California International University in Los Angeles for ten years and adjunct professor of psychology at Argosy University in San Diego during the six years prior, Dr. Haddad also served business owners, executives, and performing arts professionals as a leadership coach. Along the way he demonstrated a sub-speciality in human factors for the Los Angeles County Metropolitan Transportation Authority's emergency security operations center. Publications include contributions to the *Handbook of Transformative Phenomenology* (2022), delivering *"Transcendence as Radical Objectification,"* a peer-reviewed paper to the Society of Phenomenology and Human Sciences (2021), chapter contributions to *Deathworlds to Lifeworlds: Collaboration with Strangers for Personal, Social and Ecological Transformation* (2021), and a contribution to *Transformative Phenomenology* (2008). noema@mac.com

James Leonard Marlatt, PhD, MA, MBA, CEC, P.Eng. is an Institute for Social Innovation Fellow at Fielding Graduate University with an interest in applied social phenomenology. Jim is a certified executive coach and leadership development consultant with coaching credentials from Royal Roads University. His publications include the co-edited books *Deathworlds to Lifeworlds: Collaboration with Strangers for Individual, Social, and Ecological Transformation* (2021) and the *Handbook of Transformative Phenomenology* (2022), with Professor Valerie Malhotra Bentz. He co-authored book chapters "The Transformative Potential of Conversations with Strangers" in *Expressions of Phenomenological Research,* "The Silver Age of Phenomenology at Fielding" in *The Fielding Scholar Practitioner;* "Embodied Awareness: Transformative Coaching through Somatics and Phenomenology" in *Innovations in Leadership Coaching,* and "Coaching from Somatic and Phenomenological Foundations" in the *Handbook of Transformative Phenomenology.* Jim is also a professional geological engineer with an international career in the mineral resource industry and numerous applied geoscientific publications. He is an occasional education and training consultant to the International Atomic Energy Agency on matters related to energy supply. jmarlatt@email.fielding.edu

References

Anderson, F. D., & Althouse, M. T. (2010). Five fingers or Six? Pentad or Hexad? *Kenneth Burke (KB) Journal, 6*(2). https://www.kbjournal.org/anderson

Bentz, V. M. (2016). Knowing as being: Somatic phenomenology as contemplative practice. In V. M. Bentz & V. M. B. Giorgino (Eds.), *Contemplative social research: Caring for self, being, and lifeworld* (pp. 50–79). Fielding University Press.

Bentz, V., Rehorick, D., Marlatt, J., Nishi, A., & Estrada, C. (2018). Transformative phenomenology as an antidote to technological deathworlds. *Schutzian Research* (10), 189–220.

Bentz, V. B., Marlatt, J., Haddad, D. B., & Buchner, B., Estrada, C. (Eds.). (2021). *Handbook of Transformative Phenomenology*. Fielding University Press.

Bentz, V. M., & Marlatt, J. (Eds.). (2021). *Deathworlds to lifeworlds: Strangers to collaborators for individual, social and ecological transformation.* De Gruyter.

Berger, P. L., & Luckmann, T. (1967). *The social construction of reality: A treatise in the sociology of knowledge.* Anchor Books.

Burke, K. (1969). *A grammar of motives*. University of California Press.

Carden, J., Jones, R. J., Passmore, J. (2021). Developing self-awareness in the context of adult development: A systematic literature review. *Journal of Management Education*, 46(1), 1–38. https://doi.org/10.1177%2F1052562921990065

Cranton, P. (2016). *Understanding and promoting transformative learning: A guide to theory and practice* (3rd ed.). Stylus Publishing.

Dirkx, J. M. (2000). Transformative learning and the journey of individuation. *ERIC Digest,* No. 223. https://eric.ed.gov/?id=ED448305

Duncan, H. D. (1985). *Communication and social order.* Routledge.

Eschenbacher, S. (2020). Transformative learning and the hidden dynamics of transformation, *Reflective Practice*, 21(6), 759–772.

Goffman, E. (1959). *Presentation of self in everyday life*. Doubleday

Haddad, D. B. (2002). *Intentionality as an instrument in action research* (Publication No. 3041672) [Doctoral dissertation, Fielding Graduate Institute]. ProQuest Dissertations and Theses Global.

Haddad, D. B. & Marlatt, J. L. (2019). *Apex research: Resources for apex leaders.* https://apexresearch.ca

Hanna, T. (1988). *Somatics: Reawakening the mind's control of movement, flexibility, and health.* Da Capo Press.

Heron, J. (1992). *Feeling and personhood: Psychology in another key*. Sage.

Husserl, E. (1954/1970). *The crisis of European sciences and transcendental phenomenology: An introduction to phenomenological philosophy* (D. Carr, Trans.). Northwestern University Press.

Kegan, R. (1982). *The evolving self: Problem and process in human development.* Harvard University Press/Triliteral.

Kegan, R. (1994). *In over our heads: The mental demands of modern life.* Harvard University Press/Triliteral.

Kegan, R., & Lahey, L. L. (2009). *Immunity to change*. Harvard Business Press.

Lahey, L., Souvaine, E., Kegan, R., Goodman, R., & Felix, S. (2011). *A guide to the subject-object interview. Its administration and interpretation.* Minds at Work Press.

Laske, O. E. (2015). *Dialectical thinking for integral leaders: A primer.* Integral Publishers.

Marlatt, J. (2012). *When executive coaching connects: A phenomenological study of relationship and transformative learning* (Publication No. 3518579) [Doctoral dissertation, Fielding Graduate University]. ProQuest Dissertations and Theses Global.

Marlatt, J., & Bentz, V. M. (2020). Embodied awareness: Transformative coaching through somatics and phenomenology. In T. H. Hildebrandt, F. Campone, K. Norwood, & E. J. Ostrowski (Eds.), *Innovations in leadership coaching* (pp. 224–250). Fielding University Press.

Marlatt, J., & Noronha, J. (2021). Coaching from somatic and phenomenological foundations: From writing phenomenology to talking phenomenology. In V. M. Bentz & J. Marlatt (Eds.), *Handbook of Transformative Phenomenology*. Fielding University Press.

Marlatt, J., Rehorick, D., & Bentz, V. (2020). Transformative Phenomenology. In A. Possamai & A. J. Blasi (Eds.), *SAGE Encyclopedia of Sociology of Religion.* SAGE.

McAdams, D. P. (2016). *The art and science of personality development.* The Guilford Press

McWhinney, W. (1992). *Paths of change: Strategic choices for organizations and society.* Sage.

McWhinney, W., Webber, J., Smith, D., & Novokowsky, B. (1997). *Creating paths of change: Managing issues and resolving problems in organizations* (2nd ed.). Sage.

Mezirow, J. (2009). Transformative learning theory. In J. Mezirow, E. W. Taylor, & Associates (Eds.), *Transformative learning in practice: Insights from community, workplace, and higher education*. Jossey-Bass.

Moustakas, C. (1994). *Phenomenological research methods.* Sage Publications.

Nussbaum, M. C. (2011). *Creating capabilities: The human development approach.* Harvard University Press.

Pearce, W. B. (1989). *Communication and the human condition.* Southern Illinois University Press.

Pearce, W. B. (2007). *Making social worlds: A communication perspective.* COS Printers Pty Ltd.

Progoff, I. (1975/1992). *At a journal workshop: Writing to access the power of the unconscious and evoke creative ability.* Penguin Putnam Inc.

Rehorick, D. A., & Taylor, G. (1995). Thoughtful incoherence: First encounters with the phenomenological-hermeneutical domain. *Human Studies: A Journal for Philosophy and Social Sciences,* 18(4), 389–414.

Rehorick, D. A., & Bentz, V. (Eds.). (2008). *Transformative phenomenology: Changing ourselves, lifeworlds, and professional practice*. Lexington Books.

Rehorick, D., & Bentz, V. (Eds.). (2017). *Expressions of phenomenological research: Consciousness and lifeworld studies* (Vol. 10). Fielding University Press.

Rehorick, D., & Marlatt, J. (2020). *Leregogy. Transformative phenomenology and us.* https://transformative-phenomenology-and-us.home.blog/leregogy/

Schutz, A., & Wagner, H. R. (Eds.). (1970). *Alfred Schutz: On phenomenology and social relations.* The University of Chicago Press.

Taylor, J. S. (1998.) *Poetic knowledge.* State University of New York Press.

Torbert, W. R. (2004). *Action inquiry: The secret of timely and transforming leadership.* Berrett-Koehler.

van Manen, M. (1997). *Researching lived experience: Human science for an action sensitive pedagogy.* Althouse Press.

van Manen, M. (2019). Rebuttal: Doing phenomenology on the things. *Qualitative Health Research, 29*(6), 908–925.

Wagner, H. R. (1983). *Phenomenology of consciousness and sociology of the life-world: An introductory study.* The University of Alberta Press.

Chapter 11

Moral Moorings: Reflections for Public Service Leaders

Julie Smendzuik-O'Brien
Institute for Social Innovation Fellow

The last 5 years of American political life have been particularly turbulent due to a number of factors that have led to what David Brooks (2020, October 5) has called a time of *precarity*. There are both opportunities and risks in a time of precarity, according to his source, Albena Azmanova at the University of Kent, who first advanced the idea (Azmanova, 2020a). Azmanova and others (Azmanova, 2020b; Biale et al., 2021) have continued to debate what this means in economic and social terms. Azmanova (2020b) argued, for example, that the solution to economic precarity was to "build a more stable, secure, and sustainable society" and offered ideas for creation of the more just society. In this chapter, I have used primarily her idea that in precarity lie both risks and opportunities for civil society, political processes, and political leaders rather than explore all her routes to the just society. I explore the idea of opportunities in connection to the social justice outcome of the development of human capabilities after a broad discussion of the political precarity in the United States at the present time. The specific research question addressed is: What moral principles about the nature of civil society, political processes, and political leaders might be gleaned from religious traditions and from U.S. political traditions to aid public service leaders called upon to create contexts for the development of human capabilities?

Political Precarity

While it is not possible to detail all the occurrences that led to this time of political precarity, a sample from academic and mainstream media sources along with a journal I maintained from March 2020–June 2021, will serve to illustrate some important dimensions. One dimension is the disgruntlement of U.S. citizens that led to the election of Donald J. Trump in 2016. Working on an assignment from the chancellor of the University of Wisconsin who wanted to know what the residents of the state thought of the education system, Cramer (2016) conducted research using conversations with local people throughout rural Wisconsin for 7 years. What she found was a rural-urban divide whereby rural dwellers believed that city dwellers did not understand their lives and they were not listened to when decisions were made in the large cities of the state. She called it a "politics of resentment" that had more to do with place than with partisan identity. I question whether this attitude of "not being heard" is similar to views of people who rallied and then stormed the U.S. Capitol on January 6, 2021 to stop certification of Joe Biden's election win and who stand ready to take up arms if Trump does not win in 2024 (Freedman, 2021, December 20).

A second dimension of political precarity comes from the actions of the former president during his term of office. According to *New York Times* reporters Maggie Haberman, Glenn Thrush, and Peter Baker (2017, December 9), Trump told his aides that he wanted to view each day in office as an episode of a TV show in which he would "vanquish rivals." That perspective made the name calling of fellow Republican candidates and eventual Democratic nominee Hillary Clinton during the 2016 presidential campaign somewhat easier to understand. [1] Woodward and Costa (2021) wrote about the former president's name calling of another rival, Joe Biden, as the 2020 presidential contest got underway.

"Welcome to the race Sleepy Joe," Trump said on Twitter. "I only hope you have the intelligence, long in doubt, to wage a successful primary campaign. It will be nasty – you will be dealing with people who truly have some very sick and demented ideas. But if you make it, I will see you at the Starting Gate!" (p. 46)

In addition to this treatment of rivals, the former president created a precarious situation by failing to tell the American people for months in 2020 just how serious the coronavirus was. Rather than honestly report its status and growing ominousness, he told Bob Woodward (2020) that, while he knew that the coronavirus was serious, he wanted to downplay it so as not to have people panic. In an end of year report, the House Select Subcommittee on the Coronavirus Crisis (2021) identified a number of failures of the Trump Administration, including political interference in the work of scientific experts, failure to heed warnings about a potentially devastating public health emergency, and widespread fraud in the Small Business Administration's economic injury disaster loan program. State and local officials were upset by the failure to provide sufficient help early in the days of the pandemic (Costa & Gregg, 2020). Mauger and LeBlanc (2020) reported that the former president encouraged residents to "liberate" their states in response to governors' use of emergency powers to shutter businesses, workplaces, and churches to slow the spread of the virus before effective means could be found to address it. In several states, citizens staged serious protests; in Michigan, things went further. The Associated Press (2021) reported the conviction of one of six men who threatened to kidnap and kill the Michigan governor for her actions to keep residents safe. Governor Gretchen Whitmer was a state official who suffered greatly for trying to do the right thing.

Other lesser-publicized actions during his term that led to precarity impacted the executive branch. The New York Times (Davenport et al., 2021) catalogued the number of climate scientists lost from several agencies during the Trump years. The U.S. Geological Survey lost 8% of such employees, the Department of Agriculture lost 75% of climate researchers, and the Environmental Protection Agency lost 24% of its climate specialists. The intelligence community lost its one scientist studying ecological destruction around the world when he resigned because his scientific assessment was almost blocked from Congressional testimony. Davenport et al. (2021) noted that young scientists who were attracted to the work of these agencies were hesitant to apply because they feared their work might be subject to political rather than only scientific challenges. The former president also took aim at the U.S. State Department. In a minority report for the U.S. Senate Foreign Relations Committee, Democratic staff (2020) summarized the president's view of the department as a "deep state" that was trying to undermine him. Appointees to the secretary position, Rex Tillerson and Mike Pompeo, did little to salve the culture of fear and mistrust due to attacks on department personnel and the overall impact on their morale. Lastly, in a plan calculated to move the U.S. Department of Agriculture closer to midwestern farmlands and several land grant institutions, the Trump administration relocated two of its agencies, the Economic Research Service and the National Institute of Food and Agriculture to Kansas City, Missouri. Whatever the benefits may eventually be, a year after the relocation, The Kansas City Star (Lowry & Vockrodt, 2021) reported that numerous positions remained unfilled. Only a third of the employees had agreed to move, and recruitment was slow as there are a limited number of agricultural economists in the country. And much like the climate scientists in the other agencies, prospective recruits wanted to have a career and not be subject to random political acts should they decide to enlist.

The third and last contributor to political precarity that I offer from media reports of the previous administration was what happened near the end of the term—the presidential election of 2020. The outcome of what started out as a regular election with commonly understood results was that incumbent Donald Trump with 74,224,319 votes (46.9%) had lost to Democratic candidate Joe Biden, who garnered 81,284,666 votes (51.3%) and 303 electoral college votes, 33 more than the 270 required to win the election. From election night to the time of this writing, Trump has maintained that he won the contest and that it was rigged and stolen from him. According to The New York Times (Bazelon, 2020), he challenged election results with lawsuits in the battleground states of Arizona, Georgia, Michigan, Nevada, Pennsylvania, and Wisconsin and did not fare well in any of them. A Senate Judiciary Committee report (Majority Staff Report, 2021) found that the former president had repeatedly asked the U.S. Department of Justice to endorse his claims that the election was stolen and to assist his efforts to overturn its results. On January 6. 2021, supporters of the former president, and others, staged a combination protest and attack to halt the Congressional ratification of Joe Biden's win. Several media outlets reported on the events of that day including CNN, [2] NBC News, [3] and ABC News. [4] During that day, many of the former president's supporters and even his own children requested that he deter his supporters in an effort to stop what was being called not only an attack, but also an insurrection (Knox, 2021). One year later as I write this chapter, there are still debates about the meaning of that day.

Reflections on Author's Journal

As someone who had worked in state government most of my adult life, I often thought of those in Washington, DC and in state and local governments, who filled the ranks of the executive, legislative, and judicial branches and kept our government going through these turbulent years. I decided to keep a journal (Smendzuik-O'Brien, n.d.) noting important events of the day, such as how many were infected with or dead from the coronavirus nationally and in various states, what I was doing that day, and my thought on the day. I wondered from time to time how I would have felt as an employee somewhere in the country's governmental systems. What would have sustained me in doing my work for the common good?

This section contains an autoethnographic approach in which I offer some of the observations I made during the months I kept the journal. My reflections cover three timeframes that I named *lockdown*, the *tough summer*, and the *election*. The events described are as I noted them in my journal.

Lockdown

The lockdown started in March 2020 and lasted until May 2020. I named this the "lockdown" period because it was a time of my growing awareness of just how precarious the U.S. national situation had become, and the country did eventually lockdown in many areas. Almost overnight 30 million people were unemployed. My entries show that during this time, the former president created confusion regarding COVID-19 (hereafter "virus") by saying that no one knew the virus was coming, except Obama administration officials who had left a "playbook on pandemics" for the next administration. I noted that the president claimed doctors and nurses were hoarding protective masks and ventilators. He also claimed that if the United States only lost 100,000 people from the virus, his administration would have been successful. During April 2020, the deaths to date from the virus exceeded the number of Americans who died on 9/11 and who died in the Vietnam and Afghan wars. By the end of April, more Americans had died from the virus (in 3 months) than the number that had died in Vietnam (in 20 years). My reflection was, *"It feels like we are all holding our breath waiting for something to happen; how many of us will die?"* The president said he wanted to stop testing; some noted this idea would look like the virus was receding because the number of cases would be fewer. My reflection was, *"The president is afraid of failure so he does not act. If he does not act he cannot fail."* On April 11, 2020, then President Trump declared a national emergency. On April 17, he tweeted an encouragement to those protesting shutdowns to "liberate" their states; those states were Michigan, Minnesota, and Virginia. I had lived in Michigan and Minnesota, so the encouragement hit me hard. My reflection was, *"Why does Trump promote violence? "Liberate your state?" What? Violence to support the president. When have we ever done that in this country?"*

Tough Summer

On May 25, 2020, four Minneapolis police officers killed George Floyd, in my home state, in my home metropolis. His death led to riots in the streets for several days; there was evidence of outside influences making the situation worse. Mr. Floyd's death triggered a nationwide outpouring of protests about police brutality as other such instances were remembered. On July 3, the New York Times reported that over 4,700 protests had occurred since Mr. Floyd's death. [5] In some instances, statues of Confederate heroes were toppled; in Minnesota it was statues of Christopher Columbus and a pioneer. There was talk of renaming 10 Army bases that honored Confederate military leaders. Earlier in June the former president had gone on network news to say that he would call out the military to restore order and encouraged governors to "dominate the streets." My reflection was, *"We have had 84 days of coronavirus awareness and 10 days of hyper-racism awareness. I am worried about the president's threat to send federal agents, law enforcement and others, into cities to halt lawful protests because he claims Democrats don't know how to run cities."* Four hundred national security officials wrote to the former president to argue against turning the military on citizens. In neighboring Wisconsin, a 17-year-old from Illinois came north with a powerful hunting rifle and killed two people during a protest. Meanwhile, the virus raged on. On July 5 there were 49,000 new cases in one day; on July 21 there were 1,000 deaths. By September 11 there were 40,000 new virus cases per day and 50 deaths per hour. Hospitals were again overflowing with cases.

Arguments raged about open and closed businesses, whether to open parks and beaches, and whether and how children would return to in-class learning. I wrote, *"I hope the advocates of masks will prevail. It is sad that so many people are dying in the southern states. How can kids go back to school?"* Europeans closed their borders to us because of our high rates of infection. Economic conditions were severe in many places. In Dallas, Texas 25,000 lined up in mid-November at a distribution center to get boxes of food. [6] On top of everything else, the U.S. intelligence community said that Russians were paying a bounty to the Taliban for killing American soldiers in Afghanistan. At first, the former president said that no one had told him. My reflection was, *"Would he have listened to a briefing if it were offered?"* Later he said that Russians paying this type of bounty was a hoax.

Election

The campaign for the presidency formally started in August 2020 with the Democratic and Republican conventions. The post office began to remove mailboxes, claiming they needed refurbishing, a strange plan given that there were likely to be many mail-in ballots in a pandemic. The former president started to say that he could only lose the election if it were rigged for his opponent. My thought was, *"Why does no one respond to him that he will lose not because the election is rigged but because people do not vote for him? This is Civics 101."* Two times in early September he told his supporters to vote twice, once in person and once by mail, saying they should be denied the in-person ballot. Voting twice is a felony. My thought, *"I think the president above all else does not want to lose the election and be called a loser. That is what he calls other people."* On September 12, the former president sued five states to stop mail-in voting. Ten days later he said there would be no peaceful transfer of power because there would be a continuance of his presidency. Early voting started mid-October; long lines of people waited in Texas and Georgia. On November 1, he said that he would declare victory on election night if he was ahead no matter the status of mail-in and absentee ballots. He insisted that all ballots must be counted by the end of election night.

Meanwhile, in virus news, back in early October the former president tested positive for the virus and was admitted to Walter Reed Medical Center for 4 days. His physicians were very mysterious about his condition other than to say the next 48 hours would be critical for him. On October 26 there were 70,000 positive cases of the virus in the United States; on October 30 there were 98,000 cases. On October 30, there were 225,600 dead Americans.

There was no winner on election night. Counting continued until November 7, when Joe Biden got the required number of electoral votes. The former president did not concede. The director of the General Services Administration, Emily Murphy, had the power to "ascertain" who had won the election and to free up federal resources for the winner. She did not do it until November 23, claiming she was loyal to the person who hired her. The former president was busy in the weeks following the election. He hired a young supporter to remove federal employees who were "insufficiently loyal" and made it harder to reinstate environmental regulations suspended during the pandemic. My reflection was, *"Trump fumes while people are dying from the virus."* The minority leader in the House of Representatives was happy with the election results there. My reflection, *"So it is a good election or not? Is the only problem with the votes for president?"* The former president filed lawsuits in numerous states; on November 27, his record was one win and 38 losses. On December 1 Attorney General William Barr found no evidence of voter fraud. On December 9, 100 members of the House of Representatives signed onto a lawsuit about the election filed with the Supreme Court. My reflection was, *"How can these 100 individuals go home for the holiday break and tell their constituents that they filed a lawsuit instead of voting for a virus relief bill?"* On December 19, Michael Flynn called for martial law to be declared, election results in swing states to be voided, and the election to be re-held. On December 30, the drumbeat began when Senator Josh Hawley protested the acceptance of electoral college ballots. Other senators and representatives joined the chorus. On January 3, the former president called the Georgia Secretary of State asking for 11,780 more votes. My thought was, *"I hope the Congress will rebuke the president. If anyone else did this they would be prosecuted for election interference."*

On November 9, Pfizer drug company announced a 90% efficacy vaccine for the virus. A week later the company announced that it was 95% effective, and the Moderna company announced a vaccine with a similar effectiveness rate. Doctors without Borders (Médecins Sans Frontières) planned to send doctors to the United States because our pandemic was so bad. In El Paso, Texas over

200 bodies were placed in refrigerator trucks because mortuaries and funeral homes in the city could not keep up with the deaths. Affluent hospitals recruited around the country and offered bonuses to medical staff to join their facilities. My thought was, *"The poor are at a disadvantage again."* On December 30, the Delta variant of the virus was discovered in Colorado. It had been discovered earlier that Russian hackers were attacking hospitals for ransom money. It was discovered later, on December 13, that Russian hackers had attacked a wide range of federal agencies and corporations for the previous 8–9 months.

On January 5, two Democratic senators were elected in Georgia to succeed two Republicans. On January 6, the former president said again to a gathered crowd of supporters that the election had been stolen and encouraged them to fight like h--- or they would not have a country. The assault on the Capitol building and the Congress to halt the counting of the electoral ballots ensued. Consequences of that day were a second impeachment trial of the former president and an affirmative vote in the House of Representatives on January 13. At the time of this writing, follow up investigations are still being conducted by the FBI and by the Select Committee to Investigate the January 6th Attack on the United States Capitol. [7] My thought was, *"I hope the former president does not pardon all the rioters at the Capitol."*

Overall Reflection

Each of these periods held not only political precarity but personal precarity for me and likely for a number of Americans. No one knew how the virus would spread, who would be susceptible, and whether or not the U.S. government would be able to address it effectively. Beyond the unknowns related to the virus, many people lost their jobs, their income, their health insurance, and sometimes their dwelling, which added to their personal precarity. At the core, political arguments about what to do were difficult because the national leadership did not take the effects of the virus seriously, calling it a hoax for weeks. Governors sprinted into action to find medical equipment and to support frontline workers who were wearied by the hours and the loss of life that they could not allay. Beyond the problems of the virus were the concerns about racial injustice and concerns about the election. Many in the country were stressed and fearful. It was wearying for me to consider all of it again for this chapter.

Inspirational Leaders

While the foregoing may seem to depict a concerning period of political precarity, it is not the first such period in the history of the United States. Jon Meacham (2019) has written about other volatile, unjust, or otherwise troubling times. In some of them, the president of the country has pointed the way to a brighter future, and in other instances those who "witness, protest, and resist" have led the way to possibilities. The latter group includes individuals like the Reverend Martin Luther King, Jr. and John Lewis, who led the 1960s civil rights movement, and Gloria Steinem, who led the women's rights movement. About the presidents, Meacham (2019) wrote,

> A president sets a tone for the nation and helps tailor habits of heart and of mind. Presidential action and presidential grace are often crucial in ameliorating moments of virulence and violence – and presidential indifference and presidential obtuseness can exacerbate such hours. We are more likely to choose the right path when we are encouraged to do so from the very top. (p. 13)

Meacham (2019) wrote about Abraham Lincoln, who called on the nation during the Civil War, and at its end, to live so that others would not have died in vain and to heal the wounds of those who suffered during the conflict. He also described other presidents closer to this time in history, who used the language of religion, country, and hope to remind the nation of its promise. He cited Ronald Reagan, who spoke of the shining city on the hill during a national "crisis of confidence" (p. 260) and Bill Clinton, who responded to the Oklahoma City bombing in April 1995 by quoting St. Paul to "not be overcome by evil but overcome evil with good" (p. 261).

Included also by Meacham (2019) was an account of George W. Bush, who after the attacks of 9/11 said, "This world He created is of moral design. Grief and tragedy and hatred are only for a time. Goodness, remembrance, and love have no end" (p. 262). In another instance Meacham (2019) noted that speaking in the aftermath of the shooting of nine African Americans during a church bible study in Charleston, South Carolina by a White supremacist, Barack Obama argued that, in the Christian tradition, grace is not earned. Rather, it is a favor of God, and "out of this terrible tragedy God has visited grace upon us … allowed us to see where we've been blind. He has given us the chance, where we've been lost, to find our best selves" (p. 263).

American Ideals: Religious Traditions

Meacham's (2019) examples include a mix of religious ideals, primarily Christian, and political ideals. However, in an increasingly diverse country, it is useful to look at religious traditions for moral principles that can sustain public service leaders from all three great Abrahamic and monotheistic religions: Islam, Judaism, and Christianity.

Islam

This section relies on the work of Hassan Hanafi (2002). According to Hanafi (2002), there are a mix of Islamic views of civil society. He identified one view that rejects the idea of "civil society" as a Western concept, a second view that considers it a universal idea no matter the source, and a third holds that it may be possible to combine classical Islam with modern social needs. Hanafi (2002) observed that a key ingredient for all of them is the idea of umma, a nation without boundaries, to which all Muslims belong. Islam holds that different nations, societies, or sects may be part of the Muslim umma. The author noted that the "People of the Book," Jews, and Christians, historically held a special place for Muslims because of their common belief in the God of Abraham. Members within the Muslim umma have responsibilities to each other, but rights and obligations may also extend to non-Muslim groups. Hanafi clarified that classical Islam identified different institutions that acted in civil society. The first group was the wielders of power, the second group was the intellectuals and legal scholars, and the third group was the judges. Hanafi (2002) also identified the equivalent of foundations for the arts and sciences. Essentially, there was an integration of a "politico-religious" community with power distributed among its parts. Society was a unity of equal individuals with the same rights and duties. According to Hanafi (2002), there are four main values in society. The first is the protection of life. The second is the use of reason for open scientific and spiritual inquiry. Third is the defense of human dignity. Last is the preservation of wealth against corruption, excessive spending, and negligence. Public servants are expected to hold to high standards of honesty and integrity. The social justice aims are not only pursued by the state, but they are also more often advanced by non-governmental organizations such as mosques, Sufi orders, and charitable organizations. The author argues that religion in Islam is a political system, an economic theory, and a social structure and that, accordingly, values should not be separate from the business of the state. Political power should be freely-elected; common interests and public welfare should be protected; and the social order should not have great differences between classes.

Judaism

Suzanne Last Stone (2002) is the primary resource for my comments in this section on Judaism and the socio-political order. Stone (2002) observed that since Jews for much of history had no state, few conceptions of a civil society with requirements were developed. She noted that Jews did, however, have numerous ideas of what constituted a "civilized society." The Jewish people operated under the covenantal law, which prescribed behaviors and obligations for all of Jewish life. According to Stone (2002), this law included not only the law of the first five books of the Hebrew Bible, or Pentateuch, but also the 613 laws that were developed by the rabbinic tradition from the original Noahide laws. The Noahide laws required Jews to make additional laws, and prohibited blasphemy, idolatry, adultery, bloodshed, theft, and eating the blood of live animals. The author noted that Jewish law recognized three types of non-Jewish people within their communities: the heathen, the stranger, and the resident stranger. The stranger enjoyed social solidarity and sometimes followed parts of the covenantal law. The law obligated Jews to love both fellow Jews and the stranger. Stone (2002) wrote that the law governed these relationships because human nature was too frail to be relied on to do the right thing. While the bible did not call for the establishment of communal associations to foster human well-being, the idea of a beneficial public community arose during the medieval period. These associations could provide for local public needs, such as synagogues, schools, and police protection; they could also legislate for the public good. I would add that another idea of the "good" in Jewish thought was the idea of tikkun olam, which means "repair of the world." [8] This "repair" includes harmonious relationships with others—people living together in peace, justice, and prosperity. This connection is based on the idea that because the whole world belongs to God, the obligation also includes the duty to take care of the natural world.

I would also add here that the Ten Commandments guided Jewish life and were part of the Pentateuch. The first three commandments described what should be the relationship with God and the remaining seven covered relationships with others in the community. Topics of these seven were honoring parents, bloodshed, adultery, theft, false witness against a neighbor, and covetousness of property or spouse (Ignatius Bible Edition, 2016, Exodus, chap. 20; v. 1-17).

Christianity

For this section on Christianity and civil society, I have relied on Michael Banner's (2002) chapter discussing that relationship. Banner (2002) characterized the contemporary understanding of civil society as the set of "structured associations, relationships, and forms of cooperation between persons that exist in the realm between the family and the state" (p. 113). But the author clarified that the relationship between Christianity and civil society is complex because of the variety of Christian thought about the nature of human community. He offered the example that St. Augustine conceived of two cities, one earthly and one heavenly. The former was characterized by self-love while the latter was created by the love of God; in the heavenly city is found just and certain peace. Banner (2002) suggested that in that same Catholic tradition, Thomas Aquinas later wrote that the relationship between earthly and heavenly cities was closer and that all the parts—marriage, family, private property, political rule—had their appointed place and could be woven together into one will for the common good. The author described the idea of subsidiarity in the Catholic Christian tradition, which is that action in society should be taken at the lowest possible level and not assumed by a higher entity. In the Protestant tradition, Banner (2002) reported John Calvin's position that God ruled over sinful humanity, and the social order consisted of a divine-human covenant, divine commandments, and divine offices. For Calvin, order required the constant exercise of power, and in the churches of New England there developed forms of self-government and association that protected them from the power of the state.

Finally, in the Lutheran conception, according to Banner (2002), Augustine's two cities became two spheres, the outer and the inner. The outer sphere was where the state and civil society have their influence and the inner sphere was the concern of the church. He noted, however, that both traditions emphasized the importance of the sociality of human beings and their need for human community. Banner (2002) added that it was also important to both ideas that believers have the freedom to associate and to worship in societies as God intended and not be identified with imperfect societies that recognize other authorities or no authority.

The Catholic tradition has considered an encyclical by Pope Leo XIII written in the early days of the industrial revolutions as the start of its modern social teaching (O'Brien & Shannon, 2016). Associates at the Jesuit Center of Concern have condensed the seven major aspects of that social teaching into a slender volume titled *Catholic Social Teaching: Our Best Kept Secret* (DeBerri et al., 2003, pp. 18-34). Those aspects and their areas of emphasis are

- the dignity of the human person (authentic human development; love of God, love of neighbor; love and justice; dialogue),
- the dignity of work (the priority of labor over capital; religious and social development),
- the person in community (common good; human freedom / social structures; structures of sin / structures of grace; liberation; participation; the role of the Church),
- rights and responsibilities (human rights; responsibilities; private property / social mortgage; resisting market idolatry; the role of government; the principle of subsidiarity),
- option for those in poverty (biblical justice),
- solidarity (unity of humanity; peacemaking; pacifism or non-violence; just war), and
- care for creation.

It is my observation that these religious ideals from the Abrahamic religions and their views of the social order can provide encouragement for public service leaders when they are challenged by the vicissitudes and volatility in the governmental sector as described at the start of this chapter. Each of the traditions holds views that can lead to wholesome practices focused on the common good in human community. I turn now to the American political tradition for more ideals that can sustain public servants.

American Ideals: Political Traditions

Though this chapter began with a discussion of the US presidency, leadership in the public service of the United States occurs in all three branches of government—legislative, judicial, and executive—and it also occurs at all levels—local, state, federal, special district, tribal, inter-agency, and inter-sectoral. In each of these branches and at all of these levels, skilled professionals exercise leadership in their positions. What ideals from US political traditions can sustain public service employees in their work during turbulent times?

Morgan et al. (2019) have identified four sources of public morality to support actions. The first is for the leader to know the structure of the legal authority of their job. The authors clarified that legal authority may come from constitutional law; statutes passed by legislative bodies; administrative law (sometimes called regulatory law, regulations, or administrative rules); judicial law; and executive orders, proclamations, and signing orders. The second source of public morality they identified is to know what is prohibited, specifically ethical matters such as rewarding partisan loyalty, incompetence, or inefficiency. The third type of public morality is to know the type of leadership discretion warranted in the position. The authors provided examples of the range of discretion. On one end of a continuum, they described engineers or scientists who usually have technical discretion to do their work and professionals such as physicians or lawyers who often have authority to self-regulate their practice. On the other end of the continuum, the authors described those who work in social planning areas, where disagreements abound, as having the least discretion. For example, how clean should the air be? How much mercury in fish can pregnant women eat? Answers to these types of questions are often hotly debated.

Morgan et al. (2019) also identified the fourth source of public morality, which is to know the moral legacy of the founding of the United States. The authors described several rationales for this fourth source. The founders of the country experienced several problems and wanted to avoid them in the future. The founders wanted to avoid concentrations of wealth and power that would disadvantage the poor. They wanted to avoid a federal government that had no resources and would thereby end up unable to provide for the citizenry. They worried about the tyranny of a majority who might act against the best interests of the new nation. Lastly, the founders wanted to ensure that people would get engaged at their local level and participate in its government.

In addition to these sources of moral authority to support the actions of public leaders described by Morgan et al. (2019), Ingle and Normand (2018) developed a companion workbook with an assessment for public leaders to use to determine their personal alignment with public values. The public values in this assessment are stewardship, voice, fairness, integrity, respect, trustworthiness, caring, loyalty, humility, and balance.

The last political tradition that I identify as useful for sustaining public service leaders is the Code of Ethics of the American Society for Public Administration. [9] These eight principles address the intended goals of public service leaders who serve at all levels and in all branches of public service. I would assert that, along with an individual's personal religious beliefs, these values and ethical statements from the American political tradition can serve to support the work of public service professionals even in challenging circumstances.

1. **Advance the public interest.** Promote the interests of the public and put service to the public before service to oneself.
2. **Uphold the Constitution and the law.** Respect and support government constitutions and laws, while seeking to improve laws and policies to promote the public good.
3. **Promote democratic participation.** Inform the public and encourage active engagement in governance. Be open, transparent, and responsive and respect and assist all persons in their dealings with public organizations.
4. **Strengthen social equity.** Treat all persons with fairness, justice, and equality and respect individual differences, rights, and freedoms. Promote affirmative action and other initiatives to reduce unfairness, injustice, and inequality in society.
5. **Fully inform and advise.** Provide accurate, honest, comprehensive, and timely information and advice to elected and appointed officials and governing board members and to staff members in your organization.
6. **Demonstrate personal integrity.** Adhere to the highest standards of conduct to inspire public confidence and trust in public service.
7. **Promote ethical organizations.** Strive to attain the highest standards of ethics, stewardship, and public service in organizations that serve the public.

8. **Advance professional excellence.** Strengthen personal capabilities to act competently and ethically and encourage the professional development of others.

The Fraught Realm of Ideals

Perhaps the greatest challenge of ideals is that they evoke strong sentiment about how they are applied. Arguments for and against the use of both religious and political ideals applied to leadership can be found. One end of the spectrum, as to the utility of ideals, is the idea that there should exist only an altruistic approach to life based on love. This idea casts aside the overburden placed on human beings from religious and scientific sources. In *A Letter to a Hindu*, Leo Tolstoy (1908/2021) wrote to the editor of *Free Hindustan* about the oppression foisted by both. He argued that for centuries people were taught through various holy books that the highest act of holiness was to love fellow human beings. Yet at the same time, they witnessed violence by the state ostensibly to protect its members but, in reality, to preserve the power of leaders whose power was believed to be divinely bestowed. According to Tolstoy (1908/2021), later justifications for violence over love were rationalizations that he called "scientific" or "practical" and supposedly permitted by the will of the governed. Tolstoy was having none of it. He wrote:

> This is what we need, this is the only thing we need: We need the knowledge and understanding of the simple and direct truth which exists in every human soul that is not full or hypnotized by religious or scientific superstitions, the truth that for our life one law is valid, one law is to be obeyed and that is the law of love, which brings the greatest happiness and fulfillment to every individual as well as to all of mankind as a whole. (p. 65)

Political philosopher Martha C. Nussbaum is also found on the cautious end of the spectrum in connection with religious ideals. Nussbaum (2011) argued that many religions create what she calls "in-groups" and "out-groups" (p. 90) which can threaten the idea of citizens' political equality. She further argued that many religious citizens believe that their method of making choices is the right one for everyone at all times, and they may offer different ideas of what that right choice is (p. 95). Rather than religious ideals, Nussbaum (2011) praised government, and I infer from that political ideals, as the body that "must treat all people respectfully" (p. 26). For a society to be socially just, it must give its members a dignified life, and it is the role of political actors to determine what that type of life requires (p. 73).

Robert K. Greenleaf's ideas about servant leadership fall along the middle of the spectrum of caution about religious and political ideals in public leadership. Greenleaf (2002) described servant leaders as ones who care for both persons and for institutions (p. 342). While he did not argue for specific religious ideals, he did identify a role for what he called the "growing edge church." He claimed that such churches could be a force for healing society:

> One of these [roles of the church] will be to become the chief nurturing force, conceptualizer of the opportunity, value shaper, and morale sustainer of leadership everywhere: in business, school, government, health and social service, philanthropy – *everywhere.* … the dynamics of leadership – the vision, the values, and the staying power – are essentially religious concerns and fostering them should become the central mission of the growing edge churches. (p. 94)

Greenleaf (2002) also addressed the idea of servant leadership in bureaucratic society, noting that "*All* institutions – churches, schools, governments, businesses, hospitals, social agencies, families – all become bureaucracies, regardless of the sheltering ideology or the specific goals" (p. 307). This view did not celebrate the bureaucracies in which many public servants toil, but it acknowledged them. He described several attitudes that could prepare servant leaders to make these bureaucracies into places for virtue and justice, to grow *beauty, momentareity, openness, humor,* and *tolerance.* These marked dimensions of a lifestyle that is rooted in an inward grace: sensitive and aware, concerned for the ever- present neighbor, both the well-fed one next door and the hungry one on the other side of the earth, and seeing and feeling what is right in the situation (p. 316). Thus, while Greenleaf did not enumerate political ideals, he identified ideals that could serve public leaders in governmental bureaucracies.

On the other end of the caution spectrum heralding both political and religious ideals for public service leaders is Robert Reich. In *The Common Good,* Reich (2019) conveyed the idea that both political and religious ideals have shaped and can shape public leaders. He wrote the following about political ideals that most Americans would recognize, although some of them have taken a beating in recent years.

> Our central obligation as citizens is to preserve, fortify, and protect our democratic form of government [...] We can't hate our government, for it is the means by which we can come together to help solve our common problems. [...] our obligation is to work to improve government, not to undermine it. [...] As citizens we are committed to the Constitution and the rule of law, to democracy based on the consent of the governed. We're committed to the Bill of Rights; to an independent judiciary; separation of powers between the executive, the legislature, and the courts; and in checks and balances among those three branches. We believe in federalism, giving states and localities significant responsibilities. We believe in freedom of speech. We are committed to a free and independent press. [...] Importantly, most of us believe in political equality. We believe that citizens should have an equal right to vote, and that no one's vote should count more than anyone else's. We believe in equality before the law, and that no one should be above the law. We don't want government to discriminate against racial or ethnic minorities. (pp. 34-35)

As to religious ideals, Reich (2019) noted that many in the United States have become confused about the difference between private and public morality. He described *private morality* as what individuals do in private and *public morality* as what leaders should do when they are in positions of public trust. He described some failures of public morality thusly:

> When executives of pharmaceutical companies gouge consumers by jacking up the prices of drugs as high as possible; bank executives defraud their depositors by opening up sham accounts; and presidents denigrate the press, seem to endorse white supremacists, and disregard conflicts of financial interest, they are all engaging in acts of public immorality. They are rejecting the common good in favor of their own selfish needs for more wealth or power. This is shameful. (p. 153)

Beside this idea that it is possible to speak of public morality in a secular society, Reich (2019) also identified a role for faith-based leaders to help society clarify public morality, thus finding a role for religious values to influence secular society as well. Ultimately, Reich identified both religious and political ideals as helpful to public leaders, noting "Moral guidance about what is right or decent can be found in both religious teachings and in our contemporary understanding of what we owe one another as members of the same society" (p. 154).

As this short journey through the ideas of Tolstoy, Nussbaum, Greenleaf, and Reich has shown, religious and political ideals are important in the formation of public leaders whether one believes in either set of ideals or in both of them.

Unexpected and Future Leadership

As noted earlier in this chapter, some executive branch employees left service during the previous administration. Messages about the virus were conflicted, non-existent, or untruthful. Yet many employees stayed, and programs continued. The military still served in Afghanistan. Retirees and others received their Social Security and disability checks. Employees and contractors of the Federal Emergency Management Administration assessed hurricane and flood damage. Border patrol officials handled the border. Perhaps the country should have expected good performance for the very reasons just outlined. But perhaps such continued good performance was unexpected because it stood out at a time when the news was often distressing.

Beyond the importance of acknowledging past good performance, ensuring future good performance matters. Scholar Martha C. Nussbaum (2011) has argued that a good measure of human progress is human development in the form of development of human capabilities. She and others have taken their ideas to the United Nations, which now requires a report on progress on human capabilities as part of its UN Development Program. She has argued that the development of these human capabilities needs a decent society, which in turn requires good political processes to create the context and environment for capabilities to flourish. My view is that those who run such processes must be practitioners who can find within themselves the personal values, including, perhaps, religious values, and the professional moral stamina to continue their efforts for the common good, no matter their critics.

Concluding Thoughts

Earlier in this chapter the two sides of precarity were raised—the risk and the opportunity. Most of this chapter has been about the downside of precarity, the fear and uncertainty that we felt in our country from the heavy hits of illness, economic distress, racial injustice, and persons in high positions who lacked the leadership capacity to inspire and pull us back to ourselves while all this occurred. So where is the opportunity? The opportunity arises from the religious traditions and the moral aspects of our political traditions.

The ideals of religious traditions about right relationships and political moral perspectives run deep in our country. Right relationships from religious traditions can be about the relationship between self and God, if one is a believer, and can certainly be about the relationship between human beings even if one is not a believer. For example, what does the charge to "not kill" mean? It can mean to live and let live as a minimum standard, or it can mean to encourage the flourishing of another. The moral aspects of the U.S. political tradition call all Americans to higher standards of crafting a polity worthy of living in.

These religious and political ideals show us what the just society can look like and the common good that public service leaders should strive to attain. This has been the history of our nation—working toward the more perfect union as our founders and our best political leaders have encouraged for these 246 years. While many lament our political and social divisions at this moment in time, it is possible to pull through the divisions by exploring anew what these long-held ideals can mean for us now. They can take us into light rather than what at present feels like the darkness. They can inspire our public service professionals who work for the common good each day and who deserve our respect. And as citizens we can remind ourselves of these ideals and expect them of those who work for us in the branches of government. To remember the idea of Abraham Lincoln, let us not be the ones to cause the government by the people, of the people, and for the people to perish from the face of the earth. Let us hold and act on our ideals.

End Notes

[1] https://abcnews.go.com/Politics/crooked-hillary-marco-donald-trumps-nicknames/story?id=39035114

[2] https://www.cnn.com/specials/congress-electoral-college-vote-count-video-landing-page

[3] https://www.nbcnews.com/nightly-news-netcast/video/nightly-news-full-broadcast-january-6th-99015237529

[4] https://abcnews.go.com/Politics/riot-jan-dangerously-close-call-trumps-plot-succeeded/story?id=81858613

[5] https://www.nytimes.com/interactive/2020/07/03/us/george-floyd-protests-crowd-size.html

[6] https://www.kbtx.com/2020/11/16/25000-people-in-need-get-food-turkeys-at-dallas-food-bank-drive-thru

[7] https://january6th.house.gov/

[8] https://www.bbc.co.uk/bitesize/guides/zfs3d2p/revision/3

[9] https://www.aspanet.org/ASPA/Code-of-Ethics/Code-of-Ethics.aspx

Meet the Author

Julie Smendzuik-O'Brien, PhD served for 25 years in mid-level and senior-level management positions in the agriculture, natural resources, and higher education agencies of Minnesota state government. She directed change efforts in policy development, organizational improvement, organization behavior, and strategic planning. She recently completed almost a decade of service on the board of the Organization Development and Change Division of the Academy of Management in three different positions. She is a board member of the North Woods and Waters of the St. Croix Heritage Area, a program of the U.S. National Park Service focused on areas of national significance in the history of the United States. She is on the graduate faculty of the Public and Nonprofit Leadership Program at Metropolitan State University in St. Paul, Minnesota and is a member of the editorial board of the *Journal of Applied Behavioral Science*. Smendzuik-O'Brien holds an undergraduate degree in religious studies and master's degrees in public administration and human development.

References

Associated Press. (2021, August 25). Man gets 6 years in prison in Michigan governor kidnap plot. *U.S. News & World Report.* https://www.usnews.com/news/politics/articles/2021-08-24/sentence-next-for-man-who-says-he-plotted-to-kidnap-governor

Azmanova, A. (2020). *Capitalism on edge: How fighting precarity can achieve radical change without crisis or utopia.* Columbia University Press. https://cup.columbia.edu/book/capitalism-on-edge/9780231195379

Azmanova, A. (2020). Precarity, not inequality is what ails the 99%. *FT.com.* https://www.ft.com/stream/4a57dfa7-4f19-4d0b-8830-3b365d55aa6e

Banner, M. (2002). Christianity and civil society. In S. Chambers & W. Kymlicka (Eds.), *Alternative conceptions of civil society* (pp. 113–130). Princeton University Press. https://press.princeton.edu/books/paperback/9780691087962/alternative-conceptions-of-civil-society

Bazelon, E. (2020, November 25). Trump is not doing well with his election lawsuits. Here's a rundown. *The New York Times.* https://www.nytimes.com/2020/11/13/us/politics/trump-election-lawsuits.html

Biale, E., Stein, M., Vergara, C., McKean, B., & Azmanova, A. (2021). Regaining control over precarity. *Contemporary Political Theory.* https://doi.org/10.1057/s41296-021-00503-y

Brooks, D. (2020, October 5). America is having a moral convulsion. *The Atlantic.* https://www.theatlantic.com/ideas/archive/2020/10/collapsing-levels-trust-are-devastating-america/616581/

Costa, R., & Gregg, A. (2020, March 22). Governors and mayors in growing uproar over Trump's lagging coronavirus response. *Washington Post.* https://www.washingtonpost.com/politics/governors-and-mayors-in-growing-uproar-over-trumps-lagging-coronavirus-response/2020/03/22/98ac569a-6c49-11ea-a3ec-70d7479d83f0_story.html

Cramer, K. J. (2016). *The politics of resentment: Rural consciousness in Wisconsin and the rise of Scott Walker.* University of Chicago Press. https://press.uchicago.edu/ucp/books/book/chicago/P/bo22879533.html

Davenport, C., Friedman, L., & Flavelle, C. (2021, September 20). Biden's climate plans are stunted after dejected experts fled Trump. *The New York Times.* https://www.nytimes.com/2021/08/01/climate/biden-scientists-shortage-climate.html

DeBerri, E. P., Hug, J. E., Henriot, P. J., & Schultheis, M. J. (2003). *Catholic social teaching: Our best kept secret.* Orbis Books. https://www.orbisbooks.com/catholic-social-teaching.html

Democratic Staff. (2020). *Diplomacy in crisis: The Trump administration's decimation of the State Department.* https://www.foreign.senate.gov/download/2020-sfrc-minority-report_-diplomacy-in-crisis----the-trump-administrations-decimation-of-the-state-department

Freedman, D. H. (2021, December 20). Millions of angry, armed Americans stand ready to seize power if Trump loses in 2024. *Newsweek Magazine.* https://www.

newsweek.com/2021/12/31/millions-angry-armed-americans-stand-ready-seize-power-if-trump-loses-2024-1660953.html

Greenleaf, R. K. (2002). *Servant leadership: A journey into the nature of legitimate power and greatness* (Anniversary ed.). Paulist Press. https://www.paulistpress.com/Products/3-064-1/servant-leadership-25th-anniversary-edition.aspx

Haberman, M., Thrush, G., & Baker, P. (2017, December 9). Inside Trump's hour-by-hour battle for self-preservation. *The New York Times*. https://www.nytimes.com/2017/12/09/us/politics/donald-trump-president.html

Hanafi, H. (2002). Alternative conceptions of civil society: A reflective Islamic approach. In S. Chambers & W. Kymlicka (Eds.), *Alternative conceptions of civil society* (pp. 171–189). Princeton University Press. https://press.princeton.edu/books/paperback/9780691087962/alternative-conceptions-of-civil-society

Ignatius Bible Edition. (2016). *The Didache bible*. Midwest Theological Forum / Ignatius Press. https://www.theologicalforum.org/Category/0/Product/516/The_Didache_Bible_RSV2CE_Hardcover

Ingle, M. D., & Normand, J. (2018). *EMERGE public leadership performance platform: Leader practices and tools for sizing-up and taking-action on wicked challenges. Portland State University.*
https://www.pdx.edu/sites/g/files/znldhr2431/files/2020-12/EMERGE_Public_Leadership_Platform-FINAL_VERSION.pdf

Knox, O. (2021, December 14). The Meadows texts and the weird PowerPoint take Jan. 6 inside the White House. *The Washington Post*. https://www.washingtonpost.com/politics/2021/12/14/meadows-texts-weird-powerpoint-take-jan-6-inside-white-house/

Lowry, B., & Vockrodt, S. (2021, April 25). More than a year after USDA move to Kansas City, hundreds of positions remain vacant. *The Kansas City Star*. https://www.kansascity.com/news/politics-government/article250889644.html

Majority Staff Report. (2021). *Subverting justice: How the former president and his allies pressured DOJ to overturn the 2020 election.* https://www.judiciary.senate.gov/press/dem/releases/following-8-month-investigation-senate-judiciary-committee-releases-report-on-donald-trumps-scheme-to-pressure-doj-and-overturn-the-2020-election

Mauger, C., & LeBlanc, B. (2020, April 17). Trump tweets 'liberate' Michigan, two other states with Dem governors. *The Detroit News*. https://www.detroitnews.com/story/news/politics/2020/04/17/trump-tweets-liberate-michigan-other-states-democratic-governors/5152037002/

Meacham, J. (2019). *The soul of America: The battle for our better angels.* Random House. http://www.randomhousebooks.com/books/554220/

Morgan, D. F., Ingle, M. D., & Shinn, C. W. (2019). *New public leadership: Making a difference from where we sit.* Routledge. https://www.routledge.com/New-Public-Leadership-Making-a-Difference-from-Where-We-Sit/Morgan-Ingle-Shinn/p/book/9780765634641

Nussbaum,M.C. (2011). *Creating capabilities: The human development approach*. Harvard University Press. https://www.hup.harvard.edu/catalog.php?isbn=9780674072350

O'Brien, D. J., & Shannon, T. A. (Eds.). (2016). *Catholic social thought: Encyclicals and documents from Pope Leo XIII to Pope Francis*. Orbis Books. https://www.orbisbooks.com/catholic-social-thought-en.html

Reich, R. B. (2019). *The common good.* Penguin Random House. https://www.penguinrandomhouse.com/books/564303/the-common-good-by-robert-b-reich/

Select Subcommittee on the Coronavirus Crisis. (2021). *More effective, more efficient, more equitable: Overseeing an improving & ongoing pandemic response. Year-end staff report*. https://coronavirus.house.gov/

Smendzuik-O'Brien, J. (n.d.). *Pandemic Journal, March 2020-June 2021*. Unpublished.

Stone, S. L. (2002). The Jewish tradition and civil society. In S. Chambers & W. Kymlicka (Eds.), *Alternative conceptions of civil society* (pp. 151–170). Princeton University Press. https://press.princeton.edu/books/paperback/9780691087962/alternative-conceptions-of-civil-society

Tolstoy, L. (2021). *Leo Tolstoy's a letter to a Hindu: The 2021 translation* (D. Westfall, Trans.). Yehoshuai Press. (Original work published 1908)

Woodward, B. (2020). *Rage*. Simon & Schuster. https://www.simonandschuster.com/books/Rage/Bob-Woodward/9781982131746

Woodward, B., & Costa, R. (2021). *Peril.* Simon & Schuster. https://www.simonandschuster.com/books/Peril/Bob-Woodward/9781982182915

Epilogue

In this epilogue, we editors reflect on what just happened. In the context of the turbulence of 2021–2022, we called out to our Institute for Social Innovation fellows, asking them to consider intersections where precarity, leadership, and greater social justice meet. We knew that these three domains do not always intersect. Precarity can surely be met with meanness and greed, not social justice. We knew also that social justice is viewed in varied ways and with different emphases, so we asked authors to consider Nussbaum's (2011) *social justice as increased capabilities* framework. We suspected that the practices of leaders at the intersection of precarity and social justice might be riffs and rills on settled theories of leadership, but we asked our authors to also look for leading that was unexpected and innovative. We share now what we've learned about unexpected leading toward greater social justice during precarity and how the chapters in this volume inform scholars and practitioners interested in change toward a more equitable and sustainable world. We look at each domain, beginning with precarity.

Precarity

Our authors wrote in the context of the COVID-19 global pandemic, the videoed murder of George Floyd, and the bitter 2020 US presidential election. For a time, these shocks drew back a curtain on fragile support systems, unrecognized but essential workers, unequal impacts, privileged access to resources, and widespread vulnerability to hunger, harm, and death. While it might be a genuine hope that we organize socially to minimize precarity for others, pervasive political discourse and social unrest suggest that we are, instead, strengthening barriers to define more firmly who has preferred status and who does not. Many North Americans, for example, are debating who can come to or stay in our countries, who can vote, who has privacy in love or in reproduction, who can work and how, what is a living wage, who has redress at work, who has health care, who gets childcare or caregiving, who gets a "good" education—who ages with dignity, eats, lives with climate change effects, is imprisoned or absolved. The lines drawn adhere often to boundaries of race, gender, mental and physical health, sexuality, age, income, ability, ethnicity, legacy, and geography. This reality conflicts with principles of justice for all and the removal of barriers to human capability so that each person can flourish. The resulting tensions are a core characteristic of our era.

Authors encountered two types of precarity. Humans experience *inherent* precarity as part of our existence, as we all live with the inevitability of sickness and death. As an interdependent species, we rely on others and we need access to the basic requirements for survival. These dependencies create vulnerabilities. Another type of precarity is what Hamington and Flower (2021) called "market-based" (p. 2). This precarity is the result of complex social, economic, and political processes that organize how wealth and value are distributed in a society and to whom. Precarity, then, can be *deliberate*—a result of power and privilege and policy—a choice. For some citizens, the outcome of inherent and deliberate precarity is a state of "fundamental existential insecurity" (Hedman, 2019, p. 2). If such insecurity is the result of decisions and entrenched systems, though, it is also subject to mitigation and reduction.

Hamington and Flower (2021) offered that the opposite of precarity is *caring*. "Care is always the response to the particularity of someone's circumstance that requires concrete knowledge of their situation, entailing imaginative connections and actions on behalf of their flourishing and growth" (p. 6). Care is responsive inquiry, empathy, and action. This kind of leading response is not conventional; it is not Western or male-dominated or based on power and competition; it is likely rooted in Indigenous and women's ways of knowing and leading. We need such counterbalancing and disruptive responses to optional precarity.

Caring was a surprising through line in this volume. In their analysis of unexpected leading in the shadow of inherent and deliberate precarity, our authors found that caring at the level of someone's circumstance was indeed present. Curran and Thompson called caring an "igniting force," along with intent, hope, and love. These forces move capacities to capabilities in service of greater justice. Southam and Harman and Buckley discussed an "ethic of care." Care ethics are practices and virtues that humans apply in a network of social relations. Our authors found scholarly support for unexpected leading in action, principle, and theory that leverages the accessible force of caring to reduce precarity and expand social justice in what our foreword author, Joan Gallos, called "all the right places."

Social Justice

In the chapters of this book, precarity and social justice met in a wide range of settings that included schools, community-based education, government, long-term care, psychological counseling, community action, corporate teams, executive coaching, religious studies, Tanzanian cultural traditions, and women's groups. Chapter authors agreed that leading toward social justice means generating support for thriving human capabilities (Thrift & Sugarman, 2019), such as those described by Nussbaum (2011) in her capabilities framework: a normal human lifespan with dignity, bodily health, and bodily integrity; senses, imagination, and thought; emotions, practical reason, affiliation, living in concern for and relation to other species, play, and control over one's environment. There were also challenges to Nussbaum's capabilities approach, particularly its bent towards individualism and sometimes unquestioned reliance on individual rights as opposed to communal care. We can look at authors' views of social justice in times of precarity.

Several studies found evidence of growth in Nussbaum's capabilities in their research participants and concluded that social justice had been increased through unexpected leadership. Sonnet and Spearman studied the presence of five of the capabilities in a self-designed post-secondary peer support group. Their research found that three of the capabilities were strengthened by participating in this self-organized peer group: (a) affiliation, (b) emotions, and (c) senses, imagination, and thought. Southam and Harman studied unexpected leadership in older women who are actively developing crone consciousness and discovered the capabilities of (a) senses, imagination, and thought; (b) emotion, (c) living in concern for and relation to other species, and (d) the ability to reach the end of a normal human life with dignity. These capabilities are stronger in women who are committed to the continuous development of the crone archetype in later life than they are in older women leaders who are not committed to becoming a crone.

Gebhardt found a range of injustices in the small community he studied, such as discrimination, inequity, bias, and exclusion that affected minority groups and members of non-majority social classes. He proposed that the two capabilities most important for small communities engaged in social change are (a) to think, imagine, and reason and (b) to live in concern for and relation to others. Eugene et al. focused on racial injustices in society, including those supported by psychologists, arguing that to ensure clients experience Nussbaum's capabilities by living free from emotional and psychological oppression, psychologists need to actively engage in anti-racism dialogue. Parker stated that the phenomena related to poor indoor air quality in U.S. schools are fundamental to life experiences in the classroom and constitute a moral issue in the educational social-ecological system.

Are Nussbaum's (2011) Capabilities Too Individualistic?

The moral foundation of leadership has been critiqued for focusing on individual rather than collective justice (Dakin, 2013; Simola, et al., 2010). Two of the monograph's authors, Wilson and McAlpine, referred to African mindsets that arise from collectivist cultures: the Tanzanian mindset, ujasiri—doing the right thing—and the South African approach to justice, ubuntu—the philosophy or ethic of a people that our humanity is tied to that of others. Ujasiri and ubuntu originate in interdependent communities, which makes an individual rights-based justice impractical.

Wilson calls into question the theoretical usefulness of Nussbaum's capabilities as an individual rights approach to social justice. Individual flourishing divided from collective solidarities is problematic. According to McAlpine, ubuntu individual freedom is realized as interdependence. As a collective capability, ubuntu is relating in appropriate ways. In fact, there may be an entirely different set of capabilities if one was to assume a collectivist stance. Wilson stated, "When social justice is discussed, we are talking about freedom in all its forms and relationships are at the heart of those experiences." It is possible that social justice itself may be impractical based solely on an individual rights-based approach.

Buckley, Curran, and Thompson, as well as Southam and Harman, link social justice to an ethic of care. For Buckley, the rights of caregivers and those who receive care cannot be extricated from the communities around them. Buckley poignantly asserted, "So, where do families turn? They turn to their communities." In discussing an ethic of care as it arose in mutual aid groups during the pandemic, Curran and Thompson said we must "focus our concern on the good of the whole."

Does Social Justice Have a Moral Foundation of Care?

Southam and Harman found that an ethic of care is one of the defining characteristics of the crone archetype. Following on Simola et al. (2010), they proposed an ethic of care as an alternate moral foundation for individualistic social justice efforts. These researchers found an ethic of care more collectivist and thus aligned with the good work of crones.

The notion of an ethic of care was first coined by Carol Gilligan in her book, *In a Different Voice* (1993), as a paradigm of inclusion and health stemming from the feminine. Nel Noddings (2002) went on to write about an ethic of care's implications for education as building relationships between instructors and students. She said that the object of education "is to develop a caring community through modeling, dialogue, and practice" (p. 223). Joan Tronto, a major contributor to the ethic of care, said in her 2013 lecture, *The Challenges of Medical Care in a Caring Democracy*, that "we need to think about democracy as the allocation of caring responsibilities." In her book *Caring Democracy*, Tronto (2013) developed five phases and associated moral elements of care. These are shown in Table 13. Tronto posited that democracy and care are not the same. This builds on the idea that fairness or justice for each individual does not necessarily lead to social justice. Tronto's fifth phase, caring with, implies the building of solidarity and trust, which can only be done as a collective.

What of Political Emotions?

It may just be a happy synchronicity that four of our authors referred not only to Nussbaum's capabilities approach, but also to her 2013 work, *Political Emotions: Why Love Matters for Justice*. Buckley said emotions like anger, fear, sympathy, envy, grief, and many forms of love can add strength and intensity to the daily lives of those living in stable democracies, or they can derail us from contributing to a just and inclusive society. McAlpine agreed with Nussbaum that emotions can be drivers of social justice, pointing out that ujasiri is an emotional response to others' suffering and, as such, has relevance

Table 13
Phases and Associated Moral Elements of Care

Phase	Moral Element
Caring about	Attentiveness
Caring for	Responsibility
Caregiving	Competence
Care receiving	Responsiveness
Caring with	Trust and solidarity

Note. Adapted from Tronto (2013).

to similar upstander movements, such as those inspired by Black Lives Matter and Generations Against Bullying, that draw on their members' courage and strength.

Gebhardt noted Nussbaum's singling out of the emotion "love" for fostering a commitment to shared goals. Love is an emotion, Gebhardt reflected, that is not in the general lexicon of the political and business leaders of his small town. However, he noted, terms like kindness, care, and fairness are often heard. Buckley calls for "revolutionary love" (Kaur, 2020), likened to the labor of birth to a new form of caring communities. We might end this section on social justice with reflections from a crone on collective social justice:

> There are so many things happening in the world that are heartbreaking—wars, the climate crisis, migration, systemic racism and other injustices, extreme poverty alongside mind-boggling wealth, greed, shortsightedness, consumerism … the list goes on. There are also so many things happening that are expanding—individuals, groups, and organizations dedicated to mindfully, lovingly, and compassionately working on behalf of all the above things and more that I've mentioned. I tend to focus my energies much more on the former than the latter.

Woman Stands Shining, a Diné grandmother, activist, and international speaker counters this tendency. She asks us to consider a life thriving paradigm instead of the paradigm of exploitation and desecration that surrounds most of us today (Woman Stands Shining, 2021). If we look around, Woman Stands Shining says, we will find so many examples of life pushing through despite the overwhelming precarity. She points to many examples of Indigenous cultures living this paradigm as part of the #landback movement and encourages us all to consider this collectivist and caring paradigm as the foundation of our social justice actions. It is leaders like Woman Stands Shining to whom we turn as we summarize the monograph's third and final theme—unexpected leadership.

Unexpected Leadership

In the monograph chapters, leadership looks different, sounds different, and feels different compared to classic constructions. In various ways, it is unexpected. Our exploration does not pose unexpected leadership as a new theory of leadership, rather we use the term as a descriptive label to illuminate what we see happening in these chapters as precarity, social justice, and leadership meet. We see three critical ways in which leadership appears as unexpected. We term these *embodiment, shape,* and *focus*. We offer some brief discussion and critique of these dimensions and consider their connections to the literature on leadership. We then consider what the authors have to say about how unexpected leadership may come about—an issue of great importance to scholar-practitioners interested in social change.

Unexpected Leadership as Embodiment

At the time of creating this volume, unexpected leadership is much in the news. Volodymyr Zelensky, a man of short stature and comedic television background, heretofore was no one's idea of a leader-in-extremis. He now holds the world's attention as an unexpected leader. Leadership in these chapters is embodied by unexpected people—in some ways similar and some ways different ways to Zelensky.

Leaders in these chapters are unexpected in terms of their social identity. They look different from the classic model of powerful White male figures (Knights, 2021). Leaders in these chapters include older women (Southam and Harman, Gebhardt), Tanzanian villagers (McAlpine et al.), teenagers (Curran & Thompson), and women and minoritized students on a doctoral program (Sonnet & Spearman). Beyond gender and social identity, leadership is embodied (or is called to be embodied) by people acting in roles not usually associated with leadership in its hierarchical and formal manifestations. These include students (Sonnet & Spearman), clinical psychologists (Eugene et al.), administrators (Wilson), bureaucrats (Smendzuik-O'Brien), and community members (Buckley, Gephardt).

The leadership literature contains longstanding critique of the classic casting of leadership in male terms (Braun et al., 2017; Heilman et al., 1995: Kerfoot & Knights, 1993) and in hierarchical terms (Pearce & Conger, 2003). That critique is not new. And yet the myth of masculine embodiment and the formal-role embodiment of leadership is strong—as a glance at any corporate organization chart or at "leadership lessons" in training videos and bookstores will show (McCabe & Knights, 2016). The chapters in this volume are showing—in concrete as well as theoretical terms—how leadership looks different and how it can arise from unexpected roles and places—if it can be seen.

The Shape and Form of Unexpected Leadership

Unexpected leadership comes in different shapes and forms to the classic model of leadership vested in a single, heroic, decisive, all-knowing individual. In these chapters, leadership often has a different, more circular shape. It is leadership in the plural, not the singular. Gebhardt, Buckley, and Wilson show us change leadership coming from groups, not individuals—faith groups, community groups, and administrators operating in concertive fashion. McAlpine showed us leadership as a collective, not an individual mindset and action-in-the-world. Curran and Thompson see leadership emerging from teams, not individual leaders, in response to needs arising from the pandemic.

Sonnet and Spearman point to what they call an "organic peer community" that arises in response to stresses of doctoral education, wildly exacerbated in the pandemic. Arising from outside a formal hierarchy, this circular leadership is described as "spontaneous and generous." This vision of leadership attaches to established theories of leadership that are shared (Pearce & Conger, 2003), distributed (Gronn, 2010), and humble (Maldonado et al., 2021). In this sense, the authors are exploring how, where, and why such leadership arises in specific precarious contexts. Many of the chapters in the volume also resonate with the notion of "leaderlessness" in decentralized social movements (Fotaki & Fouroughi, 2022).

However, we should ask critical questions about how spontaneous these instances of emerging circular or group leadership actually are. As we open our eyes to the reality and possibilities for shared, distributed, and humble leadership, we should be open also to the likelihood of individual impetus (acts of individual leadership) that may be crucial in early (and later critical) moments of collectives, including the ones the chapter authors explore. And we should be mindful of the argument of Fotaki and Foroughi (2022), in their exploration of green activism, that claims of leaderlessness and absence of hierarchy in social movements may be more fantasy than reality. Further grounding our findings, Parker described the domain of school accreditation as lacking leadership to improve indoor air quality, at students' peril.

Still, the authors in this volume are illuminating instances and forms of leadership that stand at a far distance from the classic, heroic, individual who gazes down from hierarchy. As we have seen, the shape of this leadership is more circular and collective than that reflected in much existing leadership theory and practice.

The authors in this volume also contribute to the literature on leadership in more formal terms. Many authors are posing new forms of leadership and theorizing these forms. Wilson explores what she calls *intentional leadership* as practiced by administrators of a youth development program. Haddad and Marlatt explore what they called *essence-based leadership* and draw on phenomenology to show the structure of this leadership. Curran and Thompson pose a particular form of leadership they call *emergent generative team leadership* and model key antecedents (igniting forces) and the key dimensions and outcomes of this form. In a variety of ways, the chapters are contributing to the leadership theory by showing a new shape of leadership (circular, collective, distributed) and new particular forms or types of leadership for social justice—in theory and in particular concrete instances and spaces.

Focus of Unexpected Leadership

A final key facet of unexpected leadership is one discussed earlier in this epilogue. In the chapters of this monograph, leadership is not focused on classic economic concerns of efficiency, profit, or competition. Rather, social justice, viewed through the lens of Nussbaum (2011), is the focus of unexpected leadership in these chapters. To the earlier discussion of social justice as the focus of unexpected leadership, we revisit here some concrete instances of what this looks like in the world. In these chapters, leadership's focus or aim concerns an ethic of care—including meeting human needs of connection, development, equity, and inclusion.

How Does Unexpected Leadership Come About?

What is the impetus or catalyst for unexpected leadership toward social justice in precarity? How is this leadership spurred? How can unexpected leaders step forward and thrive? The chapters offer different answers to this question. For many of the authors (Wilson, Southam & Harman, Curran & Thompson, and others) unexpected leadership … just happens, perhaps has always just happened. By its nature, it arises spontaneously, in response to needs. Sonnet and Spearman described leading during chaos "from the edge" of conventional structures. For others, particular paths or methods are proposed. For Eugene et al., a deliberate shift to anti-racism as a central concern of psychology will require exhortation, self-critique, and pursuit of prescribed models and tasks. Wilson maintained that intentional leadership can be taught. For Smendzuik-O'Brien, unexpected leadership will require public service leaders' self-awareness and moral action bolstered by the study of religious and political traditions. Haddad and Marlatt are explicitly concerned with coaching apex leaders and proposed a specific type of mentoring to achieve unexpected leadership for social justice by those in positions of great formal power in society.

Conclusion

Conventional models of leading may reinforce the structures of precarity. At this time, so full to the brim with challenges, it is in our best interest to *gentle* precarity. Acting with social justice, especially justice framed in collectivity and an ethic of care, is one way. Another is unexpected leadership, by people in non-hierarchical and informal manifestations. We hope that together, authors and editors, we have contributed to the recognition, reinforcement, and advancement of unexpected leading towards social justice—as an antidote to precarity and a path toward a more sustainable society for all.

Meet the Editors

Marie Sonnet, PhD is a scholar-practitioner with 20 years of experience in quality and process improvement, change management, project management, training, and consulting. She learned that when improvement projects failed to meet and sustain objectives, human dynamics were often a root cause. Marie researched workgroup beliefs and behaviors present when an organization is able to meet the challenges of planned and unplanned change. She found that a collective capacity for resilience is built up by everyday experiences that add to or diminish a generative response. An organization can deliberately foster or unwittingly deter this capacity. Change response, especially under precarious circumstances, is especially enhanced by fostering emergent leadership close to the problems and close to the experiences of real people. Her research on leading from the edge continues to explore how to do this. msonnet@email.fielding.edu

Theresa Southam, PhD is a 2020 Fielding graduate in human and organizational development. Her research debunks the myth that the world is facing a grey tsunami in the growing demographic of older adults. In fact, when older adults age consciously, their everyday kindnesses contribute to more sustainable communities. Recently she expanded her research as a Fielding Institute for Social Innovation Fellow to include trauma-informed teaching and learning. As department head of the Teaching and Learning Centre at Selkirk College, she is a 2020-2021 BC Campus Research Fellow and the recipient, with College of the Rockies, of the BC Campus Award for Excellence in Open Education.Theresa has contributed blog posts, book reviews, and published a blog and portfolio piece, *Is Being an Ally Enough*, for the Association for Anthropology, Gerontology and the Lifecourse. Her dissertation was *27,000 Sunrises: Everyday Contributions of Grateful and Giving Age 70+ Adults.* tsoutham@email.fielding.edu

Patrice Rosenthal, PhD is a faculty member in the human and organizational development program of Fielding Graduate University. Prior to joining Fielding, she held faculty positions at the London School of Economics and King's College, London. She is a board member of the Organization Development and Change Division of the Academy of Management. Her research on topics such as gender and work, the management and experience of front-line service work, organization change, and employee relations has been published in scholarly journals including *Organization, Human Relations, the Journal of Management Studies, Journal of Occupational and Organizational and Psychology, British Journal of Industrial Relations, International Journal of Public Sector Management,* and many others. She has provided research consultation to numerous organizations including Women's Economic Ventures, Equal Opportunity Commission, Price Waterhouse, Tesco Stores, British Petroleum, UK Department of Work and Pensions, and many others. She is dedicated to doctoral education and the development of strong scholar-practitioners in human and organization development. prosenthal@fielding.edu

References

Braun, S., Stegmann, S., Hernandez Bark, A. S., Junker, N. M., & van Dick, R. (2017). Think manager-think male, think follower-think female: Gender bias in implicit leadership theories. *Journal of Applied Social Psychology, 47*, 377– 388.

Dakin, E. (2013). Protection as care: Moral reasoning and moral orientation among ethnically and socioeconomically diverse older women. *Journal of Aging Studies, 28*, 44–56.

Gilligan, C. (1993). *In a different voice: Psychological theory and women's development.* Harvard University Press.

Gronn, P. (2010). Hybrid configurations of leadership. In A. Bryman, D. Collinson, K. Grint, B. Jackson, & M. Uhl-Bien (Eds.), *Sage Handbook of Leadership* (pp. 435–452). Sage.

Hamington, M. & Flower, M. (2021). *Care ethics in the age of precarity*. University of Minnesota Press.

Hedman, K. (2019). Strengths and support of older people affected by precarity in South Louisiana. *International Journal of Older People Nursing, 14*(2), 1–10. https://doi.org/10.1111/opn.12232

Heilman, M. E., Block, C. B., & Martell, R. F. (1995). Sex stereotypes: Do they influence perceptions of managers? *Journal of Social Behavior and Personality, 10*, 237–252.

Kaur, V. (2020). *See no stranger: A memoir and manifesto of revolutionary love.* Random House Publishing Group.

Kerfoot, D., & Knights, D. (1993). Management, masculinity and manipulation:

From paternalism to corporate strategy in financial services in Britain. *Journal of Management Studies 30*(4), 659–677.

Knights, D. (2021b). *Leadership, gender and ethics: Embodied reason in challenging masculinities*. Routledge.

Maldonado, T., Carden, L., Brace, C., & Myers, M. (2021). Fostering innovation through humble leadership and humble organizational culture. *Journal of Business Strategies, 38*(2), 73–94.

McCabe, D., & Knights, D. (2016). Learning to listen? Exploring discourses and images of masculine leadership through corporate videos. *Management Learning, 47*, 179–198.

Nussbaum, M. C. (2011). *Creating capabilities: The human development approach.* Harvard University Press.

Nussbaum, M. C. (2015). *Political emotions: Why love matters for justice*. Harvard University Press.

Pearce, C., & Conger, J. (2003). *Shared leadership*. Sage.

Simola, S. K., Barling, J., & Turner, N. (2010). Transformational leadership and leader moral orientation: Contrasting an ethic of justice and an ethic of care. *The Leadership Quarterly, 21*(1), 179–188.

Tronto, J. C. (2013). *Caring democracy: Markets, equality, and justice*. NYU Press.

Woman Stands Shining. (2021). *On Humanity's Homecoming*. https://forthewild.world/listen/woman-stands-shining-pat-mccabe-on-humanitys-homecoming-251

Made in the USA
Monee, IL
22 December 2022

23290777R00201